THE HUMAN AND THE HOLY

THE HUMAN AND THE HOLY

ASIAN PERSPECTIVES IN CHRISTIAN THEOLOGY

EMERITO P. NACPIL
DOUGLAS J. ELWOOD
Editors

Facsimile Edition

ORBIS BOOKS

Maryknoll, New York 10545

The Catholic Foreign Mission Society of America (Maryknoll) recruits and trains people for overseas missionary service. Through Orbis Books Maryknoll aims to foster the international dialogue that is essential to mission. The books published, however, reflect the opinions of their authors and are not meant to represent the official position of the society.

Philippine copyright © 1978 by the Christian Literature Society of the Philippines, Inc., 877 Epifanio de los Santos, Quezon City, Republic of the Philippines

First published by New Day Publishers, Quezon City, Philippines

All rights reserved

U.S. edition 1980 by Orbis Books, Maryknoll, NY 10545

The U.S. edition has been reproduced by photo offset from the original edition

Typeset in the Philippines and printed and bound in the United States of America

Library of Congress Cataloging in Publication Data

All-Asia Consultation on Theological Education for
    Christian Ministry, Makati, Philippines, 1977.
    The human and the holy.

    1. Man (Christian theology)—Congresses. 2. Holy,
The—Congresses. 3. Theology—Congresses. 4. Theo-
logy—Study and teaching—Asia—Congresses. I. Nacpil,
Emerito P. II. Elwood, Douglas J. III. Title.
BT701.2.A437 1977   233   80-14134
ISBN 0-88344-195-0 (pbk.)

FOREWORD

The striking contrast between the "now" and the "then" of theological education in the Third World became vivid to me as I attended the All-Asia Consultation on Theological Education for Christian Ministry held in Manila, March 1977, the proceedings of which are recorded in this volume. I felt the contrast intimately, from within, when I recalled the first consultation held in Bangkok in 1956, and I was deeply moved by it as one who has been for the last thirty years related to theological education in Asia, in one form or another. Let me just mention a few things in a telegraphic way.

I saw taking place at the Manila Consultation what our Indonesian colleagues call a "double wrestling"—on the one hand, with the Asian historical realities and, on the other, with the living reality of God in Christ witnessed by the Scriptures. I saw also what the Association of Theological Schools in Southeast Asia calls "the critical Asian principle" at work when over one hundred theological educators, church leaders, frontier-ministries workers, and theological students determined to discover *real* Asian issues, their *own* theological agenda and tasks, and an authentic Asian framework for carrying them through. Then I realized that the three sub-themes— "Man and the Holy," "Man and Nature," and "Man in History and Society"—were not just general and "universal" themes but very much Asian ones. For, Asia was seen here as the continent with every possible religion, old and new; as divided into two ideological camps, with the alluring model of affluent Japan on one side, on the other the challenging model of China, and in between many repressive and even oppressive governments; as having experienced the end of the colonial era, yet not quite sure that it is really over though still hoping against hope for the new Asia; and, lastly, as a place whose mother earth is now being eroded and polluted through modernization and industrialization. In short, Asia in suffering and hope.

What do we mean when we, a tiny Asian Christian community, make it part and parcel of our faith to declare that "Jesus Christ (is) in Asian suffering and hope" (the theme of the Sixth Assembly of the Christian Conference of Asia, May-June, 1977); and how do we articulate in words and deeds the Asian search for a new humanity and a new society? How are Asian suffering and hope related to the biblical perspective between Creation and new Creation in Jesus Christ, and in particular to what St. Paul describes (in Romans 8:18ff.) as the threefold "groan": of the whole creation, of the first fruits, and—the most mysterious of all—of the Spirit "pleading with God for us"? The debate on the three sub-themes of the Manila Consultation took place in the form of theological "groaning" and wrestling with the Asian realities and the biblical message. I am sure that if Bishop Rajah Manikam and Dr. Stanley Smith, who together organized the Bangkok consultation twenty-one years earlier, were still with us and could have attended the Manila Consultation they would have been both amazed and delighted.

What is the contrast all about? Briefly stated, it is the striking advancement made in the on-going threefold search—for quality, authenticity, and creativity in theological education in the Third World. True, the search for *quality* started first with the concern for academic excellence and sound scholarship—to go beyond the Bible School level. And in one sense there is no going back on that. It has been increasingly realized, however, that the quality of theological and ministerial formation could not be equated with, much less exhausted by, academic excellence alone. In fact, a one-sided obsession with it may even become a dangerous threat to the true and authentic quality of theological education.

Very soon the search for quality led on to the search for *authenticity* in theological education in the Third World. The search for authenticity must even dare to reject the borrowed and imported criteria of quality, however attractive and tempting they may be. It must "will one thing"—the integrity of self-determination which comes not through claims and assertions alone but mainly through the praxis of wrestling with one's own religious, cultural, social, and political realities.

Is that all that is required for authenticity in theological education? Of course not. But it is an essential condition to meet the Lord of history who commands "the son of man to stand upon his feet" and to serve the incarnate Lord who says, "follow me," who emptied himself and became as a servant. In the final analysis, of course, the authentic quality of theological education in the Third World depends on its rediscovery of what Christian theology is all about, of what Christian ministry and, not least, Christian education are all about—that "travail" of which St. Paul talks so earnestly as if everything depends on it, namely, "until Christ is formed in us," involving so radically one's mind, one's work, and one's life.

But this "what?" of the authentic quality of theological education involves also and only comes through taking the questions of

iv

"how?," "where?," and "when?" seriously. This is what I now hear those saying who are concerned with and involved in theological education in the Third World, which I believe to be a striking advance in their on-going search for quality and authenticity in Third World theological education. For, through this on-going interaction between the search for quality and the search for authenticity, I believe, a third search inherent from the start is now coming out into the open, namely, the search for *creativity*.

We see the signs and evidences of this search for creativity here and there in the creative theological reflection leading to original writing, in the setting up of their own ways for advanced study and research in and out of their own contexts, and in the searching for and experimenting with innovative patterns of theological education. A search for creativity is not to be confused, however, with a search for novelty. But I believe that because of the advance made in the search for quality and authenticity, the stage is now set for advance in this search for creativity. I am not saying that they have succeeded, but that they are searching for it and they are pressing on. Nor am I suggesting that the problems are over; on the contrary there may be even more. But I do suggest that they are discovering their *own* problems and are determined to deal with them in their own ways. And I believe that therein lies the hope of real and creative solutions. Let us remember also that this search is still young—one generation in many countries and in some even less—and so still rather fragile.

Shoki K. Coe

PREFACE

This volume contains the addresses, workshop reports, and papers of the Consultation on Theological Education for Christian Ministry in Asia held in Makati, Metro-Manila, Philippines in March, 1977. It is the official report of the Consultation.

The purpose of the Consultation was to find some answers to three major questions: (a) whether or not there is emerging in the Asian scene some consensus on the nature and agenda of the theological task in Asia; (b) what forms of Christian ministry must be developed to carry out this task; and (c) what kind of theological formation is needed to do it. The formulation of the purpose indicated that the consideration of the issues of Christian ministry and theological education was to depend upon the kind of answers given to the question of the nature and agenda of the theological task. As a result of this, the Consultation became decidedly an exercise in theological conversation.

In order to find out what sort of theological issues are in fact emerging in the Asian situation, the dimensions of man's relation to the Holy, to society and history, and to nature became the focus of intensive analysis and discussion. Attention was directed to the way this threefold relationship of man is conceptualized and practiced traditionally in Asian cultures and what is happening to it under the impact of the forces of social change in Asia today. By seeking to identify theological problems within a relational perspective, it was hoped that the issues might emerge in their natural form and not be predetermined by some dogmatic viewpoint. By attempting to locate the problems within the Asian setting and approaching them contextually, the Consultation was being urged to put its probing fingers upon the heartbeat of Asian life and realities. The whole process was an attempt to put to work the critical Asian principle as a theological method.

Whether or not the Consultation succeeded in achieving the purposes it set for itself may be gauged by both the process it generated and the results it achieved. The process included intensive preparation through the study of preparatory documents (most of which are reproduced in this volume), plenary addresses and Bible studies on the three major themes, workshop discussions, and the production of reports. The flavor and dynamics of the plenary sessions and the workshop discussions are of course difficult to recapture in a book, and this volume will read as lifeless as any written report on any consultation, which otherwise could be exciting and colorful, as this Consultation certainly was. The process was part of the achievement of the Consultation and, as Masao Takenaka said, "it is as important as the result." The harvest of ideas and issues and viewpoints is, on the other hand, embodied palpably in this volume and it tells whether or not the Consultation was well worth its value in funds and time and energy expended. The reader may judge for himself.

What does it mean to be authentically human? This is one of the burning questions of our time, and no clear answers have yet been given. In this volume a wide spectrum of Asian Christians address themselves to this question in relation to Asian man's sense of the sacred, his experience of nature, and his responsibility for society and history. In other places theologians have talked about the "humanity" of God. The focus at this Consultation was upon the "holiness" of the human.

But this Consultation was not satisfied to identify and analyze the theological issues. It was equally concerned with the implications of an Asian theological agenda for Christian ministry and theological education. It was agreed that theological schools in Asia should teach seminarians how to approach theology as a sacred task waiting to be done and not just a fixed body of sacred knowledge waiting to be read. This does not mean that "doing" theology can become a substitute for "thinking" theologically. What it does mean is that students are to be challenged to wrestle with live theological issues that grow out of their awareness of the context as viewed through the telescopic lens of the sacred text.

It was further agreed that spiritual formation probably should not focus on self-release, as in so much traditional Asian religion, but on dedication of the self to Christ's mission in the world—taking up one's cross and following him. The ideal of the "holy man" would then be one who, like Jesus, exists "for others." This would suggest an outgoing spirituality that breaks through the monastic mentality of both East and West, and which is open to God and the world at the same time.

Theological schools in Asia are challenged from many directions to re-examine their structural models. The two we have inherited are those of the academic community (theological college) and the monastic community (seminary compound). Questions were raised as to whether or not either of these is adequately suited to theological formation in Asia today. Is there an alternative model that will break down the seminary walls that separate it from the world, and sometimes from the church, and still preserve the positive values associated with the two inherited models? This question was left unanswered for our respective seminaries to explore in their varied contexts.

Theological education is seen to be the responsibility of the whole church, and not just one segment of it. This all-Asia Consultation encourages the creation of a wider "theological community" in which not only faculty and students but also ministers and lay members may engage in dialogue and common action. One of the obvious problems they need to face together is that of discovering a quality-style ministerial training which Asian national churches themselves can finance. This is of course part of the larger problem of contextualization. Theological schools in Asia have too often been communities of privilege, alienated from the common people as well as from their own cultural and religious history, isolated by their dependence on Western money. So acute is the problem that some delegates suggested we dismantle the traditional seminaries because they do not adequately relate to the demands of the church's mission in Asian contexts. If this, or something less radical, could be done, the new structures would need to be judged only by their effectiveness in equipping people for mission.

Our thanks are due to all who participated in the Consultation, especially to those who willingly accepted leadership roles and whose names are mentioned in an appendix on "The Leadership in the Consultation." A special debt of gratitude is extended to the Theological Education Fund and the regional agencies for their cooperative sponsorship of this venture. These include the Association of Theological Schools in Southeast Asia, the Northeast Asia Association of Theological Schools, the Board of Theological Education (India and Sri Lanka), and the Christian Conference of Asia. We wish further to express our appreciation to Mrs. Gloria Rodriguez, Publishing Editor and Director of New Day Publishers, of the Christian Literature Society of the Philippines, for the care with which she assisted in bringing this "brain child" to birth.

It is hoped that this volume will continue to stimulate theological discussion within Asia and spark new insights and perspectives in Christian thought which will illuminate the way into the future for the tiny Christian community in Asia as it makes its witness in thought, worship, and service to the lordship of Jesus Christ.

E. P. NACPIL and D. J. ELWOOD

CONTENTS

ix

x

PART ONE

MAN AND THE HOLY

1

1

MAN AND THE HOLY: A WORKSHOP REPORT

Contemporary Asia is a confusing and colorful part of our world. Since the achievement of independence in the late nineteen forties and fifties, many of the nations we represent have experienced radical social and political change. Most of us are trying to catch up with Western countries in order to enjoy similar standards of living and to use their technological and scientific discoveries to hasten our own national development.

But our societies are in a state of transition. Part of our region is still caught up in a traditional world view and societies in this area still think of "the Holy" in a religious sense. Moreover, the resurgence of interest in the living faiths of Asia, as an expression of national identity, has brought in its wake a commercialization and distortion of "the Holy"—the people being thus separated from a sense of the presence of God. Where the cultivation of tolerance has fostered religious pluralism the resulting confluence of different understandings of "the Holy" has fostered the growth of dialogue and, in some situations, social action for common ends. This new pluralism illustrates our Asian struggle to find meaning in life and the longing to bring one's life into contact with the religious ultimate. It is tragic, therefore, to note that this new phenomenon is being exploited out of a sense of self-interest by some political leaders, commercial interests, and even religious leaders themselves.

Other parts of our region are caught up in accommodating to a secular world view. Here the traditional religious outlook has been de-sacralized in the dramatic process of secularization, and the yearning for meaning in life is being confused with the pursuit of material prosperity. Basic drives and ultimate goals are being directed toward satisfying an insatiable desire for material things. A person's value and a nation's dignity are being measured by the gross national product and per capita income. To be successful has become an ambition pursued with religious conviction and fervor. This too is a distortion of "the Holy" and a denial of what it means for people to be human.

This fluid, challenging, stimulating, and disturbing situation forces upon us, with a real urgency, an analysis and discussion of the theme, Man and the Holy. What is the relationship now between Man and a sense of the presence of God in our world? What is the meaning of the gospel in and for our world today? In order to undertake a study of this theme it is important to begin with an examination of popular notions of "the Holy" which are to be found in different parts of Asia.

POPULAR ASIAN EXPRESSIONS OF THE HOLY

The word "holy" still has a religious significance on the Indian subcontinent, in Thailand, Malaysia, Indonesia, the Philippines, and Taiwan, but is to be understood in ethical terms in the more secularized countries of South Korea and Japan, as well as in the urban industrial centers which are scattered throughout Asia.

A descriptive analysis of usage in these countries includes the following ideas:

1. The Holy is a unifying cosmic force which enables people to organize their lives so as to live at peace with each other and in harmony with nature. This unifying force overcomes the barrier between the living and the dead by making that which is divine or transcendent an essential part of the empirical world in which we live.

2. Something which is known and venerated as sacred must be kept at a distance, lest it harm the people; that which is sacred is feared because of its holy power: its ability to destroy as well as to protect.

3. If persons are to be holy, then they must detach themselves from the hustle and bustle of daily life and seek through a life of separation to pursue the goal of union with a "wholly other" ultimate reality.

4. In Christian Philippines and Islamic Southeast Asia holiness and godliness are often spoken of as twin concerns of religious people. Holy persons are godly because their lives take on the char-

3

acter of the Holy One to whom they confess allegiance, and whose revealed will they seek to follow.

5. Holy people are often considered spiritual people because they live a life of devotion to the supreme and holy being which lies at the center of all that they say and do.

6. To be holy means to live a life of moral purity. Of course, different societies have varying relative standards of morality, but religious persons are expected to adhere to principles and to live a certain style of life which is consistent with their religious convictions. In this sense religious persons set approximate moral standards for the community at large to follow if it so chooses.

7. There is a sense in which a person of mature character, who leads an exemplary life, and who exercises a leadership role in a small community or even in a larger segment of society, becomes surrounded with an aura of "holiness." There is in the popular imagination something quite religious and "other-worldly" about the charismatic qualities of personality which some individuals seem to possess. Here we come across a sense of holy which is "a-religious."

Behind these descriptions of man's experience of the Holy, in religious contexts, is an awareness that the word "holy" refers to the activity of a mysterious hidden power which appears to pervade the cosmos at various places and at times which cannot be predicted, and which through different kinds of objects and things breaks into and intrudes upon our own world. Behind these descriptions, especially in secular or a-religious contexts, is the notion that what we call "holy" refers to a dimension of the human personality, and is identified with a certain quality of character, which in turn can be projected into the life of a community as an ideal or aspiration for all to follow. In this sense "holy" refers to something which stands in relative contrast to the strengths and weaknesses of humanity itself.

However, these popular views of the Holy distort the kind of relationship which should exist between Man and the Holy if people are to grow to mature adulthood as believing, expecting, rejoicing human beings. These popular views are also sometimes a hindrance to national development in countries where it is imperative to improve the livelihood of the people. When these popular views confuse the Holy with relative values, and prevent people from encoun-

4

tering the healing and transforming power of God in their own lives, then the demonic manifests itself.

To be authentically human is to be holy. In suggesting this perspective for our understanding of the theme we believe that we have grasped the meaning of Jesus' mission for the life and times of our churches in Asia. In a programmatic statement Jesus declared:

> The Spirit of the Lord is upon me, because he has anointed me to preach good news to the poor. He has sent me to proclaim release to the captives and recovering of sight to the blind, to set at liberty chose who are oppressed, to proclaim the acceptable year of the Lord. (Lk. 4:18-19).

A brief exegesis of this passage will help us to understand its significance for the theme, Man and the Holy. Jesus reads from Isaiah 61:1-2, one of the servant songs, and thus identifies himself in Luke's view with the same kind of mission performed by the exilic prophet. From its context in Deutero-Isaiah, we may conclude that Jesus did not understand his own mission in narrowly spiritual or religious terms, but with reference to the social, economic, and political realities of first century Palestine. When he speaks of the poor he is not referring to the poor in spirit (Matthew 5:3a.), but to those who were suffering economic deprivation. The good news which they hear concerns the coming of "the acceptable year of the Lord"—The Year of Jubilee, a Deuteronomic provision for the redistribution of wealth and property each fifty years. "Release to the captives" in the same way refers to people detained for various political reasons (as they were during the Babylonian exile), and the phrase "set at liberty those who are oppressed" is a reference to various kinds of social, economic, and political restrictions placed upon the exiles. From the context, the phrase "recovery of sight to the blind" originally was a reference to the restoration of sight for those whose eyes were gouged out as punishment for trying to escape capture at the time Jerusalem fell.

By using this passage, Jesus, the son of Man, discloses that he comes to bring people into a new relationship with God, and to create through his mission a new community of faith which will reflect the character of God himself and thus become through the power of Jesus' spirit the new humanity in the world. So, in this passage Jesus tells us how it is possible for us his followers to discover our true humanity in the way his Father determined from the beginning; and by living out this program, even to death on the cross, Jesus has made it possible for his followers to be as human as he himself.

To be "in Christ" (*en Christo*)—to be human as Jesus was—is to participate in the "new creation" and to be a "new person"; it is to reflect the holiness, or wholeness, of God. As part of the "new humanity" of God, Asian Christians are called to be a "holy" community, a "light" to their own nations, to enter into a covenant with God on behalf of their own peoples, and thus to become deeply involved with others who can share their aspirations in the renewal and reconstruction of national life.

In order to explore this understanding of our theme still further and to sharpen the issues with which we are confronted today in Asia we now turn to an investigation of seven important problems which concern the life of our people and ask ourselves this question: How does this understanding of the Biblical understanding of the Holy affect what we say about these issues? In raising this question we believe we are contributing to an ongoing discussion which could radically affect the future life of our nations.

MAN AS THE FOCUS OF THE HOLY

THE CHURCH AS AN INSTITUTION. The church is a fellowship (*koinonia*) of men and women and the context where the good news of grace and forgiveness is heard and experienced. Here in the worshiping community we discover what it means to be human and alive. Here we find healing for our brokenness and discover a new perspective for daily living. Here we are encountered and addressed by the Holy. However, when this healing, transforming perspective of our humanity is formalized into inflexible theological confessions or dogmatic formulations and stultified by church structures and procedures, then the sense of the presence of God is obscured for the people and they no longer hear the gospel, and the church falls under the judgment of the Holy. The need today is for the fellowship of Christ's people (the New Humanity) to be continuously renewed and revitalized by the healing, transforming power of the Holy, so that the church as an institution can become the instrument for the reconstruction of a true humanity in Asian society. The Church as the "body of Christ" is called to live this program of Jesus (Luke 4:18-19), to take up this mission in spite of the difficulties, so that the renewing power of God may be manifest in our Asian world.

POLITICS. Throughout Asia there is a search for a new socioeconomic and political order which will ensure the fullest participa-

6

tion of all in the decision-making processes which determine a nation's destiny. This yearning of Asian peoples for a truly democratic order as opposed to highly centralized if not totalitarian regimes, is an expression of a search for an authentic sense of humanity and this can be interpreted by the Christian community as an encounter with the Holy in the realm of politics.

The biblical story illustrates for us the fact that "the Holy" is the presence and power of God in the midst of human life—and of course this includes our political life. Moreover, our participation in the struggle for justice and human rights is one important way in which the presence and power of the Holy is manifest today. Authoritarian governments appear to be the norm rather than the exception in Asia today, but in the light of our understanding of the Holy we want to say that any nation which denies basic human freedoms and perpetuates social injustice through self-interested government is in danger of dehumanizing its own people and of destroying that which is Holy. A nation which acts in this way comes under the judgment of God.

POVERTY AND UNEMPLOYMENT. Poverty, brought about by the oppression of landowners, employers, or the irresponsible use of political power is seen by the biblical writers to be an affront to man's humanity. Jesus proclaimed good news to the poor, inaugurated the Year of Jubilee, and thereby called for a redistribution of resources and the eradication of poverty. Thus the right to own a piece of land and to occupy a house provides a person with an identity and a context for him to realize his potential as a human being. Work therefore is his inalienable right because it provides him with a way of experiencing the creative potential of his own humanity. Through work and leisure he discovers what it means to be human and encounters the Holy. It was because of the importance of the land to Israel's own understanding of its destiny, that the refugee and alien were to be specially cared for. Jesus places before us in his own proposal a task for us to follow, and in Matthew 25:31-46 we find a paradigm for our own situation in Asia: it is in caring for the poor, and in championing the rights of those who are deprived of the opportunity to be human, that we discover where Jesus is present in our world.

Whenever, therefore, we concern ourselves with these problems we discover what it means for us to be alive and human, and it is here that we discover and are judged by the Holy.

7

SOCIAL DISCRIMINATION. All forms of social discrimination based on color, status, religious or ideological beliefs whether obvious or subtle have dehumanizing effects on individuals and communities as well as nations. When people are singled out for deprivation by self-interested parties, a demonic power is at work destroying any human sense of dignity and self-respect. The biblical message reminds us that the Christian community, because it understands what it means to be authentically human, is called upon to struggle against such discrimination in the spirit of Jesus himself.

In our Asian world the discrimination against women and the exploitation of sexuality is of particular concern. Sex, related to the sacred in almost all religions, and used often as a means of breaking through to the realm of the divine or of providing a means whereby the divine is able to flow into the human realm, is considered by the biblical writers to be the total expression of the human personality. Man is both male and female if he is authentically human. Women therefore have the right to enjoy complementary social, economic, and political rights with men. Marriage understood in the biblical sense expresses the sacramental quality of sexuality and is itself a most sensitive expression of the Holy in the human realm. There is thus something very sacred about the man-woman sexual relationship in the Bible. Here the Holy manifests itself in a unique way as God and man meet. Any exploitation of sex therefore turns what is Holy into a demonic power which destroys our humanity.

TECHNOLOGY. Technology is one of the most astounding and astonishing illustrations of man's inherent capacity and ability to create a world for himself. Through making things for his own enjoyment and to enable him to work more efficiently, and through discovering secrets about his universe, contemporary Western man has sought to reshape his destiny, and remake his history. The fruits of this technological advance are now being placed in the hands of Asian societies in the interests of national development. A unique opportunity is thus being given to Asia to take and use this technology in the best interests of all and thereby to seek to remove all forms of poverty and suffering and to increase the potential of environmental resources, thus allowing people from all walks of life and situations to realize their true humanity, and respond to the Holy. The alternative is to be sucked into the process of secularization, to be dominated by technology, and to lose sight of the holiness of human creativity which flows from the mind of the Creator.

EDUCATION AND MEDICAL CARE. In the traditional cultures of our part of the world teaching and learning are traditionally conceived as "holy" tasks. The teacher (the *guru*) passes on to others the "secrets of life." These "secrets of life" integrate the student into his community, forming him gradually as a responsible member of it, as worker, husband, wife, mother, youth, or child. On their part, the students open up to these life-giving secrets and treat the teacher with reverence and respect. In India, especially, the process of education involves a dialogical relation between man (the teacher) and man (the learner). Both teacher and student thus realize that they are engaged in a "holy" task—the passing on and receiving of a whole complex of knowledge, human values, and behavioral patterns which go into making a person a human being in his community.

Although this traditional pattern of education is venerable, has produced generations of "holy men" in Asia, and has generated a thoroughly Asian spirituality, we discern a negative aspect in the passivity of the student. Whereas the "guru system" of education was necessary in a society and culture which was basically oral and agrarian, when this pattern of education is followed in contemporary Western-inspired educational systems, it fails to really form responsible men and women for living in today's Asian world. Thus, as a system it reveals a dehumanizing or demonic level. Education in this manner tends neither to promote responsibility of the student for the community nor community responsibility for the student.

Education in the Asian context must retain a dialogical relationship between teacher and student, the respect and honor that the student has for the teacher; and yet it must incorporate the insights of recent Third World educational philosophy in which education becomes a mutual discovery of truth and life by both teacher and student. Thus, education becomes a process of formation for men and women which is Asian, and Christian, and therefore authentically human in our context. Another way of encountering the Holy!

There seems to be something sacred in shared suffering. In most countries of Asia sickness is still a community affair, and the patient is not to be left alone. The feeling is that a person needs not only medical attention but community concern. This is the basis for the sacrament of the sick. Christ is encountered in the community's care for the sick person! In modern healing, however, such concern is de-personalized. Institutionalization, specialization, and high cost have regrettably replaced real care and concern for the sick person. It is not an arm or leg or kidney that is sick but a person!

Perhaps healing can learn from Christ on the cross. In sharing our suffering he healed us. In sharing his suffering we are healed (Phil. 3:10). God's holiness, or as we might say, God's understanding of what it means for us to be human in the way he intended, is disclosed in Jesus' suffering. Here we seem to come across an idea, hardly formed in the New Testament, which suggests that when we are human as God intended, we begin to take upon ourselves part of God's own nature. Our redeemed nature is part of what it means for God to be God!

CULTURES, RELIGIONS, AND IDEOLOGIES. Man creates cultures or life-styles as he seeks to respond to the creativity of his own nature. Thus culture is an expression of man's nature as a human being—it is the way in which he seeks to give form and structure to his own creativity. This means that the total life-style of small communities as well as larger societies becomes the expression of a people's yearning to discover themselves, to establish their own identity, and to experience their own potential. Cultures are therefore relative: they are identified with particular peoples, they are found in particular geographical locations, and they are relative to certain periods of history.

Understood in this way culture can be said to express the mind of a people, and it may as a life-style reflect either a true understanding of man's authentic humanity, and in this sense refract a sense of the Holy; or it may on the other hand reflect man's lack of authentic humanity and in this sense refract a sense of the demonic. In the early nineteen forties, Western Europe saw the creation of culture in this latter sense, and from time to time since the nineteen fifties other continents have also experienced the manifestation of the demonic in this cultural form.

There is a close interaction between culture and religion, and therefore between Man and the Holy. Many life-styles are molded by the religious faith followed by the majority of the population in a large number of countries within Asia. Culture in these instances is an expression of the way of life of Hindu, Buddhist, or Islamic people, and reflects their understanding of the Holy. A political ideology can influence the life-style of people in the same way.

This situation presents the Asian Christian community with a unique opportunity to contribute to the ultimate transformation of society, as it seeks to proclaim the gospel through its own sense of authentic humanity. The Christian community can therefore affirm elements of culture which refract a true sense of what it means to be human, and bring to other situations, where this sense is missing, a new understanding of man's humanity, as this has been illustrated for us in Jesus Christ. The Christian community can therefore point to Jesus as "the way, the truth, and the life"—the one in whom man's authentic humanity has been disclosed, and the one who makes it possible for us to be human as he himself.

MAN AND THE HOLY IN DYNAMIC RELATIONSHIP

Man and the Holy is a potential starting point for theological reflection in the Asian Christian community. In the above sections we have tried to show how our understanding of the theme can radically affect the way in which the Christian community seeks to understand the contribution it can make to the re-thinking of issues which are vital to the future development of our societies, and to the course of history in our part of the world. In this analysis we have tried to contextualize our theological reflection, and to grasp what the Holy means in the Asian context of suffering and hope. Now we look at the implications of our analysis in these following areas:

THEOLOGICAL EDUCATION FOR CHRISTIAN MINISTRY. The theology we teach in and out of the theological school needs to be more descriptive and less prescriptive. It should be seen as a task to be done and not just a matter of digesting a fixed body of knowledge embodied in textbooks. Students must be challenged to wrestle with live theological issues that grow out of their awareness of the context, on the one hand, and their study of the text, on the other hand. "Doing" theology, however, is no substitute for "thinking" theologically; what is called for is "action-reflection." This means discerning the issues arising from our involvement in the life of the people, and then examining those issues in the light of biblical faith.

There is, moreover, a need to stress spirituality as part of our theological formation. But true spirituality should be seen in terms of dedication to Christ's mission in the world, of "taking up one's cross and following him." This is an outgoing spirituality that breaks through the monastic mentality, for the "holy man" is one

11

who exists for others and not one who concentrates only on self-release.

The theological community can grow intellectually and spiritually when it pays attention to the historical life of the church (the study of Church History). We must encourage writings on Asian Church History and glean helpful insights from them for our present Christian existence.

Theological schools need to re-examine their structural models. The two most common are the theological college and the monastery. Are these suited to Asia today? Is there an alternative model that will break down the seminary walls, as St. Francis of Assisi did, and yet preserve the values of excellence in learning and spiritual inwardness which have characterized the traditional models? It is perhaps in new patterns of field education that the theological schools and the churches can be drawn together in the creative task of discovering new and viable forms of theological education. The seminary's roots are in the life of the church, so theological faculties and church leaders should be encouraged to seek imaginative forms of field training in a variety of urban and rural situations as well as in clinical pastoral exposures. Field education provides the theological student with an opportunity for emotional growth and spiritual development and in this way complements the formation of the student's mind and the development of intellectual ability and insight which is also the task of the seminary.

RELEVANCE TO THEOLOGIZING IN ASIA. It should be recognized, in the first place, that just as every woman and man has the right to education, so every member of the church has a right to theological education. Theology is not the special province of the professional, but is for all God's people.

Theologizing in Asia today does not mean that we simply adopt the Nicene Creed and other classical statements of faith and repeat them over and over. We must learn to re-appropriate the faith, rethink and reinterpret it in the context of Asian experiences of the Holy and of contemporary socio-political realities. The very inspiration for "doing" theology must spring from an Asian consciousness.

We cannot begin to theologize in Asia unless we know the focal points of the sense of the Holy in Asian life. Man in relation to the Holy is a potential starting-point for relevant theological reflection. Hopefully this would suggest a refreshing variety of experimental methods, always in the framework of our faith in Jesus

12

Christ as Lord. Examples are already available in the essays published in the books, *What Asian Christians are Thinking* and *Asian Voices in Christian Theology*. Here we see how Asian colleagues have been grappling with the challenges of re-expressing the Christian message in the thought-forms and in the context of the Asian situation.

Christian theology in Asia must also seriously consider how basic insights from other classical religious traditions can enrich at some points, and even correct at other points, some of our popular traditional Christian understandings of man in relation to the Holy, and contribute to a development of the exposition of the theme, Man and the Holy, as it has been interpreted in this paper. Such, for example, is the Hindu concept of *advaita*, which is the grand conception of a single unbroken unity of man, God, and the world. It is fairly clear that the Christian community has much to learn from the living Asian faiths because these religions mold the life-styles of many of the nations in the Asian world. Obversely, our faith in Christ commits us to examine these insights critically, in the light of both the Christian scriptures and the phenomenon of social change.

CREATING A THEOLOGICAL COMMUNITY. In order to realize a theological community in which teachers, students, pastors or priests, and lay members may engage in dialogue and common action it is important that those of us who are seminary-trained learn the hard lesson of sacrificing professional jargon as part of what it means to "deny" ourselves and "take up our cross daily." There is something "unholy" about professional language at this stage of the church's life in Asia, and there is something profoundly "holy" about the mother tongue: the latter can at least be understood! This suggests an important role for the mother tongue in theological education for ministry. Preaching and teaching seminars should be encouraged in the vernacular, with stress on the use of vivid images.

While some of our theological schools have been using the vernacular for many years in the classroom, often the teaching is done exclusively from translations of standard Western textbooks. There is an obvious need for textbooks in the vernacular. Mere translations only perpetuate dependence and tend to stifle theological inspiration in the Asian context. This does not mean that we can afford to ignore the history of Christian doctrine or contemporary theological thinking in other parts of the *oikoumene*, but priority should

13

be given to laying a solid basis for creative contextualizing in our own languages and in our own historical contexts and cultures.

We need to restore the Bible to its place at the center of the theological community as the authoritative source of our faith. It is now increasingly available in the mother tongues. The particular challenge to Asians is to rediscover the Bible as an originally Asian book and as God's word to the Asian context. Since the Bible was first of all an Asian book, Asians are in a favorable position to appreciate and understand it, and are presented with a unique opportunity to develop new hermeneutical principles which will enable it to be interpreted in a relevant and meaningful way in the thought-forms of our peoples.

There is a close relationship between theological education and the financing of theological schools. The whole theological community needs to face this problem. A careful study should be made of our schools with a view to discovering a style of theological education that it is at once resourceful and inexpensive. We would encourage the idea of a federation of theological colleges, where possible, representing different Christian communions, such as we see in the experience of Tainan Theological College where Presbyterians, Methodists, Episcopalians, Lutherans, and Mennonites work together on the same campus. The cluster idea, and the consortium, offer possibilities where federation may not be feasible.

2

BIBLICAL VIEWPOINTS: OLD TESTAMENT

D. Preman Niles *

In each of these three studies we will be exploring a particular Old
Testament viewpoint: the first on the theme of Man and the Holy,
the second on Man and Nature, and the third on Man in History and
Society.   On any given subject the Bible presents us with a plurality
of alternatives to commonly accepted presuppositions and viewpoints.
Our task is to select and explore alternative viewpoints which may
present fresh possibilities for our life of faith and challenge us to
face new responsibilities.   These three studies will attempt to present such alternatives.

STUDY I. MAN AND THE HOLY (Exodus 3:1-15)
In his book, *Man and the Universe of Faiths,* M. M. Thomas
argues that

> The sense of God accompanies the sense of self, because the sense of self in-
> volves an awareness of its transcendence not only over the world around, but
> also over itself; and self-transcendence brings with it the awareness of an Ul-
> timate Reality which makes itself spiritually "felt" or "known" to the self as
> the Holy. This Ultimate Reality, encountering the self as its spiritual origin,
> ground and destiny, calls for the response of the total self in commitment.
> Since it is a response in which the totality of the self is involved, we may
> call this the dimension of faith.[1]

The approach which M. M. Thomas recommends for an understanding of the relationship between man and the Holy is drawn
from the discipline of the philosophy of religion and has its roots in
phenomenological studies of religions.   The approach itself has certain advantages for our time in that it eliminates the specific cate-
gorizations of Hindu, Christian, Islamic, etc., and emphasizes rather
"the exploration of the faith of persons."   Furthermore, an approach

---

*Dr. Niles is Secretary for Theological Concerns, Christian Conference of
Asia, Singapore.

which presupposes that "the locus of religious truth is persons" and not religious systems *per se*[2] makes it readily possible for us to accept and work with the thesis that "dialogue among faiths at spiritual depth can best take place in the modern world at the point where they (human societies) are all grappling with the spiritual self-understanding of modern man, and the problems of true self-realization or fulfilment of true humanity within modern existence."[3]

If dialogue is to be both vital and meaningful, it should take place at the level of the faith of persons in human societies and not simply at the intellectual level of religious systems. However, if the faith of such persons is to be both distinctive and critical, it has to be informed by the religious truths embodied in each religious tradition. In the case of the Christian or the Christian *Koinonia*, the major source for such faith-perception is the witness of the Bible. It would therefore be difficult to come to a proper assessment of the spiritual understanding of a Christian with an approach which does not help us to understand the nature of the relationship between man and the Holy to which the Bible bears witness.

The insight that "self-transcendence brings with it an awareness of an Ultimate Reality which makes itself spiritually felt or known to the self as the Holy" may be true, for instance, of a Hindu's confession of the relationship between man and the Ultimate Reality. However, it is difficult, if not impossible, to make such an assertion on the basis of the Old Testament. A possible exception could be Psalm 8 where, in the context of the vastness and wonder of creation, man's self-awareness brings with it an awareness of the Holy. But the context of this confession is a hymn of praise which contrasts the magnificence of the celestial bodies created by Yahweh and the lowliness of this creature man whom Yahweh has exalted to a preeminent position in creation. In fact, man's self-awareness follows the recognition of the prior relationship God has established with him and does not precede it. Furthermore, the character of the self-awareness is not self-transcendence but rather a profoundly felt realization of his own unworthiness and the experience of God's graciousness. We have here then an understanding of man's relationship to the Holy which is different. In this study, our intention will be to explore further the character of this relationship in terms of the witness of the Old Testament in the hope that it will inform the spiritual self-understanding of the Christian and set him free

16

to participate in the vital dialogue which takes place in human activities.

We shall begin by looking briefly at the ideas concerning holiness which are expressed in the Old Testament and then turn to an examination of Exodus 3:1-15 which presents a specific encounter between man and the Holy.

In the Old Testament we find ideas associated with the term "holy" which Israel shared with other religious cultures. Holiness is the divine attribute par excellence which denotes, on the one hand, the complete separation of God from the world of man and nature and, on the other—from a human point of view—"an undefined and uncanny energy, a sense of the numinous" or *mysterium tremendum* which is experienced by man in his encounter with "the holy."[4] The term "holy," in the sense of the numinous, connotes a barrier between God and man, which man cannot transgress with impunity. In the Old Testament, the sense of "the holy" is particularly emphasized by the use of the visual imagery of fire (Ex. 3:2-3; 19:18; Dt. 4:12, etc.) The term "holiness" by itself does not denote any ethical or moral qualities, so that it cannot be equated simply with "perfection" or "righteousness" or any such character, though in particular contexts such ideas may be implied. The term "holy" denotes essentially the cleavage between God and man, and signifies the unapproachableness of God (Ex. 3:5; Num. 18:3, etc.).

While these ideas of "the holy" are demonstrably present in the Old Testament, the characteristic expression of God's holiness is in his relationship to man. For example, the holy God enters into a covenant relationship with a people and demands that they be holy (Ex. 19:5f.; Lev. 11:14f.). The holiness which is required of the people is not ethical and moral perfection as an ideal, but the concrete demand to observe faithfully God's statutes and commandments (Num. 15:40). To transgress God's demands is to invite his holy wrath (Ex. 32:10). The historical expression of God's holiness in his anger may be traced back to primitive belief concerning the numinous. However, the same cannot be said of the historical expression of holiness in mercy. For instance, when Moses pleads with Yahweh asking him not to destroy his people, Yahweh repents and is merciful (Ex. 32:11-14; cf. Amos. 7:2f.). So too Hosea sees the expression of Yahweh's mercy as rooted in his holiness and as overriding his wrath.

How can I give you up. O Ephraim!
How can I hand you over, O Israel!...

My heart recoils within me,
    my compassion grows warm and tender.
I will not execute my fierce anger...
For I am God and not man,
    the Holy One in your midst,
And I will not come to destroy. (Hos. 11:8f.)

In its historical expression, therefore, the holiness of God does not denote so much a state of being or even a supernatural energy, but rather divine will and purpose which expresses itself in judgment (Is. 1:4-9; Amos 4:2-3), in mercy and grace (Hos. 11:8f.), and in redemption and salvation (Is. 29:19-21; 41:14; etc.).

In the context of the historical expression of God's holiness, the idea of transcendence which is implied in the term "holy" undergoes a change. As we observed earlier, the term denotes the essential separation of God from man. Thus, time and again, we find references to the absolute holiness or transcendence of God (Is. 33:5; Ps. 47:4; Dan. 4:2, etc.). But when God relates himself to man, "holiness" in its sense of transcendence seems to imply not just spatial or temporal separation, but the sovereign freedom of the transcendent God. For instance, in Solomon's prayer of dedication of the temple, God's transcendence is set out in spatial imagery.

But will God indeed dwell on earth? Behold, heaven and the highest heaven cannot contain thee; how much less this house which I have built! (I Ki. 8:27)

The wonder of it all is that the transcendent God in his infinite freedom has graciously condescended to make his presence known in a temple made with human hands. In a different way Second Isaiah speaks of God's transcendence in temporal terms. Yahweh is the "first" and the "last" or the "beginning" and the "end" (Is. 44:6; 48:12; cf. 41:4), before whom there was no god nor will there be one after him (Is. 43:10). Here, too, Second Isaiah's interest is not simply in making an ontological statement about Yahweh as the one who transcends history as the eternal God. Rather, there is an immediate existential interest. Since Yahweh is the first and the last, he can declare from the beginning the outcome or end and bring to fulfillment his intention. Thus, as the Eternal God, he can do the radically new thing in history, because he is not limited or bound by the course of human history but transcends it. Previously, he had declared and brought to fulfilment the deliverance of a band of slaves from a hopeless situation in Egypt. So too now he declares his intention to redeem Israel from bondage, and he will perform that deed (Is. 42:9). Elsewhere, Second Isaiah speaks of the limitless freedom of the transcendent God by contrasting

God's intentions and activity with that of finite man:

For my thoughts are not your thoughts,
neither are your ways my ways, says Yahweh.
For as the heavens are higher than the earth,
so are my ways higher than your ways
and my thoughts than your thoughts. (Is. 55:8f.)

Besides paying attention to the fact that in the Old Testament the holiness of God is characteristically expressed in God's relation to man, we should also observe the context and reference of man's encounter with the holy. There is now wide agreement among Old Testament scholars that the mundane matters of life and the secular affairs of the world are the spheres in which God's purpose and activity are made known. This observation seems to hold true even in the encounter between man and the holy, for in the Old Testament such encounters are not said to take place, so to speak, in the inner recesses of man's being when he cuts himself away from the demands and attachments of this world. Rather, such encounters take place in the context of the world in which he lives, and do not seem to demand his dissociation from it. To be sure, such encounters are often said to take place in a specially holy place, as in the Mountain of God (I Ki. 19:9-18) or in the Temple (Is. 6), but even so the essentially secular nature of that encounter seems to dominate. This fact is evident, for instance, in Elijah's encounter with the Holy. Elijah escapes to the mountain of God to get away from Jezebel's wrath. In the ensuing theophany, God asks the prophet, "What are you doing here, Elijah?" In reply to Elijah's response that he has run away from Jezebel to this mountain for security, Yahweh states, "Go back." In that encounter, Elijah is driven back to the political involvement from which he tried to escape, to execute the task which God had entrusted to him. Again, Isaiah of Jerusalem encounters the majesty of the holy God in the Temple. In that meeting, Isaiah becomes painfully aware of the fact that he is a man of unclean lips. One of the heavenly beings touches his lips with fire, and he is cleansed and sanctified. He is then commissioned to go back with Yahweh's message to the very people from whom for a moment he had been separated: "Go, and say to this people...." In his encounter with the holy God, Isaiah like Elijah is not simply transported to another realm, but instead gains a sharper understanding of his own social and political responsibility. Furthermore, this responsibility is not stated in general terms such as participation and involvement, but rather as a task which he is called upon to execute.

In our discussion so far, we have made certain general observations about the Old Testament view of man's relationship with the Holy. We may now state these in summary form. First, the term "holy" points to the essential separation of God from man. Second, the distinctive or characteristic understanding of holiness in the Old Testament, however, is as it is historically expressed in God's relation to man. In this context, holiness expresses itself in wrath, mercy, and redemption. Implicit in this understanding of the holy is the idea of transcendence which is to be viewed as the sovereign freedom of the transcendent, eternal God, who can do the radically new thing in history. Third, the encounter of man with the Holy takes place in the context of the world of everyday affairs. In such encounters man's involvement in his world is not negated or rescinded. Rather, he gains a sharper awareness of his involvement in the world of his time. This sharpened awareness is enunciated in terms of a specific task which he is called upon to execute, often in the face of immense difficulties.

We will now turn to a closer examination of a specific encounter of man with the Holy as it is found in Exodus 3:1-15.

II

Old Testament scholars have detected in the narrative in Ex. 3:1-5 the intermingling of two, maybe more, narrative sources. But, more recently, scholars have seconded the original verdict of Julius Wellhausen, the father of the modern source critical method, that a convincing separation of the sources in this narrative is not possible. More positively, scholars now assert that we do not have a haphazard composition, but a finished literary product which should be read, as one commentator says, "with imagination and empathy, as one would read a piece of poetry, for it communicates a dimension of meaning that cannot be cramped into the limits of precise prose."[5]

3:1-6: Moses, while tending the flock of his father-in-law, wanders into a holy place and encounters the Holy God. There is an unusual manifestation of fire, which fills Moses with dread when he discovers that it indicates the presence of the holy which has broken into the human world. "And Moses hid his face, for he was afraid

20

to look at deity (*'elohim*)." The holy which encounters Moses, however, is not an unidentifiable *numen*, for the interest shifts quickly from the phenomenon of the burning bush to the voice of God, which identifies the Holy as the God of the Fathers, the God of Abraham, Isaac and Jacob. In this encounter Moses meets the God of promise who had sworn to the patriarchs to give them both land and posterity. In the subsequent speech, God declares that he will now fulfill that promise.

3:7-10: In this speech, Holiness expresses itself as divine will, which breaks into the world of man to overturn an oppressive political regime that keeps in bondage a group of slaves whose voice of anguish no one was prepared to hear. God's intervention, therefore, carries "a historical accent," which is evident in the verbs which are used in this passage.[6] "I *have seen* the affliction of my people... I *have heard* their cry... I *know* their sufferings... and I *have come down* to deliver them." The speech as a whole reflects Moses' own awareness of the historical situation in which he finds himself. Seeing the mistreatment of a Hebrew slave by an Egyptian slavemaster, he had killed the Egyptian in a fit of anger and fled from Egypt in fear for his life. Now he could feel, on the one hand, the anguish of his people and, on the other, his own helplessness in an impossible situation. The divine address to Moses meets not only the problem of the Hebrew slaves, which was uppermost in Moses' mind, but also speaks to Moses on involvement in his situation. He who had run away in fear after killing a single slavedriver, is now required to confront Pharaoh, the very source of that oppressive power. "Come, I will send you to Pharaoh that you may bring the Israelites out of Egypt." As we would expect, Moses objects, "Who am I that I should go to Pharaoh and bring the Israelites out of Egypt?" (3:11)

Embedded in the narrative skill of the writer is an important theological observation which we must not overlook. In the Call Narratives, to which form critical category this narrative belongs, we find regularly the objection of the person who is called to execute a task. In the account of the call of Gideon, which has many features in common with the call of Moses, Gideon also wavers in the face of the task he is called to execute. God says to Gideon, "Go in this might of yours and deliver Israel from the power of Midian; do not I send you?" To which Gideon replies, "Please, Lord, how can I deliver Israel? Look, my clan is the weakest in Manasseh, and I am the least in my family" (Judges 6:14f.). The same feeling of helplessness is also evident in Elijah's encounter with the Holy: "I alone am left and they seek to kill me" (I Ki. 19:14). For Isaiah it is a feeling of utter worthlessness: "Woe is me! For I am lost; for I am a man of unclean lips..." (Is. 6:5). Jeremiah is overwhelmed by the immensity of the task to which he is called as he recognizes his own inadequacy: "I am only a youth"—a mere child who is called to undertake an impossible task (Jer. 1:6). In the encounter with the Holy, there is not only a vivid portrayal of the social or political problem, but also a sharpened awareness of the nature of each person's involvement in that situation, which is stated as a specific task to be performed. In the face of that demand, therefore, each man is intensely aware of his own inadequacy to execute the task. It is this self-awareness which is expressed in the objection, "Who am I that I should go to Pharaoh?"

3:12: The objection is met with a word of promise to the individual: "But I will be with you." So too for Gideon, there is the assurance of divine help: "But I will be with you, and you shall smite the Midianites..." (Judges 6:16). Furthermore, the promise of help to the individual is not left up in the air, but is anchored down with a sign. "...and this shall be the sign for you that I have sent you: when you have brought forth the people out of Egypt, you shall serve God upon this mountain."

The sign which accompanies the promise of help is sometimes requested, as for instance in the call of Gideon (Judges 6:36ff.), but is also sometimes given without a request, as it is in the call of Moses. Sometimes the sign is demonstrated immediately (Judges 6:36ff.); sometimes it points to fulfilment in the future (Ex. 3:12). Since each sign may vary in character from the other, the more important question for us is the function of any given sign. The function of the sign becomes evident in a discussion between Ahaz and Isaiah found in Isaiah 7. In the face of the dual threat of Syria and Ephraim, Ahaz contemplates asking for outside help. In the midst of this crisis, Isaiah confronts Ahaz with the message "Take heed, be quiet, do not fear, and do not let your heart be faint because of these two smouldering stumps of firebrands..." (7:4). Ahaz disregards Isaiah's advice to stand firm in the faith that God will not allow Syria and Ephraim to prevail over him (7:8f.). In the next encounter, Isaiah requests Ahaz to ask a sign of God whether "it be deep as Sheol or high as heaven" (7:10). Ahaz responds that he will not put Yahweh to the test. To this response Isaiah replies angrily, "Hear then, O house of David, is it too little for you to weary men that you weary my God also? Therefore, Yahweh himself will give you a sign. Behold, a young woman shall conceive and bear a son and shall call his name Immanuel (God with us) . . . . For before the child knows how to distinguish between good and bad, the land of these two kings whom you fear will be deserted" (7:13ff.). Thus, the request for a sign is not an indication of unfaith but faith.[7] Ahaz would not ask for a sign because he would not believe. Nevertheless, the sign Immanuel, God is with us, is given as a concrete historical reference to the divine word spoken through Isaiah that the kings of Syria and Ephraim will not prevail against Judah. "If you (Ahaz) will not believe, surely you shall not be established" (Is. 7:9). In contrast to Ahaz stands Abraham who believed the sign which was given to him "And he believed, and it was reckoned to him as righteousness" (Gen. 15:5f.).

3:13-15: In the call of Moses, the sign extends beyond the worship, which is to be offered at the mountain of God after the deliverance, to the disclosure of the divine name. Moses asks by what name the God of the Fathers is to be identified to the Israelites; and God replies:

Say this to them, "I will be who I will be" ('ehyeh 'aser 'ehyeh).
Say this to them, "I will be" ('ehyeh) has sent me to you.
Say this to them, "Yahweh," the God of the Fathers... has sent me to you.

The parallel statements, with the wordplay on the Hebrew verb *hayah* (to be) make it evident that the divine name "Yahweh" is to be understood as the third person singular imperfect form of this verb, "he will be." In the self-presentation God declares his name in the first person singular form *'ehyeh,* "I will be." Whatever the original meaning of the divine name may have been, in this context the name is to be understood as signifying the promise of God's presence, earlier given to Moses, "I will be (*'ehyeh*) with you," and now extended to the people of Israel. The new divine name Yahweh, which is disclosed to Israel, is the symbol of hope which opens up the future and makes obedience possible. "This is my name forever, and thus I am to be remembered throughout all generations." While the form *'ehyeh* (I will be), which is juxtaposed with the name Yahweh, signifies the assured presence of God with Israel, the full statement *'ehyeh 'aser 'ehyeh,* "I will be who I will be," suggests the sovereign freedom of the eternal God who retains the initiative to make his presence known as he wills. The emphasis on the transcendence of God, which too is implied in the divine name, is evident in another account of the disclosure of the divine name to Moses. "And he said to Moses...I will proclaim before you my name, Yahweh; and *I will be gracious to whom I will be gracious,* and I will be merciful to whom I will be merciful" (Ex. 33:19). In essence, therefore, the divine name, which signifies the assured presence of God, speaks not only of the God of the Fathers, the God of the past who has made a promise, but also of the God of the present and of the future who retains the initiative to intervene and act to fulfill the promise. It is this hope which makes reengagement possible for Moses, so that he can execute the task to which he is called:

For us who bear the name of Jesus Christ, the name which is given as the sign of hope is Immanuel, God with us (Matt. 1:23). Does this sign signify for us special privilege and protection, or does it, as it should, signify God's promise to be with us as we move forward in obedience to his call?

REFERENCE NOTES

[1]M. M. Thomas, *Man and the Universe of Faiths* (Bangalore: CISRS. 1975), p. 31.
[2]Ibid., p. 32.
[3]Ibid., pp. xi ff.
[4]James Muilenburg, "Holiness," *The Interpreter's Dictionary of the Bible,* Vol. 2, pp. 617-620.
[5]Bernhard W. Anderson, *Understanding the Old Testament,* 3rd ed. (New Jersey: Prentice Hall, 1975), p. 51.
[6]Loc. cit.
[7]Norbert Lohfink. *Die Landverheissung als Eid* (Stuttgart: Verlag Katholisches Bibelwerk, 1967), p. 38.

BIBLICAL VIEWPOINTS: NEW TESTAMENT
Ben Dominguez*

Travails of a New Birth[1] would describe the thrusts of the three New Testament studies. "Travails" suitably pictures the struggles of Asians in their attempts to discover an integrating perspective that could make their experiences—dreadful, frustrating, exciting,

*The Rev. Ben Dominguez is Assistant Professor of New Testament at the Union Theological Seminary in Manila, Philippines.

challenging—direct change for the enhancement of life (development). But while "travails" may primarily suggest temporary obstacles that are to be overcome, the word is used in our Bible study to picture a continuing process leading to a perspective in the face of ongoing changes.

"New Birth" pictures the entrance of Asians into a new setting characterized on the one hand by instability, and on the other hand by the persistent quest for the new Asian capable of making the setting support life for Asians together!

While the content (message) of the New Testament texts is of course given stress, equally emphasized is the way the writers of the texts made use of their tradition to address pressing problems in their time.[2] The NT writers' creative use of tradition may bear —even tangentially—upon our quest for models of "doing" theology as Asians.

The three NT studies are man-centered in the sense that we will discuss man's posture (mode of relationship) in our approach to the main topics.

In the first lesson we will consider man as a *believer* in quest of meaningful and relevant ways of living out his faith in the Holy.

In the second lesson we will see man in nature as a *steward* trying to understand his responsibilities as one entrusted with everything that falls under the rule of God.

In the last lesson we will look at man in history and society as a *witness* trying to rediscover and recover the meaning, import, and manifestations of the Holy Spirit's empowering for service.

Hence the NT studies have the following thesis: man in relation to the Holy, nature, history, and society is a believer, steward, and witness.

TRAVAILS I.   QUEST FOR A NEW SPIRITUALITY
(Philippians 3:1-11)

THE POSTURE: BELIEVER

In relation to the Holy, man is seen by Paul as believer. Thus the mode of relationship between man and the Holy is the faith-relationship. This God-man relationship is our focus in this Bible study lesson, for we will try to listen to the text for hints, or clues, or insights for the formation of a Christian life-style (spirituality) that could be understandable and meaningful for our own historical *contexts* as Asians.

Our text (Phil. 3:1-11) starkly portrays Paul's intense reflection on man's relationship with the Holy. Here we have a transformed Paul, a persecutor of the church turned apostle, trying to articulate the change of his life-style because of his encounter with the Holy. That changed life is the fruit of the activity of the Holy!

My choice of Paul as paradigm is inspired by the belief that Paul, an Asian heavily influenced by Hellenic (or Western, if you please) education and culture, embodies in his life and experience the struggles of many of us in Asia today.

PROBLEMS IN PHILIPPI: ON RIGHT RELATIONSHIP WITH THE HOLY

In Philippians we have a picture of a Christian community pressed with problems coming from within the community and from the outside.[3] In our text (3:1-11) we have Paul's warning on the teaching of missionaries who were claiming that to insure man's right relationship with God, man must observe strictly the prescribed laws of their religion. The acknowledged symbol of compliance with this claim is circumcision.

In 3:17ff. we have what Paul calls the "enemies of the cross of Christ"—those who thought that they had already attained perfection as spiritual beings and for that reason they could do anything with their bodies. Insisting that they had been liberated from giving any importance to the body in their relationship with God because only the spirit was of any significance in that relationship, they then declared freedom from any law. They manifested their freedom in scandalous behavior and gloried in such manifestations. This group may have misinterpreted Paul's emphasis on "walking in the Spirit."[4]

In 1:15 ff. (*cf.* 2:21) we have indications of preachers who claimed that they were filled with power and could do miracles. However, those whom they helped were not led to trust in God but in these preachers themselves.[5] Asserting that an apostle of Jesus must manifest power rather than weakness, they argued that Paul could never qualify as an apostle of the Lord for he was no manifestation of transcendence. According to these preachers, Paul's imprisonment was the height of his weakness and of his bringing disgrace to the proclamation of the gospel.

While all these problems were pressing upon the Philippian

Christians, Paul, being in prison, could not go there in person. Hence this letter (or letters).[6] Here we have a good example of a Christian compelled to contextualize theology as he responded to specific problems of a local church.

THE TEXT: STRUCTURE AND EMPHASES

Paul opens his discussion with a warning (vv. 1b-2) emphasizing the crookedness of the teachings of the Law-preachers.[7] "Watch out," repeated three times in verse 2, reveals the urgency by which Paul views the problem posed by these people. He describes them as "dogs"—those who keep on sniffing at Paul's footsteps and feeding on "refuse." (And what can one expect these people to feed others except refuse?) Paul also calls them "evil doers" and "those who cut up the body."

In effect, Paul is saying here that the spirituality of these teachers radically misses what it means for man to have a right relationship with the Holy One who, in his own free will, puts man right with himself!

After his warning Paul exhorts the Philippians, covering the right relationship with God, reflecting on his past (vv. 4-6) and present (vv. 3, 7-11) experiences in his own relationship with God. And Paul presents his exhortation in such a way that the radical distinction of his *past* and *present* relationship with God is vividly emphasized.[8]

PAUL'S PAST: PICTURE OF THE OLD SPIRITUALITY

As Paul pictures his former relationship with God, he takes his personal experience as the point of departure in his theologizing.[9] This is not esoteric. Rather it is societal, at best, for in doing this Paul strongly affirms his solidarity with other peoples. His experiences with the Holy are here shared by him as a human being, in relationship with other human beings who would like to seriously consider a relationship with the Holy. In his discussion Paul is basically asserting that the holiness of God is more meaningfully understood as God's act of doing for man what man really needs but could not do for himself.

In verses 4-6 Paul summarizes his former relationship with God. It is an *achievement-based* relationship. In this relationship Paul's inherited qualifications[10]—namely, his racial, tribal, and parental privileges as a *bona fide* member of God's chosen people—

27

count significantly. These qualifications are seen to have set him over and above all other peoples of the earth in relation to God. Added to Paul's inherited qualifications are his ecclesiastical and theological achievements. He is one of the most orthodox observers, expounders, and defenders of the teachings of his own religion. His zeal as defender of his religion is shown at its height in his attempts to eradicate the Christian movement which he then believed to be based on folly (cf. Gal. 2; Acts 8-9). These achievements put Paul over and above the other members of God's chosen people.

In other words, measured by any standard that could be thought of in his religion, Paul stood second to no man in his relationship with the Holy. That was Paul of the old spirituality. That was the spirituality that secured and insured a right relationship with the Holy through the fulfilment of what is required.[11] Indeed there is *security* in fulfilling what is required, for there is *regularity*. Everything is put under control. Things are assigned where they should be and there is no intrusion of anything strange that may cause disruption. There is also a sense of *direction*. Every action has its corresponding justification and every problem its answer. Then there are signs of *achievement* in relation to the Holy. When one zealously does the requirements of that relationship, then one can claim, as Paul did in his former relationship with God, "...I was without fault" (v. 6). For what manner of man would not feel secure in relation to a God that judges his relationship with man on the basis of achievements?

It is precisely here that the irony is sharpened! Security based on qualifications and achievements becomes not a bearer of freedom but a prison house, a bondage. This security leads a man not closer but farther away from God and from fellow-human beings because one becomes incapable of perceiving God's message and his coming. One is unable to see the sufferings and needs of his fellow-human beings because he is blinded by the glory of his own achievements. In this relationship God is seen primarily as one who must be pleased by man. Man goes to God. He goes to God with his "good deeds" in order to become right with him. When God comes he comes in wrath to punish those who do not fulfill the requirements. Here God is sadly misconstrued and man's role in relation to him is indeed confused.

It is in light of Paul's new experience with God in Jesus Christ that his old spirituality is unmasked. What this Christian life-style is and where it is bound are vividly portrayed by Paul in verses 7 and 8:

> But all those things that I might count as profit I now reckon as loss, for Christ's sake. Not only those things; I reckon everything as complete loss for the sake of what is so much more valuable, the knowledge of Christ Jesus my Lord. For his sake I have thrown everything away; I consider it all as mere garbage, so that I might gain Christ.

Here Paul emphatically declares as *loss* his so-called security in his former relationship with God. He gives this declaration full significance by saying that all that he then counted as "gains" are now singularly dismissed as losses.[12] That security under the old relationship with God has been shown to be useless because its emphasis and goal were security and the praises of others rather than service to others as witness of God's love for all peoples.

Paul goes on to say that to construe God in this way as someone whom man must seek to please in order to be rewarded, is so much garbage.[13] This mode of relating to the Holy is completely "missing the mark" (sin)! To go on with this relationship is to become enslaved by the deception of trusting in one's own achievements in relation to God. For Paul, the experience of the old spirituality leaves one lasting lesson, namely, that relationship with the Holy neither originates with nor is sustained by man. It is solely the gift of God.

There is a significant point that should not be overlooked here. This is Paul's familiarity with the traditions of his people. This is the reason he is able to point out the basic fault of his people's mode of relating to God. Looking at this posture of his people *vis-a-vis* the Holy from the perspective of his relationship with God in Jesus Christ, he was enabled to expose the essence (slavery) of the made-up security of the old achievement-based spirituality.

Isn't it that regionalization demands knowing our own peoples? And isn't it true that one of the best ways we can know them is for us to reflect on what they are saying about themselves and on the questions that they are asking? Aren't their reactions to problems and forces of change better understood when seen in relation to their bases for action rather than by specific acts? These questions compel us as Asian Christians to seriously study our Asian traditions.

For these traditions could either challenge and enrich or mislead and impoverish our ways of living (spirituality) as Asian *Christians*.

PAUL'S PRESENT: EXPERIENCE OF THE NEW SPIRITUALITY

CHARACTERISTIC: TRUST. Paul's present is characterized by an entirely new relationship with the Holy, a relationship which is the total reversal of what he held as normative before:

No longer do I have a righteousness of my own, the kind to be gained by obeying the Law. I now have the righteousness that is given through faith in Christ, the righteousness that comes from God, and is based on faith (v. 9).

This present relationship is a relationship of trust—man's trust in God's love and forgiveness in Jesus Christ. This whole relationship is summarized by Paul as God's free act of putting man, the sinner, *right* with him. Knowledge of Jesus Christ (understanding God through Jesus Christ; having been known by God through Jesus Christ) is that singular event (the "gain") that rendered all other qualifications in his relationship with God as "loss." Trust in man's total dependence in God's power to act: it is in this trust-relationship that man finds true security.

Why is trust the characteristic of the new relationship with the Holy? In light of his new relationship with God Paul is saying that trust is not something that a person does. Rather, it centers on *who* a person is *in relation* to another. In trust, the whole being of a person is involved. Hence, when a person truly entrusts his whole self to God—the God who loves, judges, and forgives— he finds the right relationship. There is nothing that man can do to improve on, enhance or supplement this relationship with God other than trust.[14]

Does this promote passivity? Let us not forget the man Paul here. He trusted, and because of that trust the Good News of God's love for all peoples in Jesus Christ reached the center of the Roman Empire. Because of that trust he was empowered to continually forget himself in order to serve others. It is only in the relationship of trust that God is not misconstrued.[15] It is in this trust-relationship that God is affirmed as God and that man finds his true humanity.

GOD TAKES MAN'S SIDE. Right understanding of God's holiness ("knowledge of Jesus Christ," vv. 8-10) is given birth by God's taking the side of man. He is understood by man because in taking man's side he makes himself known, and when he makes himself known there is change. Hence the understanding of God in the new relationship which Paul is talking about does not come from human ingenuity, for right understanding of God through human ingenuity is not possible at all, since man has no clean slate in relation to God. He stands on this side of the Fall, and this means that his understanding of God, of himself, of others, and of his world is distorted. For, man on this side of the Fall is not "incurably religious" but rebellious! He is always making God in his own image (cf. Rom. 1:18ff.).

For Paul the shift of the ages—from the old to the new—was brought about by God's act of resurrecting Jesus from the dead. This is God's supreme act in taking the side of man.[16] Whoever entrusts himself to God on the basis of the Cross-Resurrection is brought into the new age. The old age of man's futile strivings to make himself right before God has given way to the new age of God's redeeming grace.

FREEDOM UNDER GOD'S GRACE. Paul's present experience of the Holy is characterized by freedom.[17] For him, Jesus means freedom, a re-interpretation of what it is to affirm, "Jesus is Lord." This is freedom to enjoy life under the grace of God. This kind of life knows only one thrust, namely, that it is motivated, tested, sustained, enriched, and judged by *love* for God and for all creation. It is, as Paul describes in Romans, "walking in the Spirit"; a living in between the first and second coming. It is a life whose present is radically determined by what God has done in Christ and what he is doing through the Spirit, expressed especially through the church. It is a life of *service* to others in gratitude for God's love and in joyful obedience to his will as seen in Jesus. This is the Christian life-style, a life of freedom which Paul describes as "living in the power of his resurrection."

THE POWER OF THE CROSS. Paul comes to the heart of the new spirituality when he says:

All I want is to know Christ and experience the power of his resurrection; to share in his sufferings and become like him in his death, in the hope that I myself will be raised from death to life (v. 10).

Knowledge of Christ—yes! This has overturned Paul's old spirituality. It is the knowledge that God in Christ has put Paul right before him—knowledge that is not abstract because it is given birth by an event. It is knowledge-event, or experienced knowledge. It is also crucial knowledge, for it is knowledge of life and death.

31

This is the Cross: foolishness to the Greeks and Romans, for what Deity would allow himself to be abused by mortals? Scandal to the Jews, for what Messiah should die helplessly such a horrible death? For Paul this is God's grace! And this knowledge of God's grace has shown him two deadly things: the *deadly reversal* wherein man's achievement and role become primary and God is pushed to the periphery; and the *deadly omission* wherein no relationship with others is possible except on one's own set standards!

Through the power of the Cross Paul unmasks the basic faults of the false teachings pressing upon the Philippian Christians: the *pretension* ensuring right relationship with the Holy through personal qualifications (and achievements) of the "work-heroes,"[18] the *illusion* (absence of suffering) of the "divine men"; and the *pleasures* (abuse of the body) of the freedom enthusiasts. For Paul, these postures before the Holy One are outright *denials* of the Cross. What should never be overlooked here is the fact that as Paul deals with the problems brought about by the sophisticated, he strives to edify the common church member.

SUFFERING: THE CHRISTIAN'S WAY OF LIFE. Only through knowledge of God in Jesus Christ is Paul enabled to sing with joy the iambics of the new spirituality: that those short *responsive* accents of man's affirmation, "Jesus is Lord!" coming up triumphantly in given historical epochs, are given birth by the strong undergirding accent of God's act. This joyous song Paul could only sing meaningfully when he shared in the sufferings of Christ. For it is only here that the power of the resurrection—the empowering of the Spirit—is truly experienced!

Christ's suffering is vividly portrayed by Paul in the preceding chapter (2:5-11). This is precisely the *context* in which Paul wants to see the Christian's suffering under the new spirituality. Sharing his experiences as a Christian with the Corinthian Christians, Paul declares that suffering with Christ means continually affirming the sufficiency of God's grace in any circumstance. This is not taking belief in God as "opium" for the suffering masses; rather it is that stubborn insistence of the Christian that God takes the side of the afflicted—to empower and liberate them—in the here and now:

Yet we who have this spiritual treasure are like common clay pots, to show that the supreme power belongs to God, not to us. We are often troubled, but not crushed; sometimes in doubt, but never in despair; there are many enemies, but we are never without a friend; and though badly hurt at times, we are not destroyed (II Cor. 4.7ff.).

Suffering with Christ means seriously undertaking as a life-commitment sharing with others the Good News of God's love for all peoples and the whole creation in Christ. This demands a radical approach to human relationships:

No longer, then, do we judge anyone by human standards. Even if at one time we judged Christ according to human standards, we no longer do so (II Cor. 5:16).

and a determination to *listen* to the world to hear God's Word:

I am a free man, nobody's slave; but I make myself everybody's slave in order to win as many as possible. While working with the Jews, I live like a Jew in order to win them;.... In this same way, when with Gentiles I live like a Gentile, ...in order to win Gentiles....So I become all things to all men, that I may save some of them by any means possible (I Cor. 9:19ff.).

Sharing in the sufferings of Christ means *shaping* a life-style that could put into its relationship of trust in God every aspect of life (cf. II Cor. 11:23ff.; Rom. 9-11). It is indeed clear, for Paul, there could be no new spirituality apart from the Cross. Because, for him, sharing in Christ's sufferings—which is basic in a believer's life-commitment to serve God in Christ—is the medium through which God empowers the Christian life-style in his/her own time and situation. Indeed, Paul emphatically claims that it is in suffering with Christ that hope takes shape, develops its content, exercises its power, and offers its blessings, because the basis of that suffering is victory that has already been won.

We Asians are in the process of rediscovering what is Asian, of taking pride in our religious and cultural heritages. Gone are the days when Asian religions were regarded as "sub-Christian."[19] Now we look at our cultural and religious heritages with eagerness, excitement, passion, and depth. In doing this we expect to express and live out more authentically our faith as Christians.

We are in the mood for celebration. If we are to take Paul as our paradigm and to reflect seriously on the message of his experience with the Holy for our situation, then in the midst of our rejoicing and our sense of confidence and pride in our cultural and religious traditions, we are challenged to trust in God—to trust in his deed for us in Jesus Christ!

REFERENCE NOTES

[1] Our lessons are labelled "new" not because they are novel; neither are they called new because they are based on the NT. Rather, we hope we will be challenged *to see the ordinary in a new way.*

² When we lay emphasis on understanding the way the NT writers used tradition. as we interpret the texts, we are saying more. We are really stressing the seriousness with which we should deal with the biblical texts so that we may be enabled to get the message for our time and situation.

Often we talk about biblical inspiration in terms of how the Word got into the printed page. Don't we need the same (or even more) force of that inspiration to have that Word *spring out* of the printed page? For, if there is any truth in what someone said—"in the Early Church faith created the NT writings; in our time the NT writings create faith"—then we have to take the texts seriously.

³ The identification of the so-called "opponents" of Paul in Philippians is at best uncertain. Cf. W. G. Kummel. *Introduction to the New Testament,* translated by A. J. Mattill, Jr. (Nashville: Abingdon Press, 1966), pp. 231-233. R. Jewett, in "Conflicting Movements in the Early Church as Reflected in Philippians" (*Novom Testamentum.* XII, 4 (1970) 362ff.), points out three separate problems in Philippians. These problems are reflected in this lesson.

⁴ This is a fitting reminder for us who are engaged in theological education. If our own students misinterpret what we teach, what can we expect from those who are "primarily" interested in looking for our faults? This reminds us of how Christianity has been measured by Christians' non-fulfilment of the Sermon on the Mount!

⁵ These were the so-called "divine men" (*theioi andres*) who tried to prove their divine nature by their miracles, visions, ecstatic speech, etc. Cf. R. H. Fuller, *A Critical Introduction to the New Testament* (London: Gerald Duckworth & Co., 1966), p. 50.

⁶ Dealing with the "partition theory" of the Philippian correspondence is not germane to our discussion. We are trying to deal with Paul's emphasis which is primarily drawn from Philippians 3:1-11.

⁷ Whether these were Judaizers or some form of syncretistic group with circumcision added to its teachings is beside the point here. What is being attacked by Paul here is man's dependence on and boasting of his achievements before God. Bornkamm's comment, that Philippians is not one of the most important documents on the doctrine of justification, is apt. CF. *The NT: A Guide To Its Writings,* translated by R.H. and Ilse Fuller (Philadelphia: Fortress Press, 1973), p. 105.

⁸ The structure of Paul's presentation of his past and present relationship with God seems to betray his emphasis. He has enclosed the description of his former relationship with God (vv. 4-6) by a powerful portrayal of his new relationship with him (vv. 3, 7-11), as if to say that the former relationship has been *supplanted.*

⁹ Sallie TeSelle, in *Speaking in Parables: A Study in Metaphor and Theology* (Philadelphia: Fortress Press, 1975), posits "an intermediary or parabolic theology—a theology that is, on the one hand, not itself parable and, on the other hand, not systematic theology, but a kind of theology which attempts to stay close to the parables. Such theology may not be the major tradition in Christian theology, but nevertheless it is an important tradition, as evidenced, for instance, by Paul's letters, Augustine's *Confessions,* ... it attempts to serve the hearing of God's word for our time by keeping language, belief, and life together in solution."

¹⁰ He was circumcised the 8th day in contrast to the Ishmaelites' circumcision on their 13th year. He comes from a pure, chosen race, Israel, and from a choice tribe, that of Benjamin—the only patriarch born in the promised land and the tribe that produced Israel's army leaders and Israel's first king, Saul. Cf. M.R. Vincent, *Epistles to the Philippians and Philemon* (ICC), (Edinburgh: T & T Clark, 1897), pp. 94-99.

¹¹ Let us take note here that Paul takes the Law as expression of God's holiness. Cf. Rom. 2:13, 18; 3:31; 7:17, 12, 14. The problem lies in com-

pletely missing the point of the Law as expression of God's will and *turning obedience into achievement*. Cf. Matt. 15; Mk. 7.

[12] K. Barth, *The Epistle to the Philippians*, trans. J.W. Leitch (London: SCM Press, 1962) p. 97, summarizes Paul's declaration in vv. 8-9 as pointing to "what Christ meant and still means for him...recognition of the indictment not on his wickedness but on his goodness—that is what came upon him *dia ton christon* (for the sake of Christ)..."

[13] *Skuoala* is translated several ways by interpreters, e.g. "dung," "filth," "excrement." Cf. M.R. Vincent, op. cit., pp. 94-97, for a detailed examination of the text.

The emphasis according to Barth is on the fact that "something which, once thrown away, is never touched again nor even looked at." And the irony lies in the fact that Paul, in vv. 4-6, had been talking about his goodness!

This may also serve as a *caveat* for us theological educators, lest we be blinded and deafened by our "pet" theological emphases.

[14] Rather than having a word-study on *pistis*, "faith," the writings of Paul could be more meaningfully understood when seen in the context of his concept of sin because he talks about sin as any alternative to trusting God. Rom. 14:23, "Everything that is not of faith is sin," is made more significant because the saying is located within the relationship of members of the community.

[15] Central in Paul's experience is the fact that right understanding of God (in Christ) and relationship with him go hand in hand. The emphasis, however, is on the God who comes and the God who initiates.

[16] Here is the climax of Paul's argument against the Law-achievement posture of relating with God. The cursed according to the Law (one hanged on a tree) has been vindicated by God himself (Cf. Gal. 3:13ff).

[17] Kaseman's description of Christian freedom is both forceful and provocative. He says: "the power of Christ's resurrection becomes a reality, here and now, in the form of Christian freedom, and only in that. The reality is opposed on earth by anything that stands in the way of Christian freedom, and only by that." *Jesus Means Freedom*, trans. Frank Clarke (Philadelphia: Fortress Press, 1972), p. 154.

[18] Bultmann, according to Barth, uses the same designation. Cf. Barth, op. cit., p. 93.

[19] This is vividly demonstrated in one of the basic readings for this Consultation, *What Asian Christians Are Thinking*, ed. D.J. Elwood (Quezon City: New Day Publishers, 1976)

The role of Jesus Christ and the Bible must be seriously given attention by us Christians in relation to other religions.

3

ADAM IN DEEP SLEEP

Kosuke Koyama*

ADAM-ORIENTATION

ADAM, THE NAMING MAN, SAYS "I AM HUMAN": ADAM-CONTEXT

"Man and the Holy" is the theme of this paper. Man—humankind—
that is, *Adam,* creates meaning in his environment. And he lives
in the network of meaning and value. He does so, as an intelligent
person, in ever *naming* all things old and new. "...whatever the
man called every living creature, that was its name. The man gave
names to all cattle, and to the birds of the air, and to every beast
of the field;...." (Gen. 2:19-20). That obnoxious flying insect he
named "mosquito." This powder that kills the mosquito he named
"DDT." That emaciating fever caused by the mosquito he named
"malaria." And this remarkable drug to fight against malaria he
named "quinine." His naming activity knows no end from mosquito to proton-neutron to "Greater East Asia Co-prosperity Sphere"
to "Maoism"—without him there are no names! Take him away
and you will have a nameless world (cosmos)! Creation unnamed!
No name means no meaning. No name means no spirituality, no
responsibility, no administration, no community, and no civilization.
Where Adam is and when he acts the cosmos is named.

The naming man is engaged in a holy act. To name is to sub-
stantiate. To name is to hallow. To name that white stuff "sugar"
is to hallow sugar. To name this woman "wife" is to hallow woman. The moment of naming is the moment of the birth of the

---

*Dr. Koyama is a Lecturer in Religious Studies in the University of Otago,
New Zealand, and is a former Dean of the Southeast Asia Graduate School of
Theology. He is the author of *Waterbuffalo Theology.*

meaning of reality. Name and reality go together. Man's ability to name, however, is tragically his ability to *misname.* Because he can name, he can misname. Because he can misname, he can name. Outside of "Eden" naming always involves the risk of misnaming. I find the Semitic concept of "name" concretely intelligible and spiritually meaningful. When man names things he gives meaning to cosmos. The cosmos is enlivened by him, for him. When man misnames things and persons he creates a "mis-cosmos," that is, *chaos.* A signpost at the entrance of the Dunedin Botanical Garden says, "No dogs and bicycles please." This is "naming." But a similar signpost at the entrance of the Bund Park in the "European section" of Shanghai once said, "No dogs and Chinese allowed." Mao Tse-tung could not forget this "misnaming"—this insult. Japanese as "honorary whites" in South Africa are much in the same line with the victims of this Shanghai signpost. And they accept it! Misnaming means to "mis-organize," "mis-rule," "mis-respond"; it is "mis-life," "mis-cosmos," and "mis-holy." All these "mis-es" make up the chaos. Man the namer is man the mis-namer. He lives between the cosmos and the chaos of his own making. Listen to Alexander Solzhenitsyn:

I credited myself with unselfish dedication. But meanwhile I had been thoroughly prepared to be an executioner. And if I had gotten into an NKVD school under Yezhov, maybe I would have matured just in time for Beria. So let the reader who expects this book to be a political expose slam its covers shut right now. If only it were all so simple! If only there were evil people somewhere insidiously committing evil deeds, and it were necessary only to separate them from the rest of us and destroy them. But the line dividing good and evil cuts through the heart of every human being. And who is willing to destroy a piece of his own heart?[1]

Man experiences the Holy in *his* heart.

I find the following paragraph in Karl Marx's *Capital*:

The manufacture of lucifer matches dates from 1833, from the discovery of the method of applying phosphorus to the match itself. Since 1845 this manufacture has rapidly developed in England....Half the workers are children under thirteen, and young persons under eighteen. The manufacture is, on account of its unhealthiness and unpleasantness, in such bad odor that only the most miserable part of the labouring class, half-starved widows and so forth, deliver up their children to it, "the ragged, half-starved, untaught children." ...270 were under 18, 50 under 10, 10 only 8, and 5 only 6 years old. A range of the working-day from 12 to 14 or 15 hours, night-labor, irregular mealtimes, meals for the most part taken in the very workrooms that are pestilent with phosphorus. Dante would have found the worst horrors of his Inferno surpassed in this manufacture.[2]

This is not cosmos. This is indeed Inferno-chaos. To "name" such inhuman conditions as "inevitable for the sake of economic development" (how often we hear this!) is demonic misnaming—mistreatment of the human. Don't we have many "lucifer match industries" in South East Asia? Don't we know the Sri Lanka tea plantation workers?

The infamous prison dreadfully named "tiger's cage" in Thieu's South Vietnam was an iron bar box 2.5 meters square and 1.5 meters high. In this iron cage were jammed 10 to 17 prisoners. Their hands and feet were chained crosswise day and night. The drinking water was given in the container for human excrement! Even a tiger would become neurotic if it were treated like this. Here no human space was given to the human. Space means the possibility of freedom and responsibility. When space is denied, humanity is denied. Drinking water comes in an excrement container! Man is here placed not in cosmos but in chaos. Human dignity—to be human—demands that water not be given in this way. Man cannot accept the "tiger's cage," no matter what!

Man names and misnames. Adam the misnamer is always confronted by Adam the namer. The sense of human dignity within man rejects the "Lucifer match industry" and the "tiger's cage." As he names he declares creatively, "I am human" and as he misnames he declares destructively, "I am human." "I am human." Is this an insight? Is this a religious conviction? Is this a philosophical conclusion? Is this a committee decision? This is the voice of man in his *de profundis*. He cannot quite understand from where this affirmation comes. But it comes from him. In it is the possibility of man's health, happiness, and future. It is a sacred affirmation. Insult is a possibility because there is this sacred affirmation to insult. Only man, then, can be insulted. In this sacred affirmation is found the universal context in which damnation (chaos) and salvation (cosmos) can be meaningfully discussed.

Man—Adam—does not have to be of a certain race, of a certain education, of a certain income, of a certain ability, of a certain religion. Adam is Adam whether he is with the *Qur'an* or the *Lotus Sutra*, the *Bhagavad Gita* or the *Bible,* the *Communist Manifesto* or the *Origin of Species*. There is neither Christian Adam, nor Buddhist nor Muslim Adam. Adam is Adam whether he speaks Japanese or German, Chinese or Burmese. Adam is plainly Adam—human being. ("...*adham* occurs well over five hundred times in the Old Testament with the meaning 'man' or 'humankind.' This gener-

38

ic term is used only rarely as a proper name for the first man.")[3] He is "dust of the earth" plus "breath of God" (awareness of the ultimate meaning in one's self) is the substance and structure of human dignity. This is the content that refuses to be insulted. "You are untouchable"—and all the many variations of that statement are a denial of this human dignity. " 'Keep to the side of the road, oh low-caste vermin!' he suddenly heard someone shouting at him. 'Why don't you call, you swine, and announce your approach! Do you know you have touched me and defiled me, cock-eyed son of a bowlegged scorpion! Now I will have to go and take a bath to purify myself. And it was a new dhoti and shirt I put on this morning' "![4] The man tragically thinks that he can produce cosmos again simply by changing a dhoti and shirt after this grave misnaming! He can? But that cosmos would be a false cosmos, which is far more insidious than an open chaos. The sense of the Holy tells us this secret. The Holy is an inspiration which maintains the full meaning of "I am human." The Holy is the mysterious *tapas* (heat) that keeps the "inalienable rights of man" warm and protected. Theology is vitally related to this tapas, ground-heat of the Holy. Theology in the Adam-context is, in its first instance, sensitively in dialogue with this tapas. Adam is neither in *Nirvana* nor in "Eden." He is engaged in naming and misnaming in this history. There the Holy is experienced. The Holy, then, is not a tranquil concept. It must be actively engaged in our confusing history. "Man and the Holy" means, then, the widest possible *meaningful* context for humanity.

WAS ADAM "ASLEEP OR AWAKE"? TWO TYPES OF EXPERIENCE OF THE HOLY

As you have noticed, I am attracted to the paired concepts of cosmos and chaos. They go nicely with what I call the "Adam orientation." That is to say, man understands cosmos and chaos if he is authentically man. The experience of cosmos and chaos is co-extensive with the quality of being Adam. (Perhaps one of the "business" expressions of "cosmos and chaos" is the world's multi-million dollar "cosmetic" industry—the selling of the elements that banish chaos and restore cosmos). I think, when we are talking about Adam—and when are we not?—we can experience satisfaction in our communication if we cast human concerns in the language of cosmos and chaos. Do not the Bible and the *Upanishads* begin with such language? Are they not "Adam philosophy" in the sense that it is

39

indigenous to Adam? After all, don't we experience everyday that we live in a cosmos threatened by chaos?

If I may interrupt my discussion just for a moment, may I say that christology which is not entwined with cosmology is unrealistic and unintelligible to Adam? When Christ is presented in the cosmological language he is presented "pre-cooked," as it were, to be taken up in the Adam context and Adam philosophy.

In Japanese the word for "man" is said and written in two ways: *hito* (person) and *nin-gen* (*nin*, person, *gen*, "in between"). Actually *nin-gen* means "person" only in the secondary sense. Primarily it means "where man lives," which comes close to the Greek word cosmos. The Chinese tradition has taught the Japanese people that the concept of man stands in an intimate association with the concept of cosmos (and therefore chaos). The notion that the cosmos is an orderly universe and that this order *is* salvation is an eminently Greek idea. But, as I have said, it is a universally acceptable Adam philosophy too. Disorder disrupts well-being and salvation. Esthetically attractive means salvationally attractive. Think of the traffic situations in the major cities of Asia! Is not traffic-chaos damnation (Bangkok) while traffic-cosmos is salvation? (Rangoon—not so many cars there).

While I am excited about the concept of cosmos and chaos and much helped by them to analyze the evil of the "tiger's cage" and the "lucifer match industry," I feel the Bible is not quite with me! I feel—infinitely—precarious. I am an adopted Semitic enough to say that to be esthetically attractive, a high-degree-cosmos cannot be the "final end of man." Genesis 1:5 makes me uneasy: "God called the light Day, and the darkness he called Night. And there was evening and there was morning, one day." *God named* too! He did so before man began to do so. This is a great objection to my (attractive) Adam-centric cosmology and structure of the meaning of human life. And God named something quite basic! Day, Night, Heaven, Earth, and Sea (vv. 6-13). Why can't Adam name *all* things including Day, Night, Heaven, Earth, and Sea? Why is there this limitation on Adam?

Look at the preamble to the naming man: "So out of the ground the Lord God formed every beast of the field and every bird of the air, and brought them to the man to see what he would call them; and whatever the man called...." (Gen. 2:19). The original intention of naming all things was initiated by God and he prepared

40

the perfect naming context for the man. That is to say that in every naming act man must remember that God preceded him. Immediately continuous with the passage quoted we find Adam naming the Woman. "This at last is bone of my bones and flesh of my flesh; she shall be called Woman, because she was taken out of Man." Is not this a moment of particular significance in view of the story that the Woman was prepared while he was in a *deep sleep*? This sleep is caused by God. Then, it is a "theological" sleep (different from sleep in theological classroom!). It is not "Adamlogical" sleep because it is *not* caused by Adam. It is a strange, unprecedented deep sleep during which the Creator worked. In the *Upanishads* "deep sleep" is dreamless rest in *sunyata* (nothingness). In Genesis, by contrast, it is dream-ful action in *sunyata*.

There are two major living outlooks current in our world today. One looks at the universe remembering that Adam was asleep at one critical moment in the story of creation, and that signifies that he cannot establish his own self-identity and his place in the cosmos unless he makes important reference to the One who put him into the "deep sleep." Here the knowledge of deep sleep makes understanding of the cosmos salvational and meaningful. (Cf. Christ, Francis Xavier and his numerous letters on Japan, Sukarno's *Panja Sila* "Ke-Tuhanan Jang Maha Esa"—Belief in the One God—, Teilhard de Chardin's *Le Milieu Divin*.) This tradition maintains the attitude of theological "enchantment" with the cosmos. The other viewpoint looks at the universe with the understanding that Adam had no such "transcendental sleep." He is therefore the center of all things and *he* named all things. If Adam did sleep, it was caused by himself, not by God (cf. The Buddha; Feuerbach, *The Essence of Christianity*; Lee Kuan Yew; B. F. Skinner, "A Technology of Behavior"). May I call the first thought "cosmology with deep sleep" and the other "cosmology without deep sleep?"

It is important to know that in both cosmologies the sense of the Holy displays its power! Both Feuerbach and Teilhard de Chardin would condemn the "lucifer match industry" at which Marx vented his "holy" indignation. (Mr. Lee Kuan Yew?) Whether one is a rationalist or an irrationalist one says somewhere in his depth, "I am human." "I am human" somehow means "I am holy." Serious dialogue is possible, then, between the peoples of these two cosmologies. Are you a man of "cosmology with deep sleep"? No doubt you engage in discussion on "all kinds of things Adam named" with the man of "cosmology without deep sleep," whether or not you are aware that dialogue is warmed by the presence of the power of the Holy. Please do not simply call the people of "cosmology without deep sleep" secularists. The Buddha was not a secularist. Please do not call the people of "cosmology with deep sleep" pious, naive, and superstitious. Christ was not. The Buddha combined wisdom and holiness in his own Indian cultural way. Christ combined love and holiness in the tradition of Israel.

At this juncture I would like to introduce one overall observation about Asia's spiritual history. Generally speaking our life in Asia has been historically enriched by two great living traditions: first, India-China. "India"—not just Hinduism or Buddhism but the total history of Indian spirituality—invites us to spiritual enlightenment by way of spiritual discipline and maturity. Here *spiritual wisdom* is the central value. "China" speaks to us of a philosophy of maintenance and change of the order in our political and cosmological life. As it does so, it emphasizes the importance of *practical wisdom*. May I say, then, that both "India" and "China" are wisdom-oriented, one spiritual and the other practical. Here wisdom is the principle of the cosmos in the personal, political, and cosmological sense. Chaos appears when ignorance rules man. Each has about twenty-five centuries of experience in expounding wisdom culminating in our day with Gandhism and Maoism. Second, the Judaeo-Christian-Islamic tradition: in contrast to the wisdom emphasis of "India" and "China," this great living tradition has given us the sense of encountering God as Thou. When God (not gods) is introduced—sometimes even as "jealous God"—the sense of encounter is strengthened. Man's individuality is discovered in the light of this Thou-God. There has been influence strong enough in this to change the historical awareness of the Asian peoples.

Asia is thus blessed with two types of truth: *Wisdom* and *Encounter*. The former tends to be "cosmology without deep sleep" (the wisdom possessed by the Awakened One, Buddha) and the latter strongly adheres to "cosmology with deep sleep." ("My help comes from the Lord, who made heaven and earth" Ps. 121:2). Over many centuries, then, we Asians have lived in the context of a historic dialogue between "Adam awakened" and "Adam asleep." We are supposed to have a great deal of experience in this. All this experience is warmed by the power of the Holy. Apart from the

42

inspiration of the Holy there cannot be confrontation between Adam awakened and Adam asleep.

What about man as the namer of all things of whom I talked enthusiastically in the previous section? The people of "cosmology without deep sleep" would say that Adam named *all* things including Day, Night, Heaven, Earth, and Sea. On the contrary, the people of "cosmology with deep sleep" would say that Adam named all, but this "all" includes the *responsible* knowledge that the most basic cosmological orders are named by God. That is to say, what has been named by God is re-named and co-named with God, responsibly, by man in the inspiration of the Creator.

MAN'S INESCAPABLE CONTACT WITH THE HOLY

THE HOLY—DEEP, PERVADING, FOCUSING: THE POWER THAT CREATES ADAM'S "AGENDA"

In the previous section on Adam Orientation I have suggested the image that the Holy is *tapas* (heat) that keeps the sacred secret of Adam and of Adam's world warm. In this section I wish to explore further our experience with the Holy. The Holy is deep, pervading, and focusing. I would like to do this before I attempt to delineate the idea of the Holy.

Do you hear the word "holy" spoken? I find the word "holy" only rarely written or spoken in newspapers, radio programs, and everyday conversation. In nation-wide debates whether or not New Zealand's rugby team should go to the Republic of South Africa to play (no! in the name of humanity; yes! in the name of sportsmanship) in July 1976, the word "holy" was not mentioned. In the critical labor dispute of New Zealand's number one industry, freezing works, the word has not appeared. Instead "travel allowance" dominated the scene. Even among today's murderous waves of advertisements we do not find this word used. I have not heard (so far) of "holy deodorant" or "holy Kentucky Fried Chicken" advertised. We do not often come across "His Holiness" in our daily life either. There are of course phrases such as Holy Bible, Holy Bread, Holy Land, Holy See, Holy Scripture, Holy Sepulcher, Holy Matrimony. But these appear mostly in the special "religious-holy" context. We can then manage our everyday life without using this word. The word "holy" has an almost esoteric sound in this "secular" environment of ours. I would like to attempt some paragraphs right here in which the words "holy" and "unholy" appear.

First, in Bangkok ("the city of heavenly being"—in Thai) a quarter of its population lives in slums, while in the "exploiting section" of the city, the most luxurious high life is going on! Name any latest, expensive model of car, you will find it there. This is "O.K.," says the exploiting section. There is something decisively *wrong* with this city of heavenly being, says the exploited section. This city is *sick*. True, there is something *unholy* about this city (cf. "wrong," "sick," and "unholy").

Second, every year in September the New Zealand hills are spotted by the millions of new-born lambs. How beautiful and pastoral! Then, at this very time of nature's lovely creativity last year, from the abyss of darkness, as it were, appeared two nuclear battleships visiting Wellington and Auckland, the ironmass designed to *destroy* everything that breathes oxygen. Sheep on the rolling hills and the nuclear monsters! What a contrast! I am not saying that there is something holy about sheep, but I am prepared to say that there is something *abominable* about this multi-million-deaths machine. Indeed, there is something *unholy* about the battleships (cf. "destruction," "abomination," and "unholy").

Third, a motorcycle has an engine. The engine produces technological (not spiritual!) power, fumes, and noise. You may ride it on Sri Ayutaya Road (in Bangkok), but you may not ride it into the courtyard of Wat Benjamabopit (Marble Temple). The engine sound and the smell of fumes must stay before the temple (*pro*, "before"; *fanum*, "temple") because they are "profane." One must not ride a motorcycle into the courtyard of mosques, churches, and *wats*, because these are *holy* zones. Don't you know there is *incongruity* between the technological and the spiritual? Mixing the two kinds of powers and two kinds of zones is an affront to the *Holy* (cf. "fumes," "incongruity," and "holy").

Fourth, Japan is a land of chimneys that spew black chemical smoke. Unless we smoke we will die! By all means increase our GNP! Solution? Export our chimneys to South East Asian countries. To Mindanao! To West Malaysia! They will welcome them! Do they? Yes. The section of people who will make money will welcome the importation of *pollution*! Both exporters and importers—pollution *conspiracy*! I find such an international situation chemically polluted. Yes. I find it *unholy* (cf. "pollution," "conspiracy," "unholy").

Fifth, some time ago I was invited to watch an open heart operation at the Otago Medical School. The patient was still and lifelessly pale. A team of doctors and technicians moved around the patient as though they formed one living mandala, at the center of which was the ailing heart. What *dedication* to save human life! I noticed the cluster of most sophisticated medical machines connected in a maze of lines and tubes. As I watched this operation I sensed an inspiring harmony of medical technology, science, skill, and trained mental concentration. Technology seemed to me something more than technology. I felt some *mysticism of technology*. Then I sensed the presence of the *Holy* (cf. "dedication," "mysticism of technology," and "holy").

Sixth, within a year from my first arrival in the United States as a student, I worked as an orderly in a State psychiatric hospital. In the surgical ward where I worked, two persons on an average passed away every month. One night I took care of a dying patient. Under the dim light, since all other patients were asleep, I—a first year B.D. student from beyond the Pacific—alone watched the last moment of this lonely American's life! I gave him his last water. I remember telling myself repeatedly: "this is a *holy moment* because a person is dying." "Holy moment" (cf. "dying," "person," and "holy moment").

In these paragraphs, in which the Holy is focused, I hope I am intelligible. I am puzzled, as you are, why there is some touch of awkwardness attached to the use of "holy" and "unholy" in these sentences. (This would hold true if I were to say these sentences in my mother tongue, Japanese). Why can't I speak about the Holy with greater ease? Why do I feel particular difficulty when I *name* the Holy? Why is it that it takes more mental strain to name the Holy than to name Marxism? Why is it that the understanding of *Panja Sila* involves less effort than that of the Holy? Why is it, for one thing, that the Holy does not come to us directly, but indirectly and gradually? "Wrong," "sick," "unholy," "destruction," "abominable," "unholy." The reason for this must be that the Holy is a depth-reality and not a surface-reality. It is present but it is hidden in depth. It is hidden but it is related and pervading. It comes to us in many forms in the context of our experience of life.

More than any other term, "holiness" gives expression to the essential nature of the "sacred." It is therefore to be understood, not as one attribute among other attributes, but as the innermost reality to which all others are related. Even the sum of all the attributes and activities of the "Holy" is insufficient to exhaust its meaning, for to the one who has experienced its presence there is always a plus, a "something more," which resists formulation or definition.[5]

Augustine's thoughts on time help me in my understanding of the Holy. "What, then, is time? (the Holy?) I know well enough what it is, provided that nobody asks me; but if I am asked what it is and try to explain, I am baffled."[6] Why do we take the Holy for granted? "For nobody moves except in time" (in the Holy?).[7] "When I measure time (the Holy?) it is this impression (that the Holy gives?) that I measure."[8] All things move in time and in the Holy. Nobody moves except in them. The critical mental and spiritual *impression* is made when time and the Holy intersect. "In the year that King Uzziah died..." (Isaiah 6:1ff.).

The power of the Holy pervades in the cosmos which man named with or without "deep sleep." The "pervading-holy" is the "depth-holy." And this "depth-holy" is a "focusing-holy." As it focuses itself *around man* it speaks the language of Deuteronomy: "See, I have set before you this day life and good, death and evil... therefore choose life" (30:15-20). That "Bangkok is unholy" means that the "I am human" is violated in Bangkok. The Holy as pervading, deep, and focusing makes Bangkok a problem-agenda. It confronts Bangkok with "the choice." That "medical technology pointed to the presence of the holy" means that "I am human" has been upheld there. There too "the choice" must be constantly remembered. This is the Holy-related choice. It comes up in front of us by the power of the Holy—deep, pervading, and focusing. This is a profoundly theological situation! Deuteronomy appears everywhere without passport and visas! Do we recognize it?

QODESH ("SET-APART"), IN PRINCIPIO (WHAT HAPPENED IN THE BEGINNING), TABOO (FEAR OF THE MANA OF THE HOLY), AND THE NUMINOUS (CORE-HOLY): "BUT THE MIDWIVES FEARED GOD...."

But what is the Holy? Holy Bible means that the book is not an ordinary book. It is an especially "set apart" book. The American President-elect does not lay his hand upon *The Origin of Species* as he takes the oath of the office at the inauguration. The Bible is used for this set-apart, sacred occasion. The Bible is a sacred book. Holy Sepulcher points to the special sacred tomb of Jesus Christ. That which is "holy" is set apart from a common use by its sacred

46

nature. The Hebrew word for holy, *qodesh*, has a meaning of "separation." That the "holy" is not continuous with the "profane" is shown not only etymologically but culturally.

The Indonesian word *kudus* for "holy" comes from the same root of the Hebrew *qodesh*. This word, with the Javanese *sutji*, carries the sense of consecrated separation. It is important to take notice that *sutji* is more than *resik* and *umbah*—the Javanese words for "to clean, to be clean." *Suk-gkah-ra*, the Thai word for the holy-separation, is more than *sa'aad'* which means "to be clean." Purification and the Holy are closely related. Yet, the concept of the Holy is substantially more than "to be clean." Perhaps a delicate variation in this line of thought is found in the Japanese use of the word *sei* for the Holy. The primary meaning of this word is not "separation" but "perfection." It means fullness of knowledge, virtue, and understanding. For instance, Beethoven is called *gaku-sei*, the musician of the order of perfection. Secondarily, *sei* means separation and unapproachability.

This delicate point with regard to the Japanese *sei* must have been influenced by the naturalistic Shinto view of *kami* (gods). The eighteenth century scholar Motoori Norinaga gave a classic expression to the Japanese concept of *kami*:

I do not yet understand the meaning of the term, *kami*. Speaking in general, however, it may be said that *kami* signifies, in the first place, the deities of heaven and earth that appear in the ancient records and also the spirits of the shrines where they are worshipped. It is hardly necessary to say that it includes human beings. It also includes such objects as birds, beasts, trees, plants, seas, mountains, and so forth. In ancient usage, anything whatsoever which was outside the ordinary, which possessed superior power which was awe-inspiring was called *kami*. Eminence here does not refer merely to the superiority of nobility, goodness or meritorious deeds. Evil and mysterious things, if they are extraordinary and dreadful, are called kami.[9]

The tradition of Mt. Sinai comes with a strong note of separation-consecration: "...put off your shoes from your feet, for the place on which you are standing is holy ground" (Ex. 3:5). It is not common ground. It is separated, consecrated, sacred ground. "You are to distinguish between the holy and the common, and between the unclean and the clean" (Lev. 10:10). "Six days shall work be done, but the seventh day is a sabbath of solemn rest, holy to the Lord; whoever does any work on the sabbath day shall be put to death" (Ex. 31:15).

...And he slew some of the men of Beth-shemesh,, because they looked into the ark of the Lord; he slew seventy men of them, and the people mourned because the Lord had made a great slaughter among the people. Then the men of Beth-shemesh said, "Who is able to stand before the Lord, this holy God?" (I Sam. 6:19-20).

According to Mircea Eliade the sacred has to do with the "reactualization" of what happened in the beginning, *in principio*.

...by its very nature sacred time is reversible in the sense that, properly speaking, it is a primordial mythical time made present. Every religious festival, any liturgical time, represents the reactualization of a sacred event that took place in a mythical past, "in the beginning." Religious participation in a festival implies emerging from ordinary temporal duration and reintegration of the mythical time, reactualized by the festival itself.[10]

The time of "reactualization" is sacred time because in it a primordial sacred event is made present. The sacred time is different from "ordinary temporal duration." It is a festival time. Eliade notes that Christianity is interested in reintegration of the historical time of the incarnate God (Jesus Christ) instead of "reintegration of the mythical time."[11] "This is my body which is for you. Do this in remembrance of me" (I Cor. 11:24). Christianity does not say: "...Do this in remembrance of a mythical sacred event *in principio.*" I find Eliade's "reactualization" as an occasion for human experience of the Holy extremely useful in my understanding of religious phenomena. Is not reactualization a moment of *qodesh*?

If Moses does not take his shoes off, he is violating *taboo* (Tongan *tabu*, Maori *tapu*, Japanese *imi*). Taboo means *restriction* of profane use of the sacred. It is rooted in the awareness of grave danger in the sacred if one approaches it profanely and carelessly. The sacred is dangerous! "Take heed that you do not go up into the mountain or touch the border of it; whoever touches the mountain shall be put to death...." (Ex. 19:12). Taboo, then, points to the holy through the words of warning: "take heed!" I do not think the sense of taboo is irrational but it cannot be explained away by reasoning alone. It touches on the "depth-holy" which focuses around man. I wish to expand the concept of taboo and apply it to our own issues.

When I saw the brutal contrast between the exploiting section and the exploited section in Bangkok, I sensed an unholiness about the city. The focusing-holy attacked me, as it were, and made upon me the "impression" that taboo (in this case the sense of restriction against the destruction of human dignity by economic exploitation) is violated. Nuclear battleships violate the taboo. The Holy ("all

48

living beings that breathe oxygen") is destructively approached. Pollution exportation violates the taboo. The Holy (health and happiness of man) is violated. Motorcycles must not violate the taboo of the holy zone. Medical technology in the heart operation theater impressed me that it approached the Holy extremely "carefully." Therefore there was no violation of taboo. *"Take heed!..."*

What is this dreadful force? At this point I wish to refer to the book called *The Idea of the Holy* written by the professor of theology at Marburg, Rudolf Otto, which appeared in 1917 (Eng. tr. by J. W. Harvey, Oxford University Press, 1923). My reference to Otto is brief and selective within the scope of our present discussion. Otto says that the idea of "the holy" has been obscured because it has been mixed with the concept of moral value. *The holy* and *the good* have gone hand in hand for a long time. In order to restore the original purity of "the holy" the separation between "the holy" (religious category) and the good (ethical category) must take place. (I am, as you see, guilty of this mixing up. Exploitation in Bangkok is an ethical concept which I mixed with the concept of the Holy.) Hebrew *qodesh*, Greek *hagios*, and Latin *sanctus* are at their point of emergence "beyond all question something quite other than 'the good.' "[12] This original quality isolated from the moral connotation is named by him the *numinous* from the Latin word *numen* which means "divine will" or "divine sway." The *numinous* is *mysterium tremendum*. It is non-rational. It cannot be controlled and managed. Otto expounds the adjective *tremendum* by introducing the qualities of awefulness, overpoweringness, and urgency, and the noun *mysterium* by two concepts: "The Wholly Other" and *fascinans·* The central element in the experience of the *numinous* is what he calls "creature-feeling." He quotes Genesis 18:27: "Behold, I have taken upon myself to speak to the Lord, I who am but dust and ashes." Creature-feeling is "the emotion of a creature, submerged and overwhelmed by its own nothingness in contrast to that which is supreme above all creatures."[13] Speaking on "The Element of Awefulness," Otto quotes from Exodus 23:27: "I will send my terror before you, and will throw into confusion all the people against whom you shall come...." "Here we have a terror fraught with an inward shuddering such as not even the most menacing and overpowering created thing can instill. It has something spectral in it."[14] This terror, as one of the characteristics of the *numinous*, "may indeed be so overwhelmingly great that it seems to penetrate to the very marrow, making the man's hair bristle and his limbs quake." It is uncanny, eerie, weird, awful, and dreadful. Have you ever had a "religious" experience of the *numinous* penetrating to your very marrow, making your hair bristle and your limbs quake? If you have, that is one aspect of the *numinous* experience.

After Otto accomplishes the separation of "the holy" from the good, he traces how the *numinous* has been gradually rationalized, ethicized, and humanized (refining development) even to the righteous and loving Father of Jesus Christ. But the *numinous* remains at the core of religious experience. He maintains that religious experience at depth is something more than the rationalized, ethicized, and humanized experience. Harold Turner applies Otto's insight as follows:

Our Father (*fascinans*), who art in heaven (otherness), hallowed (holy) be Thy name (sublime *majestas*). Thy kingdom come; Thy will be done on earth as it is in heaven (energy and urgency of the *tremendum*); Give us this day our daily bread (*fascinans*); and forgive us our trespasses (creaturehood, and *fascinans*) as we forgive them that trespass against us (moralization of religion); and lead us not into temptation (i.e., "put us not to test"—moralization? overwhelmingness?), but deliver us from evil (*fascinans*); for Thine is the kingdom, and the power and the glory (*tremendum*) for ever.[15]

In the Lord's Prayer we have the sublimely refined unity of the *numinous* and morality. I am grateful to Otto that we can see this because of his analysis of *numinous*. Theology must have such unity of the *numinous* and morality. This unity rejects both antinomianism and moralism. This unity can remain as a living principle as long as original *numinous* experience is there. The *numinous* is the core-holy. If the *numinous* dimension is not there we may have our morality gradually degenerating itself to a lifeless moralism. But with the *numinous* alone we may fall into antinomianism. The *numinous* which is *mysterium tremendum* is the sacred *qodesh* power which deepens the ethical dimension of man's existence. (In parenthesis a few naughty words: Don't you think our theological education suffers from the high-degree complex? Does not the academic degree have a *numinous* fascination among us? Is "I am Mr. Ph.D." more fundamental than "I am human" *in our churches*?! Who started this crippling evil? In theological education, should everyone run after the degree? And some of us get the *numinous* Ph.D. by writing on an esoteric subject which hardly has any reference to our own history? "How beautiful are the feet of those who preach the critical Asian principle in theological education!" This principle must include the fight against the degree-complex.)

Taboo is based on the fear of the power (*mana*) of the Holy. "Taboo-attitude"—attitude of fear before the Holy—toward the Ten Commandments, for instance, will give us a first experience of the unity of the numinous and morality. "...you shall not kill. You shall not commit adultery. You shall not steal. You shall not bear false witness against your neighbour..." (Ex. 20:13-16). Do we have the sense of taboo, the fear of the Holy? Do we know that the Holy will judge and retaliate the violators of the Holy? The Holy is dangerous! Do we feel this in our depth? If we don't we are secular and *impious*. Is *fear* a negative value in theological thinking? What is the creative and meaningful use and appreciation of fear? "But the midwives feared God, and did not do as the king of Egypt commanded them, but let the male children live" (Ex. 1:17). Is the sense of fear lost among us today? Can we have the experience of the Holy when we become "fearless"? Aided by technology and science? Is secularism "fearlessness" (absence of the sense of taboo)? Is not a taboo-less world not a cosmos but a chaos? The cosmos-viewpoint, says the Holy, is dangerous!

A KIND HELP FROM THE JAHWIST THEOLOGIANS: THE HOLY IN THE SODOM CONTEXT

You will remember that Otto baptized Genesis 18:27 with an impressive phraseology: "creature-feeling." This famous creature-feeling passage is found at the middle point of Abraham pleading with God for the salvation of the people of Sodom. Let us follow the story:

...Abraham still stood before the Lord. Then Abraham drew near, and said, "Wilt thou indeed destroy the righteous with the wicked? (A highly ethical and logical, not irrational, question.) Suppose there are fifty righteous within the city; wilt thou then destroy the place and not spare it for the fifty righteous who are in it? Far be it from thee to do such a thing, to slay the righteous with the wicked, so that the righteous fare as the wicked! Far be that from thee! Shall not the Judge of all the earth do right?" (Abraham comes to the Lord intelligently with the force of human conscience and understanding in the principle of social justice. He argues like a Reinhold Niebuhr!) And the Lord said, "If I find at Sodom fifty righteous in the city, I will spare the whole place for their sake." (The Lord accepts the form and principle of Abraham's argument. Then comes Otto's "creature-feeling" passage.) Abraham answered. "Behold, I have taken upon myself to speak to the Lord, I who am but dust and ashes. Suppose five of the fifty righteous are lacking?"

In this remarkable story of negotiation, the "Judge of all the earth" goes along with Abraham all the way from forty-five to ten! Abra-

51

ham stopped at ten. He knows that he must not go to zero because such a demand would force injustice on the Judge of all the earth. "And the Lord went his way, when he had finished speaking to Abraham; and Abraham returned to his place" (18:22-33). Abraham must have thought that the negotiation was satisfactorily concluded for the sake of Sodom.

The story is triggered off by Abraham's personal concern over the fate of the sinful city of Sodom. Sodom is a city of human indignity; social injustice; exploitation; slum life; sexual chaos; prostitution; good life for few, bad life for many; racial discrimination; Ph.D.'s in the science of bribery; the rich getting filthily richer, the poor getting hopelessly poorer; political prisoners; quashed human rights.... The "creature feeling" comes in the context of the urgency caused by the "sin which is very grave" (v.20) in the city of Sodom. This is the genius of the Bible. Otto's impressive phraseology unfortunately overshadows the grave context of the story of damnation and salvation.

I find the Jahwist contextualization helpful and realistic. The *numinous* experience is placed in the context of the Sodom dispute: The Holy and the unholy met, not destructively but creatively, in the concerned person of Abraham who felt himself "dust and ashes" as he stood before the Judge (cf. the Apostles, St. Francis of Assisi, Mahatma Gandhi, Mother Teresa, Toyohiko Kagawa). The Sodom context is one in which the Holy is experienced! When we look carefully at our social and political existence today, is it not similar to the Sodom context? He conducted his negotiation not from the position of strength but weakness. "...I who am but dust and ashes." This is wise according to the tradition of the biblical teaching. The creature-feeling has prepared him to proceed with this "secular" problem. Here the *numinous* experience has provided spiritual and psychological energy to solve the problem of the sinful city. If I put it in the language of Indian spirituality, the creature-feeling is now in possession of "the power of the *sunyata*." At this point of contextualization the experience of the Holy has become, magnificently, a social and political power. Political power? Yes. This story is a political story in the sense that it is seeking a workable, just compromise. The *numinous* is contextualized and yields power as great as that of uranium placed in the nuclear furnace. I must agree with Otto that "creature-feeling" itself does not have political implication. But, as I see it, there can be no political power without this "a-political" *numinous*, and that contextualized. The *right* "creature-feeling" in the right context produces right political power. The *wrong* "creature-feeling" in the wrong context produces wrong political power. The *numinous* is the uranium of political power. Don't we need a more careful examination of this?

MELEK AND MOLEK: DESTRUCTIVE PAGAN EXPRESSION OF THE HOLY

To feel "creature-feeling" in the presence of the Creator (the tradition of Mt. Sinai) is one thing, but to feel it in the presence of the absolutized human is another (the tradition of Mt. Fuji between 1889 and 1945). Paganism is, at its root, a demonic use of "the holy," namely, to force one to feel "dread of *mysterium tremendum*" in the presence of a human being. To feel "awed" before the *melek* (responsible king) and to feel so before the *molek* (irresponsible king) is radically different. May I make this remark in the light of the 50-year behavior from the Japanese *molek*-ideology of the imperial *numinous*. Distinguish the *melek-numinous* from the *molek-numinous*! (I John 4:1).

In Israel God's kingship (God is called *melek*, I Sam. 12:12) stands in a critical tension with earthly human kingship. There has always existed some circle within Israel which felt the presence of human kingship to be an apostasy since only God is king (I Sam. 8:7), "...they made kings, but not through me. They set up princes, but without my knowledge" (Hos. 8:4). The human *melek* must be placed under the divine *melek*. The Egyptian, Sumerian, Babylonian, and Hittite patterns of kingship do not have this dimension of God the *melek*. This judgment demands the rejection of all artificially constructed politico-ideological *numinous*. Hitler was "numinously" called the *Fuhrer* (leader) and the Aryan race *Herrenmenschen* (master race). As long as people are controlled by the fear of an artificially produced *numinous*, Israel's experience of the kingship must be remembered.

Molek (Molech) was a foreign god to whom human sacrifice was made in the midst of Israel. Israel had experience of both *melek* ("I am the Lord, your Holy One, the Creator of Israel, your King." Is. 43:15) and *molek* (one who makes one's children pass through the fire. Lev. 18:21, I Kings 11:7, Jer. 32:35). The denunciation of *molek* in the eyes of the people of *melek* was focused on the abomination of the human sacrifice. The mark of *molek* is human sacrifice! Analysis of the recurring pathological appearance

53

of the historical *molek* is a complicated one. I think the Auschwitz Hitler who made Anne Frank walk through the fire was a devouring *molek*. One of the most terrifying tales of the valley of Hinnom is *The Gulag Archipelago* by Alexander Solzhenitsyn. Stalin was not an ordinary human. He was the *numinous* in the *molek* fashion.

Evidently evildoing also has a threshold magnitude. Yes. a human being hesitates and bobs back and forth between good and evil all his life. He slips, falls back clambers up. repents. things begin to darken again. But just so long as the threshold of evildoing is not crossed, the possibility of returning remains. and he himself is still within reach of our hope. But when. through the density of evil actions. the result either of their own extreme degree or of the absoluteness of his power, he suddenly crosses that threshold, he has left humanity behind, and without, perhaps, the possibility of return.[16]

The concept of *molek* and the "absoluteness of power" go dangerously together. The *molek* crosses the threshold and becomes *numinous*. Try to make your own atlas of inhumanity! Is not this world of ours despairingly *molek*-ized? Is not the land in which human rights are denied a valley of Hinnom? Isn't it true that there is an ideologically constructed man-made *numinous* behind every denial of a human right? Isn't it true that only man must make one kind of twisted reference, or another, to the idea of the Holy in order to "justify" the devilish act of his own inhumanity?

Molek! Molek seeks human sacrifice. Such demonic *molek*-ideology is violently destructive of the basic fabric of the concept of *responsibility* in the human world. The sense of responsibility is rooted in the human conscience that one is, in what one does, answerable to his fellow-humanity. Responsibility is a deeply human concept. "I am human" means "I am responsible." And since it is a deeply human concept, it is also a social and political concept. *Molek* makes a contrast to *melek* in that *molek* is the *absolute* that rejects responsibility while *melek* is the *ultimate* that is committed to responsibility. The former grasps the Holy (the quality of personal "set-apartness," "transcendence") for his own gain, while the latter maintains the Holy as the source of blessing to all. I wish to make a distinction between "absolute" and "ultimate" in this paper. The word "absolute" implies "coldness" (unrelatedness—"free or independent of anything extraneous," "complete in itself"—closed society) while "ultimate" implies "warmness" (relatedness—open society). The absolute implies rejection of context (irresponsibility, "Mussolini is always right," Fascist Decalogue 1938) while the "ultimate" implies involvement in context (responsibility, "...government of the people, by the people, for the people...," Abraham Lincoln, The Gettysburg Address). The absolute tends to produce *molek*-totalitarianism. When the absolute is combined with the *numinous* (that is, artificial numinous!) one will soon see the smoke of the valley of Hinnom rising. Is not this the experience of Japanese people up to the annihilation point of 1945?

In the critical year of 1941 there were four Imperial Conferences held on the issue of "The Essentials for Carrying Out the Empire's Policies" vis-a-vis the attitudes of the United States, Great Britain, and the Netherlands. In all these four Imperial Conferences, including the final one (Dec. 1st, 1941) which ratified the decision to make war, the emperor consistently remained silent. The then Prime Minister, Tojo Hideki, was recorded to have concluded the Conference with the following remark:

> I would now like to make one final comment. At the moment, our Empire stands at the threshold of glory or oblivion. We tremble with fear in the presence of His Majesty. We, subjects, are keenly aware of the great responsibility we must assume from this point on. Once His Majesty reaches a decision to commence hostilities, we will all strive to repay our obligations to him, bring the Government and the military ever closer together, resolve that the nation united will go on to victory, make an all-out effort to achieve our war aims, and set His Majesty's mind at ease. I now adjourn the meeting.[17]

(During the day's Conference, according to the Record, "His Majesty nodded in agreement with the statements being made, and displayed no signs of uneasiness. He seemed to be in an excellent mood, and we were filled with awe!")

"We tremble with fear"; "We were filled with awe"—*mysterium tremendum*! The *numinous* emperor silently nods. He transcends science and democracy. He *nods* even though he *knows* that the petroleum reserve for the war operation will last only eighteen months! At the moment of grave decision-making whether or not to take the nation into war, and to engulf all Asia in immense suffering, he remains "absolutely" silent! He does not take "ultimate" responsibility. The numinous emperor (Article III: "The person of the Emperor is sacred and inviolable." The 1889 Constitution of the Empire of Japan) in the Japanese manifestation has become "absolutely" irresponsible to the world and to history. In the three major wars which Japan fought against China (1894), against Russia (1904), and against the United States, Great Britain, and the Netherlands (1941), Japanese military actions occurred before the declaration of war! It seems to me the transcendental imperial

55

numinous did not pay attention to the importance of human communication. The emperor stood outside the context of history! How could he?! For a human to stand above history "with divine dignity" is pagan! It is irresponsibility called "paganism." Irresponsible holiness is the characteristic of the *molek*-holiness. *Molek* is irresponsible yet tries to be "holy," and *therefore* he must seek human sacrifice! Holiness plus irresponsibility produces destruction. Creation means, then, holiness plus responsibility. Is not this the content of the covenant relationship—responsible life together!—about which the Law and the Prophets spoke?

The *numinous* of the Japanese emperor and the Japanese land (the "divine land") have developed from the Japanese myths! I once doubted this. How could the old myths of Japan—granted they are to a large extent political myths ("Record of Ancient Matters," *Koji-ki*, completed in 712)—generate this monstrous violence of imperial absolutism? I thought there must be some influence from the tradition of Mt. Sinai, where the concept of the divine discontinuity with the human is strongly articulated. It must take a sprinkling of such powerful material as the Mt. Sinai tradition to produce such absolutism! But my study on this point revealed to me that the absolution of Japanese imperial *numinous* was generated *within* Japan from her own myths! (See *Herman Roesler and the Making of the Meiji State*, by Johannes Siemes, Sophia University, Tokyo 1968). Be careful! Some myths can produce the power to commit genocide! When mythical imagination is politically combined with the artificial sense of the *numinous, molek* appears on the horizon. It took the total destruction symbolized by Hiroshima-Nagasaki to emancipate the Japanese people from the destructive power of a myth! (the original text of *Koji-ki* is given in 96 pages in the small paperback of Iwanami Publishing House. And perhaps 10 pages of it supplied enough material to produce the demonic *molek*-ideology which cost more than 10 million lives between 1930 and 1945! A million per page!). This observation emphasizes the importance of Israel's experience of *melek* and *molek*. Israel's insight helps us to judge the variety of pagan "imperial *numinous.*" This help from Israel I value more than other help.

What is tyranny, theologically speaking? How do we "de-humanize" the Fuhrer? How do we *disarm* totalitarian symbols? What is the *democratic* use of the *numinous*?

The "secular" means "this-worldly" in our ordinary use of the word. Secularism—"this-world-ism"—means that the entire human value must be located and appreciated by man within *this* world. This world is a puzzling world. Secularism, then, must be a puzzling "ism."

The importance of *this* world ("here and now") far exceeds that of *that* world ("beyond") in today's general mental climate. The *here and now* has received much meaning from *the beyond* in the historical structures of religious piety, be it Christianity or Buddhism. We are invited to endure the hard times of "the here and now" from the promise and glory of "the beyond." But today this "accepted" progression has been challenged. The "here and now" must receive its meaning within the same "here!" As I see it, this emphasis does not mean that people are disinterested in "religion." It means rather that they are searching for a possibility of *"here and now"* interpretation of religious truth. It is a challenging secular hermeneutics with which "secular" people are engaged in in the interpretation of the religions. The *"here and now"* is, theologically speaking, of positive value.

The secular world knows that "the beyond" cannot easily be eradicated. What it is doing is, in fact, bringing "the beyond" into the "here and now." The reason for this behavior is that the Holy is pervading, deep, and focusing in the "secular" world too. The secular cannot be free from the Holy. There is a secular experience of the Holy, but there is no secular non-contact with the Holy. Inescapably we are in contact with the Holy. Secularism is a kind of hermeneutics on the power of the deep, pervading, and focusing Holy. This is a creative secularism. The presence of secularism indicates that the Holy cannot be denied and eradicated.

Here is a short simile by the Buddha Gotama called "Turban Ablaze":

"Monks, when one's turban or head is ablaze, what is to be done?" "Lord, when one's turban or head is ablaze, for the extinguishing thereof one must put forth extra desire, effort, endeavour, exertion, impulse, mindfulness, and attention."

This simile proclaims brilliantly the fundamental message of Buddhism. Here is depicted a situation of critical urgency (not trousers ablaze but turban). And the Buddha agrees that the fire must be extinguished by the "extra desire, effort, endeavour, exertion, impulse, mindfulness, and attention" *of* and *within* man! In this simile, religious truth is one's awareness that "one's turban or head is ablaze." Is this knowledge that of the beyond? No and yes. This awareness does not necessarily come from the dimension of the beyond. Analyze yourself! Study yourself! You will know it! How precise is the analysis of the human predicament given in the *Four Noble Truths* and the doctrine of *paticcasamuppada* (conditioned origination)! "Turban ablaze" is a "here and now situation" and a "here and now experience" which the wise will notice. In this fundamental sense the message of Buddhism is "secular." The Buddha achieved his own enlightenment by the resources within himself. In this noble "here and now context" the Buddhist tradition experiences the deep pervading, focusing Holy. It "secularly" appreciates the Holy.

Yet, the fact that not every one is like Gotama Budhha and needs to be enlightened by the wisdom of the Enlightened One, confers upon the message of the Buddha the quality of "the beyond." Buddha's enlightenment was an event of breakthrough to "the beyond" for his followers. In both aspects, then, Buddhism demonstrates creative secular hermeneutics. It addresses itself creatively to "the here and now."

The Buddha says that your turban is ablaze. You can very well answer that it is not ablaze. You can live quite distant from any sense of urgency. If "my turban is *not* ablaze" is true, the person who says so is telling a simple truth. But suppose it is in truth ablaze, then he is in a fatal predicament. The Buddha experienced the latter case to be "true" in the light of his own understanding. The people of "my turban is *not* ablaze" will experience the holy differently from the way suggested by the Buddha. "Those who are well have no need of a physician, but those who are sick; I came not to call the righteous, but sinners" (Mark 2:17). If we think we are well, then naturally we do not need a physician! Then we stand at a distance from the physician (non-urgency). Man of non-urgency lives at a distance from the deep, pervading, and focusing reality of the Holy. Non-urgency means distance from the Holy. This non-urgent distance from the Holy is the spirit of impoverishing secularism. Impoverishing secularism is then a distant and non-urgent experience of the Holy. Sometimes it is so impoverished that, for it, the world ceases even to be puzzling! "The here and now" in this context is impoverished. "I know your works; you are neither cold nor hot. Would that you were cold or hot! So, because you are lukewarm, and neither cold nor hot, I will spew you out of my mouth," says the Holy One (Rev. 3:15-16).

THE HOLY MOVEMENT OF THE SECOND ADAM

I would like to point out only one aspect—which I think is of great importance—of the meaning and place of the "second Adam" in our discussion. Paul, in his Adam/Christ typology, speaks of Christ as the "Second Man" or "Last Adam." In Adam—the man of dust—is death. In Christ—the man of heaven—is life (1 Cor. 15:21-22, 45-49). A powerful typological contrast! As a member of the "culture of shame" zone (Ruth Benedict) I can readily understand how shame incurred by the head of the family would immediately engulf every member of his family. So Adam, the father of our race, committed the sin of disobedience and every member of his family is tainted by that act by reason of "being a family member." The Patristic Fathers, including Augustine, built a theological system on this "principle of family-solidarity."

I hold that the fallen man (Adam) is still "blessed" because his fallenness does not mean that he is caught blindly in damnation. Paradoxically, since he is fallen he can be saved! "Only the prisoner shall be free, only the poor shall be rich, only the weak strong, only the humble exalted, only the empty filled, only nothing shall be something" (Luther). I understand that the Last Adam came so that Adam may have life abundantly (John 10:10).

"Go and tell John what you have seen and heard: the blind receive their sight, the lame walk, lepers are cleansed, and the deaf hear, the dead are raised up, the poor have good news preached to them. And blessed is he who takes no offence at me" (Luke 7:23).

Typology is not gospel. Contrast-making is not salvific, no matter how profound. The contrast must be killed in order to live by the *movement* of poor becoming rich, weak becoming strong, the humble being exalted.... The typology is not the final word. It is only an introduction to the movement of making the "unrighteous righteous." (Luther). The Last Adam-orientation is this movement

59

taking place within the context of man's inescapable contact with the Holy. It is unintelligible apart from the "Adam-orientation." Luke genealogically (!) traces Jesus to Adam, "the son of God." Then Luke immediately continues to describe Jesus' victory over temptation (3:23-4:13). Adam is prototype ("geneology") and *anti-type* (Adam's defeat by temptation) of Christ. Between the *prototype* and the *anti-type* there is a movement toward a "new creation " (Gal. 6:15). "But if it is by the finger of God that I cast out demons, then the kingdom of God has come upon you" (Luke 11:20). "Now the tax collectors and sinners were all drawing near to him. And the Pharisees and the scribes murmured, saying, 'This man receives sinners and eats with them'" (Luke 15:1, 2). The Last Adam who receives sinners and eats with them is the one who was crucified between the criminals, "one on the right and one on the left" (Luke 23:33). The church and the apostolic preaching saw in *this* the focusing of the Holy. The holiness of God is concretized in the life and work of Jesus. In him the Holy, deep and pervading, took the form of Christ. The Holy in the form of Jesus Christ was astoundingly new, "what no eye has seen, nor ear heard, nor the heart of man conceived" (I Cor. 2:9). It was the form of a *servant*. Yes, it was in the form of the crucified one that the Holy now came into focus.

The name Jesus Christ stands for the *holy energy* that emanates from the servant of God. This "foolish and weak" energy is "wise and strong" energy (I Cor. 1:25). This energy is *distinct* from other energies! It is, in truth, *qodesh*-energy! This energy cuts through our cosmology, anthropology, sociology, economics, and politics. This energy is the *truth* that sets man free (John 8:32).

The relationship between Adam and the Last Adam is not that of abolition, condemnation, and discontinuity. It is not a typological relationship. It is more than that! It is a movement-relationship in the reality of energy. It has to do with the movement initiated by the *qodesh*-energy in the midst of man's inescapable contact with the Holy. This movement is the form of Christ; its awareness is the awareness of belonging to the Body of Christ, the Church. The content of this movement is "sacrifice" and the spirit that guides it is the Holy Spirit. The context in which this movement takes place is the Adam-context; its language is theology, its healing expression ministry.

REFERENCE NOTES

[1] Alexander Solzhenitsyn, *The Gulag Archipelago*, Vol. I. p. 168.

[2] Karl Marx, *Capital*, Vol. I, p. 246.

[3] Article "Adam," in *Interpreter's Dictionary of the Bible*.

[4] CCA, *Suffering and Hope: An Anthology of Asian Writings* (CCA, 1976), p. 19.

[5] Article "Holiness" by J. Muilenburg, *The Interpreter's Dictionary of the Bible*.

[6] Confessions. Book XI 14.

[7] Ibid., XI, 24.   [8] Ibid., XI, 27.

[9] H. B. Earhart, *Religion in the Japanese Experience*, p. 10.

[10] *The Sacred and the Profane*, p. 68f.

[11] Ibid., p. 72.

[12] Rudolf Otto, *The Idea of the Holy* (Oxford, 1923), p. 6.

[13] Ibid., p. 10.   [14] Ibid., p. 14.

[15] Harold Turner, *Commentary on a Shortened Version*, p. 36.

[16] Solzhenitsyn, *The Gulag Archipelago*, Vol. I, p. 175.

[17] *Japan's Decision for War: Records of the 1941 Policy Conferences*, edited by Nobutaka Ike, p. 283.

RESPONSE TO DR. KOYAMA'S PAPER

K. C. Abraham*

I have been assigned a difficult task. I am overwhelmed by the presentation of Dr. Koyama and have not had time to digest all the valuable insights in it. What follows is very tentative in nature.

In this paper Dr. Koyama has combined his deep scholarship, imagination, and above all his refreshing sense of humor. In all this he has given us a style worth emulating!

His paper has confirmed my suspicion about the validity of the classification of our Conference theme into Man and Holy, Man and Nature, and Man and Society. This is artificial. As we heard earlier in the Conference, when we talk about the Holy we have to discuss the struggle for justice, humanization, Marxism, and other issues of society. In fact, theological reflection in Asia, if it is to be relevant, should be based on the manifold struggles of man to affirm his humanity.

A basic perspective that emerges out of Dr. Koyama's paper, which I wish to underline, is expressed in his own words: "I am holy means I am human." This is important and we need to keep it in the forefront of our discussion. When we accept this perspec-

---

*The Rev. K. C. Abraham is Rector of St. Mark's Cathedral in Bangalore, India.

tive we need further clarification on what we mean by "human." It is a term widely used in many different contexts. I submit that in this Consultation we should give serious thought to this question. What are the contents, in concrete terms, that go into this concept "human?"

An important element of this, I suspect, is the struggle and suffering of Asian man for a more just and human social order. There is a beginning in Asia to accept this as the focal point of theological reflection. I hope we can build on it. In fact, I should like to have seen a clearer expression of this in Dr. Koyama's paper.

The next point follows from this. The christological emphasis in this paper is somewhat clouded. Toward the end, almost as an appendix, he has brought in christology. I am raising this point not from a dogmatic standpoint (in fact, I have very little interest in constructing systematic theology). But I do feel that if man is the focus of our reflection, then Christ and his crucifixion and resurrection have a lot to tell us about man. The Cross and Asian suffering are integrally related. This relation speaks to the very heart of Asia.

For many Asian Christians the context in which the Holy is experienced is the "holy company," the church. Dr. Koyama has very rightly provided us with the human context, in assuming that there should not be any difference between the church, *koinonia,* and the human context. This is theologically sound, but we are faced with a practical problem in that their separation has been with us and we need to deal with it when we discuss Man and the Holy.

I offer a final comment with some hesitation. One of the tasks before us is the development of Asian theology. It is a question of methodology. I feel that Dr. Koyama's paper, with all respect to his creative contribution, is still basically Western. All the central categories and concepts are taken from Western thinkers: Rudolf Otto, Mircea Eliade, Von Rad, and others. There are Asian thinkers as well! This is not a criticism but an observation. We are still indebted to Western thinkers for our theological discourse. When will this situation drastically change? What I am saying is that Dr. Koyama's paper has not come to grips with the Asian realities as they relate to the understanding of the Holy. This is partly due to the basic concepts with which he is working.

PART TWO

MAN AND NATURE

4

MAN AND NATURE: A WORKSHOP REPORT

Theological reflection in Asia must be concerned with man in his total context, so that such reflection may provide the resources for life and set forth the responsibilities that attend it. Here we deal, however, with the specific question of Man and Nature in the hope that clarification of this relationship will provide insights for the way in which we understand the total situation.

The man-nature relationship in Asia is complex because of its characteristic plurality of religious traditions, cultural emphases, social orders, and political persuasions each of which, and in different combinations, exhibits distinctive understandings of nature and man. The situation is further complicated by the pervasive influence of science and technology. In addition to local ethnic expressions of religious belief, many religions and philosophies such as Taoism, Confucianism, Shintoism, Islam, different forms of Buddhism, schools of Hinduism, Christianity, etc., have influenced the overall view of man in relation to nature. Some social orders, politico-economic structures, and religio-cultural practices which have arisen out of various understandings of nature, have received self-authenticity and express themselves as independent realities.

In this situation, one cannot speak of an Asian attitude to nature without making very broad generalizations. However, it is possible to identify certain tendencies concerning man-nature relationships which arise out of one Asian tradition or another.

TENDENCIES CONCERNING MAN-NATURE RELATIONSHIPS
SOME FEATURES OF ASIAN APPROACHES TO "MAN AND NATURE." Generally speaking, in Asian religious traditions there is a deep sense of kinship between man and nature. There is a notable ab-

sence of the analytic understanding of nature. Instead man's relation to nature is understood relationally, intuitively, mystically, and esthetically.

Nature is looked upon as self-ordered and self-contained, having its own laws based on an organizing principle (*Tao*). Primary emphasis is placed on the coherent interdependence of nature within itself and in its relation to man.

A number of Asian religious traditions do not place man above or apart from nature; rather he is part of it, sustaining it and sustained by it. He is expected to live in a reciprocal relation to nature and to learn from it the principles of life, virtue, and wisdom.

Even in those traditions which make a distinction between nature and Ultimate Reality, or God (e.g., schools of Hinduism), God is not understood as "outside" nature, but as manifested in and through it. Thus nature at the popular level is sometimes the object of reverence and respect. In some traditions (e.g., Shintoism) the religious cult is primarily concerned with evoking the right relation between man and the gods expressed in nature.

Philosophical formulations of some religious traditions see man as an integral part of *all* life (as exemplified by the doctrine of transmigration in Hinduism) or indeed as part of the whole cosmic process (e.g. the doctrine of dependent origination in Buddhism).

SOME NEGATIVE EFFECTS. The traditional approaches to nature also manifest some dehumanizing and even demonic aspects, both in the life of individuals and of society. Some of the rigid, oppressive social structures (e.g., caste system) and political systems (political hierarchy; emperor worship) seem to be derived from particular understandings of nature and of the order of the universe (e.g., Confucianism and Shintoism). These understandings are sustained by evoking certain distorted ideas about harmony and stability which are said to be manifested in nature.

Some views of nature lead to fatalism and a static view of life, thus undercutting the urgent need for social and political change and reform. Among still others, superstitious practices and oppressive religious institutions are fostered by particular attitudes of fear and mistrust of the processes of nature. Therefore this whole area of Asian attitudes toward nature has to be redeemed from the grip of the demonic.

The Effects of Modernization

The effects of science and technology and the drive for modernization in most of the Asian societies, attended by the spread of secularism and materialistic philosophies, add to the complexity of Asian attitudes to nature. On the one hand, people are freed from the oppressive aspects of their relation to nature. On the other, however, there is a breakdown in man's relationship to nature and of the understanding of community life that essentially is drawn from nature.

Furthermore, the ecological crisis has begun to threaten Asia as well. Pollution and the rapid exhaustion of natural resources are not only questioning the doctrine of progress in technological development, but also raise the specter of an earth which may not be able to support human and natural life. The problem is aggravated by population explosion and the unjust patterns of distribution of available resources.

A scientific view of nature fractures an essentially relational understanding of man and nature by forcing man to think of nature as a "thing" to be used and manipulated. Thus modernization tends to destroy the wider sense of community which is part of the Asian heritage. Particularly at stake are the positive values in the traditional man-nature understandings.

It is in this complex and dynamic context that Asian Christians must seek to define their theological task. In so doing they need to deal creatively with their given situation on the basis of their commitment to Jesus Christ and also appropriate from other traditions those insights that enliven the faith by mutual interaction. This is not a new task. In the Christian tradition, indeed within the Bible itself, there is a constant wrestling to relate the faith to the living context, which gives both meaning and authenticity to the Christian witness. The Asian attempts to "do" theology are thus a part of this continuous process.

Some Insights from the Biblical Tradition

In the Bible we see many streams of tradition, and therefore a variety of ways of expressing man's relationship to nature. One or another of the traditions received emphasis at different stages of religious history, depending on the situation of the church and the demands placed upon her. There has been, for example, excessive emphasis on the theme of man's dominion over nature (sometimes misconstrued as supporting uncritical technological progress) which has led to a one-sided interpretation of man and nature. Greater use must be made of those traditions within the Bible (e.g., those streams of thought emanating from the Davidic Covenant theology —Psalms, Wisdom Literature, Job, etc.) which will serve as a necessary corrective to the present situation.

One seeks in vain in the Old Testament for a clear-cut distinction between history and nature. Quite often "natural events" (the driving back of the sea of reeds; manna in the wilderness; etc.) and "historical events" (e.g., liberation from Egypt) are equally regarded as signs of God's activity. The same easy transition from "nature" to "history" is observable in the Creation Psalms. This relationship must be given prominence, even though the particular symbols of God's relationship with the people are drawn normally from the sphere of political history. In the Creation Psalms (e.g., Ps. 8) there is the sense of the whole of creation (man and nature) "rejoicing" together before God. Creation itself is seen as the manifestation of the faithfulness of God, and as something entrusted to man for faithful and responsible stewardship. In his teaching ministry Jesus drew freely from nature to illustrate and to edify; so do Paul and other new Testament writers. The New Testament, however, is primarily concerned with the in-breaking of the Kingdom of God. The expectation of the impending *eschaton* leads most of the New Testament writings to deal primarily with the tension between the "old" and the "new" order. But even here God's reconciliation is with the whole of his creation which "awaits with eager longing" for its redemption and transformation.

These traditions within the Bible must be drawn and used in the reconstruction of a theology of nature.

Some Theological Issues

The above discussion raises certain particular issues for the "doing" of theology in Asia. As far as the specific area of "man and nature" is concerned, the Asian orientation must result in the broadening, deepening, and indeed the adding of new dimensions to some of the traditional theological concepts. Here are some examples:

First, we need to ask whether there has been an over-emphasis on the transcendence or "otherness" of God over man and nature, and on a qualified transcendence of man over nature. Notwithstanding that there are other factors that have contributed to the theological crisis, we need to attempt to enrich and enlarge the understanding of God and his relation to man and nature which will speak meaningfully to the crisis. The Asian cultural emphases on the immanence of the Holy, the self-sufficiency of nature, and the need to have a reciprocal relation to nature must be taken seriously in the way we understand this relationship.

Second, what is the relationship of man to nature? Does the biblical image of responsible stewardship exhaust all that can be said about it? What light does the relational understanding within Asian faiths say about the way to relate man to nature?

Third, in what ways can we accelerate and participate in those processes that liberate man from the demonic manifestations of "nature relationships"? How can we deal theologically with the dehumanizing and "de-naturalizing" effects of technology and modernization?

Fourth, how can we understand and evaluate the process of life in Asia today? There are many attempts to understand it primarily in terms of the categories of history. Is this adequate, and true to the Asian reality? What contribution can the Asian cultures which always hold nature and history in tension make to this search?

Fifth, a purely linear understanding of time which is implied in the biblical tradition tends to absolutize a consecutive understanding of processes or events in history and nature. It also fails to recognize the positive values of seeing time in a seasonal sense which implies hopes of repetitive opportunities. It may be helpful to explore ways in which these two experiences of time can be brought together for mutual correction and enrichment.

Sixth, there is a tendency in Christian theology to consider morality and ethics in terms of given codes of behavior. Many Asian religions with their understandings of nature have developed a corpus of moral teachings. There is a theological need to relate these teachings to the biblical Wisdom traditions, which also speak of nature as a teacher.

Seventh, similarly in popular Christian understanding, man's alienation from God (sin) is seen as a failure to obey. Some Asian traditions see this alienation in terms of man's relation to nature as well. What is the understanding of sin in a nature-oriented culture and what new dimension does it open to the Christian concept of sin?

Eighth, the Asian orientation also raises basic questions about the way we understand salvation. On the one hand, the political realities of the society are pressing us to reformulate the concept of salvation. Equally important are the questions raised by attitudes toward nature. Can the search in some religious traditions for a coherent relationship between God-man-fellowman and nature serve as a corrective to the individualistic/communalistic, legalistic, and future-oriented outlook on salvation?

Ninth, what does the nature-man relation in Asia say about life-styles, concept of work, spirituality, etc?

HOW TO DEAL WITH THESE ISSUES

First, authentic Asian theology concerning man and nature (or any other aspect) cannot arise without informed understanding and meaningful participation in the context itself. We need to reflect on the nature of the essential dialogue and on the ways of exposing Christians to it.

Second, the nature of the authority of scriptures and of its interpretation is a very vital issue. It may be necessary to develop a new cluster of criteria for "doing" theology.

Third, we need to sharpen further the "Asian critical principle" and the mode of its application in different situations.

Fourth, a more sustained effort must be made to gather data and information that would be made available to those reflecting on man-nature issues (e.g., ecological crisis, population explosion, fertility cults, etc.).

IMPLICATIONS FOR THEOLOGICAL EDUCATION

Theological reflections on man and nature in Asia can meaningfully take place only in an inter-disciplinary way. Attempts must be made wherever possible for theologians to work in cooperation with scholars of other disciplines.

Theological education must be broadly based. Studies of other faiths and cultures must form an integral part of the overall program and not be merely an isolated section of the total program.

Theological students must be exposed directly to ecological issues and to the problems caused by absolutizing modernization and technology.

Greater experimentations must be made in the methods of "doing" theology.

The practice of training students to be ministers only in church-directed situations must give way to broad-based training for a variety of ministries. Included in this multiplicity of ministries is the ministry related to problems of ecology.

In some seminaries there is already an attempt to relate theology to life in nature by the inclusion in the curriculum of agriculture. This is to be encouraged.

Theological education has to be more issue-centered and take seriously the agenda provided by the world it seeks to serve.

We must encourage and foster those "nerve centers" that are dealing specifically with the theological problems relating to man and nature.

Greater emphasis must be given to continuing education of those already in parish situations. Theological education by extension is also recommended as an invaluable tool for education-in-situations.

We should encourage the formation of a theological community concerned with the issues related to man and nature.

5

BIBLICAL VIEWPOINTS: OLD TESTAMENT
D. Preman Niles

STUDY II. MAN AND NATURE (Genesis 1:26-28; Psalm 8)

In this study we will concentrate primarily on Gen. 1:26-28 and
draw Ps. 8 also into our discussion. Usually these two passages,
and particularly Gen. 1:26-28, have been interpreted in the context
of problems which have arisen particularly in the West, namely
(a) the ecological crisis and the problem of man's dominion over
nature and (b) the movement for women's liberation and equal rights
for women, which call attention to the fact that male and female have
an equal place in the special status given to mankind in creation.
While we would agree that these two issues are not purely Western
but also concern us in Asia, our intention in this study will be to
interpret these two passages within a more Asian context, namely
the setting of many cultures as manifestations of the manifold wisdom of God living together and in interaction with each other. This
is a meaningful approach to take, for the theme of Creation is not
simply concerned with the appearance of Israel on the historical
scene but rather with the phenomenon of the universe and man's
place in it.

We will begin by examining the character of the theological
tradition, i.e. the Davidic covenant theology, within which the theme
of Creation has a special place. Then we will look at the context
of worship and the mood in which we must approach the theme of
Creation. Finally, we will explore the special place given to men in
creation and the relationship between man and nature.

I

The motif of creation has a special place in Davidic covenant
theology because both display an interest in the theme of order and

71

stability.[1]   The relationship between creation and the Davidic covenant is to be seen, for instance, in Psalm 89.   The psalm begins by praising God's faithfulness which is evident in creation and in his covenant with David.

I will sing of thy steadfast love, O Lord, for ever;
   with my mouth I will proclaim thy faithfulness to all generations.
For thy steadfast love was established for ever,
   thy faithfulness is firm as the heavens.
Thou hast said, "I have made a covenant with my chosen one,
I have sworn to David my servant:
'I will establish your descendants for ever,
   and build your throne for all generations.' "   (Ps. 89:1-4)

In the next section (vv. 5-37), the manifestation of God's faithfulness in creation (vv. 5-18) is juxtaposed with his steadfast love to David (vv. 19-37).   In both, God's maintenance of order and stability in the midst of upheaval and change is emphasized.

Thou dost rule the raging of the sea;
   when its waves rise, thou stillest them.
   thou didst scatter thy enemies with thy mighty arm.
   the world and all that is in it, thou hast founded them.   (vv. 9-11)

I have found David, my servant;
   with my holy oil I have anointed him;
   so that my hand shall ever abide with him,
   my arm also shall strengthen him.
   the wicked shall not humble him.
   and strike down those who hate him.
   and in my name shall his horn be exalted.   (vv. 20-24)

Just as God ensures order (cosmos) in creation when it is threatened by chaos, so too he ensures stability in human society through the kingship.

The Davidic covenant, like its predecessor the Abrahamic covenant (Gen. 15; 17:1-4), speaks of an everlasting covenant, or a covenant in perpetuity, which Yahweh made with David.   In this covenant, Yahweh binds himself under oath to keep his covenant promise without necessarily imposing conditions on the human partner for the continuation of the relationship (Pss. 89:3f.; 132:11; II Sam. 7:13-16; 23:2-7).[2]   Because the faithfulness of God, which undergirds and sustains order, is not contingent on human behavior, there is implied in this covenant the assurance of social stability. Thus, in the so-called "last words of David," the king confesses: "For he has made with me an everlasting covenant, *ordered in all things and secure*" (II Sam. 23:5).

In contrast, the Mosaic covenant speaks of God keeping his part of the agreement only if Israel keeps hers.

If you will obey my voice and keep my covenant,
    then you shall be my own possession among all peoples. (Ex. 19:15)

The conditional Mosaic covenant places tremendous emphasis on human responsibility. The prophetic cries for social justice and their demand for a radical change in Israel's life-style arise from theological emphases found in this tradition. While the Mosaic covenant could engender in people a critical awareness of the wrongness of things in society and the need for just social behavior, it could assure no real stability in society. In the Northern Kingdom of Israel, in which this covenant theology prevailed, there was, in marked contrast to the Southern Kingdom, constant unrest and turmoil as one dynasty overthrew the other.

Besides undergirding the idea of social stability implicit in the Davidic covenant, the theme of Creation also brought into Davidic theology an ecumenical world view which is so much larger and richer than that of the Mosaic theological tradition. In the Mosaic covenant tradition, a narrow concern for the relationship between a jealous God and a particular chosen people precluded any real interest in the world and its inhabitants, or for that matter in the vastness and wonder of creation. These interests and concerns are found rather in theologians like the Yahwist, the Wisdom writers or sages, and the Priestly Writer, who belong within the Davidic covenant tradition.

The total panorama of the universe is of vital interest, for instance, in Wisdom theology. Here the critical symbols which speak of God's relation with Israel disappear. In the Wisdom books (see in particular Proverbs, Job, and Ecclesiastes), there is no mention of a covenant; nor do we find any interest in a promise-fulfillment scheme which speaks of the purposive movement of Israelite history under divine guidance. Even the particularly Israelite name of God, Yahweh, is seldom used. Instead, more general and universal terms such as Elohim, Eloah, and Shaddai are used. The God spoken of in Wisdom literature is not simply the God of Israel but the God of all peoples and of the whole creation. There is, therefore, greater interest in the natural order of things and the vastness and totality of nature and human culture. Here man is everyman, who is depicted as living his life in conversation with nature and learning from it (cf. Prov. 6:6f.). Such interest is attributed to King Solomon, who is portrayed as the great savant of Israel.

And God gave Solomon wisdom and understanding beyond measure
and largeness of mind like the sand on the seashore....
hyssop that grows out of the wall; he spoke also of beasts.
and of birds, and of reptiles and of fish. (I Kings 4:29-34)

A similar ecumenical interest is evident in the Priestly creation story (Gen. 1:1-2:4). Here too God is Elohim not Yahweh; and man is 'adam, all mankind, not just Israelite man. The focus of interest is on the whole universe: stars, plants, animals, birds, fish and reptiles; and there is no mention of the promised land. It is particularly important for us in Asia to give theological weightage to the fact that the Bible begins with creation even though, within this large framework, it goes on to tell the story of only one people, Israel. For, implicit in Creation faith is an affirmation of all cultures.

The Earth is the Lord's and all that fills it,
the inhabited world (oikoumene) and all those who dwell in it;
for he has founded it upon the seas,
and established it upon the rivers. (Ps. 24:1)

Therefore, the theme of order and stability, which is implied in creation theology, is of vital concern not only for Israel but for all cultures.

II

The Priestly creation story, unlike its Babylonian counterpart, the *Enuma Elish*, does not speak of a struggle between the forces of order and the forces of chaos. Instead, there is from the very beginning evidence of order and stability.

In the beginning God created the heaven and the earth. Now the earth was as yet without ordered form; and there was darkness upon the whole chaotic waters. And the Spirit of God was moving over the surface of the waters. And God said, "Let there be light," and there was light.... Thus creation begins. (Gen. 1, free translation)

Since creation bears witness to the faithfulness of God which undergirds order and stability, creation is very often the subject of praise in Israel's worship. (See for example Pss. 33, 89, 96, 104, 146). In the act of creation, all things—heaven, stars, birds and man—

74

are made and set free to be what they are. So, creation is a joyful event, and the whole of creation responds in praise to its maker.

The heavens are telling the glory of God;
    and the firmament proclaims his handiwork.
Day to day pours forth speech,
    and night to night declares knowledge.
There is no speech, nor are there spoken words;
    their voice is not heard;
yet, their voice goes out through all the earth,
    and their words to the end of the world. (Ps. 19:1-4; cf. Ps. 148)

Even the sea, which in ancient mythology was considered a threat and an evil, is now freed from its sinister role, to rejoice.

The floods have lifted up, O Lord,
    the floods have lifted up their voice,
    the floods lift up their roaring.
Mightier than the thunders of many waters,
    mightier than the waves of the sea,
    saying, "The Lord on high is exalted." (Ps. 93:3-4)

It is also worth observing that, in his debate with God, Job is brought to his senses not by an awesome display of divine power but by a portrayal of creation as it rejoices.

Where were you when I laid the foundations of the earth?
    Tell me if you have understanding.
Who determined its measurements—surely you know!
    Or who stretched the line upon it?
On what were its bases sunk,
    or who laid its cornerstone,
when the morning stars sang together,
    and all the sons of God shouted for joy? (Job 38:4-7)

Such rejoicing is also present in Genesis 1, although in muted form. In this account God is rather solemn. But even here there is the unmistakable evidence of divine rejoicing. "And God saw that it was good!" This formula of divine approbation occurs several times in the creation story (vv. 10, 12, 18, 21, 25) to express the joy of the Creator-God when he sees what he has done; and the whole drama of creation closes with a final statement of divine rejoicing: "And God saw everything that he had made, and behold, it was *very* good" (v. 31).

The attitude of rejoicing or praise is more prominent in Psalm 8, which is a hymn to the Creator of the Universe, than in Genesis 1.

O Lord, our God, how majestic is thy name in all the earth!...
When I look at thy heavens, the work of thy fingers,
    the moon and the stars which thou hast established;
What is man that thou art mindful of him,
    and the son of man that thou dost care for him?
Yet thou hast made him a little less than divine beings
    and dost crown him with glory and honor.

Thou hast given him dominion over the works of thy hand;
    thou hast put all things under his feet,
all sheep and oxen, and also the beasts of the field,
the birds of the air, and the fish of the sea,
    whatever passes along the paths of the sea.
O Lord, Our God, how majestic is thy name in all the earth!

O Lord, our God, how majestic is thy name in all the earth! Here, too, as in Gen. 1:26-28, man is depicted as having a preeminent place in creation; and the special role assigned to him is the basis for praise.

In the theme of Creation, then, man and nature form an interdependent whole, "ordered in all things and secure," and set free to rejoice with their Maker. If we are, therefore, to understand the special place given to man in creation, we must attempt to understand it in the context of creation as it rejoices.

III

As we observed above, the theme of praise is more prominent in Psalm 8 than in Genesis 1. Hence, we shall begin our investigation of the special role assigned to man in creation by looking first at the account in Ps. 8:5-8, which has many features in common with the account in Gen. 1:26-28.[3] In this psalm, the special position man has in creation is not only the basis for praise, but is also set within the context of praise, for man leads the whole of creation in its rejoicing. It is through man that God's majesty is proclaimed throughout the world. In the context of praise, then, the theme of man's dominion over nature should be seen in terms of man's role as leader, so that we understand his rule not simply as the domination of nature but as having a special responsibility for nature.

In this psalm, the idea of domination seems to be in the forefront because the exaltation of man, who is made as one who is only slightly inferior to divine beings, is described in language which is used for the investiture of a king. For, according to this psalm, man like a king is crowned with "glory and honor" (cf. Ps. 45:4f.); and he is made to rule (cf. Is. 19:4) over creation. All things are placed under his feet like booty (cf. Ps. 2:8), which reflects the sentiment found in Ps. 110:1 where the king's enemies are made the foot stool for his feet. However, such royal imagery should not be pressed too far in interpreting the leadership role given to man. For one thing, the beasts of the field, the birds of the air, and the fish

76

of the sea are not depicted as man's enemies; and, for another, there was no other imagery more exalted than that of the royal court to describe the preeminent position given to man in creation.[4]   More important than the imagery drawn from royal court style seems to be the idea of man's proximity to divine beings ("made him slightly inferior to divine beings") for understanding the leadership role given to man.   For, in Gen. 1:26-28, man's proximity to deity is expressed in the bolder language of man made in the image of God, while the language of royal court style disappears except for the use of the theme of man's dominion (cf. Pss. 72:8; 110-2) over the birds, the fish, and the animals (cf. Jer. 27:5f).   We shall, therefore, turn to Genesis 1:26-28 to determine more precisely, in terms of the *imago dei*, the leadership role given to man.

And God said: Let us make *man* in our image, in our likeness;
   and let *them* have dominion over the fish of the sea,
   and over the birds of the air, and over the cattle,
   and over all the earth, and over every creeping
   thing that creeps over the earth.
So God created *man* in his own image,
   in the image of God he created him;
   male and *female* he created them.
And God blessed *them*, and God said to them:
   Be fruitful and multiply and fill the earth and subdue it:
   and have dominion over the fish of the sea and over the birds
   of the air and over every living thing that moves upon
   the earth.

While it is possible, though not certain, that the man envisaged in Ps. 8 is royal man or the mythical First Man,[5] there is no doubt that in this passage Man, Adam, is everyman or mankind, both male and female.

What does it mean to speak of man as made in the image of God? In the Old Testament, the term image (*salem*) is used of something concrete like a statue (Num. 33:52; Ezek. 7:20) or of a copy (I Sam. 6:5, 11).   Therefore, the image is not something *in* man or some spiritual quality he possesses, but is man himself.   The Old Testament gives us no further help in understanding the phrase "the image of God."   However, the term "image" is used of the king in various ancient Near Eastern texts to describe the relationship of the king to the deity and the function the king has as God's representative.[6]   More specifically, Egyptian texts speak of the Pharaoh, especially in creation texts, as "the image of Re" and "the living likeness of Re."   The word of the god Amon Re to Pharoah Amenophis III is particularly helpful in understanding the function of the *imago dei*.

You are my beloved son, produced from my members,
my image which I have established upon the earth.
I have made you to rule the earth in peace.

The priestly writer draws from ancient mythical thinking the motif of the image of God to express the close relationship between God and man and the function which man has as God's representative on earth. A similar indebtedness to ancient mythical thought is also discernible in Gen. 1:2, where the author borrows the idea of the chaotic waters from the Babylonian creation story, the *Enuma Elish*. However, in both instances, the ancient ideas implicit in these motifs are changed and reinterpreted. In the priestly narrative, the image of God does not mean that man is in any sense God's offspring, for he maintains the distinction between God as Creator and man as creature: "So God *created* man in his own image." Furthermore, the motif of the image is democratized, for it is mankind, male and female, that is made in the image of God and not the king. In the Old Testament, the term "image of God" is never used for the king. The democratization of this motif is further evident in the priestly writer's account of the birth of Seth, Adam's son, who is "in his (Adam's) own *likeness* as his *image*" (Gen. 5:3). Just as Seth is Adam's representative through whom, in a sense, Adam is present, so too mankind, as both male and female, is placed on earth as God's representative to rule over the rest of creation.

If we take the total context of Gen. 1:26-30, there is no basis for assuming that the dominion or rule which man exercises is an open license to use nature as he wishes. It is important to observe in this account that both man and other living creatures have only the plants for food (Gen. 1:29f.). There is to be no bloodshed or violence. Even when, later, God permits man to eat flesh, unnecessary bloodshed is to be avoided, for blood—which in Hebrew thinking is the seat of life—is sacred (Gen. 9:3ff). The idea of force, which is implied in the term "dominion,"[7] therefore needs to be understood in the context of man's responsibility for creation, namely to maintain order and peace. This is the responsibility that was usually expected of the king.

Give the king thy justice, O God,
    and thy righteousness to the royal son!....
Let the mountains bear prosperity for the people,
    and the hills, in righteousness!
May he defend the cause of the poor of the people,
    give deliverance to the needy,
    and crush the oppressor! (Ps. 72:1-4)

78

We may now explore further the importance given to the distinction of mankind into male and female. The Hebrew word 'adam usually means mankind, unlike the English word "man" which is used both as a generic term for mankind and for the male of the human species. Therefore, it is not essential in Hebrew to add the parenthetic statement "male and female" to qualify 'adam. Something more seems to be implied in speaking of mankind as both male and female. On an obvious level of meaning, the sexual distinction is pertinent, for without it there would be no possibility for mankind to be fruitful and to multiply! But, is it possible that there is implied here a mutual relationship and interaction between masculinity (dominion) and femininity (endurance, peace), which in their togetherness (see v. 27) realize the function which Man, as the *imago dei*, has upon earth? Such an idea may not be too farfetched, for the writer suggests, on the one hand, the theme of dominion or the control which man should have over creation and, on the other, the theme of harmony and peace which is implied in the statement that man is to share a vegetarian diet with all the animals (cf. Is. 11:6-9).

The tragedy in many of our cultures is that undue prominence has been given to the masculine qualities of domination and aggressiveness. Mahatma Gandhi is one of the few who saw in the feminine qualities of endurance and peace the potential for building a culture on non-violence or *ahimsa*. He says, "*Ahimsa* means infinite love, which again means infinite capacity for suffering. Who but woman, *the mother of man*, shows this capacity in the largest measure?"[8] The Mahatma was particularly impatient of the Western tendency in India to speak highly of the warrior-like qualities of some races and to denigrate the races with smaller-made people as puny and *effeminate*. In the context of this debate, he says,

To call woman the weaker sex is libel; it is man's injustice to woman. If by strength is meant brute strength, then, indeed, is woman less brute than man. If by strength is meant moral power, then woman is immeasurably man's superior. Has she not greater powers of endurance, has she not greater courage? Without her, man could not be. If non-violence is the law of our being, the future is with women.[9]

For Gandhi, the great feminine qualities of love, courage, and endurance are to be seen in woman's role as mother.

In conclusion: Many of our Asian cultures stress the theme of harmony in nature and the need for man to live in harmony with nature. If, however, along with this emphasis, we do not recover for Asia the biblical emphasis of the special position given to man in creation and the responsibility given to him to maintain order and peace, the idea of harmony in nature would at best be a romantic notion and at worst be the basis for a fatalism which allows nature and its laws, as, for example, astrology and the terror manifestations in nature, to control man. It is unfortunate that in the West the theme of man's rule over nature should have received a one-sided emphasis which stresses the aggressive qualities of domination and exploitation. Our contribution may well be to interpret man's leadership role more in terms of the feminine qualities of endurance and peace, so that we may help to restore the balance between the masculine and the feminine principles in man's responsibility for nature. In so doing, we will be able to recover for our time a meaningful relationship between man and nature which will lead once more to a recovery of man's role to lead nature in the dance of creation and the celebration of life. In this connection, it is worth observing that the priestly writer seizes on the divine blessing, "Be faithful, multiply and fill the earth," as the sign of hope for mankind and the basis for rejoicing, at a time when Israel was in exile. Israel had been decimated in her homeland, and a small remnant now remained in bondage in Babylon. Here, then, we have the rejoicing which is not a response to a deliverance already experienced, but one which expresses the joy and hope which can transcend suffering itself. It is important for us that this special blessing is given not only to Israel (Gen. 35:11; cf. Ex. 1:7) but also to mankind as a whole (cf. Gen. 9:1). All cultures, therefore, must be seen as bearing witness in various ways to this mystery of rejoicing together which arises out of and transcends suffering.

REFERENCE NOTES

[1] See Bernhard W. Anderson, *Creation versus Chaos* (New York: Associated Press, 1967), chap. 2, especially pp. 66-68.

[2] See George E. Mendenhall, "Covenant," *Interpreter's Dictionary of the Bible*, vol. 1, pp. 715-721, for an excellent discussion of the conditional and unconditional covenants.

[3] (a) Both accounts seem to envisage the heavenly council of divine beings in which the decision to create man is first announced. In Gen. 1:26 the plural pronoun "us" presupposes God in his heavenly council, and in Ps. 8:5 too the council of divine beings is assumed. (b) In both, man's status is described in terms of his nearness to God. In Gen. 1:27 man is made in the image of God and in Ps. 8:5 "he is made to lack but a little from deity." (c) In both, man is given authority to exercise dominion over the other living beings. Therefore, both accounts must draw from a common Creation tradition found in the Jerusalem cult.

⁴ See Bernhard W. Anderson "Human Dominion over Nature." *Biblical Studies in Contemporary Thought*, ed. Miriam Ward (Somerville, Mass.: Greeno, Hadden and Co., 1975), pp. 27-45. See this study also for a comprehensive discussion of the motif of the *imago dei* in Gen. 1:26-28.

⁵ So Aage Bentzen, *Messias, Moses Redivivus, Menschensohn* (Zurich: Zwingli-Verlag, 1948), p. 12 and Helmer Ringgren, *The Messiah in the Old Testament* (London: SCM Press, 1956), p. 20.

⁶ See H. Wildberger, "Das Abbild Gottes," *Theologische Zeitschrift*, 21 (1965), pp. 245-59, 481-501 and W. H. Schmidt, Die *Schopfungs-geschichte der Priesterschrift* (Neukirchen-Vluyn: Neukirchen Verlag, 1964), pp. 136-42 for discussions of the ancient Near Eastern materials which throw light on the interpretation of Gen. 1:26f.

⁷ The Hebrew terms *radah* and *kabas*, used for dominion here, are used in other contexts for more violent actions. See, for example, Joel 3:13 and Jer. 34:15.

⁸ *Gandhi: A Man for Humanity*, edited by Etti de Laczay (New York: Hawthorn Books, 1972), p. 60. Italics mine.

⁹ Ibid., p. 61.

BIBLICAL VIEWPOINTS: NEW TESTAMENT

Ben Dominguez

TRAVAILS II: CALL FOR A NEW RESPONSIBILITY (Luke 16:1-13)

In the NT there appears to be no active relationship between man and nature outside the context of man being given the responsibility to be a steward of nature.[1] In the two major passages that deal with man and nature, namely, Romans 8 and Colossians 1, man and nature are seen together as recipients of redemption:

...that creation itself would one day be set free from its slavery to decay, and share the glorious freedom of the children of God. For we know that up to the present time all of creation groans with pain like the pain of childbirth. But not just creation alone; we who have the Spirit as the first of God's gifts, we also groan within ourselves as we wait for God to make us his sons and set our whole being free (Rom. 8:21-23).

Christ is the visible likeness of the invisible God. He is the first born son, superior to all created things. For by him God created everything in heaven and on earth, the seen and the unseen things, including spiritual powers, lords, rulers, and authorities. God created the whole universe through him and for him. He existed before all things and in union with him all things have their proper place. Through the Son, then, God decided to bring the whole universe back to himself. God made peace through his Son's death on the cross. and so brought back to himself all things, both on earth and in heaven. (Col. 1:15-17, 20)

In Rom. 8 man and nature are waiting (groaning) to be finally redeemed. In Col. 1 both are pictured as having been reconciled to God through Jesus' death. We see emphasized here that both man

81

and nature are *sharers* in God's redemption. The distinction between man and nature in Colossians lies in the fact that man is an agent of redemption through the church.

In Jesus' parables, nature is used as the vehicle through which the message of the Kingdom of God gets through to man. But it is also in the parables that we find an active relationship between man and nature. This is in the context of man being given the responsibility as a steward of nature, as seen in the parables of "absentee" landlords.[2]

Here we will try to look at the relationship of man and nature with emphasis on the responsibility of man as steward, through the parable of the Unjust Steward.[3]

IDENTITY AND MISSION OF A STEWARD

OIKONOMOS: A Word Study. We will have a brief look at the identity and mission of the steward in the NT through a word study of *oikonomos*[4] (literally, "house manager"). This term occurs only a few times in the NT. (The passages are Lk. 16:1-2; I Cor. 4:2; Gal. 4:2; Titus 1:7; and I Pet. 4:10.)

In Lk. 16 the steward's task is decidedly of a secular ring. He is in charge of everything that falls within the rule of his master (*ta huparchonta autou*). This may include the master's household and his property, the other servants, etc. The steward exercises authority over what belongs to his master to insure order and harmony, which is achieved through the steward's faithful discharge of his responsibilities. At best, then, the steward's authority is delegated, his position is temporary, and his calling is to be faithful to his master's will.

Gal. 4:2: "While he is young, there are men who take care of him and manage his affairs until the time set by his father." Here, the steward is still seen in a secular context. However, this has become symbolic because Paul is using the imagery for his theological discussion. The steward here personifies the Law. The function is clear, however, for the steward is seen as doing everything to prepare the heir, the one who is going to take over the ownership of all that belongs to his father.

I Cor. 4:2: "The one thing required of the man in charge is that he be faithful to his master." Here, the steward is seen as a church leader who primarily sees to it that the members of the church are edified. Paul, in this context, uses the phrase "stewards of the mysteries of God" to emphasize the responsibility of the church leader in proclaiming the Good News of God's love in Christ.

Titus 1:7: "For since he is in charge of God's work, the church leader should be without fault. He must not be arrogant or quick-tempered, or be a drunkard, or violent, or greedy." Here the steward is the bishop whose function it is to propagate and preserve "sound doctrine" in his teaching and life-style. This is the "content" of faith in this letter and in the other two pastoral epistles (I & II Timothy).

I Pet. 4:10: "Each one, as a good manager of God's different gifts, must use for the good of others the special gift he has received from God." I Peter democratizes Titus 1. For, in this passage, every church member is a steward sharing his/her gifts from God with other church members for the good of the *whole* christian community in their life together and in their witness.

THE STEWARD'S IDENTITY AND MISSION. We see in this brief survey that it is in Luke (and partly in Galatians) that the steward is seen in a secular context. In the other passages the steward's task is seen as exercised within the Christian community for the edification of the members and for the proclamation of the Good News to those outside the church. We see the shift from a decidedly secular to a decidedly churchly application of the steward's task. This is a logical development of the thrust of the steward's task, for the NT writings grew out of and were prepared for the use of the church.

The identity and mission of the steward, however, are clear in these varying applications. The steward's task is temporary, he being the chosen representative of the real owner; and what is demanded of him is faithful discharge of his responsibilities for order, harmony, and edification. At best, then, the steward's status is a delegated status. It is given as a trust.

THE PARABLE PROPER: DECISIVE RESPONSE TO CRISIS. The parable of the Unjust Steward minus its early interpretations that came to be added to it can be seen in verses 1 to 7.[5] We can see three movements in the parable. In the first part (vv. 1-2) the steward is sent a note of dismissal from his master. In the second part (vv. 3-4) the steward is shown planning for a strategy to save himself; and in the third (vv. 5-7) the steward executes his plans.

The first part of the parable proper emphasizes the steward's impending dismissal from his job. The master has heard that his steward has been "wasting his goods." There is no elaboration. In what sense is the steward wasting his master's goods? With the current problems concerned with man's use of what is entrusted to him today, "wasting his master's goods" is not at all difficult to define. In fact, it can be rendered powerfully today with the word "abuse." But what does it mean in this parable?

The parable of the Prodigal Son which comes immediately before this parable uses the same phrase. It is used to picture the Prodigal Son at the height of his irresponsibility and waywardness: "wasting his goods in reckless living" (15:13). "Reckless living" (*zon asotos*) may literally mean "living without any thought of life." Can this enlighten the meaning of the phrase "wasting his master's goods" in our parable? We will come back to this later.

The steward's failure to fulfill his responsibilities, which is the reason for his impending dismissal, also results in a broken relationship between him and his master. This is so because in his discharge of his responsibilities he has assumed a position that is alien to his calling in relation to his master.

His dismissal from his job and estranged relationship with his master make the steward re-examine himself. This is how the second part of the parable pictures him. Here we see a very ordinary question occupying his whole being. "What shall I do?" is now the question of life and death for him.

The picture of the steward having a dialogue with himself clearly emphasizes the seriousness with which he faces the situation, as he tries to cope with the resources available to him. He has very few alternatives: in fact, only two at first—to work (dig ditches) or to beg. At once, he dismisses these alternatives and is left with no other course for some time. Then he suddenly exclaims, "I've found it!"

The third part of the parable pictures the steward executing his new-found plan. It is here that we seem to get the meaning of "wasting his master's goods" (v. 2). The phrase appears to indicate non-production. Whereas the Prodigal Son abuses what is entrusted to him, the Unjust Steward neglects what is entrusted to him. These are two sides of irresponsibility: one is exploitation, the other laziness. The steward takes decisive action and executes it with "Seiko precision" (vv. 5-7)—and it does work for his benefit!

Our time and situation are replete with stories like this parable.[6] What then is special about it? The thrust of the parable as told by Jesus does not at all lie in the steward's cleverness in having been able to get himself out of trouble, but in his action of decisively responding to a crisis. He bet his whole life on the decision he made. This approximates, by analogy, the fitting response (decision and action) of anyone who hears Jesus' preaching of the Kingdom. The repulsive way in which the response was carried out signifies the urgency of that response. It had to be done at once!

THE PARABLE INTERPRETED: A NEW KIND OF STEWARD. The Shift: From Urgency to Exhortation. Luke changed the original urgency-emphasis of the parable. He made the disciples (not the crowd) the audience of the parable, and thus revealed his purpose.[7] Using the parable as an exhortation for the Christians of his time, he put together his comments (vv. 8-13) in order to make his interpretation come through clearly.[8] Here we see Luke struggling with a piece of tradition so that it would not remain a mere recollection of a story told by Jesus, but would convey the Word of the Risen Lord concerning man as steward of everything that falls under the rule of God to the Christians of Luke's time.[9] There are four major emphases we can draw from this shift from urgency to exhortation.

1. The steward is "wiser." There is the challenge for the "sons of light" (Christians) to be wiser than the "sons of the world" (represented by the Unjust Steward) in discerning and meeting the needs of their time. In fact, I think it is closer to the truth to say that Luke is not only challenging but reminding the Christians that they are supposed to be wiser than the "sons of the world" in meeting the demands of their time because they have all the reasons to do so. In what sense are the Christians wiser?

The parable of the Rich Fool (Luke 13) may offer us help. In this parable the non-recognition (denial) of the rich man that he is a steward of all the riches that he has acquired makes everything that he has worked for all his life in vain. He dies before enjoying them. This steward forgot the temporariness of his status. The believer should know fully well his role as steward of God and the demand for him to be faithful in exercising his responsibilities within the limits of his commitments as steward of all that God has entrusted to him. He knows that his vast authority is delegated authority. He therefore has the responsibility to be "wiser" than the "sons of the world" in handling his affairs here and now.

2. The steward's responsibility under God. The believer's acceptance of his responsibility over everything entrusted to him *re-*

flects the seriousness with which he takes his relationship with God. Stated differently, his actions as a steward reflect who his God is! This is the emphasis drawn from vv. 10-12. It is interesting to see in these verses that the relationship of small matters, big matters, worldly wealth, true wealth, what belongs to someone, what belongs to you—all take their rightful place within the faithful discharge by the steward of his responsibilities.

Good stewardship consists, then, in the believer's serious and urgent assumption of his identity and calling as a steward, wherein everything entrusted to him is seen as it should be seen, used as it should be used. In this way, as the parables of our Lord emphasize, all our goods will become vehicles of the message and blessings of the Kingdom of God to all peoples.

3. The steward and wealth. The concluding verse reads:

No servant can be the slave of two masters; he will hate one and love the other; he will be loyal to one and despise the other. You cannot serve both God and money (v. 13).

Here is a piece of tradition which Luke shares with Matthew (6:24). But, whereas in Matthew this saying is taken as an independent logion included in the Sermon on the Mount, Luke uses it to conclude the parable of the Unjust Steward. For Luke the saying serves as both warning and exhortation. In this saying Luke's emphasis on the whole parable is sharpened.

The warning is this: if you serve wealth you will simultaneously fall into two traps: you will draw away from God and you will abuse everything that is entrusted to you, even your own life! This warning is vividly seen in the parables of the Rich Fool (ch. 12) and the Prodigal Son (ch. 15). It is also illustrated by the Pharisees in 16:14 and the rich man in the parable of the Rich Man and Lazarus (16:19ff.). In these illustrations the utter disregard for other persons and the abuse of things entrusted are the concrete expressions of drawing away from God. These actions portray the height of man's denial of his role as a steward. The exhortation is this: serve God and you will be empowered to put everything entrusted to you in its right place!

4. The steward and his responsibility. As the Christian movement became more and more separated in time from the resurrection event and from the eyewitnesses, and as the Christians were hit by pressures from other movements (religious and pseudo-religious) and from the Empire, their expectation of the End was heightened.

The result of that heightened expectation of the second coming was passivity and detachment in relation to the world. The continuing influx of poor people into the church also posed some problems in the continuing life and mission of the Christian communities. This seemed to be the general climate pervading the churches that Luke addressed.

Luke, interpreting the traditions of his church to the Christians of his time, affirmed that the End had been delayed. He then enjoined his fellow Christians to take the world seriously, to participate actively in the affairs of the societies they were in. He claimed that it is only in taking the world seriously, and all the things entrusted to the believers, that their faith in the Risen Lord can be concretely expressed and tested. A major point in Luke's emphasis on taking the world seriously is the Christian's active exercise of his/her responsibility as steward. Here Luke seems to have concentrated on poverty[10] as the context in which the steward's faithfulness in his calling must be seen.

In dealing with this emphasis on the steward's responsibility, Luke presents a model-relationship between man and everything entrusted to him. It is neither abuse (exploitation) nor neglect (non-production). This is so because, for Luke, man can never have a meaningful relationship with everything that is placed in his care, that is, everything that falls under the authority of God, apart from his relationship with God in Christ and with other people. This appears to be the basis of his emphatic claim that the only right use of wealth is to help the poor.

For Luke, it is in man's urgent and serious assumption of his identity and mission as steward that all creation is made one under God's rule in Jesus Christ. The church, then, must embody in her life the identity and mission of God's steward so as to bring all creation to affirm in celebration: Behold! All creation has become new!

REFERENCE NOTES

[1] Compared to the OT, the NT writings could be said not to have given emphasis to nature. Although the apocalyptic emphasis which had influenced the NT writings may have contributed to a "meager" treatment of nature in these writings, the NT in general does not carry the apocalyptic indifference to nature. What should be given attention is the NT emphasis on the redemption of *all* creation in Jesus Christ.

2 John Dominic Crossan, *In Parables: The Challenge of the Historical Jesus* (New York: Harper & Row, 1973), posits two schemes of servant parables (Parables of Reckoning): the normal scheme, where the good servant is rewarded and the bad punished; and the reversed scheme, where the bad is rewarded and good punished, pp. 96ff. Diagram of both schemes on p. 117.

3 I considered using "manager" instead of "steward" but I have difficulty dissociating the title "manager" from profit and this may prejudice my discussion. "Steward," then, is used in the discussion. This term still captures the image of a servant, which is the basic meaning of the term.

4 This approach has its limitations because of the fact that the *context* greatly determines the meaning of a word.

5 There is consensus of scholars that there had been various applications of this parable as seen in vv. 8-13. C. H. Dodd. *Parables of the Kingdom* (Digswell Place: James Nisbet and Co., 1961) p. 17, for instance, says: "We can almost see here notes for 3 separate sermons on the parable as text." When it comes to the question of the original ending of the parable, there is no consensus of scholars. There are arguments for 16:9; 16:8; 16:7. In our discussion we are taking 16:7 as the original ending of the parable. A brief but helpful resume of the debate on this issue can be found in D. O. Via, Jr., *The Parables: Their Literary and Existential Dimensions* (Philadelphia: Fortress Press, 1967), pp. 157-160.

6 Norman Perrin, in *Rediscovering the Teaching of Jesus* (New York: Harper & Row, 1967), p. 115, translates the parable into modern (American) idiom—the parable of the Labor Racketeer. I quote the concluding part: "He was duly convicted and after he had exhausted all his rights to appeal, he finally served a sentence in Atlanta Federal penitentiary. Having served his time, he took his money and moved to Miami Beach, where he lived happily ever after."
Commenting on the emphasis of the parable of the Unjust Steward. Perrin says, "The point of the story is that we have here a man in crisis....but he is a man of decision: faced with a crisis, he acted decisively. Again. we are back to the point of the crisis of the men confronted by Jesus, his ministry and proclamation, and the necessity for decision *now*."

7 Change of audience is one of the "ten laws of transformation" of the parables of Jesus, according to Joachim Jeremias. *The Parables of Jesus*, trans. S. H. Hooke (New York: Charles Scribner's Sons. 1963), pp. 113-114.

8 Perrin, op. cit., p. 115, says: "Probably it was felt that no touching up of the story itself could make such a wholly disreputable character edifying!" R. Bultmann. in *The History of the Synoptic Tradition*, p. 200 also says, "...one can learn from the slyness of a deceiver; but in what way?" What should be emphasized here is the role of Luke as *interpreter* of tradition.

9 Cf. G. Bornkamm. *The NT: A Guide to Its Writings*, p. 146: "Thus the NT writings actually passed on Jesus' word insofar as they answer each in its own way the question. not so much of *who he was*, but of *who he is*."
Luke interpreted the parable of the Unjust Steward in a particular historical context and with a particular pressing interest. This is the basic presupposition, as I understand it, of our contextualization movement in Asia. A text, in order to be understood meaningfully, must always have a context.

10 This Lukan emphasis on poverty has been recognized by interpreters but no major work on this Lukan thrust has come out so far. Our Asian setting may prove to be a helpful context for a serious consideration of this Lukan emphasis.

88

6

TOWARD A CHRISTIAN THEOLOGY OF MAN IN NATURE

Chung Choon Kim*

One of the four philosophical questions that Immanuel Kant, in 1800 —four years before his death—put to both his contemporaries and to men of coming generations is, "What is man?" He was not, however, the first one to put such a question. The same kind of question was put to Adam, as it is recorded in Genesis Chapter 3, when God asked him, "Where are you?"

It was not a question of definition, but of asking his position or relation to his Creator, since the man (Adam) had purposely hidden himself from God because of his guilty conscience in violating God's command. This question has a religious connotation. A similar question regarding man was put to Cain when he killed his brother Abel, "Where is Abel your brother?" This question seeks to know man's proper attitude to his fellowman which is an ethical question.

The biblical writers are much concerned with both "God-man" and "man-man" relationships, but less with that of "man-nature." The Bible is indeed full of the records of God-man and man-man relationships. But it is surprising to know that very few records of man-nature relationships are to be found, and it is also true that these few records are not seriously considered or understood by Old Testament scholars.

For our discussion on the subject, Man in Nature, we must first try to find some of the implications which the biblical writers tried to draw concerning the man-nature relationship.

---

*Dr. Chung Choon Kim is Professor of Old Testament at Hankuk Theological Seminary in Seoul, Korea.

BIBLICAL VIEWS OF THE MAN-NATURE RELATIONSHIP

THE YAHWIST

The earliest record of the man-nature relationship is in the Yahwist's account of the Creation in Genesis 2 and 3, in which the writer describes the fact that man is created before nature and nature is made for man, as we read,

> There was no man....The Lord God formed man....God took the man and put him in the garden of Eden to till it and keep it....God formed every beast.... every bird. The man gave names to all cattle...birds...and beasts....

It is clear that the heaven and earth (spaces), plants and herbs (botanic world), cattle, beasts, and birds (animal world), rain and mist (climatic phenomena) were made for man. The relation between man and the other creatures (nature) is clearly seen by the Yahwist in terms of utility, preservation, appreciation, and communion.

First, the writer who seems to have lived under the influence of an agricultural society in Palestine around the 10th century B.C., sees nature as the mother-earth to produce necessities for man's daily life. He seems to understand that to *utilize* nature man must till the ground. This was God's original intention in putting him in the garden of Eden, as recorded in Genesis 2:15. However, God did not put man in the garden of Eden just for idle enjoyment without laboring.[1] The purpose of putting man in the Garden was to work. Utilizing the given resources of nature seems to be a sacred demand of God from the first man.

Second, the writer seems to understand that man's responsibility for nature is to keep and *preserve* it from all damage. The word "paradise," which most Christians equate with "The Garden of Eden," is not to be found in the Hebrew text.[2] But it is a garden which was planned only for man and is to be understood as a gift of God's gracious care for the man he created.[3] Because man is placed by God in such a garden, he has a responsibility to keep and preserve it as "the gift of God's gracious care." Nature is an object of man's care and concern to preserve it in the original form in which God created it. The Yahwist is concerned about the preservation of nature.

Third, as the original meaning of the word "Eden" suggests, man is to appreciate the beauty and goodness of nature. The Yahwist does not say that "it was good," as did the priestly writer in Genesis 1, but he tries to describe man's appreciation of God's creation. When the serpent enticed the woman to eat of the tree that God forbade, she first of all appreciated its beauty by looking at it, as recorded in Genesis 3:6b: "The woman saw...that it was a delight to the eyes." Before being tempted to eat, she saw that the tree was beautiful, which gave a strong esthetic stimulus, a motivation for artistic creativeness. With such emotional stimulation, poems, pictures, and sculptures are being created. As Dante put it, "Nature is the art of God," or, as Emerson said, "Nature paints the best part of the picture, carves the best part of the statue, builds the best part of the house, speaks the best part of the oration."

Fourth, the Yahwist in his creation story tries to describe the harmony between man and nature. Adam lived among the trees in the garden, which was pleasant to his sight and good for his food. He was also living together with the animals—cattle, birds, and beasts—and he named them as man does his children. The naming of a person, according to Johannes Pedersen,[4] means "to enter into relation with somebody, and if one knows it (name), then one must use it and thus exercise influence upon him." To give names to the other creatures is to be understood as the means of communion or fellowship between man and animals (nature).

Here the Yahwist sees no difference between man and nature, they are the same creatures and he thinks of them as a unity in the created world. In particular in the passage, "man and his wife were both naked and were not ashamed," the Yahwist tries to explain the harmonious tie between man and nature. The nakedness means that without the feeling of shame, namely without knowing the distinction of sex, man seems to have a free conversation and an intimate relationship with nature, which is akin to the Oriental view of the man-nature relationship.

THE PRIESTLY WRITER

In contrast to the Yahwist, the priestly account of creation in Genesis 1 has quite differently understood the man-nature relationship. He seems to be more interested in theological aspiration. He uses the word "God" more often than the Yahwist, while the latter uses the word "man" more frequently than the former. Both are similar in stating that man and the other creatures (nature) are created by God, but the Yahwist seems to understand God's creation more in terms of human concern; that is to say, he has an anthropocentric approach to God's creation. The priestly writer, however, seems to formulate his creation story in theocentric terms,[5] includes much more detail in the creation story, and has less concern with the man-nature relationship. And yet he has proclaimed a new aspect of the man-nature relationship, which has been historically and theoretically the main-line interpretation of the biblical view of the man-nature relationship in Western Christianity: that is to say,

> ...man subdues it (nature), and man has the power and privilege to rule over the creatures (nature). This idea has made it possible to invent science and technology, which are recognized by modern society as the power to control and change man's natural and cultural environments and even to alter his own biological nature.[6]

For the priestly writer of Genesis 1, the mythological knowledge of creation is overcome by his theological knowledge; that is to say, he believes that God created the universe in the seven-day scheme, that the creation was done by the word of God, that through his creation his invisible nature is revealed, and that he created the world in the freedom of his will. Man is not therefore one with the world; he is created in God's own image, and all the creatures (nature) are given to man to have dominion over them. So the man-nature relationship of the priestly writer is to be understood in terms of man's lordship over nature, as is recorded in Genesis 1:28.[7] He has no idea of stewardship "to keep and preserve" nature. He also does not seem to be concerned with man's esthetic appreciation of its natural beauty and goodness. He could only say, "God saw that it was good," which is no doubt God's appreciation, but not man's. For him, there seems to be no harmonious relationship between man and nature. The simple vis-a-vis attitude to nature is almost lacking, and the order of creation is clearly marked: man stands above nature; nature stands below man, and man is not at one with nature.

THE DEUTERONOMIST

The deuteronomist seems to be concerned deeply with the problem of history for the sake of reconstructing Israel's ancient past and for the sake of interpreting her contemporary history. He therefore seems to put a strong emphasis on theological expansion in understanding the man-nature relationship. In Deuteronomy and the other historical books of the deuteronomic school (from Joshua to II Kings), the writers seem to devote themselves to establishing a clear historical relationship between God and Israel in terms of the people of God.[8] That is to say, they try to let the people of God know the right God, the right place of worship, the right relationship with God, the right confession, the right politics and institution, the right attitude toward their fellowmen, and the right place to live. The deuteronomic historians seem to have much concern about the land where the people of God settled down and lived. Their concern with history is so strong that they do not seem to think much about creation. Rather, for them the people of God had an immediate and urgent need to understand their own history. It is noteworthy that the man-nature relationship in Deuteronomy can be drawn in the light of the relationship of "God's people and land." Von Rad seems to be right when he says, "Deuteronomy is dominated from beginning to end by the idea of the land which is to be taken in possession. It forms the theme both of the law and of the paraenetic discourse."[9] It seems, then, that the man-nature relationship in Deuteronomy is to be understood mainly in terms of the land. The land, a gracious gift of God given both to their ancestors and to their descendants, is so good that the deuteronomist appreciates the land with a beautiful song:

A land of brooks of water, of fountains and springs, flowing forth in valleys and hills, a land of wheat and barley, of vines and fig trees and pomegranates, a land of olive trees and honey, a land in which you will eat bread without scarcity, in which you will lack nothing, a land whose stones are iron, and out of whose hills you can dig coppers and you shall eat and be full, and you shall bless the Lord your God for the good land he has given you (Deut. 8:7-10).

Here we see the beauty, richness, blessing, satisfaction, and usefulness of the created world (nature) which is described as a good service for man's need. Here the usefulness and appreciation of nature for man are more concretely and colorfully expressed than in the Yahwist writings, and so the deuteronomist seems to expand the Yahwist's anthropocentric idea of the man-nature relationship in full scale. But this human-centered idea of nature can hardly be understood unless we recognize the deuteronomic accent on a theological view of history, based on the covenantal relationship between God and Israel which requires certain duties of Israel, as recorded in Deut. 8:6: "You shall keep the commandments of the Lord by walking in his ways and by fearing him."

THE PSALMISTS

In the Book of Psalms we find many which have a deep concern with nature and most of them are viewed in terms of a "God-nature" relationship:[10] God is "the creator,"[11] "the owner,"[12] "the protector,"[13] "the giver,"[14] "the establisher of the natural orders,"[15] "the controller or ruler"[16] of the created world.

The poet of Ps. 104 was already firmly convinced of these aspects of the God-nature relationship when he wrote this psalm of nature, which is one of three nature-hymns[17] to the Creator. It is generally accepted as having being influenced by and having an affinity with the well-known Hymn to the Sun composed by the Egyptian King Ikhnaton at the beginning of the 14th century B.C.[18] Nature in this psalm can be divided according to the following themes: the heavens (vv. 2-4), the earth (vv. 5-9), the living things on earth (vv. 10-18), moon and sun (vv. 19-23), and the sea (vv. 24-26). The psalmist tries to reflect on nature with affectionate intimacy, and his reflection seems to have been highly theological, because he understands the mission of nature as glorifying[19] the Creator who is "very great and is clothed with honor and majesty" (v. 1). The psalmist has special interest in "God the preserver of life" (vv. 27-30). The creation is waiting for God (as a hungry child for its mother). All the creatures are looking for food and care from the hands of God the Creator. Even the life and death of the creatures are in God's hand.

In this connection, we may say that the psalmists seem to understand nature as having some special mission to respond to God, which is expressed in various ways: nature is the organ or instrument through which the glory of God is to be manifested, the power of God is to be exercised, the word of God is to be heard, and the majesty, honor, power, and love of God are to be praised. So, nature as the servant of God (Ps. 119:91) is to give thanks to God (Ps. 145:10), to make a joyful noise to the Lord (Ps. 100:1), to worship God (Ps. 66:4), and to praise God (Ps. 148:7-13)—all the universe is to sing in harmony.

Now, for the psalmists, the man-nature relationship seems to be ignored or excluded because they consider so strongly the *God-nature* relationship. So it is noteworthy that they could see the meaning of the existence and beauty of nature in the light of the God-nature relationship. But in the 8th Psalm, another nature-psalm, we are reminded to acknowledge the wonder of man as "a little less than God," just as we saw in the priestly creation story in which man stands over all the creatures as ruler. The psalmist confesses that God has given to man dominion over the works of his hands, putting all things[20] under his feet. He declares clearly that

94

man is the lord over all creatures, but the original purpose in writing this poem was not to picture the sublime beauty or the elaborateness or the vastness of nature, but, as it is expressed in both the opening and closing verses, his thought is simply directed to the glory of God, who made all the creatures. He makes very clear that man who is a little lower than God is being privileged by his Creator to rule over the creatures (nature); that is to say, it is from his hand that man receives the position of ruler in the world. It seems to declare that nature has no value of its own, but has value only because it is ruled by man. Nature does not exist for its own sake, but exists only as a subordinate being to obey man. The writer does not seem to envisage that man's ruling over nature might open the way to science and technology which are able to create our modern culture.

JOB AND ISAIAH

In the book of Job,[21] particularly in Elihu's address (Job 32-37) and in God's response to the previous debates (Job 38-41), the writer seems to make an amplification of the idea of God's creatorship to the utmost and he also speaks about God as the gracious protector of nature. In Job, it is especially noteworthy that the idea of protection and care for nature is far more clearly described than that of the creation itself or of the natural order. This means that the writer of Job does not seem to believe that the creation of God is mechanically completed once and for all, but rather he believes firmly in the continuous creation of God (Job 28:12-28; 38:19-39:40). He also thinks that nature is not created just for its own sake, but it has a special mission to reveal God's will and his mysterious and yet powerful activities for man and to his benefit. The sufferings of Job, which is the theme of the book, are to be understood not as due to the cruel force of nature, but as an organ through which God's providential plan for man is known in order to live faithfully under God. Here nature seems to be a textbook for man's spiritual education.

In the Second Isaiah, nature is to be understood in connection with the idea of God's creation. This writer is the one who uses the special word "to create" (bar'a) more often than any other writers in the Old Testament. It is also generally believed that the priestly creation story, formulated in the form of a confession used on a certain cultic occasion, reflects the theological influence of the

Second Isaiah who seems to be "arguing over against the Babylonian creation myths and making Israel's creation story so distinctive that it is an ancillary to salvation history" (*Heilsgeschichte*).[22] In his understanding of creation the idea of nature does not seem to be important, but rather he emphasizes the *God-man* relationship. In other words, his concern with the history of Israel, the history of redemption, seems to be so cardinal that he can hardly spare his time for the consideration of the man-nature relationship. It is, however, noteworthy that in his frequent references to creation and the created world he seems to follow the priestly writer of the creation story just to understand the creatures and their manifold phenomena as instruments of God's revelation—to praise him (Is. 44:23), to proclaim his power even to alter the natural order (Is. 43:19), to witness to God's wisdom (Is. 40:12f), to show forth his glory (Is. 42:10-13), and to give promise of his immediate presence (Is. 43:1-7).

We have to consider also an eschatological understanding of Isaiah which is very similar to the Yahwist's, and yet is more expanded both in content and expression than the former. Here the man-nature relationship is described in terms of peace among the animals and of harmony between man and animals (cf. Hosea 2.18). The following passage is the most beautiful description of the relationship between man and the other creatures:

Then the wolf shall live with the sheep,
And the leopard lie down with the kid;
The calf and the young lion shall grow up together,
And a little child shall lead them;
The cow and the bear shall be friends,
And their young shall lie down together.
The lion shall eat straw like cattle;
The infant shall play over the hole of the cobra,
And the young child dance over the viper's nest.
They shall not hurt or destroy in all my holy mountain;
For as the waters fill the sea,
So shall the land be filled with the knowledge of the Lord.
(Is. 11:6-9. NEB)

In order to understand the passage we do not need to interpret it allegorically, as J. Skinner says,

....as if wild beasts were merely symbols for cruel and rapacious men. Neither perhaps is it to be taken quite literally. It is rather a poetic presentation of the truth that the regeneration of the human society is to be accompanied by a restoration of the harmony of creation.[23]

Is such a state of peace and harmony of the created world historically possible? As long as we ask this question in the form of the present tense, "is," the answer should be "no," but if we put

96

this question in the form of the future tense, we are to be convinced that the time will come when the idyllic picture of wild beasts and dangerous reptiles in harmonious companionship with domesticated animals and children seems to be possible. This is what Isaiah believed concerning the messianic time when God will rule over the world of human history and of the created world (nature) "with justice and with righteousness" (Is. 9:7), because his conviction is that "the work of righteousness shall be peace and the fruits of it quietness and assurance forever" (Is. 32:17).

Here man's relationship to nature has some affinity to the Yahwist's description of the Paradise where man and the other creatures are harmonious, without hurting each other. So, it may be interpreted as the state of "returning back to the Paradise" (cf. Gen. 1:30).[24] It is to be noted that in this new Paradise[25] the old enmity between man and the snake (Gen. 3:15) disappears and now the whole created world (man and nature) enjoys a new life in the "full sense of new beginning, grounded not within the historical connection, but built only by the creative action of God."[26]

Here we find no more dominion of man over the created world (nature), which is quite different from the priestly account of creation. All creatures are friendly and even wild beasts like the wolf, the leopard, and the lion cease to be carnivorous. The infant and young children play together with the cobra and viper in a friendly atmosphere. All God's creatures enjoy their lives harmoniously.

THE ENVIRONMENTAL CRISIS

With the above mentioned understandings of the man-nature relationship in the Bible, we are now to ask ourselves honestly the following questions: How faithful are we to the biblical view of the man-nature relationship? Have we not ignored or forgotten some of the points in it? Have we tried any comparative studies to find out whether our national or regional cultural views of the relationship have some differences or conformities? How much have we seriously thought of this man-nature relationship in our theological reflection and activities? These questions seem to be valid and urgent because we have at various levels and in different areas discussed the problems of "living theology" and "contextualization of theology" in the search for valid ways of "doing" theology in Asia today.

97

In the third mandate of the Theological Education Fund (TEF), the determinant goal of its work was that the gospel be expressed and ministry be undertaken in response to (a) the widespread crisis of faith, (b) the issues of social justice and human development, and (c) the dialectic between local cultural and religious situations and *a universal technological civilization*. We seem to have struggled to find an answer to (a) and (b) to some extent, but the section in italics has not been much discussed. It is time now that our theological education and ministry concern itself more with science and technology. In our modern scientific and technological world we have seen and are now forced to recognize the fact that man's unnatural treatment of nature has brought with it an environmental crisis. This crisis seems to be more serious and critical where better advanced scientific knowledge and more developed technologies are dominant.

As we enter into the last quarter of the 20th century, the ecological crisis is mounting feverishly. Natural science, regarded as the effort to understand the nature we live in, has flourished to its peak accompanied by technological skills that have grown rapidly. The idea of the subjugation of nature to man, or of man's dominion over nature, has now produced a serious environmental crisis, so that man and other creatures are unexpectedly placed in the most critical situation. As Reinhold Niebuhr once put it, "the total effect of the rise of modern industry has been the destruction of community on the national and extension of conflict on the international level."[27] Technology and its impact on society will be more destructive than creative, unless a theology of ecology can be found. We may wish that we had a prophet who, following the phrases of the ancient Amos, could proclaim to the world in the midst of science and technology which claim lordship over our environment: "The days are coming, when God will send famines on the earth; a famine of grain, of water, of air and of energy." Man seems to have lost his sense of responsibility to preserve and care for nature as steward of God. It is very important to heed the warning from Don Marquiz quoted in the *Environment Handbook*:

Man has oppressed us for a million years, but he goes on
steadily cutting the ground from under his own feet making
deserts deserts deserts....
We ants remember and have it all recorded in our tribal
lore when Gobi was a paradise swarming with men and rich in
human prosperity. It is a desert now and the home of
scorpions, ants, and centipeds.[28]

This seems to be a warning to those who regard nature only as the object of scientific knowledge and technology on the basis of man's dominion over nature.

A HISTORICAL SKETCH

How is man related to nature? The relationship between man and nature may be outlined with a few prepositions: *of, from, with, to,* and *for*. Here we have to limit our discussion to the "*of*-relationship," "*to*-relationship," and "*for*-relationship."

"OF-NATURE" RELATIONSHIP. Man is of nature. He is obliged to know *his* nature as coming from the ground, as it is recorded: "God formed man of dust from the ground" (Gen. 2:7). And when man dies, he goes back to nature, as it is recorded: "Thou turnest man back into dust; 'turn back,' thou sayst, 'you sons of men'" (Ps. 90:3). Man originally belongs to nature, and he returns to the bosom of nature when his life ends. The Yahwist gives us a clear picture of man's original substance (Gen. 2:7). Man is the child of nature. According to him, "the animals are also made out of the ground" (Gen. 2:15). As H.W. Wolff points out,

The Hebrew word for "ground" (*'adama*) is derived from the same root (*'dm*) of the Hebrew word for man (*'adam*). The original meaning of the root *'dm* is "to be reddish brown color", which expresses the color of both man's skin and the ground. Man has a threefold relationship with the ground, namely, man is created from the ground (Gen. 2:7, cf. 3:19, 23); he is to till the ground (Gen. 3:23); and he goes back to the ground (Gen. 3:19, cf. 90:3).[29]

Man's genetive relation to nature is perhaps a primitive understanding of the man-nature relationship, and yet it is still true that man is not to be separated nor isolated from nature. Man has an equal position with nature; man is part of nature in the world God created. No idea of the lordship of man over nature is permissible. When man regards himself as a child of nature, he is constantly inspired and stimulated to respond to her motherly love and care, which makes man produce artistic creations. So, we see the works of the Romanticists, in which J. J. Rousseau advocated "an idea of returning to nature" as a philosopher; and William Wordsworth wrote many poems appreciating the beauty and sublimity of nature.

In this regard, it is to be noted that the Oriental concept of nature, regardless of regional variations, has never segregated nature from man, who is always a part of nature no matter how the imported Western culture tries to separate man from nature by technology. Even without the influence of the biblical teaching, we

Orientals are not able to refuse to be a part of nature, although we enjoy fully the benefits and conveniences that the technological devices can provide. The principle of the cosmic dual forces, so-called Yin-Yang,[30] is based on the integration or harmony of man and nature. Man and nature absolutely cannot be parted, because they belong to each other. One of the striking features of the Chinese philosophy is to be seen in the idea of *feng-shui* (wind and water), which can be called a "nature philosophy" in which there is a close correspondence between the features of the landscape and the cosmic dual forces—a very complicated system of interrelationships which was the basis for the proper selection of house and grave sites. Here we find an illustration of the ideas of balance and harmony between man and nature, respect for nature, and the vital role of nature in the life of man.

"TO-NATURE" RELATIONSHIP. In the long history of the man-nature relationship, it seems to have been necessary to develop a "*to*-nature" relationship, for man had to use or utilize things that God made for him. From the very beginning of man's life, he had to know something about things (nature) given to him for his daily necessities, and such knowledge was derived from observation, study, and experimentation carried on in order to determine the nature of principles. What was studied may be called science. As a result of the accumulation of this knowledge man began to find methods and ways to apply it to practical use. From such practical application of knowledge to things (nature), techniques were developed. Thus, man has constantly manipulated and managed the "*to*-nature" relationship, from which scientific knowledge and technical skills have found their functions in history. With such findings and development, culture and civilization were born.

The Yahwist introduces the ancient traditions regarding man's knowledge and techniques in relation to the tribal history, in which we find the origins of the artificial tools and necessary instruments for the ancient civilization. In Gen. 4:20-22 three names are mentioned for the people of ancient civilization. These men are to be understood as *homo faber* (artisans of humanity) : Jabal who was the ancestor of those who lived in tents as shepherds; Jubal his brother, as the inventor of the lyre and pipe, the oldest and simplest musical instruments, which made nomadic people dance and sing in rhythm; Tubal-Qayin, as the originator of smith or metal work, who may be regarded as the inventor of farming tools and of weapons. As H.

100

Gunkel points out, here we may observe "the origin of Israel's culture of antiquity," and "it was the discovery of man's skill."[31] According to the deuteronomist, the Canaanites had a much earlier history of metal usage than the Israelites (1 Sam. 13:19ff).

It seems that in the primeval stage of science and technique, man had peace with nature. Man against nature was not a serious problem and both were benefited by "giving" and "taking" principles. Man and nature were mutual helpers. Man responded to nature as a friend, although sometimes nature behaved mercilessly to man. Through the experience of the damages, destructions, and brutality of nature, man began to learn how to subdue nature as much as possible, particularly in the Western countries. With the "golden rule" of domination of man over nature, given by God, he felt a strong demand to conquer nature by his scientific knowledge and technical devices. So, now, man tries to be master over nature and as a result of this idea of the subjugation of nature, man and nature have begun to separate from each other, and thus "man against nature" and "man's mastery over nature"—this famous dichotomy—came to prevail and was applied to our understanding of the man-nature relationship. It seems that in order to have a "*to*-nature" relationship, man has to be separated from nature and consequently the harmony between man and nature is broken. Although the Eastern, Greek Christianity seems to maintain the harmony and union with nature, the Western, Latin tradition has freely accepted the concept of dominance over or oppression of nature.

The victory of Christianity over primal religion is to be understood in terms of man's dominion over nature which has now become an impregnable doctrine. On the basis of such a concept of man's mastery over nature, all the mythological ideas of equality and harmony between man and nature are rejected to the extent that no item in the physical creation has any purpose save to serve man's purposes. According to Lynn White,[32] "By destroying pagan animism, Christianity made it possible to exploit nature in a mood of indifference to the feelings of natural objects." About the feeling of natural objects, Theodore Roszak gives us an inspiring story of an Indian woman, which speaks to what the white people have done to nature:

The White people never cared for land or deer or bear.... We don't chop down the trees. We only use dead wood. But the White people plow up the ground, pull up the trees, and kill everything. The tree says, "Don't. I am sore. Don't hurt me." But they chop it down and cut it up. The Indians never

101

hurt anything, but the White people destroy all.... How can the spirit of the earth like the White man? Everywhere the White man has touched it, it is sore.[33]

In the history of the man-nature relationship "man-against nature" or "man's mastery over nature" is generally understood as the "guilt of Christianity." White is quite confident in saying that Christianity is responsible for fostering "an imperialistic attitude toward nature," and "arrogance toward nature."[34] Frederick Elder, supporting White's opinion, maintains that "Christianity has fostered a dangerous subject-object attitude toward nature, which separates man from nature and promotes a utilitarian mentality, leading to exploitation."[35] Of course, we can hardly disagree with those who hold the opinion that "Christianity bears a huge burden of guilt."[36] As Clarence Glacken points out, reviewing briefly the thoughts of Bacon, Descartes, and Leibnitz, the dichotomy of "man against nature" and "man's mastery over nature" has a great meaning for the progress of civilization. "The struggle with and the control over nature were ways of depicting the progress of civilization."[37] And he goes on to say, "In the 19th century, the idea of man's control over nature or man against nature was closely linked with the idea of indefinite and inevitable progress."[38] But in the second half of the 19th century, the dichotomy was inclined to so emphasize the mastery of man over nature, that the world of man and the world of nature became separated. A utilitarian view of nature was encouraged and man withdrew from the responsibility of preserving and caring for nature. With this retreat man began to think only of the domination over nature by rationality and purpose. By this rational attitude toward nature, the giver of the power of man's domination over nature, God the Creator and Sustainer, was challenged, and thereafter the traditional conception of the world seems to have been rejected. In this regard, the Slussers are right when they say:

The world as the created arena of God's saving activity was transmuted into the thought that nature itself was historical through revolution.... Man was truly the pinacle of creation; glory to man the master for his mastery of things.[39]

Here we see the pride of man, forgetting the creatorship and lordship of God. Such an arrogant pride is well expressed in the words of C. F. von Weizsacker: "Modern man thinks he can breathe freely only if his conquest of the world is no longer hindered by insurmountable limitation of his knowledge and his power."[40]

The story of the Tower of Babel (Gen. 11:1-9;J) seems to be an early example of man ever trying to show his wisdom and skill to build a tower, the top of which may reach into heaven. As White expresses it, "we are superior to nature, contemptuous of it, willing to use it for our slightest whim."[41] The Israelite's wisdom had already pointed this out: "Have you observed the man who thinks he is wise? There is more hope for a stupid fool than for him." (Prov. 26:12). In this pride, though he may constantly contribute to the magnificent works of civilization and cultural creations under the name of technology, man now, because of his technological devices, faces a fatal crisis of environment where he himself lives. The environmental crisis seems to have originated from "the anthropocentric view of nature,"[42] which conceives of man as standing over against nature, and consequently carries with it a basic exploitative attitude toward nature. In the crisis of environment, it is evident that man—the modern industrial man—forgetting or neglecting his Creator, is worshiping technology as his new god.

It remains now to see clearly what the anthropocentric view of nature has brought us. Because of the dissolution of any sense of stewardship responsibilities for nature, man is allowed to use the things of nature in any way to please him and recklessly to extend his own desire for his own convenience, prosperity, and happiness. Man's greedy egoism and ever-increasing desire for the more convenient and the happier life, by means of technology, have recently been endangering our environment and making our life uneasy! The Slussers are right again when they say:

The result of man's pride in his science and technology and in his neglect of wisdom...has actually been a serious deterioration of the quality and possibility of life. He has paved over the land, stripped the forests, and left the soil naked for erosion.[43]

The Slussers go on to speak about the environmental crisis in concrete terms: the overplowing and overplanting of the once fertile soil has poisoned the soil with over-fertilization; artificial dams have not only destroyed the beauty of natural valleys and inundated priceless lands but also have stripped away forests and grass lands; rivers have been polluted, and water shortage is at hand. Thus the concept of the endless frontier and the idea of limitless progress have led to an ever-increasing rate of depletion of resources by our proliferating rate of consumption and expanding technology.

In the advanced and developed countries of the West, the problem of the environmental crisis recently has led to ever-increasing and deepening issues not only for the scientists and politicians but also for philosophers and theologians as well as for the ordinary people. The degree of importance and necessity of the issues, however, is much greater in the underdeveloped countries. For us Oriental people the crisis is more serious and grave, because both our traditional concept of nature and our Christian understanding of nature, received from Western Christians, are simultaneously challenged by modern science and technology. In the countries threatened by Communism, however, the challenges are visible and inevitable, militant by the ideological strivings of the Communist, for they do not see the validity of and flatly reject both the traditional heritage and the Christian teachings. Taking an example from Red China, appearing in Rhoads Murphey's article, "Man and Nature in China," the Communist tries to see the revolution under the conception of man's relation to his physical environment, namely:

The dialectical conflict and struggle of the "permanent revolution" which is the touchstone to so much of contemporary China has replaced traditional notions of harmony and adjustment which underlay equally much of the traditional order. In no respect is this radical change more apparent than in the attitude toward nature.[44]

There is an instructive and inspiring book written by M. M. Thomas in which he has efficiently and critically analyzed and elucidated all the potential phenomena which are apt to take place in human community in such a time of technological revolution. He seems to be rather critical of more or less negative attitudes toward technology, thinking of underdeveloped countries, when he says:

There is serious doubt whether the attitude of "exploitation" towards nature, of "limitlessness" to economic growth and of "modernization" to the organic aspect of traditional society are necessary or desirable in any absolute sense of human community in a technological age.[45]

Asian countries are being benefited, as are countries in the West, by scientific knowledge and technology. The ideas of progress and development, in particular the growth of the Gross National Product and the welfare state, seem to be the ultimate goals of the Asian countries. Achieving these goals depends upon more technological benefits. It is, however, also an evident fact that the more we depend upon technology, the more we are thrown into the environmental crisis. Without any exception, we are now well aware of the problems of all kinds of pollution, overpopulation, the depletion of the land, shortage of resources, dehumanization, oppression of the poor, tendency toward totalitarian government, the process of secularization, and the like, which eventually appear in direct proportion to the development of technology. Here we have a critical moment when man has faced his own crisis, as the Slussers point out:

Man has become, along with one thousand other species, an endangered species. The frail biosphere housing terrestrial life has revealed that it is neither entertained by nor tolerant of *homo faber's* industrial drama....Suddenly many thoughtful, intelligent, and alarmed people have discovered that the industrial revolution has turned its cannons around and they are pointing squarely at mankind and life itself.[46]

With this consciousness of the environmental crisis we may be able to understand the groan of the creation, expressed in Romans 8:22, 23: "We know that the whole creation has been groaning in travail together until now; and not only the creation, but we ourselves...."

THEOLOGICAL CONSIDERATIONS

"For-nature" Relationship

Lynn White suggests a new religion in order "to get us out of the present ecological crisis."[47] But why should we have a new religion? Has our Christianity failed to meet the crisis? Or have we been wrong to understand the man-nature relationship as the Bible teaches? Is it not rather that our theological considerations have departed from a right understanding of the biblical view of the man-nature relationship? We are not sure whether White is right, when he says: "We are so tinctured with Christian arrogance toward nature that no solution can be found from science and technology." And he goes on to say: "Hence we shall continue to have a worsening ecological crisis until we reject the Christian axiom that nature has no reason for existence save to serve man." In order to find a new relationship or restore an old one, he proposes to follow St. Francis who is "the patron saint of ecologists," and advocates appropriating his concept of the "democracy of God's creatures" as a model for "an alternative, nonexploitative view of nature."

What White says on the reason and causes of the environmental crisis may have points, but we do not agree with him fully on the issue because he, as others, has put too much emphasis on "man's mastery over nature," supported by a partial understanding of the biblical view. Since a lengthy discussion against White has already appeared,[48] we need not repeat here the criticisms. But it is worthy of note that White makes it clear that "the Bible designates man's role as that of a steward or manager of creation, not as a sovereign owner or manipulator."[49] Second, he understands the conception of man's dominion over nature as "responsible stewardship" and sees no place in the Bible for the justification of the "exploitation of nature." Third, he refuses the idea of "an anthropocentric view of nature," for although the meaning of "image of God" implies a certain quality of transcendence over nature, the biblical doctrine of man implies the God-given responsibility for its care and preservation, and "respect for all forms of life, appreciation of natural wonders, and esthetic delight in its beauties."[50]

It is evident also from the discussions of Bruce Wrightsman that the doctrines of creation and man, and the teaching about nature, are to be reconsidered theologically; that is, ecology and theology must work together on the basis of the biblical view of nature. Man, as one of the fellow creatures and as a responsible steward, is required to think and act in a *"for*-nature" relationship. Man is created for God, on the one hand, and for nature, on the other hand, because man is responsible for it as the caretaker commissioned by God. Natural resources are given to man by God, and man is by all means requested to keep and preserve nature. The only responsible stance in view of the ecological crisis is a deep sense of *"for*-nature" relationship. What man does for nature will certainly be found in the ways that he tries to keep and preserve it. Nature cannot be exploited for man's own disposal, for ecological crisis is always pregnant where God's creatures are maltreated by man, their caretaker. Here it seems that a new ethic is needed, as Fisher says:[51] "An ethics more attuned to ecology is called for—an ethics that recognizes the inter-relatedness and interdependence of all living things with the natural environment." How can this new ethic be formulated? It must be based on the concept of the God-man relationship which will eventually be turned into a *"for*-nature" relationship. This is a matter of theological consideration.

A THEOLOGY OF NATURE

One of the greatest failures in the works of biblical Theology (especially in the Old Testament field) is the fact that writers have kept silent about the man-nature relationship. It is true when we read the greatest works of the scholars, such as W. Eichrodt, O

Procksch, G. E. Wright, R. Bultmann, and Von Rad. Although both Eichrodt and Procksch describe Israel's *"Gedankenwelt"* (thought-world), of which "God and world" is one of the themes, they never properly or extensively discuss what we call "a theology of nature"—that is to say, a theological consideration of the man-nature relationship—in either their discussions of creation or of man. For instance, Eichrodt sees nature only in the context of the "Creator-creature relationship,"[52] "nature standing over against man,"[53] and understands the man-nature relationship in terms of the "covenant relationship."[54] Von Rad sees nature as a sphere of God's action and therefore as "one of the principal subjects of the hymns...only an object which calls forth praise."[55] Although he outlines five points from special statements on the beauty of Israel,[56] he does not seem to be interested in the man-nature relationship because he over-emphasizes man's "response before Yahweh." Paul Santmire also recognizes this when he says:

Virtually all of the most renowned biblical scholars of our era—the names of G. Ernest Wright and R. Bultmann come to mind—either have not investigated the biblical theology of nature or have "discovered" that the biblical approach to nature is substantially the same as the modern theological approach.[57]

It is also strange that Karl Barth does not seem to consider the man-nature relationship seriously as a theological subject. In all the statements and assertions of his doctrine of creation he only concerns himself with "God-world," "the word of God," and the "God-man" relationship. Let us quote a few sentences concerning our theme:

Those who have claimed to have a world-view have always derived it from other sources than the word of God.... The word of God does not have any account of the cosmos;....[58]

The reason why there is no revealed or biblical world-view characteristic of and necessary to the Christian *Kerygma* is that faith in the word of God can never find its theme in the totality of the created world.[59]

The word of God speaks of God himself and also of man, but does not contain, either directly or indirectly, any disclosure about an independent nature of the cosmos.[60]

Barth regards the created world only in connection with the doctrine of man:

The created world surrounding man, the totality of created existence above and below him, is the prototype and pattern of that for which he is addressed by the word of God, of his life in communion with his creator.[61]
For this reason the doctrine of man has always been the central element in the dogmatics of the church.[62]

As we have seen, Barth seems to concentrate so much on the God-man relationship that he rather ignores or is unaware of the meaning and significance of the man-nature relationship. Gordon Kaufman's view reaffirms this position when he says:

> It is in fact these two terms, "God" and "Man," which provide the basic framework within which the Christian drama is worked out; the notion of "World" (heaven and earth) remains vague and largely undefined, referring to the context within which. or the stage upon which. the drama of salvation is worked out, but does not itself have a significant role within the drama.[63]

It is natural to discuss the possibility of "a theology of nature"— which has certainly been barred by the theology of Barth—in view of recent changes. As Professor Nam Dong Suh of Korea well observes,[64] this is the time, first, of environmental crisis; second, of the maltreatment of nature by the development of technology; third, of having a closer relationship between the Eastern and the Western cultures, as a result of the ecumenical movement; fourth, of a wide-open horizon for closer dialogue between Christianity and other religions; and, last, of the changing tendency of biblical studies turning from the exclusive accent on *Heilsgeschichte* to a generous and open-minded study, considering the Bible as collections of the various traditions and theological interpretations of the contemporaries of the writers. The problem we have now is to find possible ways of formulating a theology of nature. There seem to be essentially two ways of approaching it: one is to reconstruct our theological formulations with special reference to the ecological and environmental crisis, and the other is to bring the traditional and indigenous cultural heritages of our own nations to the forefront of our theological considerations.

RECONSTRUCTION OF THEOLOGY

It is certainly not easy to reconstruct our traditional theological framework which seems almost to be indigenized or at least viable to our own religious considerations and activities. As we think of such reconstruction, we have an immediate reaction from our own theological thinking, but the necessity of formulating a "theology expressing a proper place for nature" is urgent. The following are to be considered:

NATURE WITH HISTORY. First of all, as Kaufman points out, the theological focus on "history" should be moved to "nature" as well.[65] But an immediate question should be asked: how do we make a distinction between history and nature? When St. Paul mentions that "their women exchange natural relations for unnatural (contrary to nature)" (Rom. 1:26), he means that what those women in Rome did was "an abrogation of the order given by God."[66] It seems that "something natural" signifies doing something in the way of the inherent and inborn nature according to the order God originally established. "Natural" means simply eliminating the artificial. Therefore, when we say "something natural" it means that we should find things as God created them. Here we are to consider a theological motivation for understanding the very nature of things as God originally created them. In nature, therefore, we can hardly eliminate the will and action of God. Without God's will and action, nothing could exist. The question concerning nature is really both an ontological and an existential one, because we see its very nature as created substance and its existence as unchanging. Neither is man to be excluded from nature, as Kaufman says: "Man would seem to be included within nature. Certainly the material and vital dimensions of his being are directly rooted in natural processes and must be regarded as natural."[67]

Man is "a part of nature and sustained by it and cannot be conceived apart from the natural order in which he is ensconced."[68] He is at the same time a historical being. He makes his being and activities as historical reality, which is formed and conditioned in relation to his physical and material environment (nature). In him nature and history cannot be antithetic, but synthetic. History can hardly be understood correctly apart from nature, and vice versa. History is to be understood as "an account of what has happened in the life or development of a people, country, institution etc.," and the world is the stage where these happenings or events occur. For the people of Israel, the world was the land of Palestine where both the acts of God and the responses of the people were interwoven in the history of Israel. History is, for Israel, to be understood in terms of the God-man relationship, which is called a "covenantal relationship." In this covenantal relationship the land where the covenant was made possible and kept between God and Israel was considered as one of the main pillars from the beginning of its history, as it is recorded: "Go from your country and your kindred and your father's house to the *land* that I will show you" (Gen. 12:1; J.). As discussed earlier in this paper, the idea of land, in particular, comes to the foreground in the deuteronomic concepts of history in many passages such as the following:

"Behold, I have set *the land* before you" (Deut. 1:8).
"The Lord your God has given you this land to possess" (Deut. 3:18).
"You shall go over and take possession of that good land" (Deut. 4:22).

It is true also that when the history of the people came to an end, because of the breach of the covenantal relationship, the living environment (nature) of their life was believed to have been cursed by God:

I looked on the earth, and lo, it was waste and void; and to the heavens, and they had no l'ght. I looked on the mountains, and lo, they were quaking, and all the hills moved to and fro....there was no man, and all the birds of the air had fled....The fruitful land was a desert, all the cities were laid in ruins.... (Jer. 4:21-26).

Here the final destiny of man's history and his nature are not to be separated into either blessings or curses. History and nature go together and meet in man's final destiny. It has been a great mistake therefore, for Western theology to put more emphasis on man-oriented society in the concept of history than on his relation to nature, his life environment, for this is certainly not biblical. Nature as "our own home" should have its proper place in history, which is preeminently the human story. It has been wrong to separate nature from history. The Western technological culture seems to have sided only with history and in so doing has led to a false contrast between the West and the East where history and nature are conceived to be as one and in harmony.

The dichotomy of history against nature, therefore, seems to be wrong, as Santmire points out.[69] Nature is more than "the servant of history" or "the stage for history." Too much emphasis on history, therefore, pushes us in the direction of ecological collapse. If we theologians are to develop theologies with a tangible and comprehensive ecological dimension, we must formulate a "theology of nature," as Kaufman suggests:

Theology of nature enables us to understand the orders of life and being within which we live and of which we are part.... That will illuminate for us, and teach us properly to worship, the God implicit in nature.[70]

"Salvation today" has got to widen its scope and dimension in nature as well as in history, so that it will have an ecological connotation. God's redemption is never satisfied with historical categories.

It will also be helpful to learn from the teachings of Eastern Christianity which claims to believe in a God who is not transcendent over all things, but who lives and acts in, with, and through all the things created by him. The doctrine of *Theosis** must now be reconsidered for a theology of nature. Joseph Sittler is right when he says,[71] "That means that theological categories may no longer be

---
* The ultimate absorption of the human soul into Deity.

110

only historical categories. They have got to deal with man as history and as nature."

THE DOCTRINE OF CREATION. Karl Barth says that creation "includes not only the action of the Creator but also its product, the creature.... Creator and creation belong together as an integral whole."[72] If this statement is true, why does he say, "the doctrine of man has always been the central element in the dogmatics of the creation?"[73] Is it right to view man as the goal and center of the universe? As we saw in the Old Testament priestly writings, the Creator-God is the author's main concern in the form of confession. But, in the Yahwist's doctrine of creation, although man is the primary concern, the nature surrounding him is also an important element in understanding man's original nature. He is made of the dust of the ground, finds his environment of life by living in harmony with nature, and is aware of his sacred responsibility to till or cultivate the soil in order to preserve its original form as God created it and to meet man's needs for this earthly life. And, above all, in the Psalmist's doctrine of creation all the creatures are called to praise God and reveal the mysteries and wonders of God to man in order to serve the Owner of the creation. As mentioned above, the emphasis on man's dominion over nature as something "to rule" or "to subdue," as recorded in the priestly creation story, is certainly only one aspect of the doctrine of creation. Because this one aspect seems to have been dominant in the teachings of the doctrine of Creation in Western Christianity, the other important elements appearing in the other biblical writings have been ignored and buried until now, when man has begun to realize the ecological crisis.

Here we have to recover the original meaning of the doctrine of Creation, as Andre Dumas has attempted:

...I believe this operation ("to resurrect an ancient dogma") can be justified, if it offers any chance...of recovering the original substance which has to some extent been eclipsed by other interpretations certainly no more faithful to the original belief than the one we are now attempting.[74]

Although Dumas only surveys briefly the history of the doctrine of Creation in three periods,[75] he seems to give us a concrete scheme of reconstructing a doctrine of Creation in terms of "an asceticism' together with "ethical reflection and action." He views the created world as

...still intact as at the blessing of the human beings for whom God continually structures nature, inviting these human beings to recognize his own image in

111

themselves when they conduct themselves as attendants of their brothers and sisters.[76]

The doctrine of Creation in connection with an "ecological theology" seems to be clearly expressed in the 104th Psalm, which was mentioned above. We see here the Creator of the air, the sky, the small and then great animals, etc.; all these creatures are celebrating the Creator; the earth is full of God's creatures, they all look to the Creator, and they are filled with good things that the Creator gives. How beautiful to see the grace of the Creator bestowed upon the creatures. How wonderful to know the genuine dependence of all the creatures upon the Creator! Here in this "ecological doxology"[77] man does not seem to be central, as Barth believes.[78] In Psalm 194, it is not true to say that "anthropology has to do with man in the cosmos."[79] Rather, man is just one of the creatures in the cosmos. In Psalm 104, it is not true that "God alone and man alone are its theme";[80] on the contrary the created things, and nature itself, are the sole theme of this hymn to the Creator. An outspoken conversation without a word seems to be exchanged between the Creator and the creatures in this psalm.

The doctrine of creation is to be properly reconstructed in such a time as the "whole creation" is "groaning in travail together," because the disastrous ecological and environmental situation of today "requires of us a freshly renovated and fundamental theology of the first article whereby the Christian faith defines whence the creation was formed, and why, and by whom, and to what end."[81] One more point remains to be noted in connection with such "renovated and fundamental theology," that is, peace and harmony between man and the created world. The doctrine of Creation is not only to say something about the beginning of time but also something about the end of time. The Yahwist has a story of Paradise within the scheme of his account of creation. The Paradise is a place where man and other creatures had complete harmony without hurting each other. Although we may hear the echoes of the Babylonian mythology in the story of Eden, the writer with his theological emphasis on Yahweh as the only Lord of man, demythologizing the sources, tries to consider the Garden of Eden as being created by God for man and being given to man as the best environment in which to live. The garden of Eden, for the Yahwist, was understood as a place where man could live with joy and satisfaction without any kind of ecological disasters or calamities.

Isaiah, however, seems to fail to see that such a paradise as the ancient garden of Eden is possible to appear in the historical life of Israel by man's efforts and wisdom, because he was told that man's deterioration had already driven him out of the first paradise by the breach of a proper relationship between God and man. And yet Isaiah seems to have a firm conviction of God's power of *creatio ex nihilo* (creation out of nothing) and so he expects and hopes that such a paradise might be possible, if God wills, in an eschatological time of the Messiah who shall judge the poor with righteousness, decide with equity for the meek of the earth, and reign over the world with righteousness and faithfulness (Is. 11:4-5). In his picture of a utopia (Is. 11:6-9) man and nature are in harmony. There is no sign of "man's mastery over nature." The man-nature relationship has now recovered as it was in the beginning in the garden of Eden. Here we see that the doctrine of Creation has recovered its original form, such that neither man's dominion over nature nor nature's mastery over man exists, but only God rules over man and nature. Under God's power and grace, man and nature become friendly brothers and sisters. This implies a new creation of God who desires to see a peaceful harmony in his created world, in particular in the man-nature relationship in a time when man faces an environmental crisis. This means that the Kingdom of God can be established on earth only by God's grace, but it also means that man's positive evaluation of human capabilities is to be fully exercised in connection with the creative power of God.

Finally, the book of the Revelation of John sees a "new creation" with Jesus Christ who makes all things anew (Rev. 21:5). With this conviction of a "new creation" we have honestly to face the eschatological dimension of ecology,[82] that is to say, with Hans Schwarz,[83] first, our participation in the New Creation of Jesus Christ will

...enable us to arrive at a positive evaluation of human reason and, second, the Judeo-Christian tradition will enable us to bring into focus the goals and limits of all human endeavours and of our involvement in the ecological crisis.

The focus and goals seem to be attainable in the reinterpretation and reformulation of the doctrine of Creation in the light of our ecological crisis.

A NEW ETHIC. It has been a wrong orientation to understand the doctrine of Creation in Genesis as focusing only on man's role as a ruler of nature, and not also as a steward to care for nature. The moral responsibility toward nature has been ignored. To keep and preserve nature with affection was supposed to be the primary duty for Adam. In the traditional scheme of Christian ethics, the relationship between man and man—man's behavior toward his fellowmen, man's duty to another man, and man's concern for man—have been main subjects to discuss, and the man-nature relationship has hardly been considered as a valuable subject in the discussion of ethics, except in that of public morals. Now, the direction and concern of man's duty has to be directed toward nature along with the traditional attitude toward man. In particular, the ever-growing ecological crisis of today has awakened us to seek a proper attitude toward nature. Andre Dumas points toward a restoration of ethical reflection by indicating the distinctive phenomena which have brought about the ecological crisis. Interpreting the original meaning of the doctrine of creation in Genesis, he points out that man has "responsibility for and toward the natural world entrusted to his care."[84] So, he concludes, "we are living at a moment when such ethical reflection is urgently needed."[85] However, he does not make any concrete suggestions on ethical reflection. Why ethical reflection?

In the Bible it seems that not much attention is given to man's attitude toward nature, except in one particular passage of the Holiness Code, in which every seventh year the land is to lie fallow. The source seems to be very late, later than the priestly writings. It has, however, an affectionate concern for the land:

...in the seventh year there shall be a sabbath of solemn rest for the land, a sabbath to the Lord. You shall not sow your field or prune your vineyard... it shall be a year of solemn rest for the land (Lev. 25:4, 5).

The idea of giving rest to the land for a year has a religious motive: the land belongs to God. But besides this motivation we have to see here an ecological motive, namely, that the farmer should keep the soil from exhaustion by taking due care of it. The idea is to be noted that natural resources should not be consumed. Any one who has read "Technology and the Limits of Growth"[86] will know how seriously scientists are now facing the limits of both "energy and resources." According to Michel Bosquet in his report on "The UN Stockholm Conference on Environment,"

If iron and steel production continues to increase at the present rate...the resources will be exhausted in 73 years.... Reserves of other industrial metals will be exhausted much more rapidly...supplies of mercury will be exhausted in 13 years, lead in 15 years, gold in 17 years, zinc in 18 years, silver and platinum in 20 years, tin in 25 years, copper in 40 years.[87]

Here we see something of St. Paul's vision of "the whole creation groaning and travailing in pain together until now," waiting for its own redemption along with the final unveiling of the sons of God (Rom. 8:19-21). It is rightly pointed out by Eric C. Rust that the

...Christian church...has been so concerned with getting out of hell into heaven, that it has forgotten 'that Christian life has to be lived out on earth. It has emphasized man's moral responsibility to his fellows...but it has forgotten that it has an ethical obligation to its natural environment and all living things.[88]

If God sees all the things which he created and says they are "good," man has to fulfill the divine joy by learning to live on "only one earth." What are the theological grounds for reconstructing our ethics in regard to the man-nature relationship? First, man should have a sense of guilt because he has been treating nature more and more destructively and not as "brother and sister."[89] As Rust points out, man commits sins against nature:[90]

We upset the circle of nature, polluting our air and our water. We denude the earth of vegetation and upset the balance of oxygen and carbon dioxide. We pour our noxious fumes into the atmosphere, ...poison our fish, destroy our bird life, contaminate our water table, kill our oceans...all for greed and selfish exploitation.

The traditional concept of sin in Christian ethics is focused on man's behavior toward his fellowman as an individual or toward community as a part of humankind. He has to speak and act according to the demand of conscience or to the biblical norm of morality. But the first sin of man, according to the Yahwist, seems to have been committed not only by disobedience of God's command, but also by eating the fruit for the sake of his own personal ambition and desire. In other words, man seems to break the natural man-nature relationship prior to his breaking the God-man relationship, because man's "natural" relationship to nature is to eat the fruit that was allowed but not to eat the fruit that was forbidden by God. This is the problem of man's freedom to choose, which is the basis of ethical decision. This is what Andre Dumas is trying to say:

...ethics is neither the perpetuation of misplaced principles nor the pursuit of unattainable absolutes.... We are now confronted with choices to be made collectively in favour of our survival as a race. They call for a human control over nature which is more than man's capacity to discover and exploit and includes the wisdom to use and manage. This is why ecology provides ethical reflection and action with a framework.[91]

We have to make drastic decisions as to the extent to which technology should be encouraged "as a solution to environmental problems when the ultimate effect may be to cause more problems than it solves."[92] We have to make a clear statement on "the ecological sins" which are caused by "a distinct strengthening of selfish values, such as one's

115

own pleasure, physical well-being and comfort, economic security, convenience, and leisure."[93] We have to keep not only mankind but also nature, not only history but also our environment, from the damage leading to the total destruction of both man and the world by "technocratic tyranny (socialist countries) or of stimulating our sinful and greedy impulses, that is, the profit motive, national pride, and national or class paranoia (Western capitalism)."[94]

We may be asked by God, if the present ecological predicament should bring an end to our survival, "Where is nature your brother?" We cannot say, "I do not know him. Am I my brother nature's keeper?" It is a serious question that we have to answer. But the right answer may not be possible unless we become "responsible selves" (H.R. Niebuhr), "co-workers with God,"[95] persons with love and concern for nature. It seems worthwhile to follow the principle of Albert Schweitzer who lived through a special ethical stance of "reverence for life," which includes reverence and respect for nature. Man should be a keeper and a steward of nature in order to preserve both himself and his environment for survival.

THE STUDY OF INDIGENOUS CULTURE

For the reconstruction of theology we have been reviewing some of the features of Western theology which are dominated by a dichotomy of man and nature, "man against nature," or "man's mastery over nature." We have also been suggesting some of the elements of a theology of nature which should be seriously considered.

It gives me a great shock to realize that our theology until now seems to have nothing to do with the Eastern cultural heritages, which have rich resources to formulate a theology of nature expressed in terms of the cosmos and nature. It is unfortunate that Christian theology should not have originated from the ground of the Eastern or the Asian countries. Had it originated from the heritages of the Asian cultures it might have been far better in understanding the original meaning of the creation and, in particular, the relationship between man and nature.

In formulating a theology of nature we Asians have the privilege of understanding the biblical conception of nature far better than the Western people. Many theologians are now interested to ask such questions as, "Is an Asian theology possible?" The question seems to be attractive not only for the Asian theologians[96] but also for Western theologians.[97] Although there are a good many articles and monographs on subjects related to an Asian theology

116

in each nation, the main thrust will not be that of patching up the theological ideas and concepts of the Western churches with Asian ideas and concepts, but obedience to the word of God as Asians understand it in their own cultural and religious context, which is called "contextualization of theology." An Asian theology must begin with the realities confronting the Asian communities, although these realities differ from one nation to the other.

Our task here, however, is not an attempt to formulate an Asian theology. Our aim is only to try to find a way of reconstructing a theology of nature in the Asian context. In doing this, it seems to me to be necessary to make a study of man's relation to nature in the Korean context, which might give a model for doing theology to other nationalities in Asia. Before formulating an Asian theology, it is absolutely necessary to make a proper study of the cultural heritage of each nation. We have to study the raw materials of our culture *without* Christian presuppositions, which means that we should read and interpret our traditional heritages of culture and religion from our own indigenous or national viewpoint. In order to understand the idea of the man-nature relationship in Korea, for example, we must first of all do research on how this relationship is expressed in the original writings of the Koreans, and then we have to understand the biblical views on the man-nature relationship from the traditional perspective of our own culture as we have understood it in our indigenous studies. The following are a few selections from the original works written in Chinese characters, in which we shall find one of the typical Korean attitudes toward nature.

KOREAN ATTITUDES TOWARD NATURE IN THE WORKS OF YI-WHANG. Yi-Whang (1501-1570) has left us 59 volumes of books in which his philosophical works, his literary works of poetry, diaries and essays, and his commentaries on the Chinese classics are included. He spent most of his life as a government officer and died in his first year of retirement. He loved nature and very often he spent many days in the deep mountains and valleys to appreciate the beauty of nature about which he wrote many poems and essays. He was a well-known scholar trying to formulate an indigenous philosophy called *Sil-hag*, and as an esthete, was fascinated with natural beauties. When he was 18 years of age, looking at a clean and calm lake he lamented that human beings are playing a childish mischief on natural beauty so that they change it into ugliness. He seems to have understood nature as being animated and able to make a friendship with man:

117

In the midnight, when I awake from sleeping,
The fairy comes to the cottage over the river:
The wind welcomes me with affectionate feeling,
And the moon sends me a cup of wine.[98]

Here we see that nature has become a friend of man, having an intimate fellowship with him.

In one of his lectures to the emperor he explains the royal ideology referring to heaven and earth, which is an example of the man-nature relationship:

Three duties are always required for a king and he must never fail to keep them: that is, to respect heaven,[99] to fear heaven and to give service to heaven.... The wisdom of heaven is penetrated in everything and at any moment. Man's daily behaviour should not violate the wisdom and if he waves away from it because of his desires, he does not keep fearing the heaven.... As the heaven watches over carefully, how does man live without fear of heaven?... In the book called *Su myung* it is told that the heaven and the earth are the great parents of man. Besides our own parents, the heaven and the earth are the parents for all things un er the heaven. Because of this relationship, every man is my fellowman and all the things are with man. This means that man and all things are sharing the same body.... The reason that we fear heaven is like we respect our parents.... Although man is alone and unseen by others, he should keep away from the shameful action.... The fullness of heaven and earth in my body and mind is to care for them.[100]

Here we see the harmony between man and nature: and man is part of it, he must not violate the natural order, and he is also required to take care of nature. Man shares everything with nature. So the best attitude of man toward nature is to respect, fear, and give service to nature. It is to be noted that the idea of the man-nature relationship expressed by Yi-Whang is not so different from that of the Bible, although it gives no idea of the creatureship of nature, which the Bible makes distinctive from the beginning.

In the literature of the primitive religions and the folk religions, and of the main body of Shamanism in Korea, there are many references to nature, but without any exception there seems to be only the God-nature relationship in which nature is to be worshiped by man as "the Holy." And yet it is also to be noted that these old religions of Korea are full of references to the idea that man is of nature, he is harmonious with nature, he is born out of nature, lives in nature, and returns to nature when he dies.[101]

IN THE "SHI-JO" POETRY. An indigenous type of poem in Korea is called *Shi-jo*. It originated at the end of the Koryu Dynasty (918-1392) and has been continuing and developing as the typical form of Korean poetry.[102] Since our alphabet was invented in 1443, it has given a great contribution to the development of Korean literature. It is much concerned with the ordinary people's life, in particular

118

the life of the oppressed and the afflicted, while the poems written in Chinese characters were for the intellectuals. Nature was the most popular and favorite theme for the Shi-jo writers and the commonest idea expressed in the Shi-jo poems in regard to nature seems to be the harmony between man and nature, which is of course common to all the countries in Asia.

There is no dichotomy, as we see in Western culture, for man and nature are not separated from each other; man feels at home in nature and nature comes to have meaning and is alive when it has an intimate relation with man. It is the most natural way of thinking to say that man is in nature and nature is in man.

The man-nature relationship sung by the Shi-jo writers may be classified into several categories according to their theme or content.

The Lament of the National Decay. When the Koryu Dynasty was ruined by the first king of the Chosun Dynasty, a poet called Won-Chun-Sok lamented the national decay, comparing it with the grass of autumn. Nature teaches the poet that man's political activities and success are not to be counted as everlasting. Just as the grass in the field, it should fade away leaving tears to man:

When I see the grass in autumn on the tower of Man-wol,
A nation's destiny is ever calculable.
The royal works of five hundred years have now turned
Into a sad melody of the shepherd.
A visitor to the royal city toward sunset
Is not easy to pass by without tears.

The circles of man's life are to be compared with that of grass in autumn and the magnificent achievements of 500 years of the kings are compared with the setting sun, and the glorious works of the dynasty become an elegy of the shepherd. Here we see a harmony of man and nature. Man does not seem to be separated from nature. Through nature man reads his success and failure, and the rise and fall of a state. Nature is a mirror to man.

Poems of Loyalty. The highest virtue for a subject before his king is loyalty. It is a common phenomenon to see some betrayers and traitors when the political power moves from one person or group to another, and yet there are also some loyal subjects who devote themselves to the king whom they have served. The author, Sung-Sam-Moon, was one of such loyal subjects who never changed his loyalty to the exiled king Dan-Jong (1453-1455), who was killed by his uncle, the usurper Soo-Yang. The following is a poem praising the loyalty of the author, when he was killed (1456) with five other subjects by the usurper Soo-Yang:

119

What shall I be, when I die?
I will be an evergreen pine tree of the Bong-nae mountains,
And I will alone keep green forever,
Even though the world is covered with white snow.

Here we have another comparison, between an "evergreen pine tree" and the loyalty of a faithful man. It seems that man can be satisfied with his dying, if he keeps his loyalty like a pine tree. The mountain "Bong-nae" is a mythological mountain which stands in the middle of the East Sea, where a medicine-grass for never-growing old and of never-dying is found. And there is an ironic analogy between the white snow and the violence of a man filled only with lust for power. There seems to be a reference to the idea of transmigration in Buddhism, when he mentions "becoming an evergreen pine tree," but it is rather to be understood as the expression of unity between man and nature. Such unity or harmony is more clearly expressed in other poems.

The Idea of Harmony between Man and Nature.

Do you know why
The blue mountains keep blue forever,
The flowing rivers keep moving forever?
So, let our life be green for ten thousand years.

This is a poem, written by Yi-Whang, whom we mentioned above. This question "why?" seems not be an inquiry expecting any answer, but it implies an affirmation of truth which is unchangeable. The writer seems to consider human life as the unchanging blue, the primary color in nature; and his activities in the world as moving forward unceasingly. Thus, "the blue mountains" and "the flowing rivers" are the symbols of life, which should contain the original color that nature has given to man and should produce a new creation by its constantly moving forward. The author hopes to have such meaning and value of life for ten thousand years; that is to say, man's life is not a limited one, though it may be "threescore and ten" or "fourscore," but it implies a timeless duration of mankind, as the Bible records: "With the Lord one day is as a thousand years, and a thousand years as one day" (II Peter 3:8). The author seems to believe that man and nature can live together even ten thousand years.

One of the poems which admire the spring scenery, written by Chung-Keuk-In, shows concretely that nature and man are one and the same:

Is it made by cutting with a sword?
Or is it painted by a writing brush?
The elaborateness of the Creator shines through everything.

120

The birds are singing in the forest and excited with spring,
And the coquettish melodies are spreading over the sky.
Nature and myself are one and the same,
Are we both not overwhelmed with the same mirth?

We notice here that nature and man are one and the same—overwhelmed with pleasure, and enjoying the beautiful melodies and elaborateness of the Creator's skill. No idea of man's mastery over nature is allowed. The idea of "man against nature" is clearly foreign to the poet. Another poem written by Han-Hweg shows that nature is a home for man, where he lives and meets friends:

Don't bring out a straw cushion,
Fallen leaves are better to sit on,
Don't bring a torch light;
The moon of last night will come to shine.
O, just bring a cup of rice wine and appetizers of wild greens.

The poet seems to reject all the artificial things, such as "a straw cushion" and "a torch light," but wants to enjoy only the things of nature: the fallen leaves, the moon, rice wine, and wild greens. Happiness seems to come with raw materials of nature and not with the productions of technology.

Lastly, one more poem should be quoted in order to see how happy is the man who enjoys having friends from nature. The following poem is written by Yun-Sun-Do and is entitled "A song of five friends":

Do you know how many friends I have?
Water and stone, pine tree and bamboo,
And the moon on the eastern hill are they.
That is enough! No more to be added!

The author seems to have a deeper insight than Henry Adams who said: "One friend in a lifetime is much; two are many; three are hardly possible." He does not seem to consider a human friend as necessary, but he considers the typical themes of the Oriental painting—the moon, pine tree, bamboo, stone, and water—to be his real friends. He seems to have a common feeling with Job who says, "I am a brother of jackals, and a companion of ostriches" (Job 30:29). His friendship is to be found neither in society nor in history but in nature. If we really understand the true meaning of friendship we will affirm these phrases of William Penn: "Friendship is a union of spirits, a philosophic ripeness to live with an open heart toward nature. Nature becomes man's friend, his home, and his body to love. Man belongs to nature and vice versa."

These are some of the evidences showing a clear picture of the man-nature relationship in the "Shi-jo" poetry of Korea. It is, however, worth noting that in these indigenous studies of Korean cultural heritages it is not clear whether nature was created by God or it happens to have appeared contingently. Although Chung-Keuk-In asks, "Is it made by cutting, or is it painted?" we can hardly discern any definite Creator of nature. He also mentions "the elaborateness of the Creator," but he does not clarify whether or not nature is created. He seems to have no idea of a doctrine of Creation. He simply accepts the fact that there is nature of which man happens to be a part. The wonders, beauties, and mysteries of nature which the Korean poets affectionately appreciate seem to be dedicated "to an unknown god" as with the "men of Athens" (Acts. 17:23). Christianity has a mission to let this people know "the God who made the world and everything in it" (Acts. 17:24) and let them know that "he himself gives to all men life and breath and everything" (Acts. 17:25). And also, as with the Psalmists, the Korean Christians—including theologians and pastors—have to teach these people that all the creatures under heaven, and even the whole cosmos, have to give thanks and praise to the Creator. It is just not enough to let the people be aware of the serious environmental crisis. We as theologians have to find implications for Christian ministry and theological education in dealing with the man-nature relationship.

PRACTICAL PROBLEMS

What should we do with the ecological crisis? We feel rather impatient to take up our proper responsibility with this critical problem for mankind because, as St. Paul says, "the whole creation has been groaning" (Rom. 8:22) and must be "set free from its bondage to decay" (Rom. 8:21). We—theologians, ministers, and leaders of the church—are not called to solve this problem as specialists, and yet we are called that the gospel may be preached and ministry undertaken in response to a technological world which is faced with a serious environmental crisis. Therefore we have to find some implications for theological education and ministry.

SOME GUIDELINES

First of all, we have to have an optimistic view on the issue. Man is entrusted to meet and solve human problems, through God who makes all things new and who challenges men of despair. God the Creator asks us the same questions as he puts before Job (Chapter 38) :

Who settled the earth's dimensions?
Who set its corner-stone in place?
Who watched over the birth of the sea?
Who has cut channels for the thunderstorm?
Who sired the drops of dew?
Who put wisdom in depths of darkness?
Who is wise enough to marshal the rain-clouds?
Who provides the raven with its prey?

There are many other similar questions which challenge man's capability in regard to the works of creation. Our answer to these questions would have to be like Job's:

What reply can I give thee?
I put my finger to my lips. Job. 40:4)

Knowing man's limitations, we have to confess the omni-competence of God, as did Job:

I know that thou canst do all things
And that no purpose is beyond thee. (Job. 42:2)

Although we are forced into a position in which man seems to be left behind as being powerless and incapable of solving such a human problem as the environmental crisis, yet we are assured that God would not let us remain as pessimists but would want us to be optimists who hope that "we can do all things through him who strengthens us."

When man was created to rule over nature, it was not the purpose of God that man's dominion should damage or destroy it as we see now in the ecological crisis. We are assured that God would also give us the knowledge and skills to preserve and take care of it; for man is created for nature as a steward and a keeper of it. As we have seen, the historical roots of our ecological crisis have now become patent, caused mainly by the anthropocentric view of nature, which implies sins against the Creator. This anthropocentric view of nature has to be changed into a theocentric view which could eventually change man's selfish values into a passion "for the glory of God." So, the practical solutions to our ecological crisis do not seem to depend solely upon science and technology, but also upon the spirit of both scientists and technologists who can restore their own religious values according to the biblical view of nature. It also depends on the policy of the political administrators who are in a position of decision-making for a new world, as described comprehensively in Lynton Caldwell's book *Environment*.[103]

It is true and clear that we theologians and ministers are not to engage in the work of scientists, technologists, and administrators. But the purposes and values of our technology should be theologically and ethically reoriented; that is to say, not so as to rule over it for man's selfish purposes, but to preserve and keep it for God and man and for nature itself. It is unthinkable to know and love God apart from man and nature, or to know and love man apart from God and nature, or to know and love nature apart from God and man. Joseph Sittler seems to be right when he says, "Salvation is an ecological word in the sense that it is the restoration of right relation which has been corrupted."[104] God's drama of redemption is never satisfied with purely historical categories. The salvation history of Israel is not to be understood only in terms of the historical dimension. For instance, the exodus event of *Heilsgeschichte* has to include the land, sea, water, and wind—nature itself in its process. Likewise the incarnation of God in Jesus Christ is not to be understood only in terms of divine-human encounter. "Surely we need to regard it as the climax of the whole creative purpose for man and his world."[105] Eric Rust is right when he thinks of nature as an integral element of the incarnation: "The incarnation affirms the world in affirming man. It comes to us as an historical disclosure in the midst of our human history, and thereby it reminds us that God's purpose is fulfilled in human history and its natural environment."[106] Our theology, therefore, needs to be reconstructed in a "trinitarian" form to restore the right relation between *God* and *man* and *nature*. This requires a rethinking of our theological education and ministry.

THEOLOGICAL EDUCATION

It has been reported that the freshmen of the University of California are more inclined to learn the subjects related to ecological studies than any other cultural subjects.[107] This means that the younger generation of today regards the ecological problems as more important than other problems.

Speaking from the writer's experience, it is true that ecological problems have not been a concern of the ordinary seminarians of Korea. This indifference and lack of awareness can also be said to be true for the ordinary ministers of the churches. It is true to say that theologians, both ancient and modern, have forgotten or overlooked a great subject of theology, namely, the man-nature relation-

124

ship in theological education. Although they have done their part in supporting the idea of "man *and* nature" or "man *against* nature," they certainly have not contributed much to the idea of "man *in* nature."

CURRICULUM. In a time of environmental crisis the problem of seminary curricula must be seriously reconsidered along with what we already have discussed concerning the reconstruction of theology, namely, the formulation of a theology of nature. Recently theological curricula have been much renewed by adding new courses to the traditional subjects. In order to formulate a theology of nature, the following are to be considered:

Preseminary course: an introduction to natural science. This course always has been in the preseminary curriculum, but three points are to be noted: first, "nature" should not be a mere adjective to "science," but it must get the same emphasis as that of science. The name of the course should rather be called "Nature and Science" so that both are to be studied on the same level of importance. Second, its content should not only be concentrated on the development of science but also on the relationship of interaction and mutual influences of all the phenomena of vegetation, animal life, minerals, and the meteorological world. Third, the course should deal with the recent findings of ecology which is to be defined as "the study of the biology of environments, the structure and function of nature."[108]

Preseminary course: history of culture. This course is usually divided into two subsections: Western culture and Oriental culture, and in the latter for us an Asian national culture is to be included. There are many ways or viewpoints to observe in the history of culture but, with a concern for ecology, the activities of men should not be traced only in historical stages but also in the human environments where men have been making history. In the pattern of the "nomadic" and "agricultural" stages nature has a closer implication for man's activity in history, and such concern for nature should be resorted to in all the patterns of culture of mankind. The pollution of nature in industrial societies and the fast, reckless exploitation of limited natural resources should be a concern in the study of cultural history.

Preseminary course: an introduction to ecology. This can be a new subject for preseminarians. The students should obtain a primary and basic knowledge about ecology, and their *Weltanschau-*

125

ung and ability in evaluating things either natural or artificial must be reoriented in the light of the ecological crisis.

Theological Studies. All the courses in the major fields of theology must be reformulated in the light of ecological concern. For instance, in Systematic Theology the doctrine of creation and of man must be reoriented with a keen concern for ecology; and in Biblical Theology, Christian Ethics, and Church History[109] ecological concerns should be seriously attended to.

TEACHING METHOD. First of all, the professors must be aware of a proper preparation for adequate rearrangement of their teaching materials as much as possible, but there are subjects for which a specialist should be engaged. By all means, an interdisciplinary approach to teaching may be required in order to have a close dialogue between theology and the subjects related to ecology. It is advisable that the students should make a report at least once a year on the facts related to the environmental crisis, seen either on the national level or in their cities and countrysides, so that they feel the problem personally.

MINISTRY. The ministry is a life-style in the spirit of Jesus Christ, which is expressed not only by the ministers but also by all Christians who confess God as Father, Jesus Christ as Savior, and the Holy Spirit as guide leading to the right relation to God, to man, and to nature. It is told that St. Francis gave a sermon to the birds, calling them "my sisters," and the wolf, "my brother" when he rebuked the action of killing men. This seems to be real ministry orientated even to nature. The Slussers are right when they say, "What the church needs is an ecologically viable theology coupled with cultic practices that assist people in opening themselves to the presence of life and of God in all things."[110] The ministry of our churches now must begin and open another dimension of service orientating the environment where men are living as the children of God. We Christians are called "for nature" as stewards and keepers, just as a gardener to his garden, a farmer to his crops, and a breeder to a zoo. The ministry must give awareness to the congregation of realizing the aliveness of nature and the unifying presence of God in all things, and of learning the praises of nature to thank and glorify the Creator. In such stewardship for nature our ministry will give "a new set of values, a new ethic, a new set of goals for our life."[111] The idea of "reverence for life" of Albert

Schweitzer seems to be a fresh insight toward nature, but for us Asians, in general, it is the way of life learned from the traditional religions and customs. If we love one another and love nature, and if we consider nature as our "brother" and "sister," why don't we have the same solemnity for life as the Pueblo Indians Gray Snyder tells about?

They go out hunting in an attitude of humility.... They sing aloud or hum to themselves while they are walking along. It is a song to the deer, asking the deer to be willing to die for them.[112]

REFERENCE NOTES

[1] The original word for "to till" ('abedah) is to labor for something. Tillage is physical work.

[2] The Hebrew words for "the Garden of Eden" are gan-'eden, which means "garden of delight" as it is rendered by the LXX and Vulgate. Later writers, based on Gen. 2:8-15, describe this garden as "The Garden of God" where every precious stone (lokinds) is found (Ezk. 28:13, cf. Is. 51:3). "In early times such spots of natural fertility were the haunts of the gods or super-natural beings." (J. Skinner, Genesis, 1951. 2nd ed. p. 75f.). It is a highly mythological expression for a utopia.

[3] G. von Rad, Genesis (The Old Testament Library, 1961), p. 76.

[4] J. Pedersen, Israel: Its Life and Culture, Vol. I-II (1946 WND ed.), p. 252.

[5] "It speaks, therefore, with highest concentration about God (God created, God spoke, God separated, God made, God blessed, etc.), G. von Rad, op. cit., p. 65.

[6] W.C.C. Official Report (Geneva, 1967).

[7] The original word for "to subdue" (akarash) means "coercive submission or rule" (Westermann, Genesis 1-11, 1976, 2nd ed.), p. 222.

[8] G. von Rad, "Das Gottesvolk in Deuteronomium," Gesammelte Studien zum (A.T. 1929), p. 94.

[9] G. von Rad, "Promised Land and Yahweh's Land" in The Problem of the Hexateuch and Other Essays (1965), p. 90f.

[10] The references quoted here are to be examined in the light of their context and each phrase should be carefully and critically understood in the proper methods of interpretation. But here we only try to look on the psalmists' understandings of nature by the expressions they used.

[11] Pss. 146:6; 89:10; 95:5.

[12] Pss. 24:1; 50:10-11; 95:4.

[13] Ps. 36:6.

[14] Ps 147:9

[15] Pss. 74:13. 14. 16. 17; 136:8. 9; 147:4.

[16] Pss. 65:2; 72:8; 74:15; 78:47; 107:25, 29.

[17] Pss. 8. 19A, 104.

[18] A. Weisen, Die Psalmen, ATD 1950.

[19] This is the same in Pss. 8 and 19A (vv. 1-6). Kirkpatrick says on Psalm 8: "Nature is wonderful as the reflection of God's glory, but man is more wonderful still". A.F. Kirkpatrick, The Psalms (1927 9th ed.), p. 36. On Ps. 104, he says: "the Wordsworth of the ancient, penetrated with a love for nature, and gifted with the insight that springs from love" (Ibid. p. 605).

[20] Sheep, oxen, the beasts, birds, and the fish.

[21] H. Richter, "Die Naturweisheit des A.ts in Buche Hiob", ZAW Bd 70, 1958, pp. 1ff. In this article, Richter understands nature in two categories:

127

"Animated nature" (*belebte natur*) and "Unanimated nature" (*unbelebte natur*), and he discusses them with special reference to the problem of *Gattung*.

22 G. von Rad, "The Theological Problem of the O.T. Doctrine of Creation," in *The Problem of the Hexateuch and other Essays* (1966), p. 142.

23 J. Skinner, *Isaiah I-XIX* (*The Cambridge Bible*, 1954), p. 106.

24 G. Fohrer, *Das Buch Jesaja*, Bd. III (Stuttgart, 1966, 2nd ed.), p. 119.

25 In the trito-Isaiah such paradise is understood as "new heavens and new earth." and following these ideas the writer of *The Revelation* sees also "a new heaven and a new earth" (Rev. 21:1).

26 V. Herntrich, *Der Prophet Jesaja*, Kap. 1-12, (ATD. 1954). p. 208.

27 "The Present Disorder," in *Church and the Disorder of Society* (SCM, 1949), p. 17f.

28 Don Marquiz. "From the Life and Times of Archy and Mehitable," in *Environment Handbook*, ed. by G. De Bell (1970), p. vii.

29 H.W. Wolff, *Anthropologie des Alten Testaments* (Kaiser, 1973), p. 143.

30 This particular principle D. J. Elwood has already mentioned in his article, "Emerging Themes in Asian Theological Thinking," herein.

31 H. Gunkel, *Genesis* (1922), p. 51.

32 Lynn White, Jr., "The Historical Roots of our Ecologic Crisis," *Science*, Vol. 155 (March 10, 1967), p. 1205.

33 Theodor Roszak, *The Making of a Counter Culture* (1969), p. 245.

34 Lynn White, op. cit., p. 1205.

35 Frederick Elden, *Crisis in Eden: A Religious Study of Man and Environment* (Nashville, 1970), p. 19.

36 Lynn White, op. cit., p. 1206.

37 Clarence Glacken, "Man Against Nature." *The Environmental Crisis* (Yale University, 1970), p. 131.

38 Ibid, p. 132.

39 Dorothy M. Slusser and Gerald H. Slusser, *Technology, The God that Failed* (Westminster, 1971), p. 29.

40 C.F. von Weizsacker, *The History of Nature*, trans. by Fred D. Wieck (The University of Chicago, 1949). p. 67.

41 Lynn White, op. cit., p. 1206.

42 Hans Schwarz, "The Eschatological Dimension of Ecology" *Zygon*, Vol. 9, No. 4 (December 1974), p. 331.

43 D.M. Slusser and Gerald Slusser, op. cit., p. 47f.

44 Rhoads Murphey, "Man and Nature in China" in *Modern Asian Studies* I. (1967) 4. Quoted from Harold W. Helfrich, Jr. (Editor), *The Environmental Crisis* (Yale University Press, 1970), p. 139.

45 M.M. Thomas, *Man and the Universe of Faiths* (CLS, Madras, 1975), p. 10.

46 D.M. Slusser and Gerald Slusser, op. cit., p. 60.

47 Lynn White, op. cit., p. 1206.

48 Bruce Wrightsman, "Man, Manager or Manipulator of the Earth?" in *Dialog*, 9 (1970), pp. 200-214.

49 White, op. cit., p. 203.

50 Ibid.

51 Joseph L. Fisher, "Dimensions of the Environmental Crisis," *Journal of Religion and Science*, Vol. 5, No. 4 (December 1970), p. 282.

52 W. Eichrodt, *Theology of the O.T.*, Vol. II (Old Testament Library, 1967), p. 108.

53 Ibid., p. 119.

54 Ibid.

55 Von Rad, *Theology of the O.T.*, Vol. I (1962), p. 361.

65 Ibid., p. 367f.

57 H. Paul Santmire, "Ecology, Justice and Theology: Beyond Preliminary Skirmish," *The Christian Century*, XCIII, No. 17 (May, 1976) p. 461f.

58 K. Barth, *Church Dogmatics*, III, "The Doctrine of Creation," Pt. 2 (Edinburgh, 1960), p. 6.

59 Ibid., p. 8.

60 Ibid., p. 11.

61 Ibid., p. 12.

62 Ibid., p. 13.

63 Gordon D. Kaufman, "A Problem for Theology: The Concept of Nature," *Harvard Theological Review*, 65 (1972), p. 349.

64 Suh. Nam Dong, "A Theology of Nature" in *Theology in the Time of Change* (in Korean), appeared after he was imprisoned on March 1, 1976. (The Korean Theological Study Institute). p. 285f.

65 Gordon D. Kaufman, op. cit.. p. 337f.

66 O. Michel. *Der Brief an die Rcmer* (Gottingen, 1963, 3rd ed.), p. 66.

67 G.D. Kaufman, op. cit., p. 341.

68 Ibid., p. 342.

69 H. Paul Santmire, op. cit.. p. 462.

70 G.D. Kaufman, op. cit., p. 337.
The following have a common emphasis with Kaufman: Joseph Sittler. "A Theology of Earth." *The Christian Scholar*, 37 (1954). pp. 307-118. Conrad Bonifazi. *A Theology of Things* (Philadelphia. 1967). John E. Cobb. Jr., *Is it too late? A Theology of Ecology* (Beverly Hills. California, Bruce, 1972). *New Theology*, No. 8 (New York, 1971), pp. 29-312.

71 Joseph Sittler, "Ecological Commitment as Theological Responsibility," *Zygon* (June. 1970), p. 178.

72 K. Barth. op. cit., p. 3.

73 Ibid., p. 13.

74 Andre Dumas, "The Ecological Crisis and The Doctrine of Creation," *Ecumenical Review*, 27 (1975). p. 32.

75 Ibid., p. 32ff.

76 Ibid., p. 35.

77 J. Sittler, op. cit:. p. 178.

78 K. Barth, op. cit., p. 13.

79 Ibid., p. 15.

80 Ibid., p. 19.

81 J. Sittler, op. cit., p. 179.

82 Hans Shwarz, "The Eschatological Dimension of Ecology," *Zygon* (Dec. 1974), pp. 323-338.

83 Ibid., p. 334f.

84 A. Dumas, op. cit., p. 32.

85 Ibid., p. 33.

86 *The Limits to Growth*, A Report for the Club of Rome's Project on the Predicament of Mankind. by Donelle H. Meadows, Dennis L. Meadows. Ifhragen Randers, and William W. Behrens III (1974, 11th printing), p. 129f.

87 A. Dumas, op. cit., p. 25f.

88 Eric C. Rust, "Nature and Man in Theological Perspective." *Review and Expositor*, Vol. 69 (Winter, 1969), p. 11f.

89 A. Dumas, op. cit., p. 35.

90 Eric C. Rust, op. cit., p. 18.

91 A. Dumas, op. cit., p. 24.

92 Joseph Fisher, op. cit.. p. 281.

93 Hans Schwarz, op. cit., p. 324.

94 Ibid., p. 325.

95 Eric C. Rust, ibid., p. 18.

96 See the articles, books, and authors introduced in the study materials or "Background Papers" for CTECMA published herein. (March, 1977); J.A.

129

Veitch, "Is an Asian Theology possible?" p. 5 note (mimeo). See also D. Preman Niles, "Toward a Framework for Doing Theology in Asia," Background Paper No. 1; Kazoh Kitamori, *Theology of the Pain of God* (John Knox Press, 1965); Yun, Sung Bum, *Christianity and Korean Thought* (Korean CIS), 1964: also *The Korean Theology* (in Korean); Ryu, Tong Shik, *The Korean Religions and Christianity* (1965).

[97] Douglas J. Elwood, "Emerging Themes in Asian Theological Thinking," Background Paper. Van Leeuwen, *Christianity in World History* (London, 1964). G.C. Oosterhuizen, *Theological Battleground in Asia and Africa* (London, 1972). Kim, Kwang Shick, *Mission and Indigenization* (1975).

[98] This is a literary translation of section III of the collection in the *Tae-ge-jip* (Tong-wha Publishing House 1972), p. 388.

[99] "Heaven" is here meant to be equated with nature. According to Shang-ju "Heaven" is the interpretation when he says, "It is called nature that a cow and horse have four legs, but the reins of a horse and a cow's nose-ring are called the artifice. So the artifice must not hurt nature."

[100] The *Tae-ge-jip*, p. 402f.

[101] Moon, Sang Hee, "The View of Nature in Korean Folk Religions," *Theological Forum*, Vol. XI (1972), p. 61.

[102] Some of its collections can be listed: *Chung-ku-yungeun. Hae-Dong-ka-yo, Ka kog-won-ryu,* and *Yo-kum-ka-kok.*

[103] Lynton K. Caldwell, *Environment: A Challenge to Modern Society* (1971). In this book the policies of the environmental crisis for the decision-making person are fully discussed.

[104] Joseph Sittler. op. cit., p. 177.

[105] Eric C. Rust, op. cit., p. 12.

[106] Ibid.

[107] William Connell. "All About Ecology." *The Christian Magazine* (Jan. 1970). The statistics show that among 500 freshmen 85% of them are for population problems, 79% for pollution problems, 71% for the science of heredity, and 66% for ecology. These are the desired courses out of 25 different subjects in natural science.

[108] D.M. Slusser and G.H. Slusser, op. cit., p. 20. The function of ecological study is well described here.
The Slussers' book. *Technology—The God that Failed* is to be recommended as one of the side-reading books for the course in Natural Science.

[109] Min, Kyung Bae has attempted to see the Korean church in the light of the ecological view: "The View of Nature in Early Korean Church History," *Theological Forum* (Vol. XI), (1972), pp. 27-40.

[110] D.M. Slusser and G.H. Slusser, op. cit.. p. 153.

[111] Ibid., p. 154.

[112] Ibid.

RESPONSE TO DR. KIM'S PAPER

Hsien-chih Wang*

A CLARIFICATION OF THE MEANING OF NATURE

The term "nature" has been repeatedly mentioned in Dr. Kim's paper without a clear definition. There are different understandings of

---

*The Rev. Hsien-chih Wang is a Lecturer in Systematic Theology in Tainan Theological College, Tainan, Taiwan.

the concept of nature in the histories of science, philosophy, and theology. For examples, the scientific understanding of nature from Newton (1642-1727) to Laplace (1749-1827) mainly interprets it as a law-abiding machine with deterministic implications, and correspondingly man is interpreted as a micro-machine. Again, Stoic philosophers in the Fourth Century B.C. conceived of nature as a living, divine, all-encompassing cosmos which was derived from the Ionian nature-philosophers' concepts of nature as "divine," "boundless," and "full of air." Werner Jaeger termed this concept of nature as a "philosophical theodicy," which can also be applied to the ancient Taoist concept of nature (ca. 6th B.C.). Therefore, when we come to wrestle with the problem of the relationship between man and nature theologically, we have to make clear what specific understanding of nature we are talking about. In the Bible we cannot find any term which precisely corresponds to the Greek or Chinese understanding of Nature as *kosmos* or *physis*. The terms used in the Bible are very loosely defined notions, such as heaven or heavens, earth, all inhabitants of the world, land and all that abide on it, *kosmos* or *ktisis* (creation), *panta* (all things) etc. Although they are loosely defined, there is a common denominator among them, that is, they are "created." This presupposes a certain concept of an ultimate, transcendent Reality which is qualitatively different from those which are not created. Here I only invite your attention to the different understandings of the concept of nature in the history of dealing with the man-nature relationship in scientific, philosophical, and theological settings. To deal with the problem of man and nature in Christian theology in Asian settings, the different viewpoints mentioned above should be carefully evaluated.

GENERAL OBSERVATIONS OF THE ISSUES RAISED BY DR. KIM

I find that the main issues which Dr. Kim has raised are: first, ecological crisis; and second, esthetic values of nature. He draws from both biblical sources and Korean philosophy, from literature and poetry, for a reconstruction of the theological understanding of the man-nature relationship. This has been achieved by Dr. Kim with a certain satisfaction. Nevertheless, he seems to lay more stress on the esthetic values of nature and harmony, without paying enough attention to the "fatalistic" element which is inherent in the

131

experience of nature of Asian peoples. No matter how people interpret the "fatalistic" element, this aspect of the experience of nature should be taken seriously into account.

Besides the ecological problem, esthetic values, and the fatalistic element in nature, we have also to examine the relation between the formation of the political ideology of the Oriental Monarchy and the divine hierarchical understanding of nature as a sacred "Heavenly Dynasty." This understanding of politics-based-on-nature has been the dominant official ideology in many Asian countries and has caused people to suffer for thousands of years. This theme has also been comprehensively dealt with in Frankfort's *Kingship and Gods* which exemplifies the Oriental understanding of the relation between King and Cosmos. In the biblical patriarchal sagas this residual to the problem of divine kingship is a very serious issue which the Asian contextual theology has to take into account.

The last point in my general observation is that the "historical context" from which the biblical Creation faith emerges is not fully considered in Dr. Kim's paper. For example, the Creation faith in II Isaiah and the priestly Creation story have been located by scholars in the period of the Exile or Post-Exile, that is, about the 5th-6th centuries B.C. It was a time of worldwide socio-political turmoil. In the same period China was in the so-called age of "Warring States" and it was exactly in that age of awful suffering that the Taoist theory of nature as the ultimate source of life and virtue emerged. The Greek Ionian nature-philosophers appeared also at this time with a message of hope, derived from the "Logos" of Cosmos, for the suffering Atheneans who had faced the invasion of foreign powers. This means that the theme of Creation versus Cosmos or Nature which appeared in China, Greece, and Israel in the 5th-6th century B.C. serves as a doctrine for national salvation; and it cannot be interpreted fully and significantly if it is not interpreted with a reference to the concrete secular "historical context." Without that context the interpretation of the text will inevitably fall into intellectualistic or speculative explanations. This kind of "theologizing" or "philosophizing" should be consciously avoided in our Asian contextual theology.

SPECIFIC ISSUES FOR FURTHER ELABORATION IN DR. KIM'S PAPER

Dr. Kim has nonetheless offered us abundant resources for clarifying and identifying the theological issues in the area of the man-nature relationship. The following points seem to me to be of particular interest for further development in our coming discussions.

MAN'S ATTITUDE TOWARD CIVILIZATION IN "J." 1. *The "Promethean archetype" embodied in the descendants of Adam and Cain:* The rebellion of Adam's family against God seems to be the beginning of sexual life; and, following the fratricide, Cain's family starts to build a city and a house, to domesticate wild animals, to invent musical instruments for recreation, to create weapons for defense or war, etc. This creation of human civilization after man's fall seems to express the Yahwist writer's ambivalent attitude toward human activity in terms of creating civilization. This attitude is manifested more ambiguously in the event of the Babel Tower. Here is a serious theological issue to pose for biblical theological understanding of the rise and history of civilization.

2. *Division of labor:* In connection with the civilizing activities of Cain's family is the problem of the division of labor. The Yahwist writer's attitude toward this problem is not clear. He seems to depict the human civilizing labor as something natural. Karl Marx states the whole of his doctrine of alienation as "sin" in terms of the division of labor. And he says the division is "natural" because it begins from the division of labor of male and female functions in the ancient human family. Now that the Asian countries have been caught in the Communist complex in recent decades, a thorough theological reflection on the problem of the relation of the division of labor and man's attitude toward nature is urgently needed.

3. *"Breath of life"* (Gen. 2:7): This point has not been emphasized enough in Dr. Kim's paper. He did mention something about the Yahwist writer's concept of man as "land-tiller" and "land-caretaker," which is very significant for dealing with ecological issues. But an examination of the concept of "breath of life" reminds us of the similar important motif in the Greek concept of soul which has its original meaning as "breath," according to Werner Jaeger, which becomes a crucial concept in connection with the Greek idea of "air" in Anaximenes' philosophy of nature as an all-encompassing, organizing, and constituting principle of the universe. The concepts of soul, air, and *pneuma* (spirit) constitute the later Stoic doctrine of salvation in a cosmic scheme. A similar concept of nature as "divine breath of life" is rooted in the ancient Taoist

133

philosophy of nature as the Ultimate Reality and Ground of all beings and becomings. In the Bible itself the motifs of *ruach, pneuma,* and "wind" have their crucial roles in relating to the doctrine of Creation and Salvation as well. There is no need to repeat how importantly and how often the motifs of "storm" and "wind-god" have been mentioned in the cosmogony/theogony/anthropogony myths of the ancient Near East. I would like to pose this motif as a possible theological issue in the Asian setting.

MAN'S DOMINION OVER NATURE IN "P." Dr. Kim has reinterpreted the concept of man's relationship to nature in the priestly writings. Most of the scholars who have been interested in ecological issues, I think, will heartily agree with him. But there are still two important themes implied in "P" which can be drawn out for more significant elaboration. Originally in the context of the frame of Pentateuch/Hexateuch, the "P" writer's main concern is "holiness": "And ye shall be unto me a kingdom of priests, and a holy nation" (Ex. 19.6). But the concept of *imago dei* has been interpreted by Luther and Calvin as a holy, human, functional capacity in their doctrine of "vocation," which Max Weber considers as an important contribution to the secularization of European Christendom and indirectly a contribution to the rise and development of early Capitalism. No matter how controversial Weber's interpretation is, the concept of vocation is an important power in the shaping of the Euro-American (technocratic) civilization. This motif is also a significant point of entry for Asian theology, specifically in relating to the Asian concept of labor as something "artificial" and "unnatural" in many traditional religious or philosophical systems.

The second motif is the "mythopoeic" (myth-making) experience of God as a Creator in "P" with its historical background rooted in the context of the worship of nature-gods in the ancient Near East. The priestly writer/redactor deliberately uses the name "Elohim" in Genesis 1:1, which, according to B. W. Anderson's interpretation, embraces a complexity or cluster of *el elyon, el shadday* (nature-gods), etc. Does this mythopoeic experience of the Creator-God in "P" reflect in some way Israel's struggle with the divinity cf nature which has been understood, in the ancient Near East and China as well, as the Ultimate Ground of life, order, and political authority. This is the area where Asian religious faiths and political ideologies encounter the Christian theological understanding of man, nature, and society.

134

NATURE/CREATION & SALVATION IN THE PSALMS & II ISAIAH. Most of the Old Testament scholars stress the gravity of Salvation instead of Creation. Von Rad, for example, says that the Creation motif is only "ancillary to" the salvation history. But by a careful examination of Psalms, such as 74, 89, 104, and 148, we can easily find that the Creation motif almost serves as a "turning point" for the mediation of the sufferings of Israel and its hope. Following the prologue of God's promise, mercy, covenant with David, etc., Creation faith quite often turns the reality of suffering into a deeper trust in God's promise with a new dedication to the coming future.

More significantly, Second Isaiah speaks of Creation faith as the all-powerfulness of God in creating "new things" which are beyond human imagination and control. It becomes the "foundation" for the reinterpretation of the whole of so-called salvation-history. God has the complete freedom to reshape human history because he is the Lord of the whole universe. From this argument, there follow new covenants, a new image of servant, new witness to all of the nations. In connection with Second Isaiah's Creation faith, the "P" Creation story works hand in hand as a "new hope" for the suffering people of God. Even Isaiah and Third Isaiah talk about the "new heaven and new earth," which are undoubtedly derived from the Creation faith.

THE COSMOLOGICAL THEMES IN THE APOCALYPTIC WRITINGS. Dr. Kim seems to pay less attention to the cosmological themes in the apocalyptic writings which have influenced the New Testament in many ways. The historical context for the emergence of the apocalyptic cosmological themes is also during a period of worldwide political and social disturbances. Martin Hengel, in his *Judaism and Hellenism,* points out that the apocalyptists' negative attitude toward the world and history projects an intention to negate or escape the reality of suffering by providing some sort of "other-worldly" hope for the oppressed. From about 200 B.C. till the coming of Christ there were interpenetrations of the various cosmological ideas between Judaism, Hellenism, and Zoroastrianism. It is said that the Gnostic understanding of the creation as a "fall" emerged from the complex of these interpenetrations. This inter-Testamental idea of trans-worldly universal salvation has a lot of implications for our rethinking of the man-nature relationship in terms of searching for an authentic life and vocation in the present world.

THE PROBLEM OF REASON AND WISDOM IN JOB 28 AND PROVERBS 8. Wisdom literature mentions nothing about covenant as a condition of salvation. These writers are more individualistic and intellectualistic. They try to appeal to human experience of nature for discovering the mystery of wisdom as a means of salvation, which means to achieve the highest life in this world. Technical use of nature in Job 28 does not guarantee the achievement of wisdom which is unsearchable (Job 28:20f). "The fear of the Lord is the beginning of wisdom." This theme of wisdom seems to be quite different from the natural wisdom of the many traditional faiths in Asia which derive wisdom of life from a contemplation of the cosmic order or process. But in Proverbs 8, "wisdom" as a co-creator in the creating of the universe is pervading, deep, and everlasting in the cosmic order and process. This direct appeal to man's experience of nature for discovering the authentic wisdom, without saying anything about covenant and salvation-history can serve as an important entry for theological dialogue between Christian faith and other faiths in Asia for the elaboration of the man-nature relationship in terms of wisdom rather than reason and technology, in terms of human experience of the divine revelation rather than dependence on old covenants and salvation-history.

CREATION AND COSMIC SALVATION THEMES IN THE NEW TESTAMENT. From an examination of Dr. Kim's paper it is obvious that the whole weight from the biblical side of his argument depends on the Old Testament. New Testament scholars should make more contributions to this area of concern about the man-nature relationship. For example, the Pauline theology of cosmic revelation, groaning salvation, and new creation; and the Johannine theology of Incarnation. Here are abundant resources for elaboration.

COMMENT ON THE EMPHASIS ON THE CONCEPT OF SIN IN WESTERN THEOLOGY. Dr. Kim is right in mentioning that the concept of sin in Western theology has been over-emphasized so that the man-nature intimate relationship is depreciated. In the history of doctrine, Ireneus' argument concerning creation as good, against the Gnostic argument of creation as a fall, for example, also has its basic concern with suffering and sin on a cosmic scale. It is only after Augustine's echo of Tertullian's doctrine of original sin that the center of gravity of Western theology was located around the concept of sin, especially the sin of human nature. People always talk about the redemption of human nature rather than that of man and nature in totality. Eastern theology seems to stress more the cosmic union of all beings. But this concept of cosmic redemption manifested in the archetypal image of the "Cosmic Christ" should also be carefully re-examined. This means that there are abundant resources in the history of doctrine which may provide an understanding of man and nature in the light of its historical developments.

METHODOLOGICAL CONSIDERATIONS

Having talked so much about the resources and issues concerning the man-nature relationship, we must now find out the method which may serve theological reconstruction in a more adequate way. We all agree that a method should be developed out of the nature of the contents themselves. The following areas of discipline may constitute a basic frame of reference for "doing" theology of man and nature.

HERMENEUTICS. There is no doubt about the importance of hermeneutics. But much attention should be paid to the relation between the text and the living context in which the real issues are located. A one-sided way of reading the text may result in irresponsible, unfruitful and, many times, a too speculative and all-inclusive way of thinking. The same hermeneutical principles should be equally applied to both sides, that is, the biblical text and the texts of other faiths. Authority of the scriptures should be seriously reconsidered in the light of the limitation or the relativity of human words and the historical formation of the scriptures.

HISTORIES OF DOCTRINES AND PHILOSOPHIES. It is very clear that the inter-appropriation between doctrine and philosophy in each period of Christian theology reminds us of how Western Christianity and Eastern Christianity separated from each other in the understanding of the redemption of man and nature. A historical survey of the development of the concepts of man and nature in Christian doctrine and histories of philosophies of East and West may provide us with a more comprehensive understanding of man and nature in theological formulations of each period. This may also provide us with a corrective to one-sided interpretations of the biblical understanding of man and nature.

HISTORY OF RELIGIONS AND OTHER SCIENCES CONNECTED. A phenomenological understanding of man and nature in each religion, as in Mircea Eliade's Cosmos and History, provides a basic description in which scholars of different religions may find a common

137

agreement. Here no judgment of truth may be claimed by any religion. A deeper and broader understanding of man and nature may be enriched also by other sciences, such as psychoanalysis, biophysics, evolutionary theory, paleontology, etc. The most significant development in science relevant to the theological concern of man and nature may be found in Karl Jung's theory of the "collective unconscious" in which different archetypes, such as anima-animus, god-image, etc., are stored. His analytical-scientific approach has achieved an understanding of man and nature in intimate unity, as Taoist philosophers had achieved through an intuitive-speculative approach. This means, in the area of Man and Nature, that there is a meeting point of analytical and intuitive approaches. The two approaches are not necessarily in contradiction. Victor White's *God and the Unconscious* is a good example of this case. Anyway the phenomenological approach is not adequate, and thus there should be included in our "doing of theology" the approaches of the other sciences. It is science which brings us to see the contemporary reality of man and nature.

CONTEXTUAL PRINCIPLE. Issues in different contexts require specific attention on the use of methods mentioned in the two previous paragraphs. The contextual principle commands us to see reality as a totality—a reality which has its historical, social, political, economic, and other dimensions. The principle not only commands us to perceive reality as a whole, but also to sort out the specific issues for theological reflection. Without specification of theological issues from the living context the methods outlined above can bring us everywhere as well as nowhere!

CRITERIA FOR THE TRUTH JUDGMENT. No absolutizing of faith is permissible. Criteria themselves are relative but should be worked out together by those who engage in the dialogical way of "doing theology." Without common recognition of certain criteria for truth judgment, dialogical theologization will be either one-sided or imperialistic. Personally I like to raise the "reality principle" as a basic criterion for truth judgment. When we talk about man and nature either in the situation of ecological crisis or of magical performance, any kind of theologizing or philosophizing has to be checked by the "reality principle." Of course, this principle should be worked out according to a mutual understanding of both sides. Any absolute stance can be claimed only in a personal and confessional way, which each man finally has to choose.

7

MAN IN NATURE: AN ORGANIC VIEW*

Tongshik Ryu

As I was preparing this paper, first of all I found myself quite at
a loss with regard to the term "Asian context." I wondered if there
is or even can be anything like a real consensus in this huge and diverse continent of Asia. Speaking of racial groups, for instance,
we have in Asia Indo-Aryans, Mongolians, Polynesians, and so on.
We have all of the major world religions such as Hinduism, Buddhism, the Chinese religions, Islam, and so forth. And we have enormous cultural diversity on this continent.

Thus it may well be that if we can find any degree of consensus
at all we will find it only at certain points: first, all of Asia has
been a target of Christian mission. Second, Asia as a whole is likewise in the process of receiving modern science and technology which
have been developed in the West. Because of our diversity, however, I am quite hesitant about using the terms "Asian context" and
"Asian tradition" with reference to the entire continent. Above all,
I do not understand this huge and diverse Asia of ours very well myself. Accordingly, I will speak to you as a Korean who lives in one
part of Northeast Asia, and speak from a Korean standpoint.

Likewise, the theme "Man in Nature" is just as broad and difficult to deal with as the term "Asian context." Therefore my understanding of our theme cannot reach beyond the level of common
sense. I have been told, however, that this consultation is a find-
ings-oriented gathering, and in this context I believe that even my

*Although this paper was not read at the Consultation, it was circulated to
the delegates as a second contribution to the topic, "Man and Nature." Dr. Ryu
is Professor of Religion at Yonsei University, Seoul, Korea.

own personal views based on common sense can contribute to our discussion.

A UNIVERSAL QUESTION: ECOLOGICAL CRISIS

The theme "Man in Nature" makes me think first of the issue of environmental deterioration. I live in the city of Seoul which is now inhabited by more than seven million people, but every morning I draw natural water from a well in the valley. I do this because the water supplied by the city is contaminated. And we often think about moving out of the city because we hear that the air pollution in Seoul is already at a dangerous level. Moreover, there are lots of news reports that fish and other living things are dying in the rivers and the sea. In the midst of this situation I am keenly aware that environmental problems and the ecological crisis are no longer just theoretical and no longer the problems of well developed countries only. They are now our own immediate and practical problems. As we attempt to deal with them, I believe we must begin by reconsidering our understanding of man's relationship to nature.

Scientists use the term "ecosystem" in referring to the world of nature. This term comes out of studying the intently mutual relationship between living things and their physical environment. Plants take their nutrition from the earth and animals live on the plants. Carnivorous animals live on herbivorous animals. When living things die, they are dissolved by bacteria and return to the earth. Then plants take nutrition again from the earth and the cycle continues. Man is an integral part of this cycle. Man does not live alone in separation from nature. Literally, he is "Man in Nature," a being of symbiosis living in unity with nature.

The biosphere which covers the earth's surface and provides the environment for life as we know it is delicate and can be maintained only to the extent that the ecosystem continues to remain ecologically balanced. In other words, the ecosystem can keep itself alive only when the earth itself and the living things on it—including man—function properly at their respective points in nature's cycle. If the ecological balance of nature's world is destroyed the natural world dies, and man, being a part of that world, has no way to escape the vortex of destruction and death. Unfortunately, the world today faces the prospect of just this kind of crisis because, in the name of progress and civilization, the ecological balance of nature is already being destroyed.

The population explosion and pollution problems associated with economic growth are usually cited as the chief causes of the problem. It is natural, on the one hand, that the population explosion should lead to an uncontrollable exploitation of nature's resources simply because of the ever-increasing demands for food. But, on the other hand, the roots of the ecological crisis go much deeper than this and can only be understood as we examine the concomitant phenomena of urbanization and growth-oriented industrial development.

The earth's ecosystem and man's economic system are in conflict with each other. While the former is a recycling system which conserves natural resources, the latter is a one-way system based upon the exploitation of nature. When natural resources are taken to be used in manufacturing goods for human consumption, one result is the steady accumulation of waste as the goods are used up. Accordingly, we can even say that economic growth causes the exhaustion of natural resources as well as environmental pollution and urbanization.

In fact, the development of the modern economic system has already started destroying the earth's ecosystem. Air pollution, water contamination, and the various chemicals used in agriculture are already threatening our daily life. Trees along our city streets as well as fish in our streams are dying. We can no longer safely eat rice and the fish from the sea, which are our major sources of food. The toxins we have sown in the earth have seemingly already started to destroy us.

Economic growth is supported by science and technology. Thus the development of science and technology is driving man into ecological crisis after all. Nevertheless, science and technology continue to grow all around the world. It appears that the processes of industrialization and urbanization will continue, in accordance with which the exploitation and destruction of nature will ultimately drive man himself into catastrophe, and, as many of today's scholars are now saying, the very survival of man himself will be at stake. This is what today's ecological crisis is about.

We can observe a few certain facts from the above considerations: First, man and nature are not in opposition to each other, but are mutually interdependent. Man and nature have an inherent, organic relationship to each other as part of the earth's ecosystem from which we can see that man is indeed "Man in Nature." Second, the continuing and accelerating growth of science and techno-

141

logy which support modern economic development is driving both man and nature into a crisis of destruction. Third, the ecological crisis is a universal problem faced by mankind as a whole. Thus it is also part of the present reality of Asia as a whole.

THE TRADITIONAL VIEW OF WESTERN CHRISTIANITY

It is no exaggeration to say that the development of science and technology has brought the ecological crisis upon us. And present tendencies indicate that such development and growth will continue. Unless we re-examine our fundamental assumptions and seek positive ways to control this growth, there will be no way to avoid the threat to the biosphere. At least this is the warning we are now hearing from the scholars who are concerned with such issues.

It was modern rationalism which provided the basis for the development of natural science. Concomitantly, as scholars have indicated, man's own attitude toward nature also functions in the background to stimulate the development of the civilization of science and technology as we now see it. It is said that, in the Western world, the Christian faith has determined this basic attitude. To summarize the viewpoint briefly, God is the transcendental Creator and nature is his creation. Man is found at the center of God's creation and is commanded to subdue it. This is the essential content of the biblical story of creation. The story can be interpreted in such a way that nature is viewed objectively as something for man to take advantage of and exploit for his own benefit. Because of its influence upon the development of natural science, this anthropocentric interpretation of the biblical text has been described as 'the historical roots of our ecological crisis.'[1]

Criticizing the traditional theological view as oversimplified, but also taking a basically positive standpoint, John Macquarrie presents a new theological direction for the solution of the problems of today.[2] He identifies two concepts of the relationship of God to the world which may be found in Hebrew thought. He calls one of them the "monarchical model" and the other the "organic model."

According to the monarchical view, God is a self-sufficient and transcendent being who creates the world by an act of will. This concept is clearly visible in the creation story of Genesis. Man is the primary end of creation; thus he is commanded to subdue the earth. This is an anthropocentric idea characteristic of prophetic religion. According to the organic view, however, God and the world are not sharply separated, but instead have an organic relationship to each other. This is the thought found in the story of God's covenant after the flood (Gen. 9:10). God made the covenant not only with Noah—mankind—but also with all living things. Likewise, the psalmist saw God in nature when he sang, "The Heavens declare the glory of God" (Psalm 19:1). This immanent naturalism is one of the specific characteristics of the priestly religion.

The point of view dominant in the Bible is that of the monarchical model, with the organic model mostly veiled in it. Thus the mainstream of theological discussion flowing through John Calvin and Karl Barth has centered around the monarchical model.

Now let me summarize the traditional views of Western theology:

First, God is a transcendent being not directly connected to either man or nature. Accordingly, God is not an object of cognition by means of human knowledge or effort. That we know God at all is only possible because of God's own revelation of himself to us.

Second, God who reveals himself is a personal being. He is the living God, a sovereign entity who speaks to us through Christ and the prophets. The phrase which best expresses the personality of God is "God the Father".

Third, this personal and transcendent God is the One who created heaven and earth and who likewise created man together with nature. "By faith we understand that the world was created by the word of God, so that what is seen was made out of things which do not appear" (Heb. 11:3). God is not a being within the world but instead is the Creator who is in some way outside of it. The neo-orthodox theological expression that God is the "Ground" of existence of both man and nature may also be regarded as a confession to God the Creator.

The outlook on man and nature appears as the other side of the outlook on God. And, distinctly separated from nature, only man is described as creature. The clearest expression of this is that "God created man in his own image" (Gen. 1:27). God created man by inspiring him with his own life (Gen. 2:7). And God gave man who has the divine life and image the power of dominion over nature. "God blessed them, and God said to them, 'Be fruitful and multiply, and fill the earth and subdue it; and have dominion over ...every living thing that moves upon the earth'" (Gen. 1:28). Here we find faith in the transcendent God and the anthropocentric world-view as well. This is the attitude toward nature which has provided the basis for the development of natural science.

CHALLENGE ONE: THOUGHTS ON SCIENTIFIC EVOLUTION

The Christian view of history is an eschatological one centering around the idea of development. Ever since the time of Joachim Floris in the twelfth century it has been common practice to divide the stream of historical development into three phases. Auguste Comte, for example, spoke of three phases in terms of the development of human thought: the age of myth, the age of philosophy, and the age of positivistic science. In our era, Arend van Leeuwen refers to development in terms of ontocracy, theocracy, and technocracy, while Harvey Cox uses the concepts of tribal culture, town culture, and technopolitan culture.

There is a common theme running through the various classifications according to which we can see that our era has entered into the Third Age in which man should see a new dispensation of God. In a word, we are described as being in the "post-Christian era." According to this view, the era of Christianity which has dominated the world and cultural development since the time of Constantine the Great is now over. The age in which Christianity looked upon itself as the only authentic, absolute religion is gone. Now in the secularized age mankind is out from under the control and domination of Western Christianity. The world is an *oikoumene* which belongs to universal history. The Third Age is represented by science and technology which deny the control of Christianity. Moreover, science and technology now take the position which Christianity took in the past, and in so doing present a radical challenge to the traditional Christian understanding of the world.

A modern scientific view of the world is inclined to accept neither the idea of creation by a transcendent God nor that of domination from the outside, preferring instead to accept the doctrine of evolution by the impulse of internal power. For those like myself with no expertise in the field of science, Teilhard de Chardin offers a great deal of insight concerning this viewpoint.

According to a recent article in *Time* magazine,[3] scientists have estimated the age of the cosmos to be about twenty billion years and its width to extend for about twenty billion light years. The sun and the earth, which are thought to be about five billion years old, are in the Milky Way, a galaxy which has a diameter of about one hundred thousand light years and which encompasses hundreds of billions of stars besides our own sun. It is possible for us to imagine the size and age of the cosmos by considering the fact that there are at least ten billion other galaxies in addition to the Milky Way.

Yet the cosmos does not stand still. It is expanding even now at the speed of light, and innumerable new stars are being formed while at the same time others are dying. In other words, the cosmos was created twenty billion years ago and now is still in the process of being created.

To see all this, however, is nothing more than to see the cosmos simply from an external point of view. Going a step further, Teilhard de Chardin holds that the cosmos is continuously created in such a way that it is internally evolving. It is not simply space but time-space which is evolving internally in a certain direction. If this time-space of his has a shape, it may be a kind of spiral, conic space. And the planet earth is at the apex of the process of cosmic evolution, with man finding himself in the uttermost apex.

Let us take a look at the process for a moment. On the surface of the earth which has a history of about five billion years, there was a critical point about three billion years ago. This was the point of Vitalization, which resulted in the beginning of life and the ensuing process of biological evolution. Thus, on the surface of the geosphere where there had been only material, there was formed the biosphere which was composed of living things. The biosphere then evolved over a period of three billion years to reach the point where it contained various forms of life such as plants, fish, birds, and mammals just as mentioned in the book of Genesis.

About two million years ago, there was another critical point in the evolution of the biosphere. This was the point of Hominization from which man came into being—man with the capacity for reflection about which we say, "He knows that he knows." In other words, there appeared man who does self-reflective thinking by which it is possible to have vision and invention, and to use tools. This occurrence marked the beginning of what is called the noosphere.

There were, again, two critical developments in the evolution of the noosphere. One was the emergence of co-reflection which started in man about thirty thousand years ago, and the other was the Christ-event which happened two thousand years ago. Co-reflection brought forth the phenomenon of Socialization and thereby paved the way for the beginning of the history of modern civilization. This history started when the phenomena of religion and arts began to emerge in society. Finally, Christ appeared in the world

145

as the "omega point" of cosmic evolution. And so the world proceeds in a movement of cosmic convergence toward this point.

The cosmos has evolved in a certain direction. It is the direction of evolution from non-living matter through the stages of Vitalization, Hominization, and Socialization, on to the stage of Spiritualization. And it is Christ who is the omega point in this process. He is the one in whom God the Creator is himself incarnate. His ultimate event is found in the spiritual body transubstantiated by the resurrection, where the spiritual body is the union of freedom and personality. Man and nature are now evolving toward this omega point.

God is not simply the creator from the transcendent outside but is the One who continues to create in the cosmos by means of the process of evolution. Man is not a being in opposition to nature but is an organic part of nature and is a being that progresses toward the point of cosmic consummation together with nature.

I said earlier that the Third Age, which we are in, is characterized by the dominance of science and technology. However, this does not mean that science and religion are in conflict with each other. They are seen as working together in the history of the cosmos.

In brief, the picture I have just presented represents the kind of modern scientific understanding which challenges the traditional Christian understanding of the world.

CHALLENGE TWO: ASIAN RELIGIOUS THOUGHT

To the shame of the West, it may be said that it was the Western nations which spread colonialism over the world. But colonies have been disappearing since the end of World War II. This is another characteristic of the Third Age. Since political domination is accompanied by cultural and religious domination as well, one could say that the Christian world-view which emerged in the West might have functioned at the very basis of Western imperialism. However, the Western imperialistic Christian era is over.

Liberation from political domination also brings cultural liberation, and religion lies at the very center of culture. Asian religions which had been disregarded or rejected are again finding their own places. Now we have started to concentrate our concerns on our own traditional religions in order to rediscover our own cultural traditions and values. In addition, Christians have started to acknowledge acts of God outside the church in accordance with the concept of *missio dei*. We do not think that God arrived along with the missionaries only about a century ago! I believe that God the Creator of the cosmos and the Providence of all history must have already worked in the cultural history of Asia. Moreover, Asian religions must have been important media of his activities.

However, Asian religious thought and traditional Christian thought do have different structures, and in this we see another challenge to traditional Christianity. Ideas about nature and man have a direct relationship to ideas about God. The Western world with its concept of a personal and transcendent God gave birth to an objective view of nature, while Asia with its concept of an impersonal and immanent, absolute being gave birth to a subjective view of nature. In the Western view man stands in opposition to nature and achieves self-realization through conquest of nature. The development of Western civilization culminating in present-day science and technology is a direct outgrowth of the Western approach to self-realization. In contrast, for Asians who see man as a part of nature self-realization lies in adaptation to nature and in embodiment of the essence of nature.

It is necessary to understand two basic concepts of Asian religions in order to see the traditional Asian understanding of "Man in Nature." One is the Hindu concept of *Brahman* and the other is the Chinese concept of *Tao*. In view of their depth and universality, it may fairly be said that these concepts are the cornerstones of the world-view of Asia. Let us look at them.

Brahman is *Atman*. Brahman is Ultimate Reality defined from the objective side, while Atman is the same Ultimate Reality defined from the subjective side. Atman, our inmost individual being, is the Brahman which is the inmost being of universal nature and of all her phenomena. Brahman is the Universal itself, which is immanent as well as transcendent: "The self is all existence and all existence is the self (*Isha Upanishad* 5:6). There is nothing outside it, and yet it abides in everything.

Brahman is all-inclusive. From it all things are created, by it all things are sustained, and into it all things are dissolved. (*Taittiriya Upanishad*). The world appears to be full of opposites, but this appearance is merely the movement of Brahman. Brahman transcends all relative opposition. Therefore, in Brahman there are no opposites. Oneness and harmony prevail.

Brahman is also the Creator of the world. Yet Brahman is not a person, so that Creation is not an act in which something is made out of nothing by a person. Instead, Creation is a self-projection of Brahman into the conditions of time and space. It is not an act of making, but an act of becoming.

The purpose of life is the attainment of freedom and joy. But ignorance stands in the way of achieving this purpose, and the knot of ignorance is egoism. Because we do not know the real nature of the Self (*Atman*), that is, oneness with the Universe (*Brahman*), we falsely identify ourselves with the "not-self" which desires to possess and enjoy the things and values of the vain world. This desire produces our attachment and *Karma*. Therefore, the renunciation of all desire is the condition for the free enjoyment of all. "By that renunciation thou shouldst enjoy" (*Isha Upa.*). By renunciation of ego, the false self, and its desire one realizes his union with Atman or Brahman. Upon realizing his oneness with Brahman, man enters the state of *Ananda* (pure bliss) where heaven and earth, object and subject, are one, and thus reaches the true realization of his humanness. This union with Brahman is an eternal existence free from time and death.

The Chinese concept of Ultimate Reality is *Tao*. Lao-tzu developed the most inclusive understanding of Tao, but of course the term is not unique to Lao-tzu. It occurs constantly in Chinese literature, both before his time and afterward. The simple meaning of Tao is "way" or "reason." But what is unique to Lao-tzu is his use of Tao as the name of that which is the ultimate explanation of the universe:

There are taos but the Tao is uncharted;
There are names but not Nature in words;
The Nameless Tao is the Origin of heaven and earth;
The named heaven and earth were the Mother of all things.
(*Tao Teh China*, Ch. 1)

Tao is invisible, inaudible, and intangible. It is something of absolute transcendental existence beyond all our senses. But it is also the essence of all existence which is produced by it and nourished and ruled by it. Therefore, it may be called "Mother" because all things come from it and it rules. In short, Tao is nothing but the Creative Principle.

"The things of this world come from the Being, and the Being

148

comes from the Non-Being, which is Tao" (Ch. 40).

And again:

Out of Tao, One is born;
Out of One, Two—Yin and Yang;
Out of Two, Three—Yin, Yang, and breath;
Out of Three, the created universe. (Ch. 42)

Both in China and Korea, scholars used the term Tao for translating the *Logos* of St. John. But we have to recognize that Laotzu's concept of Tao is limited to just the Creative Principle. It does not include the Creator, a person who created the world. Nonetheless the function of Tao is often described as if it contains some great personal virtues: "Quicken them; feed them; quicken but do not possess them" (Ch. 10). Tao does everything but desires nothing. The manifestation of this virtue of Tao in humans is called *Teh*.

The purpose of life is in holding this virtue of Tao. In order to achieve this, one must give up attachment to ego and obey Tao. In short, it is "Inaction in Nature (*Wu Wei Tzu-Jan*)." This means, "Let the Tao be Tao in you." That is, do nothing with artificiality, but simply follow the way of Nature (Tao). Then man will be content with what he is. Here again renunciation or self-negation is the center of Chinese religion, as it is also in Hinduism.

Thus there are common threads in Indian and Chinese thought. First, Ultimate Reality is not a transcendent personal Creator but an immanent Creative Principle. Second, self-realization of man is to be found in becoming one in union with Ultimate Reality. Here one can obtain freedom and joy and thus achieve the true purpose of life. Third, the renunciation of attachment to ego or the false self, that is, self-negation, forms the center of religious thought.

THE THEOLOGICAL TASK IN ASIA TODAY

I think that theology is a product of contextual reflection upon the biblical text. Accordingly, theological understandings have changed as a result of changes of context. The theology of the Middle Ages emerged out of the context of the Roman Empire, and the theology of Protestantism emerged out of the context of modern culture. Then what is our context today?

It is helpful to think of our present-day context in terms of two levels: the universal context and the local context. What we call the post-Christian era or the era of science and technology is the universal context according to which theology in the world as a whole

149

is taking on new forms. Secularization or "religionless Christianity" may be seen as symbols of change in this context.

On the other hand, there is also the local context. Among American Blacks, for example, there is a particular local context associated with problems of racism. Here we find Black Theology being formulated. And in Latin America there is another kind of local context in which a revolutionary theology of liberation is being formulated. Last summer I had an opportunity to visit Central America, and even from a superficial observation of the continuing economic exploitation and the ignorance and poverty of the people there, I came to an understanding of what this theology of liberation means. But what, really, is the nature of our local context in Asia?

Of course, our local situation is affected by worldwide issues and we must therefore participate in theological reflection at the universal level. At the same time, we have our own specific context in which to operate as well. In terms of the Third World, our local context in Asia overlaps to some extent with those of other areas. But Asia has a cultural context different from that found in Africa and Latin America. One outstanding difference is that we have highly developed religious cultures, such as those coming from India and China, and this is not necessarily the case with the cultures behind Christianity, which simply have different dimensions. However, in the modern age this fact has been disregarded and even suppressed in our encounter with Western civilization.

The theological task of the Third World, which is still partly under the domination of Western Christian civilization, seems to be conceived mainly in terms of socio-political theology. We have much to learn from this. But the specific task of theology in Asia with its strong traditional cultures is different. Of course, we are living in an age of unrest characterized by rapid socio-political change. In this context Christians who are serious citizens cannot help but participate in their own social realities. It is well known that many Christians are suffering in confrontation with political reality in Korea, for instance, and it is also true that we can carry out our Christian witness very well through such confrontation. We learn a great deal from socio-political theology. But I think this kind of confrontation comes because of one's conscience as a citizen before it is a theological task. A great number of educated people outside the church are also concerned about political reality, and it is not the Christian church itself, but ordinary educated people including Christians who raise the GNP, conduct systematic education, and carry on an organized struggle for social justice. And, in spite of many defects, socio-political activities in Asia have also been developing without any help from the church.

But there are some problems. Technicians, for instance, who may have an abundance of knowledge about their socio-political activities represent a real problem to the extent that they may also lack concern for the ultimate values of man and for religio-cosmic issues. At present there seems to be a much greater importance attached to the socio-political dimensions than to the religious dimensions of man. I think this is the point at which we find the pastoral task of the church important in Asia today. We must preserve human rights not only with respect to the political dimensions of man but also with respect to his religious dimensions. And I think that the theological task which the Asian church faces now is not the development of a socio-political theology, but the development of a religio-cosmic theology.

As for the contents of this religio-cosmic theology, I would like to make the following observations in relation to the theme, "Man in Nature." My first point concerns the organic view of nature which I mentioned earlier. Man is confronted with the threat of destruction because he has exploited nature for the sake of economic growth as measured simply in terms of GNP. In view of this threat, John Macquarrie has recommended a new theological direction as the basis for mankind's salvation: "As far as Christian theology is concerned, my thesis is that we need to move away from the monarchical model of God toward the organic model."[4] By providing a perception of the world in its organic relationship to God, this model gives both dignity and mystery to nature. Accordingly, we will be able to overcome our narrow anthropocentrism which leads us to regard nature simply as an object of human exploitation. I think we must fully accept this recommendation in our context today, not only because the perspective it gives us about God and nature is congruous with that which modern science has discovered, but also because it reflects the viewpoint of Asian religious thought. Nature is seen not as something produced by the self-will of a transcendent God, but instead it is understood that there is an organic relationship between nature and Ultimate Reality. This may not be the dominant theme in the Bible, but then it is not an unbiblical theme either. Moreover, the theology of Incarnation provides us

151

with a positive basis for the organic view: the body is composed of the same material as nature, and thus if we believe in the incarnation of God we must admit that there is an organic relationship between God and nature. The Incarnation changed Hebrew theology into the Christian gospel; the same Incarnation now provides the basis in Christian theology for the development of an organic view of nature.

My second point concerns the cosmic view of history. If today's crisis is caused by a self-centered and near-sighted world-view, then in order to save the world from destruction we must begin by looking at history from a cosmic perspective. Social confusion and international wars seem to result from a short and narrow understanding of history. Therefore, I fully welcome the cosmic evolutionary view of history which Teilhard de Chardin presented to us. First, it is a cosmic view which has scientific relevancy. The cosmos and its history are not objects that can be dealt with hurriedly in terms of some kind of millenial theory or according to the anthropocentric concepts of social science, but as far as the magnificent appearance of God's economy in the cosmos is concerned present-day science explains it rather well. Second, Asian religious thought presents us with a cosmological viewpoint in preference to one concerned with human society and politics. And it teaches us to see nature and man on the basis of this cosmology. Third, together with its dominant theme of human salvation, the Bible has numerous texts which indicate that the appearance of mature man with a cosmic view is awaited. Christ is a cosmic being. All things are created by him, sustained in him, and evolved toward a spiritual body of freedom and peace manifested by the Resurrection. All things now wait for the coming maturity to reach the glorious freedom of the children of God. (Cf. Rom. 8:18-25; Col. 1:15-20; Eph. 1:22ff.).

Finally, my third point about the development of a religio-cosmic theology has to do with *pneumatikos*-religion. By this term I do not mean spiritual life in contrast to material life, but a mode of human existence. In such a mode of existence one denies attachment and egoism and lives by committing his whole being to God. Religious effort leads to becoming a new being by means of self-negation. Accordingly, *pneumatikos*-religion means pursuing acts leading to freedom, love, and peace by means of self-negation. The root of the world's problems today lies in self-assertion and egoism. Therefore, we must seek salvation today in *pneumatikos*-religion.

And Asian religious thought focuses upon just this theme. It is the Asian religions which teach man to reach freedom and joy by renouncing the false self or human artificiality and to become one in union with Brahman or Tao. But the theme is also directly connected to the truth of the Bible in that the gospel is concerned both with the event of the Cross and that of the Resurrection.

Christian faith is to die with Christ on the cross and to take part in his resurrection (Rom. 6:3-5). Here, then, at the very core of Christian faith we find the idea of becoming one in union with the Cosmic Christ by renouncing any attachment to oneself and the world, by living to enjoy freedom and peace, and by loving one another. This is a cosmic event which goes beyond simply the spiritual gratification of a particular individual, because Christ who lives in us and in whom we come to live is really the Cosmic Christ who creates, rules, and leads the cosmos to its consummation.

The age in which man could be satisfied with individual salvation is gone. Gone also is the age in which sociopolitical theology caused a new sensation. Having entered into the cosmic age, that which is demanded of us today is a religio-cosmic theology. I believe that those who will step forward in response to this demand are Asian theologians.

REFERENCE NOTES

[1] Lynn White, Jr., "The Historic Roots of Our Ecologic Crisis," *Science,* Vol. 155 (1967), pp. 1203-1207.

[2] "Creation and Environment," *The Expository Times* (October 1971).

[3] *Time Magazine* (December, 1967).

[4] Macquarrie, op. cit., p. 8.

PART THREE

MAN IN SOCIETY AND HISTORY

154

8

MAN IN SOCIETY AND HISTORY: WORKSHOP REPORTS

Workshop A

THE GOSPEL IS FOR ALL

After independence and nation-building Asia, with 55 per cent of the world's population, still sees most of its people denied meaning in life and enjoyment of their share of life's necessities.   Cultures have recovered from colonialism and some self-direction has been regained, but the majority of Asians are still deprived.

The churches have continued to support intentionally and unintentionally the exploiters and those in power, and neglected the needy far too often.   The majority of churches are middle class institutions preaching a gospel identified with middle class values.   When the church does minister to the poor, the effect is very often that of an other-worldly religion.   Church people and ministers should be aroused to the awareness that the gospel and the goodness of God's world are for all, not merely for the privileged few.   Our mission to the poor must be clearly defined and ministries adjusted to better serve the people.

THE PEOPLE

The church's responsibility is to claim God's right for *all* people.   But society is stratified in such a way as to let some Asians exploit other Asians.   The church very often refuses to recognize the class distinctions and class oppression as a fact of life, and thus fails to recognize the need for different approaches and formulations, and often the need to take sides.   This refusal and failure restricts and isolates the Christian community.   A biblical understanding of the people is required, an education toward prophetic involvement, and the nurturing of community.

LAW AND POWER

In Asia political and economic, racial and regional powers almost always express and exert themselves in the form of law. As such, they pervade every aspect of life. They may indeed strengthen social order, economic development, and social justice. But they may also result in repression of rights and unequal distribution of wealth. The church which claims God's right for all people has to respond.

The God-given task of the church demands that she act on the side of the victims of repressive laws. Yet the church is more often than not a beneficiary of the system legitimized by the law. The question is not merely how she should respond. It is whether the church *can* identify with the poor and the oppressed. The church should seek an understanding of power, both secular and biblical, and of her own power, for the benefit of the victims of power and the unjust execution of law. For example, the church's stewardship in using its inherited property and assets for the benefit and welfare of the poor, in the church as well as in the community at large. What you have determines what you are, not only with regard to theological institutions, but also to the church as a whole. The exercise of power should also be studied in relation, for example, to the question of violence.

HUMAN RIGHTS

Side by side with those of other movements and religions, Christians are growing aware of universal human rights. In the light of God, our Creator, Redeemer, and Hope, all people are equally precious, having the right and responsibility to live the way God intends—in love, freedom, and hope. This right cannot be taken for granted in the face of economic and political oppression, cultural denial, social, ethnic, and racial oppression. It calls for struggle. The churches must struggle to safeguard and foster the rights of every human being. These are constantly threatened in the name of national security or development. Theological education must be directed to a sensitive awareness of human dignity and worth, and alerted to their constant erosion.

IDEOLOGIES AND RELIGIONS

Asia is the seat of many great religions of the world (Hinduism, Buddhism, Islam, etc.). The church in Asia is thus confronted with one religion or another. In our time we face the resurgence of these religions, and the church's exclusive claim is being challenged. The church in Asia is also confronted with many modern ideologies such as Marxism, Maoism, socialism, *Panja Sila* (Indonesia), and secularism.

The church is called into existence to witness to the coming of the Kingdom of God, the *Shalom* which proclaims the salvation of the whole world. The church as a *koinonia*, as a worshiping community, is to be a mission and servant. Thus the function of the church is in service and mission to the whole world, the whole *oikoumene*. Does the church communicate and at the same time confront the world where other religions and ideologies are also making their claims concerning the ways and means for the salvation of the world?

The church in its ministry in Asia today must consider seriously the claims of these religions and ideologies and take into account their potential and validity. The church must enter into dialogue with people espousing them. It is time for theological education to take seriously the context in which it is situated. Theological students as well as the members of the church at large are to be enabled to relate to these religions and ideologies in light of the ministry of the church in Asian contexts. This means reorientation. There is disagreement over the use of Marxist social analysis as a tool for understanding. This disagreement too should be dealt with seriously.

MULTINATIONAL CORPORATIONS

An important power which is operating today in Asia is the power of multinational corporations. Working closely with the political power of national elites the MNC combines economic and technological power to an uncontrollable extent. Since it operates beyond the national boundary, it is difficult to check. Quite often the decisions affecting the lives of people are made in a foreign country. These decisions include the relocation of resources—natural, human and financial—made with little regard for the well-being of the majority of the people of the land.

This raises the need to understand the comprehensive operation of the power of MNC as it shapes the pattern of living of the people. How can we consolidate our effort to face this enormous concentration of power? Isn't it just like the story of the small boy David facing the gigantic power of Goliath? We propose developing an interdisciplinary working group related with the grass roots,

157

among theologians, social scientists, and those who are connected with action groups, to grasp the effect of the MNC, especially its influence on the human value of people. We further propose relating such concerns and actions in regard to the MNC to similar groups from other countries and international agencies such as SODEPAX* so that an international counter-network on the people's level can emerge.

CHURCH AND FRONTIER GROUPS

For witness and service among the poor and the oppressed, the institutional church needs to support the frontier action group to do the penetrating work. On the other hand, the action group needs to be reminded constantly of biblical perspectives. We quite often see tension or even a split between the institutional church and the frontier group. The basic reason is that they serve different constituents. How can we promote a healthy relationship between the two?

MINISTRY

The church has developed many ways of expressing the gospel. There will be differences among Christians about the most appropriate form in the light of the situation and their conception of the gospel itself. Changes in society and the concrete challenges of history present ever-new demands for the church if she is to be faithful to her call to witness in word and deed. Christians are called to constant reassessment of the adequacy of their attempts to bring the gospel to the people of their time and circumstances. Ministry must take the gospel to human beings where they are, without dislocating or uprooting them from their context, actualizing their total fulfillment, and inviting all to participate as subjects in the Asian historical process.

TRAINING FOR MINISTRY

The challenge which is stimulating self-reliance demands new forms of ministry and a viable pattern of theological education in Asia. The inherited pattern was largely based on that of the old West, and does not fit today's Asia. In spite of the repeated plea

*Joint Committee on Society, Development and Peace, of the World Council of Churches and the Pontifical Commission on Justice and Peace.

158

to find a viable pattern suitable to the Asian context, we see little actual change. In many cases, the seminaries are still dependent on foreign help and personnel. We recognize a diversity of situations which demands a variety of responses. We encourage the seminaries to make use of existing information in the viability study already available (TEF, Zorn Study on *Viability in Context*) and to reassess its own task in the light of ministering to the poor. Also, further experimentation in self-reliance in ministerial training is to be fostered, even if that involves some risks.

SUFFERING AND HOPE

The process of faithful evangelization, humanization, and the formation of genuinely Asian church communities among the deprived is not automatic. There will be suffering and struggle. Today in Asian reality we see such suffering and struggle in people oppressed by powers and structures. There are challenging insights in the resurgence of traditional religions. But inherited attitudes of passive resignation in Asian traditional culture increase the sense of despair and other-worldliness among Asian peoples.

The gospel is the Good News, proclaiming the manifestation of the Kingdom through events of history. It destroys every false promise uttered by earthly principalities and powers. The gospel encourages the oppressed, who are struggling to become human, by the power of Immanuel—God *with* us. Through the Cross we perceive God's transforming presence among suffering people. Victory over principalities and powers has already been brought to humankind through his Resurrection, where the "impossible" becomes possible. We move toward the future with Asian people anticipating the full actualization of human fulfillment promised by the Holy Spirit.

How is this outlook of life and struggle manifested in the day-to-day life of the seminary commuter community? Today on the frontier of art and literature artists are creatively depicting the crying search of suffering people for hope in the Asian context. How is our theological education making concrete response to the challenges brought about by the human search for hope today in Asia? How do we manifest, both personally and structurally, the life-style which exhibits "struggle in hope" with the suffering people?

THE HISTORICAL SITUATION

Asia entered a new era with the ending of colonial rule. This was accompanied by an upsurge of human expectations. Significant advances have been made, but the task of creating a new order of society is much more difficult than had been anticipated. As a result, many hopes remain unrealized. Frustration and cynicism are widespread and the temptation to withdraw into fatalism is always present. Even where Asian peoples have emerged from old political and economic captivities, new captivities continue to threaten. The influence of multinational corporations is all-pervasive. Many governments, in their concern for economic growth, institute authoritarian or repressive structures. Modern social systems show their own forms of unfreedom and injustice. Even the church is caught in stultifying structures and shows forms of religious life that are unfree. There is no going back to the old ways. Nor are we to resign ourselves to impotence in the face of present turbulence. Our way lies forward, but where is the living hope that can empower our advance?

THE PRESENT OPPORTUNITY

Today the Asian peoples are engaged in struggle. In all parts of Asia the common people are demanding participation in power and a full share in decision-making. Different models are present. All demand the right to live in dignity, freedom, justice, and peace. This struggle is the decisive reality in the Asian scene, and is a dynamically positive way of affirming the emergence of Asian peoples today.

Many dangers are present because people are wrestling to bring to life their hopes for a new order of society, and they find themselves in frustrating and ambiguous situations. People may lose hope, thinking the struggle to be endless and the task meaningless. They may identify the form of the emerging society with the goal of the "new creation," which remains beyond every new order of society. They may be ensnared by the will to power, or by the vested interests of class, or by absolutizing an ideology. They may be enslaved by principalities and powers which are subtle but monstrous in their imprisoning evil. In spite of these dangers and the ambi-

160

guities always present, Asian peoples continue to work in hope for the new order struggling to be born. The question stands, however, as to whether or not the struggle is worthwhile.

Many signs of hope are also present, which can be recognized and celebrated even in their ambiguity. Even under authoritarian rule with its corruptions of power, people are still aware of the great changes taking place. Their aspirations are heightened and they challenge the status quo by responding to the decision-making processes open to them. Conviction leads to courageous opposition which is not silenced even by imprisonment and torture. The word of hope is heard in people who witness to their concern by challenging oppressive injustice. China stands over against all Asian nations as a constant critical challenge to all other responses in the Asian struggle, in spite of the ambiguity which seeks justice at the expense of freedom. The forms of the Chinese revolution in self-reliance, people's power, and the radical re-evaluation of tradition and culture are, for some, signs of hope which question their own models and ways of thinking.

The secular responses of the technological revolution in Asia raise different questions which are still, also, signs of hope. A new spirit of social responsibility is present. Past superstitions are being replaced by people's determination to work out their own destiny. The vigor of modern industrialization, for all its ambivalence and injustice, can provide a new capacity for creative responses. All of these are imperfect signs of hope.

THE STRUGGLE AND ITS PAIN

Bringing the new order to birth is accomplished in struggle and is accompanied by pain. This is a form of suffering which all Asia experiences today. Where this takes place it can be affirmed by Asian people as a sign of hope that the new order is emerging. Suffering here is a mark of the intensity of the effort, as the new order groans in the travail of birth.

But suffering is also a mark of oppression and injustice. In their struggles for a just society, people are subjected to indignities which violate their efforts for human dignity. In their work for justice they suffer injustice. Suffering here is a sign of the destructive power of the old order resisting the new order coming to birth. The cries of the oppressed are the groanings of people suffering under heavy burdens, yearning to be free.

161

The church is involved in this struggle for a new society. Her own members share the expectations and demands for an open and just social order. Church people are caught in the same ambiguities and frustrations as others. The pain of the struggle goes through the life of the church. The church, however, can read the signs of hope present in the struggle. She confesses with joy the struggles as marks of the emerging new creation. The cries of pain can be heard as the sounds of the creation groaning for freedom.

The church knows that this struggle is deeply ambiguous. The realities of power can be demonic and deny the hope that is present. The forces of self-centeredness constantly seek to frustrate the aspirations of hope. In every new order struggling to be born we are tempted to identify our own ideological expectation with the hope of the "new creation." Nevertheless we rejoice in the signs of hope that the struggle presents, while we also know that every movement forward involves us in the risk of being overcome in the conflict.

We celebrate many signs of hope in the church in Asia today. We are glad that her leaders are free to affirm the struggle and seek in many places to be part of it. The church is committed to development programs and educational advances which raise the consciousness level of local communities. The church is rediscovering that she can speak with prophetic authority from the midst of the struggle. Where she is involved, informed, and committed she wins again the right to share her good news. The church is also discovering the imperatives of action. She is theologizing "on the run" as she reflects on the tasks of mission and ministry in which she is urgently involved. Creative programs in rural and urban ministry are reported from many countries. Ministries on the frontiers, in situations of high risk and great danger, encourage the church just as they bring hope to deprived and oppressed groups. Faith is life in action for the sake of the gospel where the struggle is fiercest and the human need is greatest. All these are signs of hope for the living response of the church's witness.

The struggle is lightened by the renascence of the religions of Asia. A new openness to each other is present and creative dialogue is possible. All these religions are seeking ways of responding to the struggle in the midst of life. Past traditions are reinterpreted with a new awareness of the present task. The church herself is able to share this religious resurgence in rediscovering the

162

Asian cultural heritage and in developing a new spirituality in which to live fully is to live in suffering love, enfleshing the life of the servant Lord.

The ecumenical movement is yet another sign of hope in Asia. The church in the midst of frailty and polarization is beginning to speak with fresh authority whenever people suffer indignity, oppression, and injustice. Her development programs are attempts at strengthening self-reliance in the Asian struggle, along with social justice and economic independence. Her dialogic stance has encouraged the Asian churches in their rediscovery of the other religions of Asia, in their common humanity, and in their shared commitment in the common struggle. These visions and concerns are definite signs of hope.

With the perception of so many signs of hope in the midst of the struggle, we believe the church to be the *first fruits* of the "new creation." She can be a witness to the inbreaking new order, but to be able to do this the Christian community needs to give sustained evidence of her commitment to the struggle. When the church accepts suffering inflicted on her and bears up those who are imprisoned and tortured for Christ's sake, she accepts the burden of suffering. Where people live dangerously with the deprived and dispossessed, the church acts credibly. Those who live on the frontiers and those who suffer are living signs that, for all her weakness, the church is demonstrating that the Asian struggle is her own. Indeed, it is as she is involved in these struggles that she embodies the life of the crucified Christ who is the suffering Lord.

The church is given strength to carry the burdens of a struggling world, by the Spirit of life and freedom. The Spirit leads on, frees from bondage, gives confidence in the struggle, and "bears witness with our spirits that we are children of God." "We do not know how to pray aright, but the Spirit helps us in our weakness as we groan inwardly," waiting for the freedom of the new humanity (Rom 8:16, 26). The Spirit calls us to the way of suffering that we may inherit the joy of the Kingdom.

The cross is our sign of suffering, of victory, and of hope. Christ wrestled with the principalities and powers which sought to overwhelm him. His sufferings were a groaning anguish which he accepted and which he bore. His struggle was intense. We rejoice in the victory he won. However, we confess before his Cross that we are afraid of the costly obedience that his way of struggle de-

163

mands. We pray for courage to become a people who live with Christ, suffer with him, and go the way of the Cross.

Christ rose in triumph over the forces of evil. His wrestling burst asunder the bonds of death. In his rising, the hope of the new creation in "a new heaven and a new earth" is made present in his glorious body. He is our guarantor that the victory is assured, but the risen Christ bears in the body of his new humanity the marks of his sufferings. We pray that we may so experience the power of his resurrection-life that we may be living signs to the world that the new creation has come to birth and that the cries of pain can become shouts of victory.

The Agenda for Theological Education

The theological task which the reality of the Asian struggle brings to focus is directly related to the nature of the struggle itself. The context for the activity of mission and theological reflection is the turbulence and ambiguity of the emerging Asian social order. The Word of God in this situation comes with revealing power when biblical text and this context confront each other in a double wrestling—to understand both the text and the world to which the Word comes. This has major methodological implications since the "wrestling integrity" which is needed to live on this theological frontier is often lacking. The way in which the scriptures are shielded within the church suggests that they do not often penetrate a world struggling to bring a new order to birth.

The struggle is an *Asian* struggle. Again, this has major implications for the ways we theologize. We are not free to set limits beyond which the questions from our Asian culture may not come into an inherited Western tradition. Just as the Old Testament is a paradigm of the Hebrew responses, so we have other paradigms to bring into this dialogue. Just as the Christ-event was interpreted in Judeo-Hellenistic terms, we bring other paradigmatic responses from within our own cultural heritages. We do not know how far this work will take us as the Word of God speaks with renewed power within our Asian struggle.

Theological education is a serving ministry and its task is to equip those who, in turn, are to enable the whole people of God including youth and women to be effective in their mission and ministry. The question arises, who the people of God are in this time of struggle. Clearly, theological education has grown away from the

common people. They have not helped to shape theological education nor has it reflected their life and aspirations. In many cases
the seminaries have become elitist, Westernized communities of privilege, alienated from Asian cultural and religious history and isolated by their dependence on Western money.

In order to serve the people, seminaries must be rooted in the
life of the people. To relate to the people they must move quickly
toward self-reliance in financing. They must provide flexible structures which enable them to respond to the declared mission priori-
ties of the local church. They must demonstrate a life-style which,
in its simplicity, openness, and involvement with the people, rivals
the familiar style of religious teachers from other Asian traditions.
The Christian *ashrams* (religious communities) of an earlier time
are a helpful model here. This will entail a commitment to spiritual
formation as a quality of life with resilient flexibility, courage, and
simplicity to relate deeply to the local church.

The structures of the seminary need to be remodelled so that
they are functionally adequate to serve the church in mission. These
structures should be inexpensive, but resourceful and effective. They
will be judged by criteria of excellence which will evaluate the seminary in terms of effectiveness to equip people for mission. Professional education for ministry will include self-reliance in encourag-
ing "tent making ministries" and involvement in facilitating developmental ministries. In fact, the question was sharply raised whether
we should not dismantle traditional theological seminaries since they
do not relate to the present mission demands of the church! Restructured theological education will opt to support the hopes and aspirations of the people. Part of their task will be to see and reinforce the signs of hope present in the local situations and to become
catalysts able to actualize those hopes that the people articulate.
The need for a well-educated ministry will increase since the task
of interpreting the living Word of God out of involvement in the
ongoing struggle is a demanding, creative work. The Word comes
to focus within the context of the struggle.

Theological education will be for the whole people of God as a
means of enabling them to participate effectively in the struggle.
Among the many current models and experiments, the following
examples were discussed:

India. A seminary which restructured its work to cooperate in
a total enabling of the church in mission. The teaching minister

works in a team with the developmental officers, the lay pastors, and the lay witness teams. The theological college relates educationally in all these areas.

Hong Kong. A seminary which encourages its students to become professionally trained in another sphere so that they can support themselves both in theological college and in ministry.

Indonesia. A theological college which integrates rural developmental ministry with theological training so that the ministers are able to relate in the local rural communities.

Sri Lanka. A program of community reformulations with a comprehensive approach in which the emphasis is on the people's participation.

Philippines. An interseminary field education program which pools seminary resources to engage students in frontier ministry in rural and urban areas, among mountain tribes, and in prisons and hospitals, relating to church and other agencies.

Several countries. T.E.E. Programs which necessitate a total restructuring of the role of the seminary so that it can serve its students where they are.

Many other models are present giving reason for hope that the church has the confidence and resilience to respond to the expressed needs, demands, and opportunities of the situation and to reflect on its involvement in the action of mission. By the *ortho-praxis* of their own responses theological colleges will demonstrate that they have a role in responding to the Asian struggle in living hope.

9

BIBLICAL VIEWPOINTS: OLD TESTAMENT

D. Preman Niles

STUDY III. MAN IN HISTORY AND SOCIETY
(Jeremiah 45)

In the first of these three studies we looked at the context and nature of man's encounter with the holy God by examining the "prophetic call" narrative in Exodus 3:1-15. In this study we will move on to an examination of the prophetic ministry itself. We will do this by looking at the ministry of the prophets in general and Jeremiah in particular, and pay special attention to the oracle in Jeremiah 45 which attempts to understand theologically the suffering which the prophet Jeremiah had to undergo. My interest in the subject of the ministry and suffering of the prophet came about as a result of a particular situation in the theological college where I teach. Instead of taking a more systematic approach to the exposition of the character of the prophetic ministry, my intention is to take you along the road which I travelled.

Those who come to our college for their ministerial training are convinced that God has called them, but they are not always sure as to the context within which they have been called to exercise their ministry. To be sure, most of them feel that there is only one ministry, namely the cultic ministry within the church, and that they should adapt and train themselves for this ministry. Without necessarily denying the validity of this form of ministry, our task as theological educators has been to expose our students to various social contexts, so that they may discover the specific situation within which their ministry is to be exercised. For it is our conviction that the total context within which God's love is expressed is not just the church but the world. "God so loved the world that he gave his only son so that those who believe in him should not perish but have everlasting life" (John 3:16). In terms of ministry and mission, this means that we have to work toward the creation of situations within which the good news can happen and indeed become a reality so that men may experience the good news. The theological position we have taken can best be stated in the words of a New Testament scholar, J. Christiaan Beker.

The Gospel is not simply a message aimed at the winning of souls for the church; it is the announcement of the coming of God with his kingdom, who already claims historical reality for himself and who, since the resurrection of Christ, is engaged in destroying the hostile powers and in establishing domains of freedom in his creation.[1]

Our task then is to share in this ministry of Jesus Christ. As a consequence of this approach to ministerial training, several of our students have moved beyond the confines of the church to exercise a ministry within the world, that is, society.

Several months ago, at a meeting of the past students of the college, there was a session on "The Story of My Ministry." Repeatedly, those who participated spoke of failure and not of success. One past student put it this way:

I came to the college with certain ideas about the ministry. When I was in college, my ideas changed, and I began to realize that God in Jesus Christ is not only concerned with those in the church but with all those outside, especially the down-trodden and oppressed among whom I realized I had a special ministry to perform. Near the church to which I was sent there is a slum. I began working in the slum and tried to get the help of my church people. My concern was to bring to these slum dwellers a recognition of their worth as human beings and to help to build leadership among them, so that they could recognize and fight against those forces which keep them in these conditions. While I was engaged in this ministry, some of my church members accused me to the Bishop for not being a good priest to them; and I was thrown out of that church. All that I can now say is that my ministry is a failure.

To be sure, it would have been possible for us who were present at this session to analyze each "story" and show why so-and-so had failed. But the total impact of the whole session was to convince us that we were so geared to success in our ministries that we could not handle failure. Implied in our approach was an unduly optimistic assessment of history and society, so that we felt a prophetic ministry exercised in society would inevitably result in a change for the better. In other words, it had become our conviction that *we* could build the Kingdom of God on earth, so that failure led almost necessarily to despair: "Why have I failed? What is God doing?

Why did he let me down?" In one of his confessions, Jeremiah poignantly expresses this experience of failure:

O Lord thou hast deceived me, and I was deceived;
thou art stronger than I, and thou hast prevailed.
I have become a laughing stock all the day;
everyone mocks at me. (Jer. 20:7)

It was with this feeling of failure that I turned to the passage before us (Jer. 45).

I

Scholars consider the section, Jer. 37-44, as essentially the passion story of Jeremiah written by his secretary Baruch to which he has added an oracle given to him (ch. 45) as a theological comment on Jeremiah's suffering.[2] Before we turn to ch. 45, it will be helpful to look briefly at the account of Jeremiah's suffering in chs. 37-44. The Babylonians have surrounded Jerusalem. During the siege, word comes that the Egyptians are preparing for battle against the Babylonian forces, and the siege is lifted. During this time, King Zedekiah sends word to Jeremiah asking whether there is any real respite. Jeremiah replies that the Babylonians have gone away only for a time to drive away the Egyptians, and that they will return to take Jerusalem. After this meeting with the king, Jeremiah takes advantage of the lull in the fighting to leave Jerusalem and go to his hometown of Anathoth to examine a piece of land he has bought. He is arrested as a deserter, and is beaten and imprisoned in a dungeon. Shortly thereafter, the king sends for him for a secret meeting. The king asks whether there is any new word from God; and Jeremiah repeats his earlier message that the king will be delivered into the power of the Babylonians. Jeremiah then speaks of his own suffering.

What wrong have I done to you or your servants or this people that you have put me in prison? Now hear, I pray you, O my lord the king: let my humble plea come before you, and do not send me back to the house of Jonathan the secretary, lest I die there. (37:18, 20)

The king orders that Jeremiah should be committed to the court of the guard and a daily ration of a loaf of bread be given to him. The hope which Jeremiah experiences at this time is through a human agency, through a weak and vacillating king. Again, the nobles accuse Jeremiah as a traitor and condemn him to death. He is let

169

down into an empty cistern and left there to die. Hope comes again through an Ethiopian eunuch—through the compassion of a foreigner who is not even allowed to participate in the cult. Jeremiah is rescued from the cistern, and remains in the court of the guard till Jerusalem is taken. After the fall of Jerusalem, the Babylonians, considering Jeremiah to be a friend and not a foe, entrust him to the care of the governor Gedaliah. This hope for his life is short-lived, for Ishmael kills Gedaliah. Although Ishmael is of the lineage of David, his motive for killing the Babylonian appointee as governor is not to restore the throne of David but for personal profit. He seizes the people who were in Mizpeh as slaves, and sets out to go over to the Ammonites. Hope rises again when Johanan overtakes Ishmael and rescues the people Ishmael took captive. The question now arises as to whether they should stay on in the land or run away. To stay on may mean facing the anger of the Babylonians who would be incensed at the killing of their governor. After a ten-day period of waiting, Jeremiah gives them God's message.

If you will remain in this land, then I will build you up and not pull you down; I will plant you, and not pluck you up; for I repent of the evil which I did to you. Do not fear the king of Babylon...for I am with you, to save you... (42:10f.).

At this time of crisis and turmoil, the actual word of hope from God is too strange to believe. Those with Jeremiah refuse to trust this word; and they take Jeremiah prisoner and go away to Egypt. Thus, Jeremiah's path of suffering ends, as one commentator aptly remarks, "not in the light, but in the night."[3]

The narrative stresses the completely this-worldly nature of Jeremiah's sufferings. The suffering is not a prelude to a miraculous divine intervention (cf. Dan. 6:14-24). God is completely silent. The hope which Jeremiah experiences is through human agents; even the divine assurance of protection if they stay in the land is repudiated by Jeremiah's companions. So, the lights dim and disappear almost as quickly as they are lit. There is no picture of great human endurance, but only the portrayal of the agony and uncertainty of a very human character who is forced to tread this path of suffering because of the word he is called to proclaim. Inevitably, the question arises as to what God is doing at this time; or, in other words, what this suffering means. It is as an answer to these questions that Baruch appends to the passion story an oracle which he had received.

170

Baruch had earlier asked why his own suffering was unceasing and had received the following reply through Jeremiah:

You, Baruch, said: Woe is me! for the Lord has added sorrow to my pain;
I am weary with my groaning and I find no rest.
Say thus to him: Behold, what I have built, I am breaking down, and what I have planted, I am plucking up.... And do you seek great things for yourself? Seek them not; for behold I am bringing evil upon all flesh, says the Lord. But I will give you your life as a prize of war in all places to which you may go. (Jer. 45:3-5)

By placing this oracle at the end of the passion story, Baruch raises the question "Why?" for the now silent Jeremiah. The oracle, however, seems not to be a direct answer to the question itself, but an attempt to set the whole ministry of the prophet within a divine perspective. The oracle implies that the frustrations and hopes of the prophetic "I" have to be subordinated to the purpose and activity of the divine "I." What I have built I am breaking down.... And do you seek great things for yourself? Seek them not." The same emphasis is found in one of Jeremiah's confessions (15:15-21). In this confession Jeremiah states at the outset that he has completely subordinated himself to the divine will, for he has made the divine word, which spells out his own ministry, part of himself (15:16). He then raises the question of his own suffering:

Why then is my pain unceasing, my wound incurable, refusing to be healed?
Wilt thou be to me like a deceitful brook, like waters that fail? (15:18)

God's reply to this petition is to ask Jeremiah to return to him and re-accept his position as God's prophet, for it is precisely in finding his own identity in the divine mission that his personal questions concerning his safety can be answered.

If you return, I will restore you, and you shall stand before me.
If you utter what is precious, and not what is worthless,
    you shall be as my mouth.
They shall turn to you, but you shall not turn to them.
And I will make you to this people a fortified wall of bronze;
they will fight against you, but they shall not prevail over you,
for I am with you to deliver you, says the Lord. (15:19-29; cf. 1:18f.)

It is, therefore, within the total context of the divine sending of the prophet, that is, his ministry, that the specific answer to the prophet's suffering, caused by his apparent failure, can be sought. Hence, we shall turn first to an examination of the prophet's ministry, and here we shall view the ministry of the prophets as a whole, and then come back to the question of the prophet's suffering as raised specifically by the prophet Jeremiah.

171

II

In the oracle in Jer. 45, God speaks of himself as the agent in the actions of breaking down and uprooting. In the call of Jeremiah, this is the task to which the prophet himself is called:

See, I have set you this day over nations and over kingdoms
to pluck up and to break down,
to destroy and to overthrow.
to build and to plant. (Jer. 1:10)

To Jeremiah is entrusted not only the task of breaking down and uprooting, but also the task of rebuilding and replanting which too is within the divine mission (see Jer. 24:6, 42:10). In essence, then, the task of the prophet is to incarnate in the present situation both God's word of judgment and of hope. Therefore, he does not express his own opinion, but is called to be "an agent in the politics of God."[4] The role of the prophet as an agent in the politics of God becomes evident, for instance, in Jeremiah's contest with the popular prophets of his time (Jer. 23:9-32 and Chs. 27-28). Jeremiah states bluntly that these have not stood as he has in the Heavenly Council of Yahweh (Jer. 23:18; cf. I Ki. 22:13-23). Therefore, their message was a human message which was just a popular evaluation of the present situation and an empty promise of peace and well-being to bolster nationalist aspirations (Jer. 23:17). They had failed to understand the present political situation in a dimension of transcendence, that is, in the way God views it. The true prophet was called to proclaim God's word for the present and to summon the people to respond immediately.

I did not send the prophets, yet they ran;
I did not speak to them, yet they prophesied.
But if they had stood in my council,
then they would have proclaimed my words to my people,
and they would have turned them from their evil way,
and from the evil of their doings. (Jer. 23:21-22)

As an agent in the politics of God, the prophet is called, first, to proclaim God's judgment in the present, "to pluck up and to break down," and, second, to build up hope for the future, "to build and to plant." We will examine briefly these two aspects of the prophetic ministry.

A. Although each prophet performed his ministry in a situation different from that of the other, all of them display remarkable similarity in the way in which they perceived the lack of responsibility in human society. In forsaking Yahweh and turning to the worship of gods who would not question her social behavior, Israel had not only broken the covenant but blatantly exhibited her complete disregard for social justice. Amos denounces those who are willing to sell into slavery the needy for a pair of shoes (Amos 2:6). Isaiah decries the moral depravity of his people, for in places where God looked for justice (*mishpat*), there was only bloodshed (*mizpah*); and where he expected righteous behavior (*zedaqah*), there was only the cry of anguish of the downtrodden (*ze'aqah*). (Is. 5:7). Micah depicts Israel's social irresponsibility and unrighteous behavior as a failure to do justice, a refusal to show mercy, or to practice *hesed*, and to walk humbly with her God (Mic. 6:8). In refusing to practice *hesed*, Israel had forgotten that Yahweh had rescued her from bondage in Egypt, and required of her to show the same concern and mercy for the downtrodden and oppressed (Ex. 23:6-9). The prophets were unanimous in calling Israel to repentance, that is, a radical change of her life-style, for her perversity had not only corrupted society but also polluted nature (Hos. 4:1-3; Jer. 3:2-3). Unless Israel repented, disaster would inevitably follow. So Jeremiah proclaims:

Your ways and your doings have brought this upon you.
This is your doom, and it is bitter;
it has reached your very heart. (Jer. 4:18)

In launching their unrelenting attack on the social evils of their time, the prophets did not think of themselves primarily as social reformers. We look in vain in their message for a comprehensive program for a social revolution. Rather, they addressed themselves to the actual specific problems evident in their society, and called on those who had the power to act, namely, kings, priests, prophets and particular groups of people, to set things right.[5] They attacked those with economic power who were not above grabbing the property of the poor (Is. 5:8-10; Amos 2:6f.). They denounced nobles and prophets who were willing to pander to popular nationalist demands (Jer. 23). They upbraided corrupt judges for miscarriages of justice (Amos 5:10-12; Is. 3:9-12). They served notice of the judgment of God on kings who acted with complete disregard for the welfare of the people (Jer. 22:13-19). For them justice was not an abstract ideal to be realized in a future society, but a specific demand to put things right *in the present*, in every situation in which there was wrongdoing. In their message, there is an unmistakable note of urgency, for the judgment of God is imminent: "Prepare to meet your God, O Israel!" (Amos 4:12).

B. What of the future? In the prophetic message, there are portrayals of the new society which is to be born in the future. A poem found in Isaiah and Micah speaks of the New Jerusalem to which many nations will go, for in it there will no longer be injustice and strife but peace and well-being; and the weapons of war will be turned into instruments of peace (Is. 9:2-7). However, these future realizations of the new society will not be human accomplishments, but the result of the wonderful divine intervention of God (Is. 9:7). Since the new society will be a divine gift and not a human accomplishment, the contours and structures of that society are not sharply drawn, but ideally and poetically portrayed to evoke hope in "the new thing" which God will do in the future.

The new thing to which the prophets point is not an event predicted for the end-time when the course of human history will be abrogated and a new age will dawn. The prophets were not millenialists who held out hope for an indistinct future. The new which they saw in the future would be realized within actual historical conditions. Thus, Second Isaiah, in asking Israel to forget the things of the past and look to the future event of liberation, could actually point to the rise of Cyrus through whom God would perform this wonderful deed (Is. 41:2-4; 44:28; 45:1-6). Since the new would be realized in history, even in times of judgment and darkness, the implications of that future could be recognized and affirmed in the present. At the height of the siege of Jerusalem, the prophet Jeremiah was offered a portion of his family estate in his home town of Anathoth. This was hardly the time to invest in real estate. But he was persuaded to buy this land as a pledge for the future when God would again make it possible for fields to be bought in the land which was at present a desolation without man or beast (Jer. 32:43). Such visions of the future, as one commentator observes, "serve as testimonies that Israel's history is under the purposive direction of God even though, according to the same prophets, the present stands under his catastrophic judgment."[6]

III

We observed earlier that when Jeremiah raised the question of his own suffering and failure, God's reply to him was to turn again and re-accept his role as God's prophet. In terms of our discussion of the prophet's role, we may now state more sharply the context within which the question of the prophet's suffering needs to be viewed. Since the future is in God's hands and he has already given concrete signs of hope for that future (Jer. 32:43), the prophet is free from anxiety concerning the realization of that future kingdom. Therefore, personal questions of success or failure in terms of that future are essentially irrelevant. Instead, the meaning and relevance of his ministry are to be evaluated in terms of his present task, namely to break down and uproot, which is to destroy all those beliefs, practices, and institutions that thwart the realization of the Kingdom of God and its justice and peace. At the present time the corruption in human society is so pervasive that the judgment of God is directed against "the whole land" (Jer. 45:4). In this situation the prophet raises the question of his suffering: "I am weary with my groaning and I find no rest." God replies by pointing to his *own* suffering: "Look! What I have built I am breaking down, and what I have planted I am uprooting." This is not the time when the prophet, who himself is called to execute this task, can look for "rest," or even for personal rewards: "Do you seek great things for yourself? Seek them not." The prophet has to be reminded of the fact that the ministry which he is called to perform is more distasteful and painful to God, because God has to destroy what he himself has built up (See also Lk. 13:34f.). The present society, with all its injustice, still belongs to God; and he refuses to disclaim his love for it even though he has to punish it. In a sense, we find here the terrible cost of loving one's enemy. Therefore, in performing his ministry, the prophet comes to share in the suffering love of God; or rather to understand that God is also suffering with him. This is why God is silent; and there are no miraculous deeds of divine intervention.

There is, however, an assurance of personal safety to the prophet who is engaged in this ministry: "But I will give you your life as a prize of war (booty) in all places to which you may go." The prophet is present in places where the battle is most furious. He can have no other gain or booty except his life. This much safety is assured if the prophet continues in the task to which he is called. This is the assurance which is given to Jeremiah and his companions when they ask for God's guidance. "If *you will remain in the land,* then I will build you up, and not pull you down; I will plant you, and not pluck you up" (Jer. 42:11; cf. 31:27f.). They are now called to

175

participate in the rebuilding process, but human doubt engendered by human failure leads to a tragic course of action.

Let me conclude by saying that central to the prophetic ministry is the call to deny oneself and to subordinate one's desires and hopes to the demands of the Kingdom. Our problem, however, is that we find it ever so difficult to give up anything *we* think is important. Some years back, an American missionary addressed a Christian congregation in my hometown in Jaffna, Sri Lanka. Since many of those present could not understand English, a translator had to be employed. The translator was excellent, so that, for those of us who understood both languages, it was a special treat. During the course of his address the missionary indulged in a bit of verbal humor. The translator very wisely left it out, but gave in his usual excellent manner the main point which was made. Of course, nobody laughed when the translation was made. The missionary turned to the translator and said, "Brother, didn't you tell them my joke?" The translator hesitated for a moment, and then said in Tamil, "My missionary friend here just said something which is funny in English. But, if I translate it into Tamil, it will sound stupid. However, the poor man is upset. So, would you mind laughing for him?"

In contrast to us, who are perhaps not even prepared to give up a bad joke, stands the paradigm of him who so completely subordinated himself to the divine will that he gave up his divine status and assumed the condition of a slave. He accepted the limitations imposed on us by all those things which keep us in bondage. In that manner he became a man and carried his obedience to the extent of being willing to die on the cross, and sharing the fate of a common criminal (Phil. 2:6-11).

REFERENCE NOTES

[1] J. Christiaan Beker, "The Role of the Biblical Theologian in the Theological Curriculum," a paper presented to the Faculty Seminar, Princeton Theological Seminary, Nov. 5. 1975. Quoted by Bernhard W. Anderson in "Biblical Faith and Political Responsibility," *Theological Bulletin* (McMaster Divinity College), Vol. IV, No. 2 (April 1976), p. 11.

[2] Heinz Kremers, "Leidensgemeinschaft mit Gott im Alten Testament." *Evangelische Theologie*, XIII (1953), pp. 122-40.

[3] Kremers in "Leidensgemeinschaft."

[4] G. Ernest Wright, "The Nations in Hebrew Prophecy," *Encounter*, 25 (1965), pp. 225-237.

[5] Bernhard W. Anderson, "Politics and the Transcendent," *The Political Science Reviewer*, I (1971), pp. 1-29.

[6] Ibid., Section IV.

BIBLICAL VIEWPOINTS: NEW TESTAMENT

Ben Dominguez

TRAVAILS III: CALL FOR A NEW WITNESS (Acts 4:1-22)

THE WITNESS-THEME IN ACTS

The book of Acts opens with the promise of power to the disciples. This is the power of the Spirit which, according to Luke, is given only for one purpose and that is for the apostles to be the Lord's witnesses "to the ends of the earth" (1:8).[1] The gift of power through the Spirit is the gift *par excellence* for the disciples. Luke is careful to show this at the point of transition between the Gospels and the Acts. Whereas in the Gospels the Holy Spirit resided only in Jesus, this same Spirit is now empowering the apostles as witnesses in the Acts. Herein lies the very close identification of the mission of Jesus and that of the apostles (the church). The implication here is that the thrust of Jesus' mission shown by Luke in Jesus' opening message at Nazareth also underlies the mission of the apostles as witnesses of God's Kingdom.

The Spirit of the Lord is upon me.
He has anointed me to preach the Good News to the poor,
He has sent me to proclaim liberty to the captives,
And recovery of sight to the blind,
To set free the oppressed,
To announce the year when the Lord will save his people! (Luke 4:18-19)

Luke further emphasizes the witness-theme in Acts by ending his book with Paul, a prisoner in Rome, preaching the Kingdom of God *unhindered* at the Empire's capital.[2] I sense the influence of Luke's version of the *ekklesia logia* (sayings of the church) in Matthew: "And I tell you, Peter: You are a rock and on this rock-foundation I will build my church, and the gates of hell shall not prevail against it" (16:18). Luke seems to have drawn a more vivid picture: the gates of hell are no longer contending, for the witnesses' proclamation of the active exercise of God's rule in the world is unhindered!

THE TEXT: A DRAMA IN TWO SCENES

Our text is a drama in two scenes. The first scene includes verses 1 to 15, and the second, verses 18 to 22. Verses 16 and 17

177

provide the transition between the two scenes. In these transitional verses Luke subtly and yet vividly describes the reaction of the powerful opponents of the witnesses. In the first scene the *identity* of the witnesses is emphasized. In the second scene the emphasis is on the *mission* of the witnesses.

THE IDENTITY OF THE WITNESS (Scene 1). The first scene (vv. 1-15) opens with the arrest of Peter and John. Verse 2 indicates that the arrest is caused by the apostles' preaching of the resurrection. The Sadducees, the ones in control of the Temple as priests and political leaders at the same time, ordered the arrest, and the reason appears obvious. The Sadducees did not believe in the resurrection. This act of the Sadducees, however, seems to indicate more their passion to preserve their political powers than their zeal for their religious beliefs. They arrested Peter and John for disturbing the peace!

In verse 7 the question centers on the healed man: "What power do you have and whose name did you use?" Here we see the hand of Luke preparing a setting for the speech of Peter which contains the *kerygma* (proclamation) in a nutshell: "Jesus Christ of Nazareth whom you crucified, whom God raised from the dead...." (v. 10). What preoccupies Luke in the first scene, however, is the description of the Lord's witness. He describes the witness solely in terms of his relationship with Jesus. Luke takes pains to show us that this is his preoccupation. He makes verse 13 (let us call it the identification saying) the answer that the religious and political leaders, who were trying Peter and John, arrived at to explain their amazement at the disciples' fearlessness. Certainly this reflects the significance that Luke wants to give to the saying: "they realized then that they had been companions of Jesus" (*sun to Iesou esan*; literally, "they used to be with Jesus" or "they remained with Jesus"). Acts 1:21-22 states this Lukan emphasis more clearly. When the believers agreed to choose someone to take the place of Judas among the twelve, they said:

Someone must join us as a witness to the resurrection of the Lord Jesus. He must be one of the men who were in our group during the whole time that the Lord Jesus travelled about with us, beginning from the time John preached his message of baptism until the day Jesus was taken up from us to heaven.

Here it is emphasized that a witness is an eyewitness of the resurrection and a follower of Jesus in his earthly ministry.

In our text (Acts 4) we note that the identity of Peter and John as companions of Jesus is only traceable through the basic characteristic of their witness, that is, fearlessness. They were unafraid in declaring what they believed and in acting out the implications of the faith they declared! Luke's description of Peter as "full of the Holy Spirit" (v. 8) before he answered the question of the authorities—"What power do you have or whose name did you use?"—already sets forth the basis of the apostles' fearlessness in their witness. It is the *empowering* by the Holy Spirit, and nothing else, that identifies the witness. Luke also wants to emphasize to his readers the fulfillment of Jesus' promise to his disciples in Luke 12:10-11:

When they bring you to be tried in the synagogues or before governors or rulers, do not be worried about how you will defend yourself and what you will say. For the Holy Spirit will teach you at that time what you should say.

This is more significant for Luke than mere fulfillment of Jesus' promise, for this is undoubtedly the concrete sign of the presence of the Risen Lord in power accompanying his witnesses.

In the first scene, then, we have the description of the identity of a witness.[3] He was a companion of Jesus (*now* accompanied by the Risen Lord, through the Holy Spirit). He has a message to declare: Jesus Christ crucified and risen for the salvation of all peoples! His message is accompanied (vindicated!) by concrete manifestations of the power of God at work.

Luke endeavors to emphasize in the first scene the portrait of a witness as the church launches into a new setting. And certainly there will be new demands in that new setting. The church will be moving from the narrow confines of the Jewish setting in Palestine (Jerusalem) into a wider world of mission: a world characterized by pluralism; a world where *The Way* (the Christian movement) is not known. A new witness is needed, the witness that Luke has described in the first scene: a witness whose only identification is in Jesus!

In Asia we are making the transition from being mission churches sitting on the lap of mother churches of the West, to becoming "self-reliant" Asian churches. The demands of this transition on Asian Christians as witnesses are already legion. To aid the social, political, and economic upheavals in our region will certainly demand of us an awesome responsibility!

POWER PLAY: IDENTITY OF THE WITNESS TESTED (Scene 2). In the transition (vv. 16-17) from scene one to scene two Luke endeavors to portray the *effect* of the apostles' boldness in their witness. The powerful, hostile authorities, strangely enough, are shown confessing to one another: "We do not have the authority to deny it!"[4] This effect of the apostles' witness is all the more significant for Luke, because he had earlier described both groups in a contrasting manner. In verses 5 and 6 one gets the picture that *all* the people exercising authority and influence in the affairs of Jerusalem are in the group that tried Peter and John.[5] On the other hand, the apostles are described as ordinary men and of no education, obscure and unknown.

Seen in that contrasting situation, the fear, anxiety, and helplessness of the authorities in the face of the boldness and steadfastness of the apostles could never be attributed to any qualities of the apostles themselves. These could only be attributed to that powerful description of Peter—"full of the Holy Spirit!"—filled with the presence of God, which is the only power that makes one a real witness.

The Mission of the Witness

The second scene (vv. 18-22) portrays how the apostles dealt with the pressure exerted by the authorities. The height of the apostles boldness as witnesses is shown through the affirmation:[6]

You yourselves judge which is right, to obey you or to obey God. For we cannot stop speaking of what we ourselves have seen and heard! (19-20)

I notice here an interesting display of literary finesse that succeeds in portraying a desired emphasis. In verse 17 (a transition verse) the helplessness of the authorities is summed up thus: "We have no power...." In verse 20 the affirmation of Peter and John is summed up in the same day: "We have no power...." But, whereas in verse 17 the authorities confess that they do not have the power "to deny" the effect and spread of the apostles' witness, here in verse 20 the apostles confess that they do not have the power "to stop" proclaiming their message. Stated positively, the apostles' power is only for declaring what they have seen and heard!

Here lies the dilemma especially of theological students. They expect to put content into what they have "seen and heard" that they may experience the Spirit's empowering. But instead they often experience alienation. With the demands for a new witness in our region, theological education for empowering is a priority.

Concrete manifestations of the validity of what the apostles have seen and heard are placed at strategic points in our text. In verse 4 we see the growing number of those who joined the followers of "the Way" *after* the arrest of Peter and John. We also see the healed man (v. 14) whose presence led to the helplessness of the authorities. The climax of all of these manifestations of a powerful witness is the release of the apostles (v. 21).

POWER: THE CHARACTERISTIC OF THE WITNESSES' MISSION

The whole passage (Acts 4) is a concise portrayal of the working of the Holy Spirit through the apostles' witness. In this witness, God's active exercise of his power results in the overturning of the natural course of events. Hence we see a persecuted community growing rapidly; powerful authorities becoming helpless in the face of plain, obscure, non-violent apostles; a man lame since birth not only healed but saved![7]

Here the affirmation of Christ's *triumph* over all opposing forces (principalities and powers) is visibly pictured. The authorities are emptied of their power. This does not mean that they were overthrown but that they were rendered powerless (despite their threats) to stop the apostles' witness. To be *emptied* of power in the New Testament sense can be pictured by a water pail that is not only without water but also *without bottom*! Thus it can not really hold anything, although it still appears to be a pail.

Here is pictured God's active exercise of his power in the total realm of human endeavor. And, although this power is exercised through ordinary people and events, the ordinary is turned into manifestations of extraordinary power. To use an old expression, history is "his story." Here we see Luke's emphasis on being "secular." To be truly secular, for Luke, is to be able to put everything in life (in society and history) within the scope of one's commitment to God in Christ.

Luke's witness-theme appears to be his unique way of presenting history as God's story. He approaches faith and history by looking at the witness-theme in relation to his portrayal of the story of salvation. Whereas Paul takes the second coming of Christ (not a NT phrase) as imminent (it may happen during his lifetime!), Luke emphasizes only that it will come. When the coming will be is not within man's province to know. This is made clear by Luke at the opening of the Acts and in relation to the command for believers to witness. The emphasis, then, lies in witnessing, not in waiting for the second coming.

Whereas John internalizes history and puts it in the realm of deciding for or against the proclamation of God's love in Jesus, Luke presents a linear history divided into epochs with the period of Jesus' ministry as its center.[8] The period of Israel serves as the time of preparation and the period of the church as the period immediately preceding the second coming, the time and manner of which is totally in God's hands. The witness-theme in Acts, then, takes on both urgency and seriousness in this picture of the story of salvation. The command of the Risen Lord is urgent that, after the apostles receive the gift of the Holy Spirit, they will be witnesses to him before the whole world. They have to carry far and wide the proclamation of God's love for all peoples in the Empire; they have to propagate a life-style based on that proclamation, and characterized by love for one another. This mission is to be seriously undertaken by the witnesses, for they are agents of the Christian movement to offer the answer to the problem of the disintegration of life in the Empire in the midst of the so-called *Pax Romana*. The proliferation of mystery cults, schools of philosophy, and concocted religious movements were but symptoms of the "failure of nerve"—cries of the deepest human longings waiting to be fulfilled. The seriousness of the mission is seen primarily through the boldness of the witnesses. Boldness (*parresia*) includes not only fearlessness in speech but also confidence, clarity, and frankness. These are the elements of communication. Their seriousness is spelled out, for instance, in the way they dealt with their Christian tradition.[9] They dug deep into their tradition, immersed themselves in it, and did not wait for the "modern" man to offer superficial approaches to the problems of the times. They took modern man seriously by pointing him to what is basic in human existence, that is, new life in Christ! This message not only healed the lame man of his sickness but saved him, that is, made him whole again—made him a fully *human* being.

The witness has to communicate both the urgency and the seriousness of what he has seen and heard. Here success is not the question. The Devil also succeeds! The emphasis is rather on fearlessness in witness that grows out of grateful obedience to the Risen Lord. One significant illustration of the probable failure of a witness is in Acts 17—the Sermon on Mars Hill. The witness is Paul, no less. The probable failure is made more significant because the Acts emphasizes the success of early Christian preaching. This story is a classic example of a witness saying one thing and the people hearing another![10] Isn't this problem within the orbit of contextualization?

It is fitting that Luke includes this probable failure within his discussion of the boldness of the witnesses. For, if there is one message from Mars Hill that we must not forget, it is this: the urgency and seriousness of witnesssing is really taken in dedication and commitment by the witness when he is willing to *risk failure*.[11] It is here, too, that the witness becomes all the more aware that the power of his witnessing is not *his* possession. It is rather a gift from God.

POWER AND THE CHURCH

The Holy Spirit empowers not only Peter and John in their witness, but the whole community. Even if Luke appears to give emphasis to Peter and Paul as *the witnesses* in Acts, he lays equal stress on the witness of the church. In fact, he is quick to point out that the witnesses are sent and sustained by the Christian communities. The witness of Peter and John is pictured as sandwiched by two instances where Luke describes the fellowship (*koinonia*) of the Christians in Jerusalem (Acts 2:43-47 and 4:32-35).

> Many miracles and wonders were being done through the apostles, and everyone was filled with awe. All the believers continued together in close fellowship and shared their belongings with one another. They would sell their property and possessions, and distribute the money among all, according to what each one needed. Day after day they met as a group in the Temple, and they had their meals together in their homes, eating with glad and humble hearts, praising God, and enjoying the good will of all the people. And every day the Lord added to their group those who were being saved. (Acts 2:43-47)
> The group of believers was one in mind and heart. No one said that any of his belongings was his own, but they all shared with one another everything they had. With great power the apostles gave witness to the resurrection of the Lord Jesus, and God poured rich blessings on them all. There was no one in the group who was in need. Those who owned fields or houses would sell them, bring the money received from the sale, and turn it over to the apostles; and the money was distributed to each one according to his need. (Acts 4:32-35)

Notice the effect of the witness of the church as a whole on those outside the church: "And every day the Lord added to their group those who were being saved." Paul, whom Luke presents as the super-witness in Acts, had the church at Antioch as his home base in his missionary endeavors. Luke wants to emphasize that the Christian community is *the* community of the Holy Spirit, that is, the community bearing and proclaiming the active exercise of God's power in individuals and in society.

When our ecclesiastical organizations are doing well and producing good results, is there still a place for the working of the Spirit? Isn't it tragic that we tend to use the standards of business and industry to measure the work and power of the church?

Luke wants to emphasize that God's presence communicates power and such power unites the church into action. His summaries (Acts 2 and 4), however, emphasize above all that the results of God's presence through his Spirit are *ethical* as shown in the life of love and sharing in the early church. To be sure, this Lukan description of the early church is an idealization of the Church in Jerusalem, for immediately following his summaries are the violations of Ananias and Saphira (Chapter 5) and the neglect of the widows of Hellenists (Chapter 6). As an idealization it becomes even more significant, for it does not confine itself to one geographical setting but pictures what the Church universal under the Spirit should be! That Church universal should be characterized by sharing and love.[12]

Witnessing as exercise of power means that it is an expression of freedom. The reply of Peter and John, "We are empowered in order to proclaim what we have seen and heard," is the height of freedom for the witness. (This is also vividly demonstrated by Paul as prisoner in Rome, witnessing unhindered). This is the freedom to witness for the liberation of peoples from *all* kinds of bondage! That exercise of freedom in witnessing led Peter and John to create a situation so that their words of witness might be seen and heard. The situation for witnessing was created by the proclamation of their faith and by the concrete expression of their witness. When Christians risk acting on their affirmation they will discover that witnessing situations are created for them and that God's Spirit is with them. It is through witnessing that the power of God is concretely seen and experienced.

In creating witnessing situations the poor and the outcasts are the targets. This is a basic emphasis in the witness-strategy of Luke. The poor in Luke's situation (the Greek world) were really poor. They were needy, yet helpless to meet their needs; they were helpless and ignored. Their helplessness was really tragic because they didn't have anybody to turn to, for even the Greek gods would not come to their rescue!

In the healing of the lame man Luke does not use the verb "to heal" but the verb "to save" (vv. 9 and 22). This is made even more emphatic when he links the healing of the lame man with the offer of salvation for the whole world through Jesus Christ, in verse 12 (interpretation of the "cornerstone" passage). Here it is emphasized that the deepest longings of man are expressed in the *inner man*, and no human ingenuity and technological know-how can fulfill such longings. Fulfillment can come only from the outside, from what is not already here. And it comes as an offer, as a gift! John and Paul stress in christological affirmations what Luke pictures through the healing of the lame man. In their "pre-existence christologies" Paul and John emphasize that only a Christ who is not within and a part of all that is on his side of the Fall could really offer a way out. Hence the Incarnation!

What is said to be Mark's theology of history—namely, that Christ's victory over the evil spirits in his healings symbolizes the overthrow of the forces of death on man and creation[13]—and what the writer of Colossians claims as Christ's lordship on a cosmic scale (cf. 1:15ff.) are concretely presented by Luke in *microcosm* through the lame man who is saved. Luke is not content to say, "the man who has been lame since birth is healed of his infirmity," rather, Luke is *only content* to say, the lame man is healed of his lameness and much more! His deepest longings, the longings of the inner man, are fulfilled. He no longer sits at the Temple's gate, begging and ignored. He now stands with Peter and John, causing the authorities to panic and the believers to praise God!

Shouldn't this offer redirection for our massive development programs in our countries? What kind of witness is demanded of our churches?

For Luke, the witness is not bereft of power. He has the power, but it is power to declare and live out what the witness has seen and heard. In the epoch that Luke is reporting, what the witnesses had seen and heard was clear. They were companions of Jesus in his ministry and they were eyewitnesses of the resurrection. Through them the Power empowering them to liberate peoples from different enslavements was clear. In Luke's own time the witnesses were still close to the period of the eyewitnesses. And the witness done by Christians who upheld their conviction that "Jesus is Lord" in the catacombs and in the face of persecution and death under emperors, as well as those throughout the Empire who committed themselves to join the Way, were part of what they saw and heard.

How about us? What can we declare concerning what we have seen and heard? We have seen and heard of Christians oppressing each other, nay, devouring each other. We have heard of Christians having crusades not for but against non-Christians—killing them and making the act appear right before God. We have seen and heard of Christians exploiting both natural and human resources for profit. This is part of what we have seen and heard. But this is *not* our message. Rather this is the reason for the urgency and seriousness of fearlessly proclaiming and living out the demands of the One who has caused us to see and to hear the manifestations of God's presence and power. For we have also seen and heard of witnesses who have given everything they can offer—even their lives, that others may be enabled to know how it is to live as human beings in the presence of God. We are not bereft of power. It is given because we need it for our witness!

GOD IS NOW HERE!

The witness-theme of our text finds its home in that single affirmation that all the NT writings want to declare, namely, that "Jesus is Lord!" And whether it was Paul or John or Matthew or Mark or Luke—to affirm that Jesus is Lord is to say: God is now here! This is indeed a very timely and needed affirmation of faith for our own age and situation. For our faith keeps on insisting that *God is,* in a world in which belief in God does not go hand in hand with the affirmation of the freedom of man. Belief in God is sometimes the weapon of those who have power to oppress and to go on with what they are doing. We insist that to affirm that *God is* is to confess that he is love, life, and everything that human beings desire and aspire to bring about.

Our confession is not only that God is. We affirm that God is *now.* He is among us and that presence is no less significant than was his presence with the apostles. To affirm that God is *now* is timely for a world where man runs like a machine, where his daily activities are directed so much toward making himself feel secure.

We not only affirm that God is now. We further affirm that God is now *here.* To affirm the *here-ness* of God is to affirm that God cannot be deafened by sounds of jumbo jets and spacecrafts and

186

titanic machines; by cheers and shouts of "Long Live," "Banzai," "Mabuhay," or "I've Found It," in order to prevent him from hearing the faint groanings of the poor and the oppressed. To affirm the here-ness of God is to insist that God cannot be pushed into retirement. He is actively at work: creating, re-creating in a world which declares in various ways that God is dead—from outright denial to burial by silence and indifference.

To affirm that God is now here is to insist that God is not only Lord but Maker of history in every age—the primitive age or the age of the computer and the technocrat.

What Luke has shown us in our text should not make us glory in the past, nor merely rehearse a historic heritage. He is sounding a challenge and a warning: be a witness or do not be at all!

REFERENCE NOTES

[1] This single purpose of the gift of power is emphasized by Luke, for he uses it as *the answer* to the disciples' question on the coming of the Kingdom (cf. Acts. 1:6-8).
Leander E. Keck, *Mandate to Witness: Studies in the Book of Acts* (Valley Forge: the Jordan Press, 1964), Chapter 2, forcefully deals with this theme of witness in Acts.

[2] The Greek text of Acts ends with *akolutos*. This significantly betrays Luke's emphasis on the church's continuing witness and growth.
J. C. O'Neill, *The Theology of Acts in Its Historical Setting* (London: SPCK, 1961), develops this Lukan emphasis in relation to preaching to unbelievers (especially the powerful).

[3] The vivid picture of the identity of a witness, drawn by Luke, should be seen on two levels. Luke presents the incident with the apostles Peter and John as the protagonists and through them the identity of a witness is etched. This identity of a witness is what Luke wants to impress upon his readers—the members of the church of his day.

[4] This is emphasized by the Greek: *ou dunametha arneisthai.*

[5] Ernst Haenchen, in *The Acts of the Apostles*, trans. Bernard Noble and Gerald Shinn (Philadelphia: The Westminster Press, 1971), calls them "powerful opponents," p. 215; and in F. J. Foakes-Jackson. *The Acts of the Apostles* (New York: Richard R. Smith, Inc., 1931), "aristocracy," p. 35.

[6] Here, Luke makes use of a saying familiar to his readers. The first part of the apostles' affirmation, "...to obey you or to obey God," is parallel to a known saying of Socrates, "I shall obey God rather than you." Cf. F. F. Bruce, *Commentary on the Book of Acts* (Grand Rapids: Wm. B. Eerdmans Publishing Co., 1955), p. 104.

[7] Luke uses *zoso* for the healed man, especially in Peter's answer to the question of the authorities (v. 9). Haenchen, op. cit., p. 217, connects healing and salvation at this point.

187

[8] As advanced by H. Conzelmann, *The Theology of Luke*, trans. Geoffrey Buswell (New York: Harper & Row, Publishers, 1961). This thesis of Conzelmann has gained wide acceptance among NT scholars.

[9] This should be a constant reminder for us Christians as we relate with other religions in the Asian region.

[10] Keck, op. cit., p. 117.

[11] Ibid., p. 126.

[12] This could be for us Asians a caveat against "extreme" contextualization. May our endeavors toward "Asianization" of the Christian faith not lead to "assassination" of the faith!

[13] Cf. James M. Robinson's brief and helpful essay on *The Problem of History in Mark* (Naperville: Alec R. Allenson, Inc., 1957).

10

SOME PRENOTES ON "DOING THEOLOGY": MAN, SOCIETY, AND HISTORY IN ASIAN CONTEXTS

C. G. Arevalo, S.J.*

The theme "Man in Society and History" is so central to contemporary theological concerns all over the world, and so much has been written on it, that one risks simply repeating what has been said a hundred times over, in dealing with it. Let me begin by noting that I believe we gain nothing (for our purposes for this Consultation) by attempting a bibliographical exercise. Essay after essay in the two excellent reference books which form the broader ideational background of the present consultation, Dr. Anderson's *Asian Voices in Christian Theology* and Dr. Elwood's *What Asian Christians are Thinking*[1] address themselves to the relationships between Man, Faith, Society, and History.

The background paper Dr. Elwood has prepared for our more immediate orientation has given us a good selection of themes, from writings of Asian theologians, which emerge within this area of discourse.[2] Dr. Preman Niles' paper, as well as the Dar-es-Salaam statement of Third World theologians, deals almost entirely with the same concern.[3] At the beginning of this section, I wish to express our gratitude to Dr. Elwood for the work he has done,[4] and I would like to use his summary as the point of departure for the reflections I here (albeit with considerable hesitation) suggest for your discussion.

We might start with something of a summary of the section on

---

*Fr. Arevalo is Professor of Ecclesiology and Theology of Atonement at the Loyola School of Theology, Ateneo de Manila University, Manila, Philippines. He is also a member of the Pontifical International Theological Commission.

"Man in Society and History" in Dr. Elwood's survey paper, with the following paragraphs:

1. *Asian Man.* Asian man is today summoned *by the gospel* to the responsibility of transforming and humanizing society. *"By the gospel"*: It is Jesus, in the light of his vision of a new order of things under the Kingdom of God, who frees man and announces that he has been given the authority and responsibility to alter his society and make it more truly human, more just, more fraternal.[5] He must have a vision of the direction and goal of history, and of his past, in shaping the future. He thus needs a "new eschotology" which will deliver him from what is dead and unfree in the Asian past and the Asian tradition and which will help him toward the freedom with which he is enabled to take part in the transformation of his world and the shaping of his future.

2. *Jesus.* Jesus, in and through the Incarnation, is "God permanently residing in creation, bringing to birth a new order in creation." The new creation in Jesus Christ has personal, social, and cosmic dimensions. Christ's creative and redemptive activity goes on in the happenings of contemporary life and world events. In and through this activity a new humanity is in the making, in which all persons are being reconciled to God (Christians and non-Christians alike). The new creation in Christ is a process that takes hold of human history from within, and gives it shape and direction. "It makes it possible for faith to look for the signs of God's new creation in Christ not only in the transformed lives of individuals, but also in the struggles and purposes of men to renew structures of society, culture, and religion, and to transform earth and heaven in the name of the dignity and destiny of man."[6]

3. *The Church.* The church must endeavor to discern how Christ is at work in the revolution of contemporary Asia, in the quest and struggle of Asian man for creating a new humanity—the quest for human identity and human community, in and through which modern religious and secular movements are being driven into the orbit of the process of the new creation in Christ. It is the mission of the church to participate in the Asian social revolution, discerning the presence of Christ (and anti-Christ) in it, and witnessing to the new creation in Christ as the fulfillment of the quest of modern Asia. It is the task of the church to participate in the creation of an "integral humanism" as a common framework for joint action

in the creation of a new humanity and new societies in Asia. This integral humanism should be spiritually informed by the insights of the prophetic Christian faith and by the humanism of Asia's indigenous religions and cultures.[7]

4. *The World.* For Asian man there must be the effort to hold both history and nature as equally important in his experience of God's activity in relation to the world, since man's world is both natural and historical viewed from different perspectives, and God is Lord of the world as "nature-history."[8]

The points just enumerated are, I believe, commonplaces in contemporary theology. We have said that in some way or another they have been said and re-said by theologians, by conferences and assemblies here in Asia in the last ten years. We can assume, I believe, that (even if there are points where the formulation might invite revision) they carry the consensus of most of the participants in this Consultation.

If I may be allowed a *confirmatur* from Roman Catholic sources here in Asia, I might refer first to a rather encyclopedic presentation of the theme of evangelization by the Indian theologian D. S. Amalorpavadass,[9] where the same general themes are developed at some length: the struggle for the construction of a new humanity in a new society; the efforts toward human development and liberation; Christ and his eschatological Kingdom; the meaning of the salvation of the whole man and of all men and the re-creation of a new earth in and through the humanization of man in the whole range of his relationships; the church and its role as sign of Jesus Christ here and now, making present his liberating action in the building up of a new society in accordance with God's design; the relationship between evangelization and humanization (development/ liberation) in the church's task; conscientization as part of the task of evangelization in Asia today.[10]

It is in the statement (of considerable influence in the Philippines above all) of the Asian Bishops gathered in Taipei in the FABC* Plenary Assembly in 1974, that we find perhaps one of the best articulations, from the Roman Catholic side, both of the situation wherein the gospel is to be proclaimed and of an attempt to respond to the situation.[11]

---

*Federation of Asian Bishops' Conferences.

Modern day Asia is marked today by swift and far-reaching transformation, a continent undergoing modernization and profound social change, along with secularization and the break up of traditional societies. Side by side with undeniable benefits and positive values, these processes have brought most serious problems. Industrialization and all that goes with it violently threatens our peoples with irreparable alienation and the disintegration of patterns of life and social relationships built up over the centuries. Stable meanings and values which have supported their lives are deeply shaken, and Asian peoples today are left in confusion and disorientation, even in despair and darkness of spirit.

We who make up the Church in Asia today are inextricably part of this new world, since we are bound to our peoples by a common history and a common destiny. With the light which God's Spirit and his Word provide us, we seek to read the signs of the times, and to discern with our peoples what, in their present situation, they must accept and foster, and what they must reject and refuse.

We know that in the hearts of our brothers there are these quests today: to find new meanings in their lives and endeavors, to overcome destructive forces and to shape a new integration in our societies, to free themselves from structures which have created new forms of bondage, to foster human dignity and freedom and a more fully human life, to create a more genuine communion among men and nations.

It is our belief that only in and through Christ and his Gospel, and by the outpouring of the Holy Spirit can these quests come to realization. For Christ alone, we believe, is for every man "the Way, the Truth and the Life" (John 14:6), "who enlightens every man who comes into the world" (John 1:9). We believe that it is in him and in his good news that our peoples will finally find the full meaning we all seek, the liberation we strive after, the brotherhood and peace which is the desire of all our hearts.

It is because of this that the preaching of Jesus Christ and his Gospel to our peoples in Asia becomes a task which today assumes an urgency, a new necessity and magnitude unmatched in the history of our Faith in this part of the world. It is because of this that we can repeat the Apostles' word, and repeat it joyfully. "Woe to me if I do not preach the Gospel" (1 Cor 9:16), for it is "the love of Christ which presses us" (2 Cor 5:14) to share with our peoples what is most precious in our hearts and in our lives, Jesus Christ and his Gospel, the unsurpassable riches of Christ (cf. Eph. 3:8).

To preach the Gospel in Asia today we must make the message and life of Christ truly incarnate in the minds and lives of our peoples. The primary focus of our task of evangelization then, at this time in our history, is the building up of a truly local church.

For the local church is the realization and the enfleshment of the Body of Christ in a given people, a given place and time. . . .

The local church is a church incarnate in a people, a church indigenous and inculturated. This means concretely a church in continuous, humble and loving dialog with the living traditions, the cultures, the religions—in brief, with all the life-realities of the people in whose midst it has sunk its roots deeply and whose history and life it gladly makes its own. It seeks to share in whatever truly belongs to that people: its meanings and its values, its aspirations, its thoughts and its language, its songs, and its artistry—even its frailties and failings it assumes, so that they too may be healed. For so did God's Son assume the totality of our fallen human condition (save only for sin) so that he might make it truly his own and redeem it in His paschal mystery.

In Asia especially this involves a dialog with the great religious traditions of our peoples.

In this dialog we accept them as significant and positive elements in the economy of God's design of salvation. In them we recognize and respect profound spiritual and ethical meanings and values. Over many centuries they nave been the treasury of the religious experience of our ancestors, from which our contemporaries do not cease to draw light and strength. They have been (and continue to be) the authentic expression of the noblest longings of their hearts, and the home of their contemplation and prayer. They have helped to give shape to the histories and cultures of our nations.

How then can we not give them reverence and honor? And how can we not acknowledge that God has drawn our peoples to himself through them?

Only in dialog with these religions can we discover in them the seeds of the Word of God (Ad Gentes, c. I, 9). This dialog will allow us to touch the expression and the reality of our peoples' deepest selves, and enable us to find authentic ways of living and expressing our own Christian faith. It will reveal to us also many riches of our own faith which we perhaps would not have perceived. Thus it can become a sharing in friendship of our quest for God and for brotherhood among his sons.

Finally, this dialog will teach us what our faith in Christ leads us to receive from these religious traditions and what must be purified in them, healed and made whole, in the light of God's Word.

On our part we can offer what we believe the Church alone has the duty and joy to offer to them and to all men: oneness with the Father in Jesus his Son, the ways to grace Christ gives us in his Gospel and his sacraments, and in the fellowship of the community which seeks to live in him; an understanding too of the value of the human person and of the social dimensions of human salvation—a salvation which assumes and gives meaning to human freedom, earthly realities, and the course of this world's history.

A local church in dialog with its people, in so many countries in Asia, means dialog with the poor. For most of Asia is made up of multitudes of the poor. Poor, not in human values, qualities, nor in human potential, but poor, in that they are deprived of access to material goods and resources which they need to create a truly human life for themselves. Deprived, because they live under oppression, that is, under social, economic and political structures which have injustice built into them.

This dialog has to take the shape of what has been called a "dialogue of life." It involves a genuine experience and understanding of this poverty, deprivation and oppression of so many of our peoples. It demands working, not for them merely (in a paternalistic sense), but with them, to learn from them (for we have much to learn from them!) their real needs and aspirations, as they are enabled to identify and articulate these, and to strive for their fulfillment, by transforming those structures and situations which keep them in that deprivation and powerlessness.

This dialog leads to a genuine commitment and effort to bring about social justice in our societies. In turn this will include an operative and organized "action and reflection in faith" (sometimes called "conscientization"). This is a process which seeks the change and transformation of unjust social structures. Through it the deprived and oppressed acquire responsibility and participation in the decisions which determine their lives, and thus are enabled to free themselves. Through it those who (consciously or unconsciously) maintain these structures may be made aware of them, and hopefully be converted to justice and the freedom of Christian love for their brothers.

The Synod of Bishops of 1971, in the document Justice in the World, has affirmed that "actions in behalf of justice and participation in the transformation of the world fully appear to us as a constitutive dimension of the preaching of the Gospel, that is, of the mission of the Church for the redemption of the human race and its liberation from every oppressive situation" (1971 Synod of Bishops, Justice in the World, Introduction). We affirm this teaching again, for we believe that this, in our time, is part and parcel of "preaching the good news to the poor" (Mt 11:5; Lk 4:18). It is our belief that it is from the material deprivation of our poor people, as well as from their tremendous human potential, and from their aspirations for a more fully human and brotherly world, that Christ is calling the churches of Asia.

Engaged in tasks for justice in accordance with the spirit and the demands of the Gospel, we will realize that the search for holiness and the search for justice, evangelization and the promotion of true human development and liberation, are not only not opposed, but make up today the integral preaching of the Gospel, especially in Asia.

We pledge ourselves to a continuing and large-hearted encouragement and support for those who are engaged in these tasks and for those who we believe have a special call from God to identify with the poor, especially when their work meets with difficulty, failure and opposition.

Evangelization is the carrying out of the Church's duty of proclaiming by word and witness the Gospel of the Lord. Within this context we have spoken of these tasks which are of particularly crucial importance for most of the local churches in Asia, for through them our local churches can most effectively preach Christ to our peoples.

Indigenization renders the local church truly present within the life and cultures of our peoples. Through it, all their human reality is assumed into the life of the Body of Christ, so that all of it may be purified and healed, perfected and fulfilled.

Through the second task, the Asian religions are brought into living dialog with the Gospel, so that the seeds of the Word in them may come to full flower and fruitfulness within the life of our peoples.

Finally, through the "preaching of the good news to the poor" (Lk 4:18), Christ's renewing life and the power of his paschal mystery is inserted into our peoples' search for human development, for justice, brotherhood and peace.

The texts need no comment, I believe. They are cited (as we indicated) as confirmatory: these are accepted as tasks of the Christian churches in Asia. Participation in the "Asian social transformation," as a task deriving from the Christian vocation in the world; Jesus Christ the Lord of history as summoning Christians and the churches to take part in the effort for the creation of the new humanity in new Asian societies; the church as a community which seeks to share in the tasks of transforming and humanizing society, to recall constantly in the name of the gospel the dignity and rights of man as primary values which must be fostered (and never sacrificed) in the process of transformation—these are accepted without question as forming part of the agenda for the Christian and the church in Asia, and (the inference is not gratuitous) as forming part of the theological agenda of Asian Christians.

This is our point of departure. It is my impression that we have gone beyond the general statements of this consensus. We are *in* quite a bit more deeply than this. Dr. Nacpil's letter assigning this topic to me says:

The main concern of the paper will be to raise the logical issues that seem to emerge out of the impact of change on the traditional concepts, attitudes and relationship about man in society and history or in the Philippines, using it as a special case in point. The paper is intended to raise issues and stimulate thinking rather than to put forward positions.

II

By way of a rather personal contribution to this discussion, I would like simply to make a few seemingly disparate points which, though they take some tentative positions, have no pretensions to being anything but points of departure for discussion. "Seemingly disparate": I believe that when seen together they converge, and have a certain coherence.

First, some remarks along methodological lines: Let me begin by referring to a note which Fr. Antonio Lambino, current President and Dean of the Loyola School of Theology, wrote some years ago, "On Asian Theological Reflection." Discussing the construction of an Asian theology, he suggests that "the task of constructing an Asian theology will not be achieved...through the direct formulation of theological principles 'in an Asian way.'"[12] Applying the current distinction between theological "principles" and theological "imperatives," he believes that the present moment in Asian theological reflection is a moment for formulating imperatives rather than principles.

The distinction is made nowadays between theological principles and theological imperatives. An imperative is born of the interaction between principle and the actual human situation. The imperative is characterized by a greater "contingency" or "modifiability" because of its closer dependence on the sociological, economic, political, etc, factors of the concrete historical situation. When these contingent factors change, the imperative also changes with them.

One could say that whatever new developments are taking place in Western theology today have been set in motion by the continual need to form imperatives in accordance with the contemporary historical situation. Of this, Vatican II is a good example. This Council did not start off by directly formulating theological principles in a new way (or, if it tried to, it soon discovered this was not the way to go about it). But in its efforts to face up to the concrete situation, it arrived at the realization that the existing theological structure was no longer adequate to provide the basis for needed imperatives. This led to the reexamination and reformulation of theological principles.

It would seem to me that the construction of an Asian theology will have to follow an analogous process. (In any case, the urgency of the Asian situation calls for imperatives and allows no leisure for a principle-oriented theology). There is a particular complexity about the problem here: the theological principles which provide the basis for imperatives have come to the Asian in Western form. As he searches, then, for imperatives he will realize time and again that he does not feel at home with his theological principles. But the fact that the Asian has realized the non-indigenous character of the theological structure shows that the process of constructing an Asian theology has begun.

195

Principles without imperatives tend to be irrelevant. Imperatives not built upon the foundation of solid theological principles tend to degenerate into mere ideology (in the pejorative sense of the term). There must be a dynamic interaction between the two. Just as imperatives are in some way drawn from principles, so are principles formulated and reformulated out of insights derived from imperatives. The West constructed its theological system in responding to historical challenges which called for imperatives and led to the formulation of principles "in the Western way." For instance, the heresies were the occasion for the formulation of dogmas. The contemporary challenge of secularization is a call for Western theology to re-examine and re-formulate its principles.

For various historical reasons the Christian East picked up the Western theological system without experiencing that interaction with imperatives which was necessary for the growth of that system in the West. This is analogous to the adoption of the democratic system of government by some Asian countries. It was not, for the most part, out of their national political experience that these countries adopted Western democracy. This led to a clash between indigenous attitudes, values and customs on the one hand, and the tenets and procedures of the Western democratic system of government on the other. The tension could not be endured indefinitely, and it has probably contributed in no small part to the rise of authoritarian regimes in most of Asia.

What Asian theologians are realizing is the need to re-discover and re-formulate principles through interaction with particular Asian imperatives....

To my mind, Asian theology is at a phase of construction where the discovery of imperatives will be the predominant activity for a while. No rigid separation can be imposed, of course, between the search for imperatives and the formulation of principles. One cannot arrive at imperatives without some kind of interaction with principles. The endeavor to discern Asian imperatives will gradually lead to an Asian formulation of principles. This will not be achieved in a day.

Imperatives are *discerned*. They are not simply the conclusion arrived at through rational analysis of the principle in its relation to the concrete situation. Discernment is an area where Asian communities have much to contribute. The spiritual thrust and value orientation of the East possess a dimension which is underdeveloped in the West. Generally speaking, the Eastern attitude and mentality should make the Asian better equipped to do discernment (in its theological and Ignatian sense) than the Westerner who is heir to so much rationalism.

An important part of the discernment process is listening to the testimony of the behavioral sciences, economics, political sciences, etc. Discernment is, therefore, an interdisciplinary affair. So is theological reflection of which discernment is an integral aspect.

If the discernment of imperatives is an important element of theological reflection, the carrying out of these imperatives is even more important. Only through contact with human experience can the validity of theological principles be verified. Moreover, only the experience of reality can lead to further valid theological reflection.[13]

Though the language of "principles" and "imperatives" seems to be especially related to the field of Christian ethics, the point has applicability on a broader scale. The question it raises, I think, is whether we embark on too ambitious (too imperial?) a project when we try to bring into being a full-grown Asian theology (or Asian theologies) with some large framework or scheme of reflection as

196

the principal objective of the construct, instead of working "from the ground up" by formulating imperatives, one by one, in the face of concrete demands of a situation.

This would seem to be especially relevant in reflecting theologically on the themes which emerge under the general rubric, Man in Society and History. I believe there are major frameworks already drawn up (political theologies, the theology of hope, the various development and/or liberation theologies, and the like) from other— even First World—contexts. Is it necessarily to be too dependent on "foreign constructs" to accept such previous frameworks, *by way of working hypotheses,* and by asking very concrete questions raised from within real situations Asian Christians and Christian communities face, little by little—too dependent to allow our own larger themes (and our own major framework) to emerge?

Edicio de la Torre, SVD, who gave what was considered the main paper in the Theology in Action Workshop[14] here in Manila some years ago, used to speak of "guerilla-style" theology, one which does not immediately look for a larger and "finished" theological construct, but is willing to take a piece-meal (even a "hit and run") approach, thus building more realistically—less academically but ultimately more solidly—in trying to create an Asian theology.

The second point I raise grows out from the first. I cannot be rid of the feeling (if that is all it is) that the main focus of Asian theological reflection in our present age—for most of post-colonial Asia, at any rate—will be found in the general area of the theologies of development and (especially) "liberation." Certainly the joint Dar-es-Salaam statement of the Third World theologians is a piece of liberation theology, even of liberation theology "with a vengeance," spanning now three entire continents. A cursory reading of theological journals from Latin America, Africa, and various sections of Asia will suffice to show the predominance of this theme. D. Preman Niles' paper is at base a suggested Asian approach to liberation theology,[15] and Dr. Niles does call himself (in the course of his essay) a liberation theologian. The same might be said, I believe, for Dr. C. S. Song's basic theme, which Dr. Niles uses as a point of departure.[16]

It will cause no surprise, I think, when we note that liberation theologians, especially in Argentina (Lucio Gera and Severino Croastoo come to mind),[17] have developed, over some five or six years, an approach to the theology of liberation through the theme of *el pueblo*, the people, which bears remarkable similarities to the Asian approaches of both Dr. Song and Dr. Niles. This in no way reflects on the originality of the suggestions put forward by the Asian theologians just cited; in fact, for me anyway, it is a remarkable point of convergence—which is rather a source of rejoicing, for obvious reasons. After all, the Christian heart of an Asian and a Latin American will, despite large dissimilarities, when placed in similar human predicaments, register basic "coincidences," be moved by similar reactions, seek somewhat similar responses, articulate similar aspirations and yearnings. They will recognize these in some major symbols and themes in the Bible and the Christian theological tradition, because these furnish us with our common Christian horizon.

But what then shall be *Asian* in this theology? One might sound facetious by saying simply "its rootedness in the concrete Asian situations"; but that would be in fact the true answer. It would seem to me that the questions should be articulated precisely as they arise (with the language and image and all the emotional overtones) out of the Asian experience, and that the imperatives which are discerned should be expressed as people, who are the subjects of this experience, in fact believe their Christian faith should be expressed in deed and life—as their Christian faith commits them to respond to this experience and the reflection and discernment which follow from that experience. To me, the operative words here are "just as they arise out of their experience" and "as they in fact believe *their* Christian faith commits them."

You will see that I am not asking anything very different from what the Theology in Action Workshops asked, from what Ian Fraser asks in his stimulating book, *The Fire Runs*,[8] which is something of a *summula* on this "close to the ground" approach. I would only ask insistently that Asian Christians be allowed to experience and respond to the realities they encounter *without being decisively programmed* to a response already worked out for them by some ideological or theological construct coming from Euro-American, Latin-American or African contexts. As much as possible, the response should arise from their own struggling with the Scriptures and their reflections on pertinent data from Christian history and experience (tradition).[19]

A large order, and some might think a naive and impossible one. For, want it or not, the "programming apparatus" (mainly the ideological and theological constructs) is already very much in operation, no matter which way we turn. And yet, must not the effort be made? Would any genuinely *Asian* theology (of liberation or any other concern) be possible without such an effort? Here I think we possibly have one cardinal and highly neuralgic point for discussion, which it might be quite profitable to take up.

In the third place, experience is indispensable in the effort to construct a genuinely Asian theology of liberation. We cannot insist on this sufficiently. This is the first condition for "contextualization," and perhaps many among us have failed to get onto the first solid step of a genuinely contextualized theology precisely because we have not been able to allow this experience to enter significantly into our lives. A merely token experience ("two weeks in the squatter areas") will not do; what is called for is something that *internalizes* the lot of people caught in situations of poverty and hopelessness, growing in the consciousness of the total reality in which their life-situation is inserted, and facing it (both the darker and lighter sides of it!), trying to cope with it in some measure, trying to do something about changing it, "struggling for liberation."

In our Christian communities in the Philippines at this moment there exist among a not-insignificant segment of "church people" an effort, which we cannot sufficiently praise and encourage, to enter truly into this world of the poor, the suffering, the deprived. The 1974 FABC statement, already quoted, speaks of those "who have a special call from God to identify with the poor" and to share in their struggle for a new and more human society. Surely the summons of the Spirit of God lies behind these efforts at solidarity with the poor and inspires these vocations in the church. For, who of us will doubt that this effort at solidarity and even identification with the poor is *one very genuine expression* of living out the gospel for our time and our place?

Granting all this, we must say however that sheer experience is not enough, certainly not enough for the theological enterprise and those whose task is to engage in it. There has to be a moment which follows after this, at least in the "theological community," not simply the moment of understanding or even conceptualization,[20] but the moment of discernment and of judgment which precedes responsible decision and commitment.

Is there too much (at present, anyway) of an unexamined acceptance and support of ideological perspectives out of either a sense of "being established" or, on the other hand, out of a sense of moral outrage, but not enough of the really difficult effort of hard-nosed multi-disciplinary research, analysis, step-by-step planning, as well as the exercise of "utopian imagination" in all this? Can we learn from the (admittedly rather paralyzing) investigation done, as well as the lines of further study proposed, by the sociologist Peter Berger in his book, *Pyramids of Sacrifice*?[21]

The examination of ideological analyses and constructs (mostly of Marxist provenance) which we so readily assume into contemporary theologies of liberation has to be undertaken with all possible seriousness, and it has to be not only a mesmerized study of the concepts there given, but an examination of their verification or non-verification in our concrete situations.

More, we have to have a sufficient sense of theological responsibility to see what is biblical language and Christian "consequence-drawing" from Christian teaching, and what is ideological language and concept—and the possible over-facile transition from one to the other, the possibly uncritical assumption that one set of words means the same realities, equivalently, as the *other* set of words—that, for instance, the Gospel theme of "God being on the side of the poor, the widow and the orphan" means the same thing as "God being in favor of the class-struggle."[22]

May I suggest that this is perhaps the most demanding and most crucial area for the theological reflection on "man, history, and society" in Asia today? I might point out in passing that at least among the more "leftward activists," and also in many ways the more genuinely committed segments of the Christian community in our country, this suggestion of a more sustained and empirically hard-nosed probing is taken as a sign of non-involvement, of bourgeois vacillation, of ivory-tower academicism and even a heartless betrayal of the cries and anguish of our people. And yet, unless we wish to yield to irresponsibility, must this kind of reflection not be done as our grave responsibility, as theologians and as ministers to our Christian people, lest we be as blind men *passionately* leading the blind?

But note that this effort of study and reflection cuts both ways. We have to critically apply the questions raised by people like Juan Luis Segundo in his *Liberation of Theology*[23] to our reigning and operative theological constructions also. As Segundo does, we must project the questions Marxism asks, and we must take these questions with utter seriousness. We must undertake the equally hard-nosed effort to see how our reading of the Scriptures and Christianity has suffered (liberalist) "ideological infiltrations" and to see how our conscious or unconscious ideological stances and commitments have influenced (even vitiated) our own understanding of and living out of the Christian faith.[24]

The missionary enterprise in Asia, carried out by churches linked with the colonizing powers, the church structures and theologies brought into our countries by that enterprise, the continuing influences (some would speak of domination) of the church communities of the First World in our local church milieux—their language, their mind set and concerns, even their life-styles—all of these need deeper probing and questioning, more courageous evaluation by the kind of theological reflection which few (at least among the theological people we know) have pursued with the seriousness and courage demanded by the task.

Fourth, the question of the necessity of "involvement and praxis" (even, say the liberation theologians, the *inevitably conflictive praxis* that "being on the side of the poor" thrusts one into) for the very possibility of "doing theology" must be considered also. The Dar-es-Salaam statement "rejects as irrelevant an academic type of theology which is divorced from action." "We are prepared for a theology which engages in critical reflection on praxis in the reality of the Third World." Here we touch *the new epistemology of praxis* (which the liberation theologians "prolong" from Marxist-Maoist thought) and the question of commitment to the struggle of the poor and oppressed which (so the liberation theologians argue with great power— take Segundo as an example) is and must be genetically *prior* to the task of doing theology itself.

This is perhaps the strongest challenge which theological education among us must meet and answer one way or the other: that theology must be functional to *orthopraxis*. This is the theological transposition of the Marxist norm that primacy must be given to the transformation of society and history over theoretical constructions: one is not there to contemplate reality; one seeks rather to change it. The theological norm would then be: the primacy goes to *the praxis of evangelical love* within history over the merely correct *affirmations of faith* and the constructions of theology: *orthopraxis over orthodoxy*. Theology and doctrine are functional to the praxis of effective love, and this praxis (for instance in our concrete Philippine situation) is involvement in the social and political, on the side of the majority who are poor and oppressed as they strive to bring into being (as the very meaning of history) a more human world.

It is a challenge that has been thrown increasingly at theologians of seminary and university in this country. It is a challenge not

201

to the theologian in "Teutonic captivity" only; it poses rather a crisis of identity for the entire church, her pastoral activity, her structures, her presence in the world.

Most of you in this audience are familiar with the almost complete inversion of perspectives that is demanded. On the premise that the modern world sees knowledge as functional to the control and transformation of natural and social processes, on the Marxist premise that social practice primes theoretical knowledge, these affirmations are made:

I. God reveals himself to us and through his Word. But his Word is not first of all "words" (Scripture) but an historical praxis—his action which liberates man and through man all of Creation. The real locus of divine revelation is God's liberating *action* in history.

II. This self-revelation of God in act summons from man the response of faith which is *not* notional understanding of the nature of God and his relationship with the world, but rather a response that is a praxis (of social and political liberation in history) which seconds God's own *doing* in the world.

III. When men engage themselves in this liberating action they *realize* God's own doing in history. For the liberation which God works consists above all in enabling men to make themselves free. Thus this historico-social praxis is both the doing of God and the doing of men.

IV. Faith, when it is taken to be intellectual knowledge—vehicled by words (the Scriptures. the texts of tradition, the writings of theology)—is and must be subordinate to praxis. It takes its origin from the *doing* of God in the world and must terminate in the *doing* of men transforming humanity, freeing themselves within history.

V. The liberative praxis of God, mediated in history in and through the liberative praxis of men, is solidarity with the poor and the oppressed in any given society. Hence the praxis of solidarity with the poor and the oppressed is the privileged "space" where the summons of God and his revelation of himself can be met today. The historical praxis of social and political liberation is the privileged encounter with the God of Abraham, Isaac and Jacob, the God of our Lord Jesus Christ.[25]

A good number of consequences flow from these theses. Those who espouse them hold that the entire theological enterprise must have concrete praxis not only as the privileged locus for its verification but as the only guarantee of its authenticity. Faith and its concepts are evangelically authentic, and Christian theology is similarly authentic, only when they begin with commitment to and struggle for the poor and the oppressed and only when they flow back into it.

Thus the effort to elaborate intellectual constructions and theological systems, spelling out in academic discourse one's understanding of God and his relationship to the world, is contrary to that evangelical authenticity toward which theology itself must strive. Theological faculties and schools cannot exist for this kind of work. If they do, they run counter to what the Gospel asks of them. The truth of God's Word is found only when the believer submits to it in its project and movement in history. The minister of the Gospel is not authentic because he can speak learnedly of the Scriptures, but because he can show in his life and in his sharing in the struggle for liberation that his love for his brother is effective and obedient to God's word.[26]

This position which I have just enlarged on is *not* mine. But it has been raised most insistently before people like ourselves (if perhaps not with all this explicitness of expression) again and again of late. It poses the most serious questions to our entire theological education, if it seeks in fact to be an education in involvement and for involvement in the creation of a new world of justice among men. We are told that it is only when this perspective is adopted that theology can be really liberated so that men can liberate themselves.

The points I have made so far are primarily methodological. You might regard them as outside the scope of the theme assigned to me, but I believe these issues must be faced, in the effort to create an Asian theology.

As a last point, which might be called methodological also, Fr. Lambino, in a recent talk to the 1977 National Convention of students of Roman Catholic seminaries,[27] summed up the task of theological formation for the church in the Philippines today as striving for a theology (a) *na marunong lumakad*: a theology whose first component is experience, a true sharing of the experience of our people, especially the masses of the poor, of their poverty, their suffering, their joys as well as their aspirations and struggle for a more human life; (b) a theology *na marunong umupo*, which does not shirk the agony of prolonged and disciplined study, multidisciplinary research, sustained reflection, and responsible judgment of issues—an ability "to sit down" which is of such crucial importance since theology is not a search for knowledge only, but at base a search also for the Kingdom of God. Lastly (c) a theology *na marunong lumuhod* (recall Hans Urs von Balthasar's *betende Theologie*), a theology which is finally born in the fire of prayer, enlightened and purified by prayer, by living contact with the Word of God and the presence of God in our lives.

With both clarity and force Fr. Lambino insisted (and I would agree with him) that there is finally no theological integration without worship, prayer, and obedience to the will of God discerned in prayerful reflection and in the stillness of adoration which is the noblest act of our human freedom.[28]

This point terminates in another demand: that our theological education for participation in the transformation of society be, in a way, a *formation in a spirituality for the ministry* of our time—a formation of the kind of men and women who can participate in responsibility for the world *as Christians,* who are able to integrate presence-and-action in the secular and often conflictive areas of social and political action with their vision of faith, their grasp of the presence of God in the love of persons as its privileged context.

This may sound like a cop-out on the task assigned to me: but if what we need first of all at the present time in Asia are not so much theoretical systems but efforts in the line of authentic spiritualities of participation in responsibility for our brothers, should not theological education for this participation be geared explicitly to foster *an authentic spirituality for ministry?*

A colleague of mine likes to say that the Marxist-Maoist challenge is first of all not on the level of theory (although *surely* it is that too) but on the level of commitment and deeds, hence in that area of lived theology which Christian tradition calls spirituality.[29] I have read recently where in not a few seminaries in Europe and the United States what is called "spiritual formation" has come to know a significant revival. May I be bold enough to suggest that this area deserves a certain priority in an Asian theological consultation, under the rubric, not of personal formation only, but precisely in the area of social and political action?[30]

III

For the third part of this paper I would like to indicate some themes which I believe our theological work must touch or investigate in the effort to apply "the critical Asian principle" to the theology of man in history and society.

1. It is a commonplace now to remark (I believe) that there is the need of a phenomenology of the religious consciousness of Asians as they are caught up in the transition from the traditional to the modern in the shapes and textures of Asian societies. May I hazard the impression that our social scientists, philosophers, and historians of culture have not done us the needed service of giving us this kind of phenomenological description because their work remains excessively specialized? (So much of the lack of dialog between

social scientist and philosopher or theologian stems from the different "sizes" of field of interest; apparently there are no Max Webers writing in Asia today.) I speak admittedly from the necessarily limited viewpoint of the Filipino Roman Catholic community, where I believe thinking and writing in this area have not yet developed a solid body of research and reflection. There have been some conferences and worshops which have revolved around this theme, but at least in the Roman Catholic community no comprehensive synthetic effort has yet been made to see the entire process in such a perspective and with sufficient courage to draw "the large picture' that theology might fruitfully mesh with it. This is of course as much the fault of theologians as of social scientists, because the kind of dialog that might motivate social scientists to do this kind of work has not been significant so far.

Latin American liberation theology, for instance, has created a typology of Christians and Christian groups face-to-face with the movements of social change and/or social revolution, which is quite revealing and which poses challenging questions for theological reflection: attitudes of the "official church," a "class-ist typology" of religious stances, varieties of responses, and the like.[31] In the Philippines we have not even done the spade work for such a typological picture.

Perhaps this is precisely the kind of content some of you might have expected from this paper. I wish, myself, I could have essayed something of this sort for you: it could have provided, were it well done, a table of significant signs and symptoms which would be of considerable interest and value for a "theology of the church in the Asian revolution."

2.   There is an area of our "social and political theology" which cannot, however, await the frequently retrospective scholarship of social science. I refer to the area of *the defense of human dignity and human rights* in our countries today. In situations where what has been called "the ideology of national security"[32] so readily sacrifices human rights and human dignity, and so readily labels as subversive even the defense of the most basic rights of men and women, the church must seek the form of Christians—and above all, it would seem, Christian ministers—who are truly sensitive to human rights and their violation, and ready to take stands in these matters, in the witness of Christian hope and love.

We do not speak of adolescent postures and sensation—seeking stances. We do not even rule out the acceptance of what has been called "developmental evil" and "*de facto* evil" in limited measures,[33] in a period such as the present when it seems that national development can only take place under strong and decisive governments which cannot assume the "free and open" features of relatively affluent Western democracies. But we must surely be awake, within our theological enclaves, to the reality of the ideology of "national security" constructed with equal passion by rightist *and* leftist authoritarian states today. We must be aware of how, within the perimeters of the influence of this ideology, blindness can so easily afflict us in our classrooms and seminaries, a blindness born of timidity or fear. In many ways the "specifically Christian contribution" to the effort of national development or liberation, a contribution which need not await scholarly definition, is that of never allowing strong-arm governments to forget that in all the efforts to construct a new society and a new humanity, the freedom and dignity of the human person is the supreme value which cannot be set aside.[34]

3. In spite of what I said earlier in the paper regarding a certain distrust of constructing too early a large framework for Asian theology, I believe that some such hypothesis as that offered by Dr. Niles (and Dr. Song before him) would provide an admirable base for an Asian theology. The history of a people as assumed into God's plan of creation and the history (patient of the truly new) which derives from it, or as assumed into salvation history—I do not think too sharp a distinction need be drawn between these two: I wonder if Dr. Niles does not at base agree with Gustavo Gutierrez's attempt to merge creation and salvation history into one stream— seems to me a very fruitful "story" which can serve as a guideline for an Asian theology, or for a theology for each of our peoples. Such a structure would integrate within it the reality, the development, the significance of the religions of our peoples and the histories and traditions which have been largely shaped by them. Such a structure would open our present moment of history to the movement of God's redeeming work in the world, point out where we believe the line of meaning ought to be leading, and trace where the *de facto* historical line fails to coincide with the "ought line," that is, where sin and the structures of sin are most present in our societies, as we perceive this in our reflection on the word of God and under the light of its judgment.

There is no time here to enter into the details of Dr. Niles' suggested theological framework, but I believe it is eminently worth pursuing.

4. Much has been written of late on models of the church; on paradigms for the Christian community. Avery Dulles' well-known book[35] deals successively with the church as institution, as mystical communion, as sacrament, as herald, as servant. For the Asian situation it has been suggested that *the church as first-fruits* is especially meaningful (it was Dr. Masao Takenaka from whom I first heard the development of this theme). In recent years, now, my own search for a privileged image or model of the church for our Philippine context has focused on the church as *suffering servant* (Dr. Niles has briefly but movingly developed this theme). In the last few months I have felt that the two biblical names of Jesus, *Son* and *Servant,* taken as point and counterpoint, would be a particularly fruitful combination of models for the church in the Philippines and the description of its mission.

5. The theme "son and servant" leads to the theme of a "Filipino christology' underpinning our social-political theology of the church as "son and servant." A christology for liberation, but in a Philippine setting, would be a necessary prelude. This is not a minor enterprise, surely. We are not without first essays on this, first essays of interest and value (Dr. Elwood's book is an example),[36] in our various countries. But here, in the context of Asian liberation theologies, a new and creative effort must be made.

Surely one need not argue the conviction that all Christian theology returns sooner or later to Christ as to its center, its hold on reality. It is when faced with the reality of Jesus that "out of many hearts, thoughts are revealed." Our Christian presence in the social and political contexts will be primed by our christology and our "jesusology"; who Jesus is for us, who Christ is for us, finally tells us who we are, what we are sent for, what we must do. The choice of the names of Jesus, the ascending or descending christologies we select—these determine our ecclesiology as well as the shape and quality of our Christian life and action.

Some Latin American theologians today opt for a historical Jesus whom one of them[37] seeks "beneath" all his biblical names and titles, a historical Jesus who can only be truly known in the praxis of following him, a Jesus who in the course of his life completely revises his understanding of God when he sees the suffering and oppression all around him, when he is rejected by the established people and powers of his time; a Jesus who begins by being wholly orthodox in his concept of God and religion, but ends up by seeing that the only authentic response to the one true God is not the religious one, but the human struggle on the side of the poor and the oppressed for the coming of the Kingdom of God. Surely here we have a christology "from below" (with a vengeance!) which is almost wholly functional to liberation theology and liberation spirituality as well.[38]

A christology of "Son and Servant," we have said: the name "servant," linked with the notion of the suffering servant, is especially meaningful for most Asian Christians today. The suffering servant lifts up the task of servanthood which the Christian community is called to fulfill in Asian societies today:[39] the willingness, the readiness to share in God's suffering love; the self-effacingness and seeming failure of his endeavors and the shipwreck of his mission; the total self-gift, in love and obedience, for others, in bearing witness to what God is doing for his people.

But the name "son" should be at least equally significant for us. Sonship retains a meaning in traditional as well as present Asian society which it has lost in much of the modern world (Western and socialist). I have often wondered what a fully developed "theology of sonship" would be, written in an Asian cultural context; so much nearer in spirit to the original biblical context, but nonetheless with its own particular ethos. "Son" would also underline the aspects in the Christian vocation which speak of what *"is already,"* not only of the "not yet." The relationship with the Father; the rootedness in his acceptance and his love; the sense of being from him, sent by him, into one's mission and task; the confidence of being always with him; the conviction that in one's fidelity to the Father one remains in him, even now—these are aspects of biblical christology (and Christian celebration also) which tend to receive short shrift today, when the search is for a human Jesus seen through the prism of social conflict; the human Jesus who lies even "beneath" the biblical names (or, should the names and titles be used, a unilateral and rather narrow choice among the senses of "servant"—servanthood in social history, in passion and struggle, in social conflict).

A christology of "Son and Servant" would provide a theme for Asian theology which would greatly enrich our social and political theologies.

6. The final theme I would like to bring up could have taken up this entire paper, and I apologize for this inadequate treatment. It has been said that "the effort to reinterpret Christianity today in such a fashion that can lay claim to the ethical and moral vacuum found both in science and revolution is certainly the most momentous spiritual struggle of our time." This task is far from com-

pleted. In the Roman Catholic communion the Synod of Bishops of 1971 affirmed that "action in behalf of justice and participation in the transformation of the world fully appear to us a constitutive dimension in the preaching of the Gospel, or, in other words, of the Church's mission for the redemption of the human race and its liberation from every oppressive situation."[40]   Action on behalf of justice, the Bishops are saying, action in the transformation of society toward a more human and more just world is integral to the proclamation of God's word.

The Christian churches have increasingly affirmed this in the last few years.   Yet, if Christian theology must motivate and commit men more decisively, even more passionately, to the task of doing all they can do for the poor and powerless in society and for the changing of social structures which institutionalize injustice, it must also constantly remind them that the coming of the Kingdom of God is not identical with the forward thrust of *any* economic, social or political movement in the world.   If it will teach Christians that responsibility for history and participation in the building up of a just society are integral to the presence and action of gospel and church in the world, it must yet recall to them that the fulfillment and realization of the age to come belong to the freedom and power of the Lord, and will come in the time and season hidden in his counsels.

For Roman Catholics, this is the burden of Pope Paul VI's most recent *summula* on evangelization, and one senses in it the struggle to give the project of "this-worldly" liberation its rightful place in the mission of the church and yet to be clear that it must open out to "something more" in the realms of the spirit, of the sacredness of each person, and of eternal life, if it is not to betray other basic elements in the Christian message, and the more abundant life which is the Lord's gift to us.[41]

An adequate "theology of history" or a "theology of responsibility for the world" is far from being an accomplished task in Christian theology—in Asian theology, but in Western theology too, for that matter.   Today the efforts are many but are positioned along lines of ideological polarization which seem to wait upon events for their resolution.   At the moment we are at one pole of the swing of the pendulum, but the last word has surely not yet been said, for we wait perhaps for a greater commitment of Christians to their work in the world before we can adequately formulate our theology.   Will an Asian Christian theology of liberation, drawing also on the reserves of ancient Asian wisdoms, have something by way of original contribution "to what is the most momentous spiritual struggle of our time"?[42]

My dear friends, instead of the bread you had perhaps the right to expect from me, I am afraid I have given you "a hard and resistant stone." Thank you for your patience in bearing with me all this time. I know I speak to those far wiser than myself, and thus my feeling of inadequacy is softened by the assurance that in your Christian patience and wisdom you can, in your discussions, with the Lord's help, turn this stone into bread. Our Christian people and our peoples in Asia hunger so terribly these days for the bread of earthly sustenance, true, but just as truly (this for our comfort and gratitude!) for the bread of the spirit and life.

REFERENCE NOTES

[1] *Asian Voices in Christian Theology*, edited with an introduction by Gerald H. Anderson (Orbis Book, Maryknoll, New York, 1976) and *What Asian Christians Are Thinking*, a Theological Source Book, edited with an introduction by Douglas J. Elwood, (Quezon City, New Day Publishers, 1976). Since there has been no time for the present writer to fill out this paper with adequate footnotes, the notes as appended simply try to give sources of quotations and a few references more or less indispensable for a better reading of what follows. One of the characteristics of "doing theology" in frontier situations is that there is hardly ever the time to work with one's footnotes!

[2] Douglas J. Elwood, "Emerging Themes in Asian Theological Thinking," mimeographed text distributed to participants in the consultation. Since the printed text will not have the same pagination as the mimeographed text, I have not given any exact page-reference.

[3] D. Preman Niles, "Towards a Framework for Doing Theology in Asia," CTECMA Background paper 1. "Churches in the Third World and Their Theological Tasks," text issued by the theologians "of the Third World" gathered at Dar-es-Salaam, 5-12 August 1977.

[4] I refer to Dr. Elwood's text; cf. footnote 2, above. (Henceforth indicated as Elwood, *ETATT*)

[5] Elwood, *ETATT*, refers us to Dr. Emerito Nacpil's articles here.

[6] Ibid., references to Paul Devanandan and M. M. Thomas.

[7] Ibid., reference to EACC 1959 Assembly, and M. M. Thomas.

[8] Ibid.,reference to Dr. Kosuke Koyama.

[9] D. S. Amalorpavadass, *Approach, Meaning and Horizon of Evangelization* (Bangalore: National Biblical, Catechetical and Liturgical Centre, 1973).

[10] Amalorpavadass, op. cit., 61-72.

[11] *Evangelization in Modern Day Asia*, the First Plenary Assembly of the Federation of Asian Bishops' Conferences, 1974 (Manila, Office of the Secretary-General, FABC).

[12] Antonio B. Lambino, S.J., *Approaches to Christian Decision*, Loyola Papers 4, Loyola School of Theology, 1976, 71-75.

[13] Ibid., 72-73.

[14] Oh Jae Shik and John England, editors, *Theology in Action*, A Workshop Report, 1-12 September 1972, Manila (Tokyo, EACC, 1972) "The Christian Participation in the Struggle for Liberation," 33-39.

[15] D. Preman Niles, "Towards a Framework for Doing Theology in Asia," CTECMA, March 1977, Background Paper 1.

[16] Choan-seng Song, "The New China and Salvation History. A Methodological Inquiry," *South East Asia Journal of Theology*, XV/2 (1974) 55 ff.

[17] Jose Miguez Benino, "The Theology of Liberation," Chapter 4 of his book, *Doing Theology in a Revolutionary Situation* (Philadelphia, Fortress, 1975), 65-69. "The Church does not offer a model which it has itself invented; it does not impose a system from above, *but it accompanies* the people, communicating the liberating contents derived from the kerygma" (Miguez, op. cit., 68).

[18] Ian M. Fraser, *The Fire Runs*, God's People Participating in Change. (London: SCM Press), 1975.

[19] This *freedom*, on the part of "indigenous theological projects" *to pick and to choose* seems to me an essential element in the whole matter of creating indigenous theologies. One cannot eliminate existing horizons of Christian theology in other parts of the world, in other areas of the Church's existence and life. But one may not allow them to dictate one's own concerns, approaches. bases of perception, sensibility, imagery, etc. John Mbiti says pretty much the same thing in several essays, e.g., in the paper from which I quoted at length in my preface to Leonardo Mercado's book, *Elements of Filipino Theology* (Tacloban City. Philippines: Divine Word University, 1975), xii-xiv.

[20] Cf. the remarks of Fr. Lambino, summarized in the latter part of this section (an excerpt from a longer address), "Doing Theology in Three Moments."

[21] Peter Berger, *Pyramids of Sacrifice*. Political Ethics and Social Change, (London: Allen Lane, Penguin, 1974). Cf. H. de la Costa, A.B. Lambino, C.G. Arevalo. Faith, *Ideologies and Christian Options*, Loyola Papers 7/8, (Manila: Loyola School of Theology), 1976. 16-17. 88-90.

[22] A question: is there at least a semi-conscious "glissement of vocabularies" operative in the dialog between Marxism-Maoism and Christian liberation theology? Or is this "glissement" really logical and really justifiable, as Juan Luis Segundo's work argues? (Cf. footnote 23, below).

[23] Juan Luis Segundo. *The Liberation of Theology*, trans. John Drury (New York: Orbis Books), 1976.

[24] Alfred T. Hennelly, "The Challenge of Juan Luis Segundo," in *Theological Studies*. 38/1977, 125-135 (March 1977).

[25] Luis Alberto Restrepo, "Teologia y Practica Politica" (in "Fe y Justicia)." *Theologica Xavieriana* (Bogota, 1976/4), 453-469, es. "*algunas tesis*," 463-469.

[26] These theses are drawn for the most part from Restrepo's article: cf. previous footnote. See also Jose I. Gonzalez Faus, *La Teologia de Cada Dia* (Salamanca. Sigueme, 1976), 283-292.

[27] Unpublished talk to the 1977 National Convention, Inter-Seminary Forum of the Philippines, 20 February 1977.

[28] Cf A. B. Lambino, ISPF address (fn. 27, above) and the address at the first general assembly, Loyola School of Theology, "Doing Theology in the Philippine Context," mimeographed.

[29] Antonio B. Lambino, lecture on "Liberation Theology, a New Model," to be published in Loyola Papers 10, *More on Faith and Ideologies*.

[30] From recent conversations, especially with people involved in theological education in the United States, this fact has come to my attention. Without being able to cite title and journal at the moment, I have read several recent articles on the renewal of the dimension of spirituality in seminary formation and theological education for ministry. This is certainly true of Roman Catholic seminaries; I am sure it is equally true of theological colleges of other Christian communions.

[31] For instance, cf. Cesar Aguilar, "Currents and Tendencies in Contemporary Latin American Catholicism," CICOP Position Paper, V/pc/70; Emmanuel de Kadt, "Church and Society in Latin America," *Clergy Review*, October 1971, 755-771, and November 1971, 843-866. Also, Enrique Dussel. *History and the Theology of Liberation*, A Latin American Perspective. trans. John Drury (New York: Orbis, 1976) bibliography, 183-189, of considerable interest. Dus-

sel has an even more recent volume, *Historia de la Iglesia en America Latina,*
1492-1973 (Barcelona: Nova Terra, 1974).

32 IDOC Monthly Bulletin, New Series, January-February, 1977, on "National Security Doctrine," articles by Joseph Comblin on the ideology of national security; bibliography, 17-22.

33 Edmundo M. Martinez, "Church and State in the Philippines: Martial Law, an 'Unjust Structure'?" Ateneo Lenten Lecture 23 February 1977, in mimeographed form. To be published in Loyola Papers 10, *More on Faith and Ideologies.*

34 Cf. A. B. Lambino, "On the Gospel, Human Rights and the Church in the Philippines today," in *Approaches to Christian Decision,* 88-93. Cf. Vatican Secretariat for Justice and Peace, *The Church and Human Rights,* Vatican City. 1975 (available in the Philippines from Cardinal Bea Institute, Ateneo de Manila University). The important collection of texts from the *magisterium* of the Roman Catholic Church. *The Gospel of Peace and Justice,* Catholic Social Teaching since Pope John, ed. by Joseph Gremillion (New York: Orbis Book, 1976).

35 Avery Dulles, *Models of the Church* (Garden City, N.Y.: Doubleday, 1974).

36 Douglas Elwood and P. L. Magdamo, *Christ in Philippine Context* (Quezon City: New Day, 1971).

37 Jon Sobrino, *Critologia Desde America Latina* (Mexico: Ediciones CRT, 1976).

38 To cite only one title, Jose Miguez Bonino, Leonardo Boff, et al., *Jesus: Ni Vencido ni Monarca Celestial* (Buenos Aires, Tierra Nueva 1977). Cf. the bibliography, 269-272.

39 D. Preman Niles, art. op. cit., cf. footnote 15, above

40 Synod of Bishops. Rome, 1971, *Justice in the World,* Introduction.

41 Paul VI, *Evangelii Nuntiandi,* Apostolic Exhortation. 8 December 1975. Cf. H. de la Costa. A. B. Lambino. C. G. Arevalo, *Faith. Ideologies and Christian Options* (Manila: LST 1976), 38-60; references to Philppe Delhaye's commentary, 42.

42 James V. Schall. "From Catholic 'social doctrine' to the 'Kingdom of Christ on earth'," *Communio:* International Catholic Review, III/4, 1976. 293.

RESPONSE TO FR. AREVALO'S PAPER

Raymond Fung*

Fr. Arevalo sees a basic consensus among theological educators in Asia concerning the nature and function of the Christian community in society and history. I second that. It is amazing how, within a decade or so, this subject of church and society has ceased to be a controversial subject, at least on the conceptual level.

The second part of the paper, on methodology, is extremely significant, I believe, for the purpose of this Consultation. Quoting his colleague Fr. Antonio Lambino, Arevalo starts by telling us that an Asian theology cannot be done by direct formulation of theological

* The Rev. Fung is Secretary for Christian Industrial Mission of the Hong Kong Christian Council.

principles "in an Asian way." His answer is to formulate imperatives rather than principles, and to do it one by one from the ground
up, in the context of concrete situations. I find this invaluable and
fully agree with it. It seems, however, that something is missing in
the process. I think Fr. Arevalo is hiding something from us! If
the motif of an Asian theology is not the "East-West" category, then
what is it? The logic of the paper suggests an answer. If I may
make a guess—an educated guess, I hope—I think the motif of an
Asian theology as suggested in Fr. Arevalo's paper is, in effect, the
"class" category: the haves and the have-nots, the rich and the poor,
the powerful and the powerless, the middle class and the proletarian
class. The middle-class Christians—and they are the Christians of
today—ask the question, "How can I be a good Christian?" or "How
can I be a good Christian teacher? A good Christian doctor?" The
proletarian Christian, on the other hand, asks, "How can I, as a
Christian, best serve the people?" Both formulations are legitimate,
but I believe the latter question is what we need in Asia today.

On the matter of theological formulation and its relation to political ideologies, Fr. Arevalo does not give us any clear-cut answer,
and instead encourages discussion. This is a wise decision. It seems
to me that if we formulate our theology without direct reference to
the dominant political ideologies of our situation, we may run the
danger of not being serious, of being merely marginal, even esoteric.
On the other hand, if we do formulate theology with the category of,
say, communism, we run the danger of losing the radicalness of the
gospel. This is a subject we must discuss and decide according to
our own differing situations. Fr. Arevalo leans toward giving top
preference to a process of encounter between experience and Scripture. This is legitimate. I, in a very different situation, would opt
for a formulating process with more attention given to the dominant
political ideologies of our day.

Another problem that Fr. Arevalo describes and considers very
seriously, but somehow hesitates to boldly state his position on, is
that of the necessity of involvement and praxis for theological educators. In other words, should theological educators, indeed the theological enterprise, be judged authentic on the basis of their involvement in social transformation? Fr. Arevalo has a stand, but he
does not share it. I can understand why. I suspect that if he should
tell theologians that their authenticity does not basically depend on
their involvement, theologians might take his advice too readily!
I remember an occasion with a theologian who claimed to know

something about liberation theology, and to be interested in human rights, etc. One day, after I received an urgent request to mobilize some appeal cables on behalf of the Korean poet Kim Chitta, I went to see the theologian. He told me his integrity demanded that he must be convinced of the cause. Fair enough. So I turned over four documents by Kim. He told me he was concerned and interested, but that he would need several weeks to digest the material! I wondered why I should waste time with this theologian in the first place. So I think I can understand Fr. Arevalo's hesitation. He simply says, "This position which I have just enlarged on is not mine." Fr. Arevalo, this is irritatingly short. Tell us more!

Fr. Arevalo also mentions the missionary enterprise in Asia. I like this word. I wish the term "missionary enterprise" would be used more often in this Consultation. Arevalo emphasizes the need to probe and question the missionary enterprise in Asia. His paper clearly points to a missionary involvement, not so much across geographical boundaries, but across class boundaries. His paper points equally clearly to a Christian, a missionary, who identifies with the experiences of the poor, who studies and reflects, who prays in the presence of God, and who takes a stand on injustice. For this vision I applaud Fr. Arevalo's presentation.

PART FOUR

BACKGROUND PAPERS ON THE HUMAN AND THE HOLY

11

IS AN ASIAN THEOLOGY POSSIBLE?*

James A. Veitch†

At the outset it is important to define the way in which some important terminology will be used in the arguments that follow:

Theology in Asia is the theological reflection of Asian-based or Asian-oriented thinkers, for whom being in Asia does not determine the form or style of their theological activity.

Asian Theology,‡ on the other hand, points to the possible existence, or potential creation, of a theology shaped, molded and related to a specific historical context, by particular socio-cultural and religious factors (religious here includes philosophical) so that the emerging form of this theology differs in emphasis and possibly in structure, though not necessarily in content, from other kinds of theology—for example, Western theology in either its European or American cultural form.

I admit that within Asian theology there may be sub-forms in the following sense: the way the gospel message is related to north Thailand, for example, will differ from the manner in which this

---

* This was one of the background papers for the All-Asia Consultation. Reprinted with permission from the *Southeast Asia Journal of Theology*, XVII, 2 (1976), pp. 1-14, and originally published in the *Scottish Journal of Theology*, 28:1 (1975), pp.27-43.

† Dr. Veitch is a Lecturer in Systematic Theology at the Trinity Theological College in Singapore.

‡ There is a certain amount of risk involved in using a phrase such as Asian Theology because, for many European theologians, it may carry overtones associated with *Deutsches Christentum*. But in Asia this can hardly be the case. The Christian community in Asia is a minority community and one that can never (humanly speaking) hope to become the dominant faith; it is rather the "leaven that leavens" the whole. With an Asian theology the Church "confesses its faith and establishes its historical existence in dialog with its own environment." (M.M. Thomas in his foreword to R. H. Boyd. *An Introduction to Indian Christian Theology*, Bangalore, 1969).

same gospel is related to Balinese culture, or to the lives of tribal communities in West Irian and the Philippines, and to Islamic cultural influences in such places as Malaysia and Indonesia, but the socio-cultural and religious context remains the same; it is the context of the non-Christian Asian world, and out of the meeting between the gospel and this world a type of theological reflection may arise which can legitimately be called Asian theology. Sub-forms share the general characteristics of the emerging form in the same way that the sub-forms of Western theology share the same general characteristics although there may be some differences arising out of cultural and philosophical influences in the respective geographical areas of the Western world.

In the following pages it is my aim to put the case for an Asian theology, and then to indicate the emphases and shape such a theology as it is emerging may have. There are two contrasting and conflicting views on the case for an Asian theology—one has been put in the affirmative by Karl Barth; the other, in the negative, has been argued by Arend Th. van Leeuwen.

I

In a letter to Southeast Asian Christians, Karl Barth asked two pertinent questions with reference to the relevance of his own theology in the Southeast Asian situation. "Can the theology presented by me be understandable and interesting to you—and how? And can you continue in the direction in which I believed I had to go, and at the place where I had to set a period—and to what extent?"[1] The very way in which Barth raises these questions has within it an implied answer, and the comments he goes on to offer make it quite clear that he did not consider his own theological task to be directly transferable to the Asian setting. He seems to have thought that the theologian in Asia must be obedient to the Word of God as he understands this in his own cultural and religious context. Addressing the theologian he writes:

Now it is your task to be Christian theologians in your new, different and special situation. You truly do not need to become "European, Western men," not to mention "Barthians," in order to be good Christians and theologians. You may feel free to be South East Asian Christians.[2]

The implication is obvious: Barth's own theological task has to be set within its own context, namely nineteenth and twentieth-century European theology. He set out to overthrow the influence of Schleiermacher and the theology of religious experience and to re-

217

place it with a "theology from above": a theology that adopts the word of God as its starting point. The twelve parts of the *Church Dogmatics* chart such a course and Barth develops his thinking according to new principles and, in part at least, in dialogue with other responses to the task of reconstructing a viable and meaningful theology for the Western European church. Barth's theological program is cast in a particular framework and designed to meet the needs of the Protestant church following the failure of the Schleiermacher-Ritschl-Hermann-Harnack theological enterprise.

Is it any wonder then that Barth, with considerable humor, writes to the Southeast Asian Christians: "Now I want to think a moment about you and about the task placed upon you as Christians in your world. In my life I have spoken many words. But now they are spoken. Now it is your turn."[3] How is this enterprise, envisaged by Barth, to be undertaken, except by theological reflection within the Asian context and in dialectical relationship to the *Weltanschauung* of this part of the world?

A different view is espoused by Arend Van Leeuwen in his book *Christianity in World History*. He notes that Western thought patterns have been transferred, without much change, from Europe to the Third World. He allows that the time has arrived when:

there is an urgent need for creative work on the part of Asian and African theologians—and laymen—in which they would squarely face up to their environment with its various cultural and religious currents and would think out the great questions of doctrine and ethics in a fresh and profound way.[4]

If such a program were to be undertaken, Van Leeuwen suggests that aspects of the biblical message, at the present time neglected in Western European theological thinking, would emerge, along with new heresies. He then points to what would be an interesting parallel: the emergence in the early European theological world of the "eastern theology" of the Orthodox Church. As this church has a presence in India as well as in Ethiopia it is perhaps possible that a truly "eastern theology" would have a similar emphasis[5] to that of the Orthodox Church, as distinct from both the European Protestant churches and the Roman Catholic Church. He notes also that the struggle of the early church with syncretism, gnosticism, neo-platonism, and manicheism offers a parallel to the Asian church's struggle with modern Hinduism and Buddhism.[6] Yet in the end he concludes that "none of these considerations really constitutes sufficient argument for pleading the necessity of a distinctive type of 'eastern theology,' as it were in its own right."[7] On the contrary, he argues in favor of an ecumenical discussion that sets the "missionary encounter" at the "center of our theological concern."[8] In a planetary world theological parochialism cannot be defended: "We simply must be up to date enough to bring the whole world into all our thinking"; therefore, "it would seem on the whole wise to let go the idea of a specifically 'eastern theology.' "[9]

Such a thesis is built on two main presuppositions—the ecumenical nature of the theological task,[10] and the notion that the "ontocratic" structure of non-Western civilization is being destroyed in the new missionary movement of Western technology.[11] Both of these presuppositions are open to criticism. Commitment to the ecumenical nature of the theological task does not necessarily imply a uniformity of theological expression. The confession "Jesus Christ is Lord" is a faith commitment that can be echoed in any cultural context, but the theological task of tracing out the implications of this confession must be undertaken in particular contexts where the members of the world-wide Christian community live out their faith. Such a theological task is undertaken in different languages, using a variety of thought patterns, and in dialectical relationship with particular religions and philosophical traditions.

According to Van Leeuwen's interpretation of Asian and African cultural and intellectual development, the ontocratic nature of this society (i.e. the sacred character of nature, and its corollary in man's primordial identity with the whole cosmos) is collapsing with the introduction into the Third World of a Western secular technological culture.[12] It is Van Leeuwen's idea that the gospel westernizes or secularizes, and conversely that as modern Western-secular civilization spreads, the spirit of the gospel is at work in this movement in an incognito form.[13]

Given such presuppositions and the overwhelming supremacy of Western technological skills and of Western Protestant secular values, it seems impossible that an Asian theology can, or has the right, to emerge and take its place alongside European expressions of the gospel and Anglo-American theologies. Yet such arguments overlook two main points.

First, the ability of so-called ontocratic societies to adjust to Western technology and at the same time to resist the de-sacralizing effect of technological secularism on traditional values and on the vitality of the living faiths. In fact the designation of the Eastern world as "ontocratic" and the seemingly consequent vulnerability of such societies in the face of Western technology and secularism is similar to the kind of argument in favor of Christian missions advanced by J. N. Farquhar at the turn of the century, an argument that has long since been invalidated by the resurgence of the Asian faiths alongside the growing industrialization and technology of independent Asia.[14]

Second, such arguments also overlook the very profound insights of ancient Asian civilizations such as that of India, China, and Japan, and in particular the difference in religious and philosophical reflection, as well as the difference between styles of living in the Western world and in Oriental civilizations.

It is in fact this second line of thought that suggests the possibility of an Asian theology emerging and making an important contribution to the ecumenical theological task. In this context, one may say that the movement toward an indigenous expression of the Christian faith is already in evidence and has been for some time, an obvious parallel being in the development of the "New Church Movements" in Africa and in the more distinctive theological task of translating the Christian faith in the African cultural context.

For some time now, in India,[15] and in China prior to the revolution,[16] as well as in Japan,[17] attempts have been and are being made to work out the shape and context of an Asian theology, and outside these areas preliminary work has been done to chart the course of independent reflection by Choan-seng Song,[18] Kosuke Koyama,[19] Emerito Nacpil,[20] Harun Hadiwijono,[21] Fridolin Ukur,[22] and T. B. Simatupang.[23] This is not just a matter of theology in Asia but of a theology emerging with a certain shape, with different emphases, with different insights into the nature of religious reality, and with new understanding of the contribution to be made by the gospel to Asian situations, especially in the fields of social justice, socio-economic development, and in ethical attitudes toward a whole range of religious and moral problems.

Having thus put the case for Asian theology our task now is to indicate the characteristics and form of this theology. We can tackle this by making a number of propositions and then commenting upon them.

II

1. *In the past the major theological influences on and in the churches of Asia and in its theological seminaries have been largely conservative or biblical (in the non-critical sense) in character, and this has led to the identification of Christianity with Western cultural values. One of the more important consequences of this iden-*

tification has been to divorce the Asian Christian community from its own socio-cultural, religious, and historical context. Little attempt has therefore been made to translate the gospel from its Western socio-cultural, religious, philosophical, and historical form into a form that belongs to the Asian world.

It was in the eighteenth century that the Protestant churches of Europe took up the missionary task.[24] The impetus for this new outreach came from "evangelical-minded" church groups, and the missionaries sent out naturally shared this perspective. The "free churches" were joined in time by the established churches in which smaller communities of revivalistic and pietistic sentiments had championed the missionary cause[25]—but of course the emphasis was again on piety and devotion in missionaries rather than on a combination of these qualities with academic theological excellence. It must be pointed out that the movement of higher criticism which dramatically affected biblical studies at this time and later, did much to polarize missionary zeal, so that those rejecting these methods of biblical research moved more to the conservative stream and actively promoted missions, while those accepting it tended to look on the missionary movement with unfriendly if not critical eyes.

A new appreciation of the "higher" living faiths through translations of basic and important religious texts also brought critical eyes upon the missionary movement, and even later the development of anthropological studies focused on tribal communities, and called into question the evangelism of such societies.

The missionary movement, shaped in the light of these struggles at home and confronted by an enormous educational, medical, and spiritual challenge abroad, was strongly Western in its cultural attachments and in its style of life. The missionary church used Western concepts to explain the gospel and used Western forms of argument. Its vision of history came from Europe and the symbols and rites of the Christian faith were those which seemed to the Westerner the most appropriate ways to re-enact his faith; for example, the bread and wine of the eucharist were retained, although for most of Asia rice and tea are the comparable symbols. The church of Europe was thus transplanted into Asia and Africa, and controlled by missionary influence, thus divorcing the gospel from the socio-cultural, religious, and historical background of the evangelized national.

The task is not so much to see this divorce but to discern in Asian and African society and religions, structures and values that can be preserved and built into the fabric of the church communities, thus bridging any gap that may exist. This is not transplanting the church, but transforming Asian and African society and translating the gospel into its thought forms and using its symbols and rites wherever possible. Only by running the risk of syncretism (in some form) can something new be created, realizing of course that it is not the gospel itself but Asian society that will be syncretized into the gospel by being baptized into the faith of Jesus Christ.

Another problem arising from Van Leeuwen's thesis is this: if the gospel westernizes, and thus secularizes, does this not mean that Western technology will in any case destroy social relationships, customs, traditions, and religious faith as this is represented by the living religions of Asia? This may not necessarily be the case as the following proposition indicates.

2. *Asian nations are confronted with the necessity of adopting Western forms of technology in order to accelerate development and catch up with the scientific, industrial, and commercial achievements of Europe and America. This Western technology brings with it powerful economic and social pressures and disrupts traditional patterns of life and belief. The choice confronting Asian and African countries is as follows: can the technology essential for modernization and development be separated from Western secularization? If the two can be distinguished, and I think they can, then a form of neo-colonial exploitation can be avoided and old patterns of life can be transformed by renewal from within.*[26]

Much of course depends on what is meant by secularization. The Christianity of the modern missionary movement, according to Roger Mehl, was "the Christianity of an already profoundly secularized society, that is to say, of a society where the churches had become differentiated in relation to global society."[27] One could live in this global society without being a Christian because religion was becoming very much an individual's own private choice. Such an ideology impregnated the missionaries' gospel: one could choose—indeed one had to choose—either the gospel of Christ, with its emphasis on individuality, or the faith of one's tribal unit. Asian cultures do not sharply distinguish between the sacred and the profane (to use Western concepts); life has a sacral basis and religion is a communal affair. The missionary gospel (itself the product of re-interpretation) attacked the very core of this kind of life so that conversion meant uprooting an individual from his own socio-cultural environment and placing him in a new one (the church), which lacked roots in the Asian society. This was a major weakness of the Protestant understanding of the gospel in post-Reformation Europe. Today the missionary is very often found striving to re-root the church into its Asian context and to stimulate re-thinking in terms of indigenization.

But in contemporary European Christian thinking the problem of secularization is still a central concern. Secularization is defended as a biblical concept, which began with Israel's interpretation of the exodus, and was reinforced by the priestly doctrine of creation. Yahwism is seen as the rejection of the sacral character of nature.[28] On another plane this process has been interpreted by Van Peursen as the change from a mythical society (in which man is enclosed by the sacred and magical) to an ontocratic society (in which man is freed from fear of the supernatural) whence secularized man emerges in the technological age as a pragmatic individual concerned primarily with how things can be used to build a new society.[29] This is the kind of ideology lying behind Van Leeuwen's thesis, and when it impregnates the gospel its consequence is to divorce the Asian Christian man (secular and technological man) from his own society. In other words this emphasis on secularization and the gospel reflects the dilemma of European Christianity, but it would be wrong to believe that it is universally applicable. Western Christians entering Asia enter a different world that often has different problems, and has some important presuppositions which must be taken seriously when the gospel is interpreted. It is salutary to recall some comments of Heinz Zahrnt at this point:

...secularization is neither a consequence consciously drawn, of Christian faith, nor an intentional revolt of man against God. It is the "natural consequence of the discovery and gradual extension of the rational horizon of human understanding."[30]

This is a far different idea from that espoused by Harvey Cox!

In an Asian theology secularization has to be seen in its proper context. It is primarily a Western theological idea that is used by several important theologians to tackle the problems of the church's role in Western society; there it may be valid, especially in Christian-Communist-Humanist dialogue. What may be more relevant to the Asian scene is a consideration of secularizing forces within the living faiths. In Theravada Buddhism and in the traditions of Hinduism, secularizing atheistic and naturalistic tendencies can be noted which stand in relationship to various forms of sacred expression—

this is particularly true of Hindu traditions.[31]   From the same point of view, Confucianism, Taoism, and Shintoism can be said to be secularizing in the sense that ethical norms are emphasized above that of belief in God or particular gods.   It is this kind of secularism that should be investigated more closely in the Asian context.

Western technology, so highly desired in Asia (and certainly thrust upon her by European involvement in the region) may be assimilated into these cultures, the accommodation being made possible by secularizing forces of an Asian religious nature.   It ought not to be forgotten in the Western world that both in this respect and in other ways the world-view of Asian civilization is considerably different from that in Europe and therefore presents a distinctly dissimilar context for the proclamation of the gospel.   The gospel must lose its affinity with Western culture and its identity with technological advancement, and break free from its dialogue with secularism to immerse itself into a new environment.   This leads us to the third point:

3. *The world-view of Asian cultures, their religious and philosophical patterns of thought, and their social structures differ from those of the Western European world and therefore constitute a radically different cultural-social-religious context in which to reflect upon the Word of God as this is received in the proclamation of the gospel and in the reading of the Bible.*

Such a proposition implies a re-orientation of theological reflection in the Asian context.   This does not of course mean that theological dialogue with Europe, North and South America, and Africa cannot be continued; such dialogue constitutes the very stuff of theological reconstruction.   But here attention is drawn to the context of the Asian reconstruction and to the fact that this means mapping the contours of the Christian faith in relation to the main influences of the living Asian religions, and to the philosophical insights that undergird these ways of believing.   It also implies that subsequent communication and transformation is carried out by using thought forms and ways of thinking already current in the regions.   A living Asian theology must be as "situational" or as "contextual" as that of European theology.[32]

The quest for obedience to God as he discloses himself in his Word, both proclaimed and written (systematic theological reflection and ethics), has to be mapped out anew in relation to different points of reference in the Asian world.   The philosophy of religion (in the West usually the philosophy of the Christian religion) tackled in this context takes its point of departure from the Asian religions and philosophical traditions and must be related at every point to these. Then too in the Asian world a Christian interpretation of the faith of others is part of the church's very *raison d'etre*; without this interpretation the church is afloat in a religious world without meaningful relations to other kinds of religious commitments. Moreover, there are very important implications for the study of the Bible as can be seen in the following:

4. *As the world-view* (Weltanschauung) *of the Bible and that of Asia are more closely related to each other than the world-view of the Bible and that of Western Europe, the historical-critical method of studying the Bible in Europe may not have a direct relevance to the Asian approach, especially when it is recalled that historical criticism is a by-product of the cultural and intellectual development of the West.*

The historical-critical method arose to a position of almost undisputed dominance in biblical and theological studies in the second half of the nineteenth century, and as such it was a product of the tremendous advances in human knowledge up to that time. Perhaps some kind of critical analysis of the Bible was inevitable once man began to investigate the nature of the world in which he lives, and to discover how remote the traditional view of God had become from the actual life of man. Also, with the growth of urban industrial communities the church lost the function it had once held in an agrarian society, and it was no longer taken for granted that the church held the monopoly of knowledge. Faced with such drastic changes and challenges to its authority, the church was forced to look again at the basis of authority and accommodate itself to the new changes.

In the ancient world and in the middle ages down to the Reformation era time stood relatively still: with the Renaissance and *Aufklarung* the revolution began. Theology could no longer claim a place of preeminence in the mind of man; rather it had to adjust itself to a more realistic assessment of its hitherto unchallenged claim to omniscience. Now, it was almost taken for granted that "theology, in so far as it remains true to its task, of its very own nature moves with the times, i.e. it accepts the language, thought forms, and approach of the present."[33] Theology is "bound to a definite tradition." If that is the case in contemporary Western theology and in biblical studies, it only serves to emphasize the immediate theological and biblical tasks confronting the Asian world.

The Bible must be studied and understood not so much through the filter of the contemporary Western scene, but more directly in relation to the world-view of Asian man. The direction is not: the Bible—Western critical methods—the Asian world, but: the Bible—the Asian world—Western critical methods. In other words, Asia must experience its own renaissance and *Aufklarung* and select what is legitimately helpful from European methods of biblical interpretation and what is relevant to the Asian mind. It might also be said that Asian man should feel free to express his own reaction to the biblical message and to approach it in his own way allowing its gospel to impinge upon his life where he himself is called to live.[34] It remains to be decided how much historical criticism (as this is currently understood in the West) applies to the study of the Bible in Asia. Such a decision can only be made when the tremendously powerful influence of Western theology can be seen in its true historical perspective in the Asian world.

With this new freedom the starting point of Asian theology can possibly be expressed as follows:

5. *If the Asian world is not as troubled by historical-critical considerations, theologians are still free to map out a theology in the context of Asia with its starting point in the resurrection of Jesus of Nazareth from the dead.*[35]

It is sometimes forgotten that the New Testament is written in the light of Jesus' resurrection.[36] That is to say, there can be incarnational theology only because of the resurrection. The humanity of Jesus is related to the dignity of man and his quest for social justice only because he arose from the dead. He is "the man for others" only because he first became the "man for us—the Christ." Paul puts the context of theology in a famous utterance: "If Christ be not risen from the dead, then our faith is in vain and we are of all men most miserable."[37] The question we are confronted with is, "If Christ is truly risen, then what does this mean for mankind?" and more important, "What does it mean for the majority of mankind who live in Asia?"

Reference to the resurrection contains yet another dimension; it alludes to the importance of biblical theology in the total fabric of Asian theological thinking. Biblical theology does not refer to the collecting together of verses and ideas from both testaments to demonstrate the unity of the Bible and its authority. Biblical theology is much more dynamic; as a theological enterprise it follows closely upon the heels of a study of the religion of Israel and of the early church as both minority communities struggling to discover the reality of the divine self-disclosure "given" in the history of Israel and emergent Judaism. Biblical theology is "contextual" or "situational" theology in relation to the roots of the Christian faith.

Focus on the resurrection-event, as the starting point for a theology that is rooted in the biblical witness, also brings into prominence another theological principle. "If Christ be risen from the dead," then man has hope for the future. For just as the Son of God was raised, so will the sons of God be raised to life: salvation now, in the present, is a sign of the reality of the Christian hope.[38] Through salvation man and God are reconciled, but the depth of this reconciliation can only be finally realized when the hope for mankind demonstrated in the resurrection is realized in human experience. In the resurrection, salvation becomes a reality for man in a provisional sense: "When anyone is united to Christ, there is a new world, the old order has gone, and a new order has already begun"[39]—begun but not reached completion, because the resurrection itself places faith into a proleptic context, and points to the fulfillment of what is now begun, in the resurrection of man to new life. The provisional character of salvation gives to the truth-claim of the Christian assertion "Jesus Christ is Lord" the status of a confession, and opens up the possibility of a dialectical relationship between the Christian faith and the other living faiths. Put in another way, the resurrection is an event that calls into question all experiences of salvation and liberation and all attempts (including the Judeo-Christian) to apprehend the divine presence in human experience. The resurrection negates these and fulfills the promise of salvation and liberation inherent in all these experiences, only to point once again into the future to an event (the resurrection of man to new life yet to come) that will complete what has already begun.

The resurrection of Jesus from the dead thus stands astride the historical path of the living faiths, as a key event in man's religious life.[40] But it is only when the various faiths are taken seriously as ways of salvation and liberation that the Christian can seek a theological interpretation of these living faiths from the starting point of the significance of Jesus' resurrection from the dead.

III

What then is the shape and emphasis of our Asian theology? If we summarize the issues already discussed, we can answer as follows:

An Asian theology is a way of talking about God which is created out of the Christian interpretation and appreciation of the living faiths as genuine ways of experiencing the divine, and as they can be theologically interpreted in the light of the resurrection of Jesus from the dead.

The prolegomena to an Asian Christian theology consist, therefore, in studies of the living faiths in their socio-cultural, religious, and historical context. Living faiths in this context mean the Indian religious traditions (the various strands of Hinduism and Buddhism), the Chinese and Japanese religious traditions, as well as Islam, Judaism (including its roots in Israel),[41] and the various ethnic religions. Included in these prolegomena are the philosophy of religion (here understood in its widest sense as an analysis of religious truth-claims), and the investigation of the biblical basis of the Christian faith. Asian Christian theology is thus the theological analysis of the Christian confession "Jesus is Lord" as understood in the light of the resurrection of Jesus and the theological interpretation of the living faiths and the various claims made about the nature of the divine self-disclosure, and the subsequent mapping out of salvation as the way in which man is reconciled to God the ultimate religious reality, thus realizing his own identity as a human being, and reconciled with others, thus realizing his solidarity, togetherness, and neighborliness with others in society.

The central sections of an Asian Christian theology[42] could thus be categorized broadly as follows:

I. Prolegomena:
    (a) The living faiths described and analyzed as living religious traditions embodying a divine self-disclosure and a genuine experience of liberation or freedom for the believer.
    (b) The basis of the Christian faith as this is rooted in the biblical witness to Jesus and his resurrection.
II. Christian theology proper:
    (a) The Christian interpretation of the world.
    (b) The Christian understanding of man and his hope for the future.
    (c) The Christian concept of freedom as this determines a distinctive life-style.
    (d) The Christian interpretation of the self-disclosure in human experience of an ultimate religious reality.

This is a theology from below, a theology that begins with the realities confronting the Asian communities.

It is a theology of religious experience, although not as understood in the nineteenth-century sense, because in the second section of the prolegomena the centrality of the resurrection of Jesus as the context for biblical faith is emphasized. Jesus is thus not an addition to faith but the basis of faith.

It is a theological interpretation of the religious life of man (a theology of religion and of religions) which contextualizes the Christian's talk about God and his revelation to man in the man Christ Jesus.

Finally, it is ecumenical in the sense that a new and different perspective is brought to the task of theological reflection and has important implications for theology as a whole.[43] Thus it functions as a corrective to one-sided parochialism, and together with the insight of African and Latin-American theological experience it helps to place talk about God into its proper context; a global or universal context which is the theater in which the presence of God can be perceived and encountered by all men.[44]

REFERENCE NOTES

[1] *Southeast Asia Journal of Theology*, Vol. II (Autumn 1969), p. 3.
[2] Ibid., pp. 4-5.   [3] Ibid., p. 4.
[4] *Christianity in World History* (London, 1964), p. 425.
[5] Ibid., pp. 424-5.   [6] Ibid., p. 425.   [7] Ibid.
[8] Ibid., p. 426.   [9] Ibid., pp. 426 and 427.   [10] Ibid., p. 427.
[11] For an account of Van Leeuwen's meaning of "ontocratic" see: ibid., pp. 158ff; for the "missionary nature of western civilization" with its secular and technological character see: ibid., pp. 403, 407, 411, 413, 416.
[12] Ibid., p. 409, cf. also pp. 418-22.   [13] Ibid., p. 18.
[14] J. N. Farquhar, *The Crown of Hinduism* (Oxford, 1913). See also the sensitive account of Farquhar's influence and achievements in E.J. Sharpe, *Not to Destroy but to Fulfil* (Uppsala, 1965).
[15] See R.H. Boyd, *Introduction to Indian Christian Theology* (Bangalore, 1969). K. Baago, *Pioneers of Indigenous Christianity* (Bangalore, 1969). M. M. Thomas, *The Acknowledged Christ of the Indian Renaissance* (London, 1969).
[16] See *Documents of the Three-Self Movement* (New York, 1963).
[17] C.H. Germany, *Protestant Theologies in Modern Japan* (Tokyo, 1965), and also Carl Michalson, *Japanese Contributions to Christian Theology* (Philadelphia, 1960)
[18] The most accessible of his articles can be found in G.F. Vicedom (ed.), *Christ and the Younger Churches* (London, 1972), pp. 63-82: "The Role of Christology in the Christian Encounter with Eastern Religions."
[19] Koyama has published a number of very important articles in various periodicals: some have been published in his *Waterbuffalo Theology* (Singapore, 1971). See also his *Five Minute Theology* (Singapore, 1972).
[20] See his *Mission and Change* (EACC, 1970).
[21] See his article "Theology in Asia," *SEAJT*, Vol. 12 (1971).
[22] Ukur's most important contribution is written in Indonesian and entitled *The Challenge and Response of the Dyak People* (translation of the title) (Jakarta, 1971). In English, see his article on "Salvation" in *Asia Focus*, vol. VII, no. 4 (1972).

[23] Gen. Simatupang is a prolific writer, always alert and sensitive to the importance of social and political thinking in the Asian churches.

[24] S. Neill, *Colonialism and Christian Missions* (London, 1966).

[25] R. Mehl, *The Sociology of Protestantism* (London, 1970), pp. 164ff.

[26] For the background to this proposition see B.N.Y. Vaughan, *The Expectation of the Poor* (London, 1972), chapters 5 and 6.

[27] Mehl, op. cit., p. 173.

[28] Harvey Cox, *The Secular City*, (S.C.M., 1965).

[29] Van Peursen, in *The Student World*, LVI (First Quarter) and LVI (Fourth Quarter), 1963.

[30] H. Zahrnt, *What Kind of God?* (London, 1971), p. 20.

[31] See the study by Dale Riepe, *The Naturalistic Tradition in Indian Thought*, (Delhi, 1964).

[32] See the EACC document, *Confessing the Faith in Asia Today* (Bangkok, 1966).

[33] G. Ebeling, *Word and Faith* (London, 1963), p. 26.

[34] A very good example of this kind of exegesis is demonstrated in an article by Kosuke Koyama, "Meditation on an Epileptic Child," in *Asia Focus*, vol. VII, no. 4 (1972), pp. 6ff. See also the papers from an EACC conference in Manila, 1972, *Theology in Action*.

[35] The resurrection has been an important emphasis in Indian approaches. See the articles in *The Indian Journal of Theology*, vol. 17, no. 2, 1968.

[36] cf. A.M. Ramsey, *The Resurrection of Christ* (London, 1950), p. 7: "The resurrection is a true starting point for the study of the making and meaning of the New Testament." See also J. McLeman, *Resurrection Then and Now* (London, 1965), ch. 9.

[37] I Cor. 15:8. cf. also Rom. 3:21-24; 5:1-2; 6:3-6; 8:11-12; Gal. 3:22-27.

[38] I John 3:2;   [39] 2 Cor. 5:17.

[40] I hope to expand on this point in another context in the near future. It should be noted at this stage that I do not wish to minimize the importance of the cross and suffering in any attempt to theologize meaningfully about the faiths of others. However, to me the resurrection of Jesus is a first-order theological concept, the cross is a second-order concept, as is the concept of revelation.

[41] The importance of the Old Testament background and its implications for Asian Christian thinking has been indicated by Kosuke Koyama in his collection of articles, *Waterbuffalo Theology*, op. cit.

[42] In the outline that follows it must be emphasized that the context is Asian culture and religions: it is the Christian interpretation of the world as this is grasped and understood in Asia that is determinative for the discussion.

[43] In the sense of *oikoumene*—"the whole world."

[44] G.D. Kaufman, *Systematic Theology: A Historicist Perspective* (New York, 1968), p. 114. But whenever a Western theologian offers a comment such as this he must be careful to avoid the assumption that Asian theology "must justify itself before Western theology" (M.M. Thomas, op. cit.). He must also avoid a patronizing attitude that emphasizes the importance of Western theology above that of Asia or Africa. The two (or three) styles of theological reflection must enter dialogue as equals, each bringing to the discussion its own insights to be woven into the total fabric. This will only be possible when the West is more intimately conscious of the Eastern theological contribution. It is to be regretted that Kaufman only notes the relevance of Kitamori in two footnotes. For an indication of the importance of Asia at the present time the book by G.C. Oosthuizen, *Theological Battleground in Asia and Africa* (London, 1972), should be consulted, together with that by Cecil Hargreaves, *Asian Christian Thinking* (Delhi, 1972). On the other hand, it is also important for Western theologians to examine the "objections to Christianity" as these are framed by believers from other traditions. See, for example, T. Ohm, *Asia Looks at Western Christianity* (New York, 1959; original German edition 1948), and the brilliant study by Isma'il Tagi A. al Faruqi, *Christian Ethics* (The Hague, 1967), especially the Introduction.

12

EMERGING THEMES IN ASIAN THEOLOGICAL THINKING*

Douglas J. Elwood

The new situation in ecumenical theology today, as M. M. Thomas expresses it, is that "we have come to see Christ as transcending the culture of Western Christendom and able to relate himself creatively to other cultures."[1] Others have noted that "a radical theological realignment is taking place in the Church today." The old centers of theological influence in Europe and North America are soon to become the new peripheries. The new centers of vitality in theological construction appear to be in Asia, Africa, and Latin America—where the majority of Christians will be living in the year 2000![2] Because of the new theological pluralism in world Christianity we can no longer expect to have a "trans-cultural consensus," at most an "inter-contextual unity," in our confessions of faith in Christ.[3] Emphasis now falls upon the Christian community in each place making its distinctive contribution to the theological thinking of the whole church, based on its own response to Christ in its cultural, historical, and socio-political context. As the Nairobi Assembly of the WCC affirmed, "There is no single culture peculiarly congenial to the Christian message; each culture is to be both shaped and transcended by that message."[4] The other side of the problem, as Taiwanese theologian Choan-seng Song expresses it, is

how Christians and churches will confess their faith in unison and not in dissonance, in harmony and not in discord.... The message of the Bible and the demands of the context are always held in tension. When this tension is broken, the context is stressed at the expense of the Bible or the Bible is upheld at the

---

*This was one of the background papers for the All-Asia Consultation on Theological Education for Ministry. It is largely a summary of selected emphases in the writings of Asian Christian theologians, mainly those found in the two volumes, *Asian Voices in Christian Theology* and *What Asian Christians Are Thinking*, organized around the stated themes of the All-Asia Consultation.

expense of the context. In either case the message of the Bible loses its impact on the life-and-death issues which all men and women have to face in their daily struggles.[5]

Japanese theologian Yoshinobu Kumazawa sounds a similar note of caution:

When we discuss relevance as a theological issue, we have to think of it in terms of relevance to the Word of God and relevance to the situation in which we live. That means there must be relevance to the text *and* the context.... The Christ of the text cannot be separated from the context. He who lived yesterday also lives and leads our history today, and it is our task to discover the Christ of the text in our own context.[6]

If someone should raise the question about the risk of heresy as the gospel is allowed to take its own shape in diverse Asian contexts, M. M. Thomas once again has a ready answer. He says that we need a new understanding of the meaning of "orthodoxy (or catholicity)" and "heresy" with reference to Christian theology. He begins the discussion by acknowledging that any theology that is developed on the frontier between Christian faith and the cultural and social revolutions of our time is bound to contain certain inadequacies and even blindness to some aspects of the Christian truth. Beyond this, "even the best theological definitions of the faith are necessarily fragmentary, one-sided, situation-bound, and inadequate to express the plenitude of God in Jesus Christ."[7] Therefore, to see only partial aspects of the truth that is in Jesus Christ cannot properly be called "heresy." All living theology will contain "heresies" if we continue to define heresy as one-sidedness or incomplete understanding of the faith. What then constitutes orthodoxy and heresy in theology?

Orthodoxy lies in the preparedness of the theologian and any theological community to stand within the historical community of the Great Tradition and to affirm unity with the universal community of the faithful, namely, the Church; and the heretic is one who considers his theology so absolute as to be sectarian and separates himself from the continuity of the Great Tradition and the unity of the Church.

In other words, heresy lies in absolutizing a one-sided doctrinal position, which leads to a break with the continuity and unity of the community of the faithful. On the other hand, dialogue with the theological tradition—the universal deposit of faith handed down—and submission to the consensus of the church within the situation in which theologizing is being done—these are the true marks of orthodoxy.[8] Some would want to add, of course, in the light of more recent theological thinking, that *ortho-praxis* (correct practice) is equally important. With specific reference to efforts at contextual theology in the Asian church, Thomas believes they are to be judged only "in the light of the mission of the Church" in Asia, "and need not be brought to any other bar of judgment."[9]

The purpose of this paper is to bring together some of the important ways in which the Christian faith challenges, or is challenged by, living issues in Asia. A survey of Asian theological writings indicates two broad concerns: first, to interpret aspects of Asian traditional cultures as vehicles of Christian insight and, second, to understand modernization, development, and social revolution in the context of God's redeeming purpose for mankind in Jesus Christ. "The problem of the relation between these two concerns," observes Charles C. West of Princeton Seminary, "may be the fundamental one for the Asian churches tomorrow."[10] Three specific problems that currently preoccupy the minds and hearts of Asian Christians appear to be: dialogue with Asians of other faiths; contextualization of Christian faith and life; and human development and liberation.[11] Most Asian theologians would identify these as, just now, the most pressing problems, though they may differ in the order of priority among the three. Evident in recent years is a new boldness in tackling these problems, as was manifest already in the statement of the historic Consultation convened by the EACC at Kandy, Sri Lanka, in 1965, which says: "In the past we have been...too tied to inherited traditional and conceptual forms of confession" to venture forth in extending our "theology from the study or the seminary to the world of Asian thought, philosophy, and religion—the world of the Asian renaissance and revolution...."

A living theology is born out of the meeting of a living church and its world.... The Asian churches so far, and in large measure, have not taken their theological task seriously enough, for they have been largely content to accept the ready-made answers of Western theology or confessions. We believe, however. that today we can look for the development of authentic living theology in Asia....[12]

As one of the participants in the Kandy Consultation Dr. M. M. Thomas summarizes the thrust of "living theology in Asia" in terms of four basic criteria:

1. A living theology is always situational or contextual.
2. The content of a living theology is the discernment of what God-in-Christ is doing in the situation and the interpretation of the truth and meaning of Jesus Christ in terms of the situation and its self-understanding.
3. The stuff of living theology is the life and witness of the laity in the lay world and the fellowship of the Churches' congregations responding to Christ to save the secular neighborhood.
4. The "orthodoxy" of living theology is for the Churches to stand within the consensus of the Great Tradition while sitting loose to the confessional traditions.[13]

233

When Dr. Kosuke Koyama was Executive Secretary of the Association of Theological Schools in Southeast Asia he delineated five "sacred roles" of Christian theology in Asia today, as he addressed a National Consultation on Theological Education in Bangalore:

1. To live in the awareness of travail in giving birth to the *morphe* (shape) of Christ in the Asian community (Gal. 4:19).
2. To be honest and obedient to the "puzzling reflections in the mirror," with the humility of a "dry skull" (I Cor. 13:12).
3. To be constantly "biblically accommodating" in remembering the history of God's covenant relationship...which culminated for the sake of all the nations in the *kairos* of God's accommodation in Jesus Christ.
4. To discern the whereabouts of Asia as Christ sees her.
5. To express "charismatic theological simplification" relevant to the real problems of life in Asia, and present Christ unmistakably—with the full force of his stumbling-block—before the people.

Theology travails, puzzles, accommodates, discerns, and focuses, says Koyama, but these five exciting roles make real sense, he hastens to add, only as it is seen to be "a genuinely missionary theology"— that is, a "serving theology" directed to and concerned about our neighbors. Only a neighbor-oriented theology will communicate to Asians, and Christian theology, in turn, will begin to "breathe fresh Asian air" and "speak a new language of comfort and relevance."[14]

MAN AND THE HOLY

Dr. Emerito Nacpil's treatment of theological issues facing the "new Filipino" is in many ways applicable to the coming of the new man in Asia.[15] He shows the relevance of the Christian faith to "the new man of the future" by presenting the gospel from three different perspectives: first, man's liberation from the shackles of cyclic time, a sacral world, and a kinship society; second, man's call to accept the responsibility of mastering and developing his share of the earth and changing his society as requisite conditions for his full emergence in the future; and, third, man's vision of the future as a "horizon of hope" for the direction and goal of history.[16] The "good news" is that Christ has power to form the new Asian and to bring about his arrival.

Nacpil seeks to show how the human questions related to the problems of modernization facing the new Asian man are not just economic, political, educational, and social, but fundamentally theological. Likewise, the answers to these questions, viewed as theological, must emphasize and develop their "human meaning," for it is the human meaning and "social content" of Christian faith that requires systematic exposition. By human meaning he refers to "their capacity to illuminate the human situation, reveal the truth about man, dignify his existence with freedom and meaning, and enhance his future with humanizing possibilities."[17] Here is a deliberate attempt to let the gospel speak meaningfully to an Asian situation. Nacpil is fully aware that in this effort only certain aspects of the gospel may be emphasized and developed, but he feels too that this is the only way to use theology responsibly. In this way, hopefully, dimensions of the Christian message will be uncovered which have been forgotten, neglected, or perhaps never before known. This is what the Kandy Consultation hoped for. "We have inherited the 'Great Tradition' of the gospel," the EACC statement says, "but we believe that Christ has more of his truth to reveal to us, as we seek to understand his work among men in their several Asian cultures, their different religions, and their involvement in the contemporary Asian revolution." Confessing Christ in the Asian contemporary situation "is the way to discover yet fuller riches in Christ, to appropriate 'those things to come' for which Jesus promised the Spirit of truth 'to guide into all truth.'"[18] (John 16:12-15)

Under a discussion of man in relation to the Holy we are concerned especially with that perspective of the Christian faith which sees man as "called to responsibility." This is highly relevant to Asian man's search for a "new anthropology" which Nacpil considers to be one of the three most urgent theological and missiological problems.[19] Asian man today is seeking a new self-understanding, a more authentic selfhood, and a more fulfilling community life. He is asking what it means to be a person, as well as what it means to live in a modern industrial society. The gospel speaks directly to this need when it is seen from the perspective of man's summons to responsibility for himself and the world around him. The theological basis of this call lies in the biblical account of creation which pictures God as giving to man the authority and power to master his environment. The lesser gods and environmental spirits are to be driven away so that nature may be restored to its true proportions as the creation of God and as the proper domain of man as a son and a steward of God. For man is also responsible for transforming and humanizing society. The new Asian man—if the new Filipino is any gauge—desires to be liberated from a structure of social relations dominated by kinship and personalistic ties. But Nacpil's point is that, in light of the gospel, man need not be a helpless victim trapped in his environment. "The message of Jesus is that the reign of God in human affairs shakes the foundations of social existence loose and opens them up for restructuring along lines in which man becomes a responsible person and a neighbor to, and a brother of, all men."[20]

POINTS OF ENTRY

The East Asian Christian Conference, at its first Asian Faith and Order Consultation in Hong Kong, in 1966, singled out four "points of entry" at which the proclamation of the gospel may commend itself to Asian peoples today. These are Asian man's experience of Nature, Society, Religion, and Suffering.[21] It will be noticed that three of these correspond roughly to the three main themes of the All-Asia Consultation on Theological Education for Ministry, as outlined in this paper.

Since religion has to do with man's experience of the Holy, we may consider it here as one of the points of entry for the gospel. As the EACC study document points out, Asian religions have shaped the cultures of vast numbers of people. It is important, therefore, that Christians in Asia learn to discern the types of relationship that are possible between the Christian faith and the older Asian faiths, with a view to a positive appraisal of the contributions of other religions, at the same time discovering how they can be reinterpreted and enriched in the light of the gospel. It is acknowledged that there are aspects of religious truth and experience, and categories of thought, which have played the role of preparation for the understanding and acceptance of the gospel. In India, for example, "the concern for holy living, the desire for intense *bhakti* (devotion), the desire for release from bondage, the search for a worthy *guru* (teacher), the authority of personal experience, have all been helpful points of entry for the gospel."[22] Similarly, in Islamic lands "implicit obedience to the will of Allah and the concept of the justice of God have been helpful starting points." Again, in Chinese thought "the idea of cosmic orderliness implied in the concept of *Tao* may be a good introduction to present Christ as the Word (Logos) of God."[23]

It is equally important, however, to discern those aspects of the older Asian religions which might, in turn, illuminate and enrich the interpretation of some of the basic dimensions of the Christian faith. The EACC study document singles out the *advaita* concept of transcendence in Hindu thought, which is a grand vision of God, man, and the world in a single conception of unbroken unity. An-

236

other is the *visishtadvaita* concept of grace, and still another is the mythology of the victory of God over the powers of darkness. In Islam there are the concepts of the oneness and majesty of God and the ideal of universal brotherhood. Christian thought can also be enriched by the Confucian ethic of obedience.[24]

We must be aware at the same time, the document cautions, of the risks involved in using concepts from other religions without reinterpreting them in a Christian frame of reference. Syncretism is the obvious danger here. Examples cited include ideas of renunciation which ignore legitimate participation in the world, and otherworldly ideas of redemption which ignore the necessity of responsible social action. Equally inadequate are understandings of the relation between nature and history which prevent the renewal of culture by the liberated man, and relativistic interpretations of religious truth and salvation which fail to understand the uniqueness of Christ and the once-for-all-ness of his saving work.

Suffering is another potential point of entry for the gospel, especially in Buddhist lands where the ancient religious answers to the problem of human suffering are still convincing to millions of people. When Christians learn to appreciate the sense of the transitoriness of life (*annica*), on the one hand, and the hidden frustration derived from religious legalism among Buddhists, on the other, these may become exciting points of entry for the Good News of Christ.[25]

SUFFERING AND HOPE

It is widely known that the theme of the Sixth Assembly of the Christian Conference of Asia (formerly the EACC), held in Penang, Malaysia, June, 1977, was "Jesus Christ in Asian Suffering and Hope." That Assembly gave teeth to the traditional Asian concern about human suffering, as it focused attention upon concrete forms of suffering around us today such as those resulting from poverty due to exploitation or oppression by the powerful. Although such suffering is not unique to Asia, it is more massive here and the Assembly's desire was to come to grips with the suffering which emerges from and is evident in the contemporary Asian context. General Secretary Yap Kim Hao expressed it in these words:

The phrase "suffering and hope" is not meant to convey two unrelated categories; it should be seen as suffering-in-hope or hope-in-suffering. For those who suffer there is hope and in the suffering situation there is hope.... As we all identify ourselves with these struggles we participate in the creative process of forging a new future for our peoples and societies. This calls for

237

a deeper understanding of the Christian faith and a wider involvement in the life of our people. Together with Christ we labour to build a more humane community where those who suffer can hope and where hope emerges from the suffering situations in Asia.[26]

Stress fell upon the presence of Christ "in" Asia's suffering and hope, which points to the central affirmation of our faith. Jesus Christ is in the very midst of life, not a detached bystander. "Whenever and wherever there is suffering and hope, Christ is already there."[27] And what does it mean to say that Christ is there? Dr. T.B. Simatupang, the Assembly's Presiding Chairman, answered that question in part when he said that Christ is "present and working in both judgment and grace in the midst of Asian suffering and hope, thereby offering to the Asian world that hope of which it is in need, but which it cannot generate on its own."[28]

FEAR OF SYNCRETISM

Early attempts at contextualizing Christian faith and life in Asia, especially in India, foundered on the rocks of a syncretism that was in vogue in the 1920's and 1930's. This was a major issue at the Tambaram (Madras) Conference, in 1938, where Asian reaction to Hendrik Kraemer's theology was unmistakably in favor of letting the Christian faith express itself through Asia's religious cultures. Many felt that this was an absolute necessity if the Christian message was to survive in Asia, in view of the resurgence of older Asian faiths. Since that time, however, syncretism has been an ever-present threat retarding the progress of authentic indigenization. Unfortunately, the fear of syncretism came to mean "absolutization of Western Christianity" leading to still further self-isolation of Christian churches from those of other faiths in whose midst they lived.[29] There was little hesitation, however, at the Kandy Consultation, in 1965, where it was frankly acknowledged that Christian faith and experience can be illuminated and enriched through insights from Buddhist, Hindu, and Islamic religions. "This enrichment comes," the statement from that consultation reads, "when as Christians we reinterpret, to express our own obedience to Christ, the Asian concern for asceticism and renunciation, its wrestling with the meaning of suffering, and its deep mystical experience."[30] Syncretism results only when contrary beliefs are held side by side without reinterpretation. "In the past," the statement goes on to say, "we have been too inhibited by our fear of syncretism" to enable us to interpret Christian faith in the context of Asian cultures and religions, and of the contemporary Asian revolution.

But a living theology must speak to the questions Asians are asking, as well as "in relation to the answers that are being given by Asian religions and philosophies, both in their classical forms and in new forms created by the impact on them of Western thought, secularism, and science."[31]

The collective voice of Asia was heard loud and clear at the Nairobi Assembly of the World Council of Churches, in 1975, especially during the debate over the "Seeking Community" report. As the CCA News reported it, "Asian voices challenged the negative and largely unfounded fears of some Europeans that syncretism will be entertained in the concern for dialogue with people of other faiths."[32] The Rev. Kenneth Fernando of Sri Lanka, speaking from the floor, said that "exclusivism" is a far greater danger for most Asian Christians than "syncretism." Wesley Ariarajah, also of Sri Lanka, supported his countryman in pointing out that "Christianity is itself a syncretistic religion," at least in its theological formulations, symbols, and practices, "and to say that seeking community with people of other faiths will entertain syncretistic tendencies is sheer nonsense." He and others bemoaned the fact that those who deny the reality that Christ can be experienced through the living process of dialogue are usually Christians who have not actually experienced living with people of other faiths!

The idea that Christ can be seen to be at work in other faiths, even secular faiths, is widely accepted by Asian Christian theologians. Some of the more conservative among Protestant theologians still warn of the danger of syncretism, and their warning is well taken. Dr. Bong Ro, a Korean who is Executive Secretary of the Asian Theological Association, embraces the principle of contextualization, but he is also concerned that in the process biblical and historic doctrines of the Christian church be preserved without compromise.[33] In his view, some of the attempts already made by Asian Christian theologians definitely compromise the gospel. An extreme example is cited from the theology of Dr. Sung Bum Yun, a fellow-Korean, who finds the Christian doctrine of the Trinity in the Tang-gun myth of creation. According to the Korean myth, in the beginning there was a heavenly emperor, Hang-in, whose son was named Hang-ung. The father gave his son three royal seals to rule the world. The son descended into the world near Taeback Mountain in the central part of Korea, by a divine tree, with his 3,000 tribesmen to erect a divine city. He married a female bear who bore a son named Tang-gun Wang-kum. He is the one who built the first Korean dynasty, Tang-gun Chosen. The supreme God, Hang-in; God's son, Hang-ung; and the female bear, a terrestrial goddess, were united to produce a human being. Now, Professor Yun concludes that the Tang-gun myth may be an indigenized form of the Christian doctrine of the Trinity. If Dr. Ro has understood Dr. Yun correctly, it would seem that he is entirely justified in citing this as an example of syncretism in Asian Christian theology.[34]

THE HIDDEN CHRIST

Roman Catholic theologian Raymundo Panikkar, his father a Hindu and his mother a Christian, has little fear of syncretism because he is a man who is in continuous "dialogue" with himself. In a remarkably succinct article he sets down some basic principles of inter-religious dialogue.[35] For one thing, "there is only one faith, but many beliefs." Beliefs are the different expressions of faith. Furthermore, it is faith that saves, not beliefs, for beliefs are always culturally bounded. If we try to convert our belief into faith, the result is no longer faith but only belief. Religions are sociological units of beliefs. A second important principle is that

No inter-religious dialogue can yield any fruit unless it is (at least logically and anthropologically) preceded by an *intra*-religious dialogue within the partners themselves. This *intra*-religious dialogue implies the critical awareness that my belief—which for me may be ultimate and even intentionally exhaustive —does not preclude a free interval or an intellectual perspective (a step back, one may prefer to say) from which my own belief may be seen, judged, and even criticized.

It also implies that, although I may consider my own belief the most complete expression of faith, I must consider how my own belief can make room for other relatively valid expressions of faith, and even for enrichment on my part. In other words, "only those who can critically undergo an internal dialogue within themselves are ready for inter-religious dialogue."

Fr. Panikkar expands on this view in his essay on "Christians and So-called 'Non Christians.'"[36] On the strength of the conviction that there can be no genuine human relation from which Christ is absent—nothing truly human that is alien to him—Panikkar argues that, strictly speaking, there can be no such thing as a real "non-Christian," or for that matter an actual "non-Christian religion." If indeed there are religions that have no reference to Christ, then Christianity is just another religion and nothing more. "Christ would no longer be the universal Savior, neither would redemption be an act for the whole of humanity. It would only be the 'Christian faith' for the benefit of the 'initiated' to the exclusion of all (so-called) 'non-Christians.'"[37] On the basis of Acts 17:23, where St. Paul tells the Athenians, "Whom you worship in ignorance I declare unto you," he concludes that Christ is present in other authentic religions. The essay includes the main thesis of his book, *The Unknown Christ of Hinduism*. As he phrases it in another place, "In the last analysis any religion is mysteriously oriented toward Christ, and Christ, mysteriously but no less really, works within it."[38] It is in Christianity, however, that Christ is fully revealed, and so the work of the Christian mission is virtually that of "unveiling" the hidden Christ of other religions. Christianity can reveal to Hinduism, for example, the true object of its agelong quest.[39] But "Christ is already there in Hinduism, in so far as Hinduism is a true religion." Again, "Any man who lives his own religion adheres, even if he does not know it, to Christ...."[40] Panikkar calls his viewpoint the "Christic perspective" which sees the mediatorship of Christ as present in all authentic expressions of religion. After all, he says, "Jesus Christ came not to found a religion and much less a new religion, but to fulfill all justice (Mtt. 3:15) and to bring to its fulness every religion of the world (Mtt. 5:17; Heb. 1:1f)." Just as Western Christianity is "the ancient paganism, or to be more precise, the complex Hebrew-Hellenic-Greco-Latin-Celtic-Gothic-Modern religion converted to Christ more or less successfully," so Indian Christianity should be "Hinduism itself converted— or Islam or Buddhism, whatever it may be."[41]

OUR COMMON HUMANITY

Very different from Panikkar's approach is M. M. Thomas' "theology of religious pluralism," and yet Thomas admits that they arrive at similar conclusions by diverse routes. Thomas takes more seriously than Panikkar the "rebellion against God" that is implied in religious legalism, and recognizes also the significance of the ferment of secular humanism today for the "conversion" of other religions to Christ. In Thomas' view, Panikkar is too preoccupied with religiosity to recognize the Christian significance of the "new anthropology" in the encounter of religions today.[42] Thomas' new book, *Man and the Universe of Faiths*, reiterates a viewpoint that is widely held by Asian Christians, perhaps largely due to the influence of Thomas' leadership over the years in the EACC. Broadly, this viewpoint is an emphasis on Christian solidarity with the world, which was affirmed as early as 1959 at the Kuala Lumpur Assembly of the EACC. "It is the task of the Churches to discern the presence of Jesus Christ in contemporary Asian history," the Assembly declared, "so they may respond to him and participate in his work for the world."[43]   One implication of the principle of solidarity has to do with the basis for relationships with those of other faiths.   As M. M. Thomas has often said, "The most fruitful point of entry for a meeting of faiths at spiritual depth in our time" is "the common humanity and the self-transcendence within it" (including the common response to the problems of humanization in the modern world), rather than any supposed "common religiosity, or common sense of the divine."[44]   The book is, in part, an Asian reply to the controversial thesis of John Hick in his book, *God and the Universe of Faiths,* which stresses instead the common sense of the divine among the world's faiths.   In other words, Thomas believes that religions and even secular faiths are drawn together most fruitfully in our time through a community of common concern and responsibility to build societies which realize the highest possible quality of human life.   It is in their interaction with the forces of modernity that the various faiths are being transformed and even compelled to reinterpret their apprehensions of the ultimate meaning of human existence, their doctrines of God, man, and the world.

By the same token, the traditional theological formulations of the Christian faith are being challenged to revision.   Thomas believes that the time has now come to focus attention on the "human aspect" in God's redemptive act.   There is now an urgent need to relate the New Man in Christ to the problems of community and of the self-understanding of modern man.   In fact, it is at this level of the new anthropological questions raised by modernity that the non-Christian world is either opening or closing itself to the gospel.   The doctrine of the New Humanity in Christ seems to be decisive now for the reconciliation of Christianity and the other Asian faiths. The whole book is a profound and provocative study of how the life and thought of the various religious and secular faiths of mankind today are finding expression and being transformed as they confront, respond to, and grapple with, the social forces and human self-understanding engendered by the events of modern history.

In what Dr. Thomas calls "a theology of religious pluralism" he goes back to an insight of Karl Barth in order to arrive at a "post-Kraemer theology!"   Barth had stressed the transcendence of the Word and Deed of God in Jesus Christ over all religions and quasi-religions of mankind.   At the same time, however, Barth's understanding of Jesus Christ as the "humanity" of God, rejecting and re-electing all mankind in Jesus Christ, points to a transcendent power which can renew them all. This provides Thomas with the basis for a radical "Christocentric relativization" of all religions and secular faiths—including Christianity and atheism—in the name of the grace of God in Jesus Christ. According to Thomas, this means that "people are 'already' released from the absolute claims of religions and quasi-religions, in so far as they are caught up in the New Humanity of Christ through implicit or explicit faith...."[45] It is by this same token that the religion called "Christianity" must be distinguished from Christ and, like all the others, relativized "enabling Christ to reform, and take form within" it. "If Jesus Christ transcends the Christian religion, as its judge and redeemer, it opens up the possibility of Christ reforming all religions and in-forming Himself in them."[46] Here he is acknowledging the validity of attempts at expressing the meaning of Christ in terms of the indigenous religious traditions of Asia, and in that process renewing those traditions to become vehicles of Christ. It is at this point that Thomas and Panikkar meet once more, having followed very different routes. All the religious traditions of the world are in various stages of renaissance and reformation, concludes Thomas, through which they are seeking to redefine themselves under the impact of two powerful forces: (a) the spiritual self-understanding of modern man, and (b) the urge to provide a spiritual foundation for the struggle for genuinely human community.

THE PROBLEM OF TRANSCENDENCE

We have just been discussing the views of a highly trained Roman Catholic priest and a leading Protestant layman, both of India. U Khin Maung Din of Burma is also a Protestant layman, concurrently lecturer in Philosophy at the University of Arts and Sciences in Rangoon and in Christian Ethics at the Burma Divinity School. In his essay on "Problems and Possibilities for Burmese Christian Theology Today,"[47] he boldly sets out to recast the Christian faith in terms of the Theravada Buddhist understanding of man, nature, and Ultimate Reality, in the light of the socio-political realities of our time. For him, the theological question, "Who is God?" should begin with the question, "What is Man?" In fact, the latter is the question that is understood as crucial by mankind today. It is not the purpose of his essay to answer the question, but merely to show that certain insights from Buddhism and other Oriental philosophies can be incorporated in Christian theology. It is not enough, he

243

says, to give a Burmese form to the Christian gospel. We must also "try to discover new dimensions for theology with the help of the spiritual experience and concepts of men of other faiths."[48] One such concept is the Buddhist principle of "non-attachment." According to Theravada teaching, suffering results from attaching ourselves to what we do not have or even to what we cannot have. Professor Din says that the popular belief among Christians in the continuity of the self as immortal soul may reflect a craving of the self for something it cannot have, that is, continued existence after death. Christian theology at this point has allowed itself to be "trapped by 'reward/punishment' concepts."[49] Our present Christian teaching on resurrection is clouded by a misunderstanding of immortality. In Din's view, we must learn to rid ourselves of this craving for continued existence after death.

The Christian understanding of salvation can also benefit from the perspective of Non-Attachment, especially in helping us to overcome our obsession with "over-activism" in the world. The present controversy between the "other-worldly salvationists" and the "worldly humanists" is a false problem. "If the church in Burma is faithful to its Oriental heritage, then it will not commit the error of absolutizing only one relative aspect of salvation. To the Oriental mind, salvation itself is a mystery which transcends all human ways of understanding it.[50] Therefore, no theology of salvation can make absolute claims for itself. The important problem for the Burmese Christian is that which concerns *the desire* for salvation. "A truly liberated person is not even conscious of the fact that he has attained salvation. In other words, the very desire for liberation itself must be transcended before one can acquire final liberation." With the aid of the principle of Non-Attachment the Christian can rid himself of both the desire for salvation and the craving for continued existence.

Dr. Lynn de Silva of Sri Lanka also deals with "The Problem of the Self in Buddhism and Christianity."[51] He returns to the Hebraic roots of Christian faith in order to show that the biblical doctrine of man is not that of an independent, self-existent being with an immortal soul. He finds a basic agreement at this point between Christian and Theravada teaching.

According to the biblical taching man is creature, that is, he is created like every other being. Since all things are created out of nothing (*creatio ex nihilo*) man, like everything else, can pass into nothingness.... Man is a unity of soul, body, flesh, mind, etc., all together constituting the whole man.

244

Now, if man is a unity, "none of these elements is capable of separating itself from the total structure and of continuing to exist independently after death."[52] The real point of difference between the two teachings is that, according to the Bible, the authentic "self" can exist only *in relationship.* One can cease to be a separate self by losing one's self in a genuine "I-Thou" relationship. But selfhood is always being fulfilled by being transcended. This is what Jesus meant in saying, "If you seek to save your self, you will lose your self. But if you lose your self for my sake, you will save your self." (Mk 8:35, paraphrased). Here is the basis for a Christian doctrine of *anatta* ("not-self") which "denies the 'soul' without yielding to a nihilistic view, and which affirms authentic selfhood without yielding to an eternalistic view.... The spiritual meaning of *anatta*," De Silva continues, "is the experience of self-negation, the denying of the self, which is an essential aspect of the spiritual life of Buddhists as well as Christians."[53]

He also concludes that a biblical understanding of *anatta* can locate the place of "God" in Buddhist thought, for, "if man is absolutely *anatta,* the hypothesis of the Unconditioned or some such other hypothesis becomes absolutely necessary if the error of nihilism (*uccedaditthi*) is to be avoided." It is in the emptiness of soul and even the absence of God that one discovers a Reality that transcends being. "If God is, the realization that one is *anatta* leads to the experience of emptiness and fullness (*sunnata-punnata; natthi-atthi*) all in one."[54]

Returning to Din's essay for a moment, it is clear that De Silva confirms the conviction of Professor Din that Buddhism is not atheistic. As Din contends, "There can be and there is in fact a Buddhist Theology, provided *Theos* is understood in Buddhist terms and not in terms of traditional Judaistic, Greek, or Western categories."[55] It is important to understand just what is affirmed and what is denied in Buddhism. It is true that Buddhism denies the existence of *Theos* as a personal Being or Creator. In the Buddha's teaching, theism and fatalism were rejected for the same reason, because the theists try to explain evil by appealing to the will of God, and the fatalists substitute a *karma* principle for an invisible God.

It is this sort of *Theos* that is denied by the Buddha. But this does not mean that Buddha denies the existence of what can be philosophically described as "Transcendence, or the Ultimate Reality".... If by theism is meant the affirmation of the existence of such a Transcendental Reality, then Buddhism is profoundly theistic![56]

Having established this point, the problem for Christian theology in Buddhist lands is that it usually insists on understanding God as a Personal Being. Even in Western contemporary Christian thought, however, there are some theologians who challenge the traditional language ascribing personality to God. Likewise, the concept of "Being" has been called into question by those who prefer to speak of God as "Process" or "Becoming." The Theravada Buddhist goes a step further: "the best way to describe the Ultimate Reality is not to describe it at all. The predication of Reality in human terms will distort and relativize its true nature."[57] This way of thinking is not peculiar to Buddhism, but may be said to be a general characteristic of traditional Asian thought—Buddhist, Taoist, Hindu, and Confucian. Khin Maung Din raises the question, in the light of this, whether Christian theology in Asia should continue to speak of God as a "Person," or a "Personal Being," or even as a "Personality" in any absolute sense. "Is it not closer to the truth," he asks, "to say that God is a Person as well as not-a-Person; that God is a Being as well as a Becoming; that God exists and also does not exist?"[58] He anticipates the criticism, "How can you pray to an impersonal God?" The criticism is valid, he admits, for theologies that go to the other extreme of understanding God *only* as an impersonal "That." But this should not be a problem for the Oriental mind which can conceive of God as a "Thou" as well as a "That." Also, the Oriental method of meditation can open up profound ways of entering into communion with God. "When prayer becomes more than asking, or talking, or even thinking, then it is arriving at the level of true meditation."[59]

THE YIN-YANG WAY OF THINKING

The inclusive way of thinking which can conceive of the Holy as both a "Thou" and a "That" has been referred to by Korean theologian Jung Young Lee as "The Yin-Yang Way of Thinking" in his article by that title.[60] Its opposite, the "either/or" way of thinking in the West, has not only promoted but shaped the absolute dogma of God. But "The God of dogma is less than the God of Christianity."[61] Though associated with traditional Chinese thought, this relativistic way of thinking is also found in the Indian thinker who is able to visualize a continuous stream of interrelated moments of *sive-sive*—that is, "This as well as that, in an endless series of changes and transformations."[62] The Jain School of thought in India calls their doctrine *syadyada,* which implies the relativity of all human judgments, so much so that all assertions are qualified with the prefix "somehow." As Professor Din has pointed out, instead of stating categorically that "S is P," they would rather say that "somehow S is P." But that is not sufficient. One must go on to say that "Somehow S is also *not* P," and even this statement is not final. One must go on to negate the negation and say, "Somehow it is *not* true that S is P as well as not P."[63] If this be so, then even the category of "both/and" is relative and must be transcended. This way of understanding Reality is also followed by the Vedanta school of Hinduism, according to which Brahman, or the Absolute, can only be negatively described as *neti, neti* ("not this, not this"). This method of "contrapletal logic," as it has been called in the West, was already used by Ramanuja (11th century) in his profound *Vedartha-samgraha.*

The Yin-Yang ("both/and") way of thinking in Chinese thought can be traced to the *I-Ching* (Book of Change), and may therefore have a deeper historical root than any other concept in China. The concept of *yin*, originally the cosmic female principle, came to signify the dark, cold, negative, and passive aspect of reality, whereas *yang*, the cosmic male principle, came to stand for the light, warm, positive, and active aspect. Yin represents everything that is not yang, and yang all that is not yin.

Thus in an ultimate analysis everything, whether spiritual or material, temporal or spatial, can be categorized by the symbol of yin and yang interplay. The symbol of yin and yang is then the primordial category of everything that exists in the world. The characteristic nature of this symbol is not the conflict but the complementarity of opposites.[64]

Dr. Lee advocates this way of thinking as a possible new method for ecumenical theology. He believes it can help to clarify and resolve some of the unresolved issues that have plagued the history of Western Christian thought, such as the problem of whether God is transcendent or immanent, whether he is personal or impersonal, how Jesus Christ can be both human and divine, and how man can be both body and spirit. To look briefly at the first two problems, whereas the mainstream of Western Christian thought has felt a contradiction in conceiving of God as both transcendent and immanent, the yin-yang logic feels no problem in thinking that God is both at one and the same time. Western theologians have never settled the debate over whether God is personal or impersonal. According to the contrapletal logic of the yin-yang, God cannot be conceived of as personal only, for he transcends all human categories of thought and must therefore be somehow impersonal as well. From

247

such a perspective, the "silence" of the Buddha as he contemplates a flower, or of Confucius as he responds to the queries of his students concerning the Ultimate, becomes pregnant with meaning. "To the Buddha," as noted by Professor Din, "the relatively best way of describing the true nature of Transcendence is not to describe it at all." On the other hand, "the Oriental refusal to predicate Transcendence with Western philosophical categories should not be interpreted as the denial of Transcendence itself."[65] Lee considers yin-yang the most suitable way of approaching Christian truth because "it is the most inclusive and integral symbol of ultimate reality." And if that be so, he adds, "it does not exclusively belong to the East but to all humanity."[66] So enamored is Dr. Lee of this approach to theology that he calls for a general overhaul of all the Western dogmatic and systematic treatises on Christian doctrine, and for a radical reinterpretation of the Christian message according to the category of the yin-yang principle.[67]

GOD AS CHANGE-ITSELF

In another important essay titled "Can God Be Change Itself?"[68] Dr. Lee approaches the problem of God from the perspective of "change" as a philosophical category. The idea that God is purely "changeless," he says, is a holdover from Greek philosophy and its dominant influence on Christian thought. If, however, the basic truth about life is change, as science now pictures the universe for us, and as the authors of the *Book of Change* recognized centuries ago, then it may be more appropriate to think of God as essentially Change-itself instead of Being-itself. According to the ancient Chinese philosophy of change, the whole process of creativity is anchored in Change. The creative process itself is possible because of the Change which changes and creates all things. Change is the creator of heaven and earth, heaven being symbolized in the first hexagram of the *I-Ching* (*Book of Change*) and earth in the second. Heaven's symbol signifies the infinite concentration of *yang*-energy, and earth's symbol that of *yin*-energy. However, both yin and yang owe their existence to Change which is therefore the ultimate reality of all that is becoming and in process. According to the Great Commentary on the *I-Ching*, "The Great Ultimate is in Change. Change produces the two primary forms (yin and yang)."[69]

If Change is the ultimate category, then God can be seen as the "Moving Mover" rather than the "Unmoved Mover." But it is clear that change as applied to Ultimate Reality does not suggest fickleness, which the Greeks ascribed to their many Gods, nor does it suggest decay. What it does connote is movement and creativity. It has been proposed that the lines of the hymn which read, "Change and decay in all around I see. O Thou who changest not, abide with me" be changed to read: "O Thou who changest too, abide with me!"[70] In Lee's words, "if the changing world of relativity is accepted as a basis of thinking, instead of a static world of absolutes, it is possible to define God as the Change which changes all changing phenomena."[71] In fact, he contends, this is a more congenial way of grasping the biblical idea of God, for the category of change is more in harmony with the Hebraic way of thinking than it is with that of Greek philosophy.

Having said this, however, Lee returns to reaffirm the basic truth in the idea that God is also "changeless." But changelessness does not imply a static and frozen statue that cannot move. Rather, the concept reinforces the idea of faithfulness and steadfastness. In other words, "the character of changelessness is part of the changing reality of God. God is changeless because he is primarily Change-itself." Changelessness points to the unchanging and consistent pattern of change. "The changelessness of God does not negate his essential nature as Change, but affirms the pure form of his changing activity."[72] If God is not Change in a changing world, then he is not in the world. He is only an observer, not a participant. In short, "to deny the idea of a changing God is to deny the living God."[73]

THE PAIN OF GOD

Japanese theologian Kazoh Kitamori in his *Theology of the Pain of God* may be said to emphasize the moral character of the changing God. His is the most self-consciously Japanese of theological currents in Japan, and the first attempt to work out an indigenous Christian theology. His theology represents an Asian approach to Luther's Theology of the Cross, interpreted by Kitamori as "love rooted in the pain of God." This means that God was not detached from the suffering of Christ on the Cross. "The Cross is in no sense an external act of God, but an act within himself."[74] Pain is the very "essence" of God, and "recovering this lost essence," Kitamori believes, "is the ultimate and grave task for today's theology, especially in Japan."[75] Any theology that is ashamed of this idea that pain is

249

the essence of God still belongs to the "theology of glory" (*theologia gloriae*). The theology of the Cross (*theologia crucis*) is the theology which wonders most deeply at "pain as the essence of God." This pain is that by which God embraces completely those who do not deserve to be embraced.

Kitamori first discovered the phrase "pain of God" in the Japanese literary version of the Bible (Jer. 31:20), which translates Jeremiah 31:20 with the words, "My heart is pained." "God in pain," he concluded, "is the God who resolves our human pain by his own."[76] For Kitamori, this is the perspective from which the whole of Christian theology should be understood. Most modern theology (up to Jurgen Moltmann, at least) has advocated a God who has no pain, who cannot suffer, and who looks upon the Cross without emotion.

The fact that man is no longer astonished by the news "the Son of God died on the cross" is most saddening.... In a church that has lost this wonder, unastonishing theological doctrines teach that God, against his nature, took an emergency measure and made Christ suffer for the redemption of sin.[77]

Those who would understand pain must also actually experience it in order to establish the theology of God's pain. At this point Kitamori's approach differs from a purely rationalistic, detached theology. "The theology of the pain of God," he says, "can be pursued only when we participate in it through our own suffering."[78]

One of his great concerns has been to accommodate the theology of the Cross to the Japanese mind. His theology is contextual in that it makes central a concept that is already central in the Japanese experience. For instance, the sense of tragedy in Japanese drama is present in the experience of *tsurasa* (pain), the emotion which occurs when one has to sacrifice himself or a loved one in order to save the life of another. Kitamori regards this as a splendid analogy to the pain of God in receiving the sinner in spite of his sin. Another analogy is drawn from the Buddhist attitude toward cosmic suffering, long recognized as a meeting point for the Christian and the Mahayana Buddhist. There is no exact parallel, of course, because the Buddhist concept lacks the element of "wrath," and consequently sorrow to the Buddhist is only sympathy, and not really pain. But Kitamori also finds the note of pain in God strangely lacking in the Christianity that came to Japan in the form of Liberal and Neo-orthodox Protestant theologies, even though Christianity's primary symbol is the Cross![79]

MAN IN NATURE

The EACC study document, "Confessing the Faith in Asia Today," also mentions Nature as one of the points of entry where the gospel may be expected to relate most meaningfully to the life of Asian peoples today. "Traditionally, Asian cultures have understood man in terms of his affinity to nature," the document says, "and have sought his harmony with it."[80] Now the church in Asia is faced with a new kind of challenge, for the natural sciences have shown that nature can be controlled, in part, for human ends, and a scientific world-view is growing particularly among the younger generation. Asians are somewhat in a position of advantage at this point. "Because modern science comes to Asia largely as a foreign importation, Asians can take a more objective view of it than Westerners, and can evaluate it in terms of traditional Asian humanistic and spiritual values."[81] It can be said that more recently many Western thinkers have been looking to some of Asia's classical traditions in order to find help in the face of an ecological crisis. These Asian humanistic and spiritual values can also be strengthened by a Christian sense of stewardship for the whole created world. Asian Christians are thus challenged to evaluate the development goals toward which their societies are moving.

Dr. Masatoshi Doi of Japan, in an essay he calls "Religion and Nature," bemoans the fact that under the impact of modernization in Asia, nature is being "stripped of its religious veil together with its dimension of depth."[82] He further regrets that Western theology has not yet developed an adequate theology of nature, and he believes that this may be one of the contributions expected from the Asian church, and from Japan in particular. Although such a theology of nature as Doi envisions has not yet appeared from any Asian quarter, some pointers have been set by Doi, Koyama, and a few others. For example, a doctoral dissertation under the Southeast Asia Graduate School of Theology has just been written by a young Taiwanese teacher of theology, the Rev. Hsien-chih Wang, on the Taoist contribution to a Christian theology of nature.* Dr. Doi, who is Director of the NCC Center for the Study of Japanese Religions, in Kyoto, attempts in this essay to suggest certain lines along which a theology of nature might develop. In Japanese primal communities "nature was hallowed with religion and religion was deep-

---

*See his response to Dr. Kim's paper in this volume.

ly embedded in nature." Nature worship was the heart of Shinto, Japan's indigenous religion, and this is still true of village culture in Japan. But the Western notion of nature as "something to be conquered by reason" is now penetrating the minds of the youth who study the sciences. Consequently, nature "has been turned into an object which is merely there for the free disposal and exploitation of man. As a result, man himself is alienated from nature and consequently dehumanized."[83] The task of a Christian theology of nature in Asia, as Doi sees it, is twofold: on the one hand, to emancipate the village people from the spell of nature, and, on the other hand, to correct the materialistic view which reduces nature to mere "things" which can be manipulated and exploited by man.

A LESS DOMINEERING GOD

A similar challenge comes from a Korean Christian layman, Pyong-Choon Hahn, who in a brief statement on "God, Man and Nature" challenges Christianity to "come up with a theology based on a less domineering and proprietary image of God."[84] In traditional Christian theology, he points out, God as Creator has a proprietary interest in maintaining his dominion over the earth. Man, as steward of a proprietor-God, strives strenuously to maintain his dominion over nature for fear that his failure to dominate may result in his subjugation to nature. In keeping with the European dialectics characterized by rigid "either/or" dichotomies, "either man conquers Nature or Nature conquers him." Without dominion over the material world man is nothing! But non-Christian Korea has had a different world-view.

Nature is never hostile to man; on the contrary, man without Nature is nothing, just as Nature without man is nothing.... Neither dominates the other; no subjugation, and conquest is sought by neither. Man does not seek to increase his power unlimitedly at the expense of Nature. He adjusts himself to the rhythm of Nature; a failure to do so means his death. Man knows that the dominion over Nature inevitably includes the dominion over his fellowmen.[85]

In short, there is mutuality and interdependency that keep man from dominating and exploiting nature. A Christian theology of nature based on a less domineering and proprietary image of God would help to restrict man's right to abuse nature out of his own greed for power. "God and Man must be integrated back into the Creation," concludes Hahn.

LIBERATION FROM ALIEN POWERS

One of the basic theological issues identified by Dr. Nacpil in his essay, "A Gospel for the New Filipino," focuses on the need for a "new cosmology" in relation to which the gospel can be understood from the perspective of "liberation." Under the vision of a new order it is required that Asian man today should achieve a measure of mastery over his environment, and that he learn to appreciate, understand, and apply to his advantage the relationship of man to nature implied in modern science and technology. This kind of liberation includes emancipation from "cyclic time" and a "sacral universe." The gospel frees man from a sacral understanding of the world as dominated by preternatural powers, and de-sacralizes the world so that it may be seen as God's creation given over to man as steward. This emancipation is grounded in the covenant relationship between God and man and between man and man. One of the meanings of salvation in the covenant is that of deliverance or liberation, and one of the things man is delivered from is "the worship of false gods and their images and from a sacral understanding of the world as dominated by religious powers which do not possess true divinity."[86]

As we have seen already in our discussion of man in relation to the Holy, man's freedom in Christ gives him a new relationship to nature. The alien cosmic powers and environmental spirits having been driven away, man is given the freedom and responsibility to "subdue" nature, and to develop and care for it. This is one of the means by which man fulfills his destiny as the "image" of God. Nacpil points out that man's calling to dominate nature has to be seen in the context of the ambiguous relation between man and nature. On the one hand, man is subject to the powers of nature, and he is from the beginning a part of nature (Gen. 2:7; I Cor. 15:47). Man is also nurtured by nature, and without nature he cannot exist at all. Besides providing him a habitat and food for sustenance, nature offers him esthetic delight, meditation (cf. Ps. 104), companionship, consolation, and inspiration.[87] In regard to this aspect of man's relation to nature there is much common ground between the Judeo-Christian view and that of the indigenous Asian religions.

On the other hand, man transcends nature and exercises domination over it. Man is clearly distinct from the rest of nature, in the biblical view, for he alone is given the vocation to control it, and to develop and care for it. "In man, nature has ceased to act merely naturally and spontaneously and unconsciously, and has begun to act freely and intelligently and responsibly."[88] It is in regard to this aspect of man's ambiguous relation to nature that some of the greatest differences appear between the Judeo-Christian view

253

and that of Asia's more indigenous faiths. Many of the Asian Christian theologians, some of whose writings are summarized here —Thomas, Samartha, De Silva, Koyama, and Nacpil—are forthright in saying that the new awareness in Asia of the personal, historical, and social dimensions of human existence may be Christianity's greatest gift to Asia. The Christian faith in this way provides a theological perspective for the new Asian's desire to master his environment.

But Nacpil hastens to add that this theological perspective must also be critical, for man's destiny is not simply to control nature; he also has a sacred responsibility for human development. What man does with nature affects himself and his fellowmen, and it is well known that some of the adverse effects upon nature of modern technology have seriously threatened human life on earth. It is therefore necessary, in the development of a theological perspective for the new Asian's desire to control his environment, "to ask whether the kind, aims, and consequences of technical domination which man exercises over nature does honor to man's relation to God, as a son and a steward of God and a fellow-worker in the creative process, and thus helps build up a culture and a society which are truly human."[89]

THE COSMIC CHRIST

A theological concept that a number of Asian theologians have been attracted to over the years is sometimes called the concept of the "Cosmic Christ." In the early part of this century Justice P. Chenchiah of India linked Jesus of Nazareth to the cosmic process of creation, and later Paul Devanandan, following Chenchiah in some respects, stressed the cosmic dimension of redemption in Christ. "God's act of redemption in Christ Jesus," Devanandan writes, "concerns the whole of his creation. Biblical faith repeatedly affirms that the work of Christ is of cosmic significance in that the redemption wrought in him has affected the entire creative process."[90] Devanandan extends it to other religions and secular faiths. M. M. Thomas extends it still further to embrace the entire revolutionary ferment in Asia.

Dr. S. J. Samartha, in his essay "The Unbound Christ," applies the concept in his pointers toward a christology for India today. Much of what he says is applicable to the Asian church as a whole. He believes that it is only as we share in the struggles and conflicts and tragedies of our national life and, "in that context, seek to answer what it means to affirm that Christ, crucified and risen, is the Lord of all life that we can hope to make the Gospel thrustingly relevant to human need in contemporary India."[91] It is his conviction that Christian theological thinking in India should take *advaita* seriously; that is, Sankara's grand vision of God, man, and the world within a single conception of unbroken unity. This Hindu insight into "the larger unity of all life" can help Christians to overcome a sometimes-too-narrow view of revelation "as confined to the historical, thus isolating it from nature and from human consciousness."[92] On the other side, however, he also believes that the affirmation of the lordship of the crucified and risen Christ over all life can "help Hindu spirituality to recover a sense of the personal, the historical, and the social." He rejoices that the much-too-narrow view of salvation as limited to saving *man* is now being supplemented by a recognition of the work of the "larger Christ."[93] Returning to the Letter to the Ephesians, Samartha, who heads up the important study and action program on Dialogue with People of Other Faiths and Ideologies, of the WCC, comments that God's activity in Christ, viewed in the context of *advaita,* expresses itself in the continuing act of creation and redemption and moves toward fulfillment. Ultimately, it is God who brings about the consummation of all creation. "The mystery of his will" and the purpose he has set forth in Christ as "a plan for the fullness of time" is "to unite all things in him, things in heaven and things in earth" (Eph. 1:10).

But this consummation should not be regarded as a return to the beginning but as an enrichment and a fulfilment, moving through struggles and conflicts, overcoming evil in love, gathering up values, reaching out, and finding final fulfilment in the fulness of God himself. The affirmation of the lordship of the crucified and risen Christ over all life does not involve any exclusiveness. On the contrary, it is the declaration of the universality of the unbound Christ.[94]

CREATION AS A THEOLOGICAL FRAMEWORK

The biblical theme of Creation has found fresh relevance in the work of at least two Asian theologians, C. S. Song and Preman Niles. Dr. Song relates the theme to Christian mission, attempting a radical reconstruction of missiology.[95] He does this by relating redemption in Christ to the whole process of God's creative activity. This enables him to move beyond the "spiritual provincialism" of a "mission-compound Christianity," as he calls it. From the standpoint of the biblical doctrine of Creation, a cosmic view of *missio dei* is possible, for "God is not to be identified *simply and solely*

, particular form of his manifestation and with a particular ssion of man's response."[96]

Dr. Niles, an Old Testament scholar, goes further than Song by lifting the Creation motif out of the context of discussion about "salvation history" and adopting it as a broad framework for "doing" theology in Asia. Since the Creation faith affirms the absolute freedom of the Creator-God to do "the new thing" in history, it provides "a theological framework for confessing that in Asia God is realizing in a new way the promise of salvation given in Jesus Christ for all mankind."[97] In the light of the Servant passages in Second Isaiah, Niles concludes that "in the situation of Asian suffering and hope, we are called upon to see our participation as no less an undertaking than to share in God's suffering love for his creation."[98] He believes that the motif of Creation provides an Asian standpoint by enabling Asian Christians to see the activity of the Creator-God in their midst, even if the signs of hope which point to his activity are hazy and often ambiguous. The task of an Asian Christian theology, then, is "to perceive and articulate the nature and shape of the radically new thing which God in Jesus Christ is doing in our midst."[99]

MAN IN SOCIETY AND HISTORY

The EACC study document, "Confessing the Faith in Asia Today," also mentions Society as one of the points of entry at which the proclamation of the gospel may become credible to Asian peoples. Stress falls upon the new Christian life-style required by living in urban-industrial environments. Obedience to Christ in these situations calls for alertness to the causes of social injustice, seeking to eliminate the causes while at the same time ministering to the needs of those who are victims of injustice. "Men have been freed from old restraints and patterns of life and are potentially open to the gospel," the study document points out, "but they are also open to forces of evil and social disintegration, unless the gospel is presented to them in terms that are relevant to the situation."[100] As we all know, in more recent years the gospel has sometimes been proclaimed in Asian countries through declarations of conscience and liturgical protests in situations of conflict, such as the "Theological Declaration by Christian Ministers in the Republic of Korea,

1973." The Sixth Assembly of the CCA was specially concerned with human suffering caused by social and political injustices.*

Dr. Nacpil's treatment of theological issues relevant to the coming of the new man in Asia focuses upon two perspectives of the gospel that speak to the broad theme of man in society and history. The first is that already mentioned in Part I of this summary, as man's summons to "the responsibility of mastering and developing his share of the earth and changing his society as requisite conditions for his full emergence in the future." It will be recalled that his essay has special reference to the Philippines, and the rise of the "new Filipino." He believes that the structure of kinship is the base of Filipino society. Any change at this point will have far-reaching consequences, and Nacpil purposely limits his remarks to the discussion of a theological perspective for this kind of basic change. In the first place, man as God's creation is given the responsibility for transforming and humanizing society. In the second place, Jesus, in the light of his vision of a new order of things under the kingdom of God, "announces that the absolute authority of the old order is broken, that man is delivered from the support and shackles of the old institutions, and that he must now opt for a new life and a new set of relations in the new society which now replaces the old (Mtt. 6-7)."[101] On these bases Nacpil shows how man need not be a "helpless victim" trapped in his society and history, when he has been given the authority and responsibility to alter his society and make it more truly human.[102]

A THEOLOGY OF THE NEW CREATION

Emphasis on the New Testament doctrine of the New Creation in Christ, and its application, is now recognized as an indigenous Christian tradition in India. M. M. Thomas traces its history in his essay "Toward an Indian Christian Theology."[103] It all started with a lay Christian, Justice P. Chenchiah, who was a leader of the Madras "Re-thinking Christianity Group" of the 1930's. He stressed the concept of the New Man in Christ, clothing it in the categories of emergent evolution of the creative process. He saw the appearance of Jesus in history as "the manifestation of a new creative effort of God, in which the cosmic energy, or *sakti*, is the Holy Spirit, the new creation is Christ, and the new life order is the Kingdom of God."[104] He believed that Indian christology should be based on

---

*See the preparatory issue of *Asia Focus*, a theme-issue on "Asian Theological Reflections on Suffering and Hope" (No. 661, Jan. 1977).

the discovery and recovery of the Pauline theology of Incarnation as "new Adam," and should work along the lines of the Eastern theology of the Son of Man. Jesus is the "first fruits of a new creation" (St. Paul), the first of a new race—"the sons of God" (St. John). Jesus is the pinnacle and crown of creation, and God's assumption of humanity through the Incarnation is a permanent one. From now on Jesus is the Power of God, a divine humanity transcending mankind. "Humanity did not borrow Jesus to stay a while on earth" and then return home after his mission was completed. "In that case incarnation will be an adventure, an interlude in the Eternal Son's life, leaving no permanent deposit on earth or in heaven." In Indian Christian theology Jesus belongs to man! "It is essential for our doctrine of incarnation to hold that Jesus assumed body permanently as the consummation of creative human process." What this means is that Jesus represents not merely the meeting of God and man, but the fusion into unity of God and man, so that man may partake of his divine humanity. He becomes "God permanently residing in creation," bringing to birth "a new order of creation."[105]

Paul Devanandan, building somewhat on the thought of Chenchiah, also emphasized the new creation in Jesus Christ, which for him had "personal, social, and cosmic dimensions." The special application he gave to the creative and redemptive activity of Christ in the happenings of contemporary life and world events added a new dimension to the New Creation theme. For him, all persons share in the new creation in Christ, within and outside the church. A new humanity is in the making, in which all persons are being reconciled to God—Christians and non-Christians alike. This implies, in his own words, that "the whole creation in all its being is already redeemed by the work of Christ, that the gospel is primarily the good news of this new order of being, calling men to accept what they are."[106] Any easy distinction, therefore, between the believer and the unbeliever, between the Christian world and the non-Christian world, tends to break down. If the new man in Jesus Christ has "broken down the wall of partition" between the Jew and the Gentile, Devanandan asks, does it not also mean that the new humanity in Christ transcends the Christian and the non-Christian, and that the division between Christianity, other religions, and secular humanism breaks down wherever vision of the new man Jesus Christ is transforming them? Therefore, though salvation history has to be discerned by the church, it is not to be identified solely with church history; it should be defined rather as secular history "being controlled by the purposive will of God."[107] Thomas summarizes the views of his chief mentor in this way:

Like Chenchiah, Devanandan emphasized that the new creation in Christ is not merely something that touches human history from without as a tangent touches a circle; instead it becomes a process that takes hold of the process of human history from within, and gives it shape and direction. It makes it possible for faith to look for the signs of God's new creation in Christ not only in the transformed lives of individuals, but also in the struggles and purposes of men to renew structures of society, culture, and religion and to transform earth and heaven in the name of the dignity and destiny of man.[108]

CHRIST ACTING IN OUR SOCIETY

It has been noted that there is in the churches of South Asia a striking "theological propensity for finding Christ really active *there* in society, in movements, in men of other faiths and of no faith," and this insight may point to a neglected area—at least, until quite recently—in Western theological thought.[109] The idea has been traced to Paul Devanandan and D. T. Niles, and may have first appeared in a statement from the inaugural Assembly of the EACC, at Kuala Lumpur, in 1959, where Niles was the organizing director and Devanandan and Thomas were among the leaders. The report reads as follows:

The Church must endeavor to discern how Christ is at work in the revolution of contemporary Asia, releasing new creative forces, judging idolatry and false gods, leading peoples to a decision for or against him, and gathering to himself those who respond in faith to him.... The Church must not only discern Christ in the changing life but be there in it, responding to him and making his presence and lordship known.[110]

Another source of this insight is the thesis of Raymond Panikkar that Christ is present and active in Hinduism, although hidden there in the sense that he is not yet known by the Hindu. It is interesting to note that what appears to be an indigenous Indian Christian tradition has since become a major emphasis of contemporary Western theology, by an independent route through the influence of Friedrich Gogarten and Dietrich Bonhoeffer.

This account of an Indian Christian tradition would be incomplete if we did not show how M. M. Thomas applies to his own theology of social revolution Devanandan's thought concerning the social and cosmic dimensions of the new creation in Christ. Thomas agrees with Devanandan, his predecessor as Director of the Christian Institute for the Study of Religion and Society, Bangalore, that in the quest of modern Asia for human identity and human community non-Christian religions and secular movements are being drawn into the orbit of the process of the new creation in Christ. All of these movements are alike being compelled to come to terms with the "new humanism" which is the result of the hidden activity ot Christ in contemporary history. So powerful is the force of this "new humanism" that modern Asians are obliged either to open themselves to Jesus Christ in a new way or to close themselves more firmly to him in a new way. They can no longer remain neutral or indifferent. It is the mission of the church to participate in the Asian social revolution, discerning the presence of Christ (and Antichrist) in it, and witnessing to the new creation in Christ as the fulfillment of the quest of modern Asia.[111]

One of Thomas' essays is titled "The Struggle for Human Dignity as a Preparation for the Gospel."[112] As other theologians have seen in Asia's great religions a preparation for the gospel, M. M. Thomas discerns a *preparatio evangelica* even in the Asian social revolution. The basic element in the revolution is "the quest and struggle of men for their humanity." Although there are perversions in all revolutionary movements, the basic drive behind them is the personal and historical dimensions of human existence. At the core of this new awakening there is a Christian impetus that must be taken seriously. Christ is at work in Asia's revolutionary ferment creating a new humanity. The church must be involved in the movement of the people for power as the path to justice; yet at the same time, as Thomas puts it in another essay, the church must also

...point to the Kingdom of Righteousness which always comes through Divine judgment on and forgiveness of sin in all human action, through the Cross of Christ, as the framework for the struggle itself. In this context the Church as a community of forgiven sinners, unable to identify totally any city of man with the City of God, is God's instrument of the permanent revolution.[113]

And what is the ethos or "ideology" of the Asian struggle? It is what Thomas calls an "integral humanism, spiritually informed by the insights of the prophetic Christian faith and by the humanism of Asia's indigenous religions and cultures...."[114] Such an ethos is necessary as a common framework for Christians and people of other religions and secular ideologies in Asia to engage together in action in the Asian struggle. But he acknowledges that the distinctive Christian contribution to this common framework still needs further exploration.

A continuing interest of Jesuit Fr. Arevalo of Loyola School of Theology, in Manila, has been the search for a Christian perspective on development and liberation. He first presented reflections on the theme at the Asian Ecumenical Conference on Development, held in Tokyo, July, 1970. In his paper titled "Notes for a Theology of Development," he establishes the christological basis for a theology of development, reviews the basic kinds of institutionalized violence which today crush the underdeveloped segments of mankind, and then moves on to reflect on the question, "Must Christian churches of Asia align themselves unequivocally with the poor and the victims of social injustice against the unjust structures which impede justice and development?" His answer is a qualified "yes," qualified by the consideration that "to stand on the side of the poor is not to take a stance of enmity or hate against those who possess wealth and power...but rather to take issue with attitudes of selfishness and the structures which institutionalize egoism...."[115] His colleague, Fr. Antonio Lambino, in a recent article on the subject, "Theology, Social Change and Christian Conscience," agrees with Arevalo that "Christianity is not fully compatible with any ideology of which a 'this-worldly utopia' is an essential part, whether that ideology be capitalist or socialist."[116] We saw earlier how M. M. Thomas is searching for an ethos, or "ideology," that Christians and non-Christians might share as a common framework for joint action in the Asian struggle. Thomas would agree with Arevalo and Lambino on the points cited above. It would be interesting to get their reaction to Thomas' suggestion of an "integral humanism" based on a new vision of the universality of Jesus Christ and the unity of mankind.

MISSION AND MODERNIZATION

Modernization spells "promise" to Asians, according to a report of a Working Group at the Asian Conference on Church and Society, held in Seoul, in 1967—promise of "release from the cyclical 'fate' of nature which will enable them to face the future with hope and expectation, and which will place in their own hands the right and means to shape their future." It means also the promise of "liberation from grinding poverty" and, third, the promise of "emancipation from static, outworn or inhibiting social structures." Finally, it includes also the promise of "a new life struggling to come to birth. Asians claim these promises as their goals and accept modernization as a necessary development in their history."[117] At the same time, however, they are aware of the perils of modernization, knowing that it carries with it the risk of new forms of bondage and dehumanization. But, for them it is a risk worth taking. A major concern at this Asian conference had to do with "how the Christian

261

faith illuminates human creativity and responsibility for the shaping of the ways and pace by which modernization proceeds."[118] The task of theology, the report concludes, is to articulate a Christian interpretation of history that "views modernization within the revelation of God's purpose for man in Christ."

In an essay by the title "Mission and Modernization" Emerito Nacpil views the participation of Christians in the modernization of Asia as an aspect of their missionary obedience. The argument runs as follows: Since the mission of God is logically prior to the mission of the church and is more inclusive than that of the historical church, modernization can be viewed within the larger perspective of God's mission. But, since the historical process of modernization has destructive as well as creative possibilities, it must be made the object of both "prophetic criticism" and "pastoral concern."[119] Thus Nacpil appears to build on the conclusions reached at the Asian Conference on Church and Society.

HISTORY AND NATURE

Dr. Koyama, in the light of his experience as a Japanese missionary in Thailand, was compelled to wrestle with the problem of man in relation to nature and history, in what he popularly calls his "Waterbuffalo Theology." Working directly with the biblical material Koyama brings the thought-world of the Bible into contact with the thought-world of the rural Thai. In this encounter of two "worlds" he finds points of harmony and points of "theological friction,"[120] especially around the question whether the world is understood primarily as "nature" or as "history." Although he approaches the Thai world-view with sympathetic appreciation, he allows biblical theology to do its critical task. One can see in his approach a model of balance between accommodation (the "pastoral" element) and criticism (the "prophetic" element) in Christian theology.

In his essay subtitled "Will the Monsoon Rain Make God Wet?" he shows how one can experience the world around him primarily as "nature," in which time appears to be cyclical, while events appear to have the character of "many-time-ness." This is a part of the traditional "monsoon orientation" of the rural Thai as of most other Southeast Asians. When, on the other hand, one experiences his world primarily as "history," time appears to be linear and events are characterized by "once-for-all-ness." This is a part of the world-view of the biblical writers. Are the two views incompatible? Koyama suggests that they are not. Time need not be symbolized by a straight line (linear) or a circle (cyclical), although both symbols point to two essential truths about the universe we live in, namely, its regularity (nature as cyclical) and its direction (time as linear). Both of these truths about the world can be contained in a new symbol, the "ascending spiral." Under this symbol time is circular in one sense and linear in another sense, or somehow both cyclical and linear. By locating the Thai cyclical view of time, based on nature, within the biblical linear view of time, based on history, Koyama shows how the former is illumined by the latter. Instead of forcing us to choose between history and nature, he concludes that one must "hold both history and nature to be equally important" in man's experience of God's activity in relation to the world. Man's world is both "historical" and "natural" viewed from different perspectives, and God is the Lord of the whole world as "nature-history."[121]

One of the perspectives from which Dr. Nacpil asks us to view the gospel, in relation to the rise of the new man in Asia, is "the horizon of hope." This speaks directly to the need for a "new eschatology," which Nacpil sees as one of the three most urgent problems for Christian theology and mission in this part of the world. To say that the new Asian man needs a new eschatology is to say that he needs a new orientation to time. He must now be concerned not only with the past and the immediate future but also with the long-range future and with change. He is to have a vision of the direction and goal of history, and of his part in shaping the future. The gospel can free man from a cyclical view of time, based on the rhythm of the seasons, and enable him to see his life also in relation to historical time which moves toward the future through the projection of human purposes, meaningful activity, the occurrence of historic events, and through remembering the past and anticipating and planning for the future. The gospel becomes indeed "good news" to traditional Asian man who is seeking deliverance from the past and from the lesser cosmic powers and environmental spirits, and who is seeking freedom to change the world and to shape the future.[122]

As indicated earlier in this paper, Nacpil is convinced that the gospel has power to bring the new Asian into being. This claim is based on the biblical insight that the Kingdom of God is the reign of God in human life, which "delivers man from what makes him less than human, restores him to his dignity, and places him in a climate of liberty in an environment of love and a network of fulfilling relationships."[123] This liberation and restoration pertain not only to social welfare and social action, but also to the power to heal human lives, renew society, and even redirect world history toward human freedom, justice, and maturity.

REFERENCE NOTES

[1] M. M. Thomas, *Man and the Universe of Faiths*, (MUF) (Bangalore: CISRS, 1975), p. 151.

[2] G. H. Anderson and T. F. Stransky (eds.). *Mission Trends No. 3: Third World Theologies* (New York: Paulist Press, 1976). See also David B. Barrett, "The Disciples of Africa in This Generation." in *God, Man and Church Growth*, ed. by Alan R. Tippett (Eerdmans, 1973), p. 397.

[3] Richard Campbell, "Contextual Theology and Its Problems," *Study Encounter*, XII, 1-2 (1976), pp. 11-25.

[4] Report of Section II, "What Unity Requires" (Nairobi, WCC). See a similar emphasis in the Report of Section I, Confessing Christ Today," *Breaking Barriers* (Geneva: WCC, 1976), p. 45f.

[5] C. S. Song, Editorial in *Study Encounter*, XII. pp. 1-2 (1976).

[6] Y. Kumazawa, "Seeking to Integrate Text and Context," in Anderson, *Asian Voices in Christian Theology* (New York: Orbis Bks., 1975), pp. 203ff.

[7] M. M. Thomas, *The Acknowledged Christ of the Indian Renaissance* (London: SCM, 1969), p. 310.

[8] Ibid., p. 311.

[9] M. M. Thomas, "Foreword" to *Introduction to Indian Christian Theology* by Robin Boyd (Madras: CLS, 1969).

[10] C. C. West, "Foreword" to *What Asian Christians are Thinking* (WACAT) (Quezon City: New Day, 1976).

[11] Cf. Francis Clark, S.J., "Making the Gospel at Home in Asian Cultures," *Teaching All Nations*, XIII. 3 (1976), pp.131-49.

[12] EACC. "The Confessing Church in Asia and Its Theological Task," (1965), pp. 43ff. in *WACAT*.

[13] Thomas, *Acknowledged Christ*, pp. 306-311.

[14] K. Koyama, "The Role of Theology in Asia Today," pp. 1-22 in *Addresses Delivered at the National Consultation on Theological Education* (Bangalore, 1968), Supplement to *Indian Journal of Theology*, 1968.

[15] E. Nacpil, "A Gospel for the New Filipino," pp. 117-146 in *Asian Voices*, op. cit.

[16] Ibid., p. 141.   [17] Ibid., p. 124.   [18] EACC, op. cit.

[19] Nacpil, op. cit., p. 124   [20] Ibid., p. 139.

[21] EACC, "Confessing the Faith in Asia Today," pp. 10-15 in *WACAT*.

[22] Ibid., p. 13.   [23] Ibid.

[24] Ibid., p. 14. Cf. Timothy Tian-min Lin, "The Confucian Concept of Jen and the Christian Concept of Love," *Ching Feng* (Hong Kong), XV. 3 (1972), pp. 162-172.

[25] Ibid., pp. 14ff.   [26] *Assembly News* (June 1, 1977), p.2.   [27] Ibid.. p. 1.

[28] Ibid., p. 2. The reader is also referred to two preparatory volumes on the theme: *Asian Theological Reflections on Suffering and Hope*, ed. by Yap Kim Hao (Singapore: CCA, 1977), and *Jesus Christ in Asian Suffering and Hope*, ed. by J. M. Colaco (Madras: CLS, 1977).

[29] M. M. Thomas, *Man and the Universe of Faiths*, op. cit., p. 156.

[30] EACC, "The Confessing Church in Asia and Its Theological Task," op. cit., p. 43.

[31] Ibid., p. 44.   [32] *CCA News* (Dec., 1975).

[33] Bong Rin Ro, "Contextualization: Asian Theology," pp. 47-58 in *WACAT*.

[34] See critique of S. B. Yun's view of indigenization in P. N. Park, "A Theological Approach to the Understanding of the Indigenization of Christianity," *Northeast Asia Journal of Theology*, No. 3 (September, 1969), pp. 106-114.

264

35 R. Panikkar, "Inter-Religious Dialogue: Some Principles," *Journal of Ecumenical Studies*, XII. 3 (Summer, 1975).
36 In *WACAT*, pp. 338-376.
37 Panikkar, "The Church and the World Religions," *Religion and Society*, XIV, 2 (1967), p. 62.
38 Ibid., pp. 62ff.
39 Robin Boyd, *Introduction to Indian Christian Theology*, op. cit., pp. 222ff.
40 Panikkar, "The Church and the World Religions," op. cit., p. 63.
41 Panikkar, "Christians and So-Called 'Non-Christians,'" p. 361 in *WACAT*.
42 Thomas, *Man and the Universe of Faiths* (MUF), op. cit., p. 153.
43 EACC, *Witnesses Together*. Edited by U. Kyaw Than (Rangoon, 1959), p. 7.
44 Thomas, MUF, p. vi.   45 Ibid., p. 149. See his chapter herein.
46 Ibid., pp. 150ff. The reader is also referred to an article by Wesley Ariarajah, "Towards a Theology of Dialogue," pp. 88-97 in *Dialogue* (New Series, Colombo, Sri Lanka), III, 3 (Dec., 1976).
47 In WACAT, pp. 87-104.   48 Din, p. 88 in *WACAT*.
49 Ibid., p. 102.   50 Ibid.   51 In *WACAT*, pp. 105-118.
52 Ibid., p. 110.   53 Ibid., p. 112.   54 Ibid., pp. 117ff.
55 Din, op. cit., p. 89.   56 Ibid., p. 90.
57 Ibid., p. 91.   58 Ibid.   59 Ibid., p. 93.
60 In *WACAT*, pp. 59-67. In Dr. Lee's book, *The I: A Christian Concept of Man*, he applies the yin-yang method to the Christian view of man (N.Y.: Philosophical Library, 1973). In a forthcoming book, *Theology of Change: A Christian Concept of God from an Eastern Perspective* (Orbis, 1979), he applies it to the Christian understanding of God.
61 J. Y. Lee, Ibid., p. 60.   62 Ibid., p. 65.   63 Din, op. cit., p. 92.
64 Lee, op. cit., p. 64.   65 Din, op. cit., p. 92.
66 Lee, *The I: A Christian View of Man*, p.8.   67 Ibid., p. 9.
68 In *WACAT*, pp. 173-193. See also his forthcoming book, *Theology of Change: A Christian Concept of God from an Eastern Perspective* (Orbis, 1979).
69 Lee, "Can God Be Change Itself?" p. 184 in *WACAT*.
70 Paul Lehmann in a lecture to seminarians at Silliman University (Philippines).
71 Lee, op. cit., "Can God Be Change Itself?" p. 186.
72 Ibid., p. 187.   73 Ibid., p. 189.
74 Kitamori, "Theology of the Pain of God," p. 208 in *WACAT*. See also his book by the same title.
75 Ibid., p. 209.   76 Ibid., p. 199.
77 Ibid., pp. 207ff.   78 Ibid.
79 It should be noted that Koyama and Ohki, former students of Kitamori, show the influence of their teacher—Ohki in his essay on the idea of Transcendence as Love, and Koyama in his emphasis on the "crucified mind."
80 EACC, "Confessing the Faith in Asia Today," op. cit., p. 11.
81 Ibid.   82 Doi, "Religion and Nature," pp. 119-130 in *WACAT*.
83 Ibid.   84 Pyong-Choon Hahn, "God, Man and Nature," *Anticipation* (WCC), No. 12 (September, 1972), pp. 25-26.
85 Ibid.   86 Nacpil, "Gospel for the New Filipino," op. cit., p. 129.
87 Ibid., p. 136.   88 Ibid.   89 Ibid., p. 375.
90 Devanandan, *The Gospel and Renascent Hinduism* (London, 1959), p. 47.
91 Samartha, "The Unbound Christ," pp. 221-239 in *WACAT*.
92 Ibid.   93 Ibid., p. 236.   94 Ibid.
95 See Chapter 2 of his *Christian Mission in Reconstruction: An Asian Attempt* (Madras: CLS, 1975).
96 Ibid., p. 23.   97 D. Preman, Niles, "Towards a Framework of Doing Theology in Asia," p. 22 in *Asian Theological Reflections on Suffering and Hope*, op. cit.

[98] Ibid., p. 27.   [99] Ibid., p. 28. See also the Song-Niles-West debate in *Occasional Bulletin*, I, 3 (July 1977), pp. 9-15.

[100] EACC, "Confessing the Faith in Asia Today," p. 12 in *WACAT*.

[101] Nacpil. "Gospel for the New Filipino," op. cit., p. 139.

[102] Ibid., p. 140.   [103] In *Asian Voices*, pp. 11-36.

[104] Quoted by Thomas, ibid., p. 30.   [105] Ibid.

[106] Devanandan, as quoted by Thomas, "The Gospel and the Quest of Modern Asia," *Union Seminary Quarterly Review*, XXII (March, 1967), p. 236.

[107] Ibid.   [108] Thomas, "Towards an Indian Christian Theology," p. 32 in *Asian Voices*.

[109] R. W. Taylor, "Christ Acting in Our Society," *Indian Voices in Today's Theological Debate*, edited by Horst Burkle (Lucknow, India, 1965). p. 60.

[110] EACC, *Witnesses Together*, p. 60.

[111] Thomas, *USQR*, p. 236.

[112] In *WACAT* pp. 267-276.

[113] Thomas, "Christian Action in the Asian Struggle," in *WACAT*, p. 450.

[114] Ibid., p. 451. See also his essay in *Political Prospects in India* (CLS, 1971).

[115] Arevalo, "Notes for a Theology of Development," pp. 398-424 in *WACAT*.

[116] Lambino, "Theology, Social Change and Christian Conscience," in *IMPACT*, XI, 11 (November, 1976), p. 375.

[117] ACCS, "Theological Foundations of Modernization," pp. 379-386 in *WACAT*.

[118] Ibid.

[119] Nacpil, "Mission and Modernization," pp. 277-288 in *WACAT*.

[120] Koyama, "Points of Theological Friction," pp. 65-86 in *Asian Voices*.

[121] Koyama, "Will the Monsoon Rain Make God Wet?" pp. 131-144 in *WACAT*.

[122] Nacpil, "Gospel for the New Filipino," op. cit.   [123] Ibid.

13

TOWARD A FRAMEWORK FOR "DOING" THEOLOGY IN ASIA*

D. Preman Niles

Asian theology is suffering from a crisis of identity, for it is often dominated by theological thinking in the West and, more recently, by Latin American and Black American Liberation theologies. Indeed, it is difficult to perceive what is distinctive about Asian theology. If theology in Asia is to have its own identity, it must cease to be merely an extension of Western theologies, and instead speak meaningfully to and within the context of Asian suffering and hope. The true identity of Asian theology will emerge only when we begin to perceive and articulate the relevant word in our situation. Hence, it will be helpful to look at the issue of the identity of Asian theology through the experience or consciousness which has engendered this conviction.

I

Many of us who are caught up in the task of articulating a theology for Asia have learned "the tools of our trade" in Western scholarly circles. In this process we have gone through an experience which may be deemed a theological version of culture shock. Through this experience we have become more sharply aware than before of the continuities and discontinuities which exist between the Western part of our heritage which is ours as Christians and the Asian part of our heritage which is ours culturally and politically. Somehow we have to come to terms with the fact that we are heavily "Western" precisely in the area of the articulation of faith which is the task of theology. This Western heritage poses a problem in that our

---

*This was one of the background papers for the All-Asia Consultation. A condensed version was published in *Asian Theological Reflections on Suffering and Hope* (CCA, 1977), pp. 16-28.

faith calls us to live and to witness to Jesus Christ *in Asia* and in relation to everything which that situation demands culturally, socially, and politically. The problem we face is not alleviated even by the fact that the Asia of today has been influenced by secular movements and ideologies beside Christianity, which also have originated in the West. Two demands have arisen out of this experience. The first is the call to break away from what is described as "the Teutonic captivity of theology."[1] This call is not so much a reaction to Western theology as such, as it is a warning to us, for too long we have depended on Western theologians to do the primary task of providing us with the insights which we could apply in the Asian situation. In other words, in relating the gospel to the Asian situation, we have worked and still work with theological presuppositions developed in Western contexts.

The second call is to discover our functional relevance and identity as scholars in the Asian situation within which God in Jesus Christ is present and active. From this new stance has come a proposal for doing theology in Asia which has been called "the critical Asian principle." We have as yet not worked out all the implications of this method, for we are still in the period of searching and struggling to find a model for "doing" theology within the religiously and politically pluralistic Asian context. But the main thrust of what this principle implies may be stated in the words of Emerito Nacpil of the Philippines.

For one thing it is a way of saving where our area of responsibility is, namely. the varieties and dynamics of Asian realities. We are committed to understand this context both sympathetically and critically. For another thing, it is a way of saving that we will approach and interpret the Gospel in relation to the needs and issues peculiar to the Asian situations. It functions therefore as a hermeneutical principle. Third, it is a way of saying that a theology worth its salt at this time in Asia must be capable not only of illuminating the Asian realities with the light of the Gospel, but also of helping to manage the changes now taking place along lines more consonant with the Gospel.[2]

We may now state succinctly the task for theology in Asia. First, there is the conviction that we should not simply operate with the theological presuppositions which have arisen and still are operative in the West, but rather develop our own theological framework which will take into account "the varieties and dynamics of Asian realities." Second, if theology in Asia is indeed to be Asian, and not simply a revamped version of a theology from elsewhere, it must relate the gospel in its redemptive and judgmental power to the particular Asian realities of our time. It is only when we take these two factors into account that we will be able to come up with a theological framework or model which will be ecumenically valid for Asia as a whole without abdicating the necessity of being relevant in particular local situations. We will, therefore, begin by focusing upon the issues emerging from a local situation, in this case Sri Lanka, and then come to the question of a framework for doing theology in Asia.

II

Asia as a whole is a complex phenomenon. Some of the major historical factors which contribute to the complexity are: (a) the resurgence of religious culture in Asia; (b) the struggle of the Asian peoples for a new life which often has to contend with racial discrimination and various forms of oppression; (c) the challenges posed by Marxism and other secular ideologies; (d) the tremendous pressures of scientific and technological development which influence all the factors noted above; and (e) the increasingly authoritarian governments in Asian countries and the limitations of liberties. Admittedly, the Christian response to these trends should be and indeed is being articulated for the Asian context as a whole because these factors in varying degrees are present in each national or local situation. However, the issues for theology in any local situation are not posed by these factors in isolation. In each local situation, these factors interpenetrate and combine to form a distinct entity. It is out of such a situation that the issues for theology emerge. Hence, a model for doing theology must help us to understand and deal with issues in their particularity and reality. A general theological response to the trends noted above is not sufficient. In other words, we have to proceed toward the development of a model for "doing" theology in Asia from the base of our experience in local situations.

Let us look at some of the theological issues emerging from Sri Lanka. Last year a bill proposing the organic union of the major Protestant churches in Sri Lanka was presented in the National State Assembly. The bill was challenged in the constitutional court as embodying elements which are contrary to the constitution of Sri Lanka. The challenge was upheld, and thirty years of painstaking theological discussion and careful negotiation came to nothing. The Scheme of Union in essence was a simple one. Denominational churches preserving a Western historical identity are an anachronism in Sri Lanka. Furthermore, a divided church cannot be effective in its mission. The Scheme of Union was intended, on the one hand, to bring together the best in all these traditions and, on the other, to engage in the task of mission as one church. There have been varying reactions to this failure, but let me single out one particular reaction. In conversation with one of my friends I expressed my personal disappointment. His comment was, "We have enough problems with the church structures we have. Why now ask for a superstructure?" His comment is indicative of a feeling among some younger Christians that the church as it is in Sri Lanka is more concerned to preserve its past identity, with its inherited Western baggage, and less concerned with understanding the historical realities in Sri Lanka and relating the gospel to these realities. For him and many like him, church union was simply another effort to hang on to the past rather than to seek the relevance of the church in the present. The failure to achieve union, instead of being understood as a setback, was to be construed more positively as an opportunity to break away from the past. The church in Sri Lanka must seek to divest itself of this past and the problem of division, which is Western in origin, and incarnate itself in the present so that it begins to discern the ways in which the Kingdom of God is breaking into the situations in Sri Lanka with its message of judgment as well as hope.

One may dismiss this opinion simply as a quaint minority viewpoint except for the fact that it represents those groups in Sri Lanka who have freed themselves from the institutions and structures of the churches and have moved, so to speak, into the frontiers of mission. Among these there is a greater awareness of the fact that the sphere of God's activity is the world and not just the church. This awareness has been engendered by the new political and social trends in Sri Lanka, which stress the necessity for social justice and freedom from want. There are ambiguities and contradictions within the political and social movements themselves, for they are also creating new forms of oppression and discrimination. It is these areas of oppression and discrimination that these frontier groups recognize to be the proper context for mission. Some have chosen to work among city workers and trade unions, others with the exploited coolie labor on the estates, or the low caste people in the north of Sri Lanka, and some others with youth in rural community farms. In all these cases, it has been an adventure in faith, "the Abrahamic model" as some have chosen to call it. In doing so, none of these people felt that they were the bearers of a special message of salvation. Rather, they moved into critical situations where they saw oppression or discrimination, or into situations where people had lost hope in the confidence that God in Jesus Christ would meet them in those situations in the midst of their struggles. Because they moved into those situations and settled there, they became the church in that situation, entrusted with the task of witnessing to the presence of Jesus Christ in that situation as both redeemer and judge. Several insights have emerged from these groups, of which three are particularly important for our discussion.

First, persons who are involved in proclaiming the Good News about Jesus Christ in these situations increasingly find that a mere verbal communication of the gospel is not sufficient. They find that they often have to question, change, and restructure existing social mores and conditions if the gospel of liberation is indeed to become a reality and a means of hope. For those engaged in this ministry, evangelism, the proclamation of the Good News, is an *activity* which is concerned with creating situations where the Good News can happen. On the one hand, this means to identify and articulate the signs of new hope and, on the other, to resist the factors which tend to frustrate or deny the realization of hope. The second insight, which is a corollary of the first, is that the task of mission is not simply to indigenize the gospel, that is, to make native to a situation that which is essentially foreign to it. Rather, it is to recognize that God in Jesus Christ is meeting these people through the thought-forms and liturgical symbols which communicate the hopes, aspirations, and fears of these people. As a consequence of the two factors, there is the recognition of a discontinuity between the present situation and the past religious traditions found in other religions as well as in the Bible and church history.

In the light of these issues we will attempt to construct a framework for "doing" theology in Asia. To do this we will examine the biblical traditions, and in particular the way in which Second Isaiah handles them, for in addressing his message of hope to a people in bondage he employs a method which may provide us with a model for doing theology in Asia today. Before we do this, however, we have to clarify the presuppositions with which we as Asians approach the Bible.

While we speak of the redeeming and judging activity of God in Jesus Christ in the present, we have to recognize the fact that the primary and sole witness to what God has done in Jesus Christ is enshrined in the biblical witness. However, since the Bible is basically confessional material which reflects the faith and belief of a particular people at a given time, it is not possible to state that the

271

Bible has the unchanging nucleus of belief and practice which is valid for Christians and others at all times and in all places.[3] Hence, we are presented with the problem of re-understanding the lines of continuity and discontinuity between the Bible and the present situation. For us in Asia, the problem centers on our understanding of the status of Israel whether it be the Israel of the Old Testament or the Church as the New Israel. The question arises as to what is the entity in Asia which is coterminous with the Israel of the Bible. *One approach* would be to see the church, the new Israel, as the entity so addressed. God's message of salvation would then be addressed primarily to the church; and others would share in it in so far as they confess, "God is with you only." While such an approach would enable us to see our situation in a theological line of continuity with Israel, it is precisely this approach which is under fire in Asia. If the God declared to us in Jesus Christ is the Creator-God, the God who is graciously concerned with the whole world and its peoples, such a reduction of his salvific concern to Israel as *the* people of God would be unacceptable. In terms of mission, the basic mistake here is pointed out by the wry comment of Sarvapalli Radhakrishnan, "You Christians are very ordinary people trying to make extraordinary claims!"

A *second approach* would be to see the poor and the suffering as the New Israel, for in the Bible these are the special concern of God. This tendency is particularly evident in Liberation Theology. While it is true that the God of the Bible does declare himself to be on the side of the poor and the oppressed and against the oppressor and that this concern becomes a revolutionary impetus in human history, we should not make a different kind of reduction on that score and speak of another group of people as the New Israel. As many have observed, there is nothing as frightening as the new forms of oppression which the newly liberated can manifest! Any revolutionary movement contains within it possibilities of death as well as of hope and new life. To reduce the concern of the God of the Bible to any one group of people in this way would again present us with the problem of exclusivism which seems to be endemic to the term "Israel" as we use it now. As G. Ernest Wright so properly warns us, we cannot claim for any group the exclusivism which belongs to God alone.[4] And if we learn our lesson rightly from the experience of the old Israel, while God did deliver her from bondage in Egypt, he was also on that score equally harsh with Israel's arrogance (cf. Am. 3:2).

A *third approach* which is emerging in Asia is that God is concerned with the whole people of Asia which is a part of his universal concern for all mankind and that this concern is expressed directly and immediately. We will examine briefly the theological undergirding for this approach. Although there are glimpses in the Old Testament of God's redemptive concern for other people which is not mediated through Israel (e.g. Amos 9:7), the basic thrust of "the missionary message" of the Old Testament is that other nations will share in Yahweh's salvation when they come into Israel (cf. Is. 2:1; 45:14-15). In the New Testament, as Johannes Blauw observes, the missionary movement is outward from Israel to other nations; and this emphasis he sees worked out particularly in Paul's apostleship.[5] While this is true, a recognition of this fact alone does not do justice to the New Testament message. For in moving out among other nations, the new Israel has in fact created pockets of "chosen people" who keep inviting others to join them. The radical nature of the new reality introduced into history in Jesus Christ becomes evident when we turn to the events recorded in Acts 10:1-11:10. First, Peter is forbidden from making his own prejudices the basis for relating to God's creation. Later in his encounter with Cornelius, he is led to the conviction that God's redemptive concern for others is not mediated through the church, but is immediate and operative within their own realities. It is the recognition of this fact which astounds the early church, "So for the Gentiles also!" What is revolutionary is not the fact that the nations could share in God's salvation, for this was always possible by establishing their continuity with Israel. Rather, it is the fact that God's redemptive concern can become operative among other nations within the realities of their own situations. But having made this point, we also have to make a distinction between God's redemptive concern for Israel, which is but a part of his larger concern, and his call to Israel to be the witnesses to his creative and redemptive activity in history. This is a special task to which the church is called. Unfortunately, the identity of the church as it is manifested in Asia is made known less in the performance of this task and more in making exclusive claims for itself.

Before setting out our own proposal for a framework for doing theology in Asia, we should examine a proposal made by C. S. Song for such a model. An examination of his model will help us to clarify the issues for our proposal. In his several writings, Choan-seng Song makes a perceptive analysis of the changing situation for mission in Asia.[6]   He stresses the fact that a particular era for mission is over.   This change, he observes, permits us to look at the task of mission in Asia through Asian eyes; and he goes on to suggest several theological motifs which will be helpful in reconstructing the task of mission.   Although in the course of this discussion I will have occasion to disagree with some of his conclusions, I should also state that many of his insights have been seminal in my thinking.

For Song, the significance of the changing missionary situation in Asia is not that Western missionaries are being withdrawn to be replaced by Asian missionaries, but that a particular era is over and that with its end has come a recognition of a decisive break with the past.   He states that in Asia:

> We have experienced two radical breaks in historical continuity: the breakdown of the effort on the part of the Western churches to incorporate the masses of humanity in Asia into "salvation history" as they saw it; and the resolute rejection of Christianity by China, which has become a communist state.

He understands such discontinuities not simply as historical accidents but as endemic to the very nature of God's activity in history.

> History in the Bible derives its meaning from God's redemptive acts.   Events and experiences taken into the orbit of redemption interrupt the normal course of history.   They become the bearers of a meaning which anticipates fulfillment in the future.   Redemption is the power which enables us to leap into the future and frees us from slavery to the sinful past and from an absurd fate.[8]

He uses the idea of discontinuity to argue that Asian religions and historical traditions could be seen alongside those of Israel so that these too may be interpreted as valid salvation histories; and he rejects the assumption that salvation comes to Asia only in so far as it agrees to fall in with one particular stream of salvation history. In order to make this point he appeals to Creation as the theological framework within which redemption is to be understood, and denies the connection usually advocated in theology between election and redemption.   He states that it is only when we see that "the experience of redemption is an experience ultimately related to the experience of creation" that we will be able to liberate ourselves from the religious isolationism and spiritual provincialism which have been engendered by the old missionary consciousness.   For, Israel's creation story, he asserts, speaks of Yahweh not simply as the redeemer of Israel but as the Creator of the world.   Thus, in the context of Creation other religions and cultures can also be viewed as manifestations of the creative activity of God.[9]

More specifically, Song is interested in the theological significance of the New China for world history, since he sees the New

China as presenting a viable alternative to the gospel of salvation developed in Western Christendom.

Just as the Western nations, under the profound influence of the spirit of the Christian Bible, have set the norms of values and consciousness for the Western world and even beyond, here is now the New China which seems to have every potentiality of radically changing the course of history for future centuries.[10]

This is a commendable shift of emphasis, for it attempts to take seriously for theology an Asian historical reality. However, it is questionable whether a "salvation history" model, even if it be an Asian salvation history, is the most suitable theological framework within which we should perceive the theological significance of Asian historical realities, because to juxtapose salvation history and an Asian history is to give theological weightage to the former. For instance, he elicits the theological significance of the Long March in terms of the "symbolic significance" of the exodus. In arguing against Oscar Cullmann's view of salvation history, Song asks,

Is the salvation history intensely exhibited or demonstrated in both the Old and the New Testaments to be looked upon as the absolute norm by which events in secular world history get chosen arbitrarily to be incorporated into God's salvation history in Christ, OR, is it to be regarded as a pattern or a type of God's salvation manifested in a massively concentrated way in ancient Israel and in the history of the church and therefore to be discovered in varied degrees of intensity and concentration in other nations and peoples also?[11]

In preferring the second approach, Song still makes an understanding of Israel's salvation history normative for an understanding of Asian history. If indeed the theme of creation permits us to see other histories also as manifesting the creative activity of God, we must then allow them to speak on their own terms.

The difficulties inherent in taking a salvation history approach may be shown by examining Song's methodological discussion.

In the light of the experiences unique to Israel, other nations should learn how their histories can be interpreted redemptively. An Asian nation would have its own experiences of exodus, captivity, rebellion against Heaven, the golden calf. It would have its own long trek in the desert of poverty or dehumanization. *What a nation goes through begins to take on redemptive meaning against the background of the history of Israel,* symbolically transported out of its original context to a foreign one. An Asian nation will thus be enabled to find its place side by side with Israel in God's salvation.[12]

While the suggestion is attractive, it also poses a problem. Here are we not going back to an old method in a new form? The old method was to declare that what is potentially good and redemptive in any culture or history becomes in fact so only when it is appropriated into a Christian viewpoint. Thus, for instance, J. N. Farquhar in his book, *The Crown of Hinduism,* develops the thesis, "if

Christ is able to satisfy all the religious needs of the human heart, then all the elements of pagan religions, since they spring from these needs, will be found reproduced in perfect form, completely fulfilled, consummated in Christ." So too Raymond Panikkar in his book, *The Unknown Christ of Hinduism*, sees Christian theological motifs foreshadowed in Hinduism, and asserts that Christianity is Hinduism which has died and risen again transformed.[13] While this method may be of some value in trying to describe the similarities and dissimilarities between the Judeo-Christian religious tradition and other religions, as a theological approach it savors of spiritual imperialism. In fact, when the figure of Jesus Christ and his teachings were appropriated into other faith structures, the tendency has been to find a place for the gospel in these faith traditions with the required accommodations rather than to radically change the traditions themselves so that they may be accommodated within a Christian faith structure.[14] Song's approach, which tends to operate in the area of history rather than religious faith, will also be found unacceptable, for he makes "the experiences unique to Israel" normative for interpreting other historical traditions. This method has a further shortcoming in that it was designed to answer not the question we are facing but a different question, namely, how do we understand *historically* other cultures and histories as manifesting the activity of the God who revealed himself in Jesus Christ? Song himself poses the question we are facing, in excellent fashion:

It is of paramount importance to know how other people can see and experience redemption and hope in the sufferings which descend on them with cruel consistency. They want to know how the chains of suffering can be broken, and to experience salvation in the present and the future. It is to these people that Asian Christians must address themselves, sharing their longing for liberation.[15]

More briefly, the question is, "How do we speak theologically to and within the context of Asian suffering and hope?" From the standpoint of this question, the model Song proposes is too restrictive, because an Israelite salvation history model will do violence to what is unique or particular to Asian traditions by only picking up motifs which could be handled properly within it. To put it differently, while we may find some experiences reflected in Asian histories and religious traditions which are parallel to those in Israel, we will also find elements present in Asian traditions which are not found in those of Israel. Some of these elements may be of significance in our theological understanding of the present Asian situations, so

276

that a method which is not essentially open to this possibility will h
serious drawbacks.

Let us highlight in summary form the breakthrough which Song's thinking represents, and indicate the way in which we will want to build on his insights. *First,* he makes the valid point that we cannot do justice in our theological thinking to the new historical realities in Asia unless we take into account the break with earlier ideas about salvation history which have been implicit in the old missionary enterprise. *Second,* he legitimately attacks the triumphalistic claims made by the church: "the theology which regards Israel and the Christian Church as the only bearers and dispensers of God's saving love must be called into question."[16] In order to break out of this trap, he suggests that redemption should not be institutionalized within a framework of election theology, but should be seen against the background of Creation. While agreeing with this point, we should also move on to a reappraisal of the motif of election which would be valid in Asia today. *Third,* he argues that other religious and historical traditions should be understood more positively and not dismissed as theologically of no consequence by looking at them from a Christian salvation history standpoint. If we attempt to see these religious cultures from the standpoint of creation, we will then understand these also as reflections of the redeeming activity of the One who is Lord of creation. While agreeing with this emphasis, we find that the theological framework Song uses to interpret these traditions is basically restrictive, because the Israelite salvation history model implies a certain principle of selection which will not allow these traditions to speak for themselves on their own terms. In the next section we will attempt to develop a theological framework which will allow such openness. To do this, we too will begin with a discussion of the motif of Creation, as found particularly in Second Isaiah, but push beyond Song's own assessment of this motif.

IV

Let us begin our discussion of the framework for "doing" theology in Asia by examining Song's thesis that "it is only when we see the experience of redemption as ultimately related to the experience of creation" that we will be able to understand that the God who acted in Israel's redemption also acts in the redemption of other peoples. He sees reflected in Second Isaiah's theology Israel's recognition of herself as a part of a larger *oikoumene* of God's redemptive concern. Israel recognized this truth when she lived in the midst of another nation in exile. Under the influence of this context, Song argues, Second Isaiah read back into Creation a theology of redemption, so that Israel's redemption is to be seen alongside the redemption of other peoples.

There are two issues implicit in Song's evaluation of the theme of Creation. *First,* Creation is the backdrop against which Israel's salvation history and that of other nations is to be understood. He who cares for Israel cares also for other nations. This insight into God's providence, which is concerned with creation as a whole, is found in Ps. 104, for instance, which speaks of the providential care of the Creator-God for his whole creation. *Second,* there is the assumption that a theological evaluation of the motif of Creation is possible only from the standpoint of an understanding of redemption, in which case, Creation would be no more than an extrapolation on a larger scale of Israel's understanding of history. Thus, Creation will remain at best a sum total of all histories and not a theological motif in its own right.

The thesis implied in Song's thinking that Creation is ancillary to redemption is expressed particularly by the Old Testament theologian Gerhard von Rad, who states,

> ...in genuinely Yahwistic belief the doctrine of creation never attained to the stature of a relevant, independent doctrine. It is invariably related, and indeed subordinated to, soteriological considerations.[17]

And with particular reference to Second Isaiah, he declares,

> ...at no point in the whole of *Second Isaiah* does the doctrine of creation appear in its own right; it never forms the main theme of a pronouncement, nor provides the motive of a prophetic utterance.[18]

Von Rad's thesis needs to be examined critically, especially since he begins his investigation of the motif of Creation with the assumption that "The Yahwistic faith of the Old Testament is a faith based on the notion of election and therefore primarily concerned with redemption."[19] Given this procedural starting point, which dictates that other motifs be understood in relation to redemption, it is not surprising that he should come to the conclusion that Creation is always to be seen as ancillary to redemption. However, his general thesis concerning the relationship between redemption and Creation has been challenged.[20] To be sure, Israel moved toward a full-blown articulation of her Creation faith through the experience of Yahweh's covenant presence with her. However, when she came to speak of Creation in this way—and here we have in mind the priestly creation story—it was not simply an insight into how God deals with other nations. Neither was it simply the opening act in the drama of redemption. Rather, it stands on its own as the supreme declaration about the God who can realize his purpose ("and God said let there be...") into ordered reality ("and thus it was"). After a careful study of the Priestly creation story, in which he takes into consideration the inter-relationship between its structure and content as well as its relationship to the Pentateuch as a whole, Bernhard Anderson concludes:

The creation story is the preface to the primeval history. It sets the stage, and provides the theological and anthropological presuppositions, for the ensuing story (world history, patriarchal history, folk history) which, in its received edition, comes from the hand of the Priestly Writer/Editor. In the Priestly presentation, then, creation is not the beginning of history. It is proto-historical, for it lies in the realm of the mystery which belongs properly and exclusively to God.... Thus the Pentateuchal story of redemption, in which Israel has a special role, is grounded in the prior affirmation of faith that God is the Creator.[21]

We may reasonably expect to find the same theological emphasis, namely, the grounding of redemption in Creation faith, also in Second Isaiah who was an approximate contemporary of the Priestly writer. Such expectation is enhanced by two further observations. *First,* Second Isaiah announces in a prologue (40:1-11) the decisions taken in the heavenly council of Yahweh. Israel is comforted with the words that she has paid doubly for all her sins and that Yahweh is about to redeem her from her present bondage. But, having made this preparatory opening statement, Second Isaiah begins his message of hope with a long poem celebrating Yahweh as Creator (40:12-31). It is particularly noteworthy that there are no references in this poem to the theme of redemption. Furthermore, Israel's cry of dereliction, "My way is hid from Yahweh, and my right is disregarded by my God," is met with the response, "Have you not known? Have you not heard? Yahweh is the Everlasting God, the Creator of the ends of the earth." In fact, the poem asserts that it is because Yahweh is Creator that one can indeed hope in him (40:28-31). *Second,* we do not find in Second Isaiah the self-presentation formula, "I am Yahweh who brought you out of the land of Egypt from the house of bondage," which is found so often in the Pentateuchal redemption story (e.g. Ex. 20:2; Dt. 4:20; 6:12; Joshua 24:6; etc.) and in pre-exilic prophecy (e.g. Amos 3:2). Instead we find the formulation, "I am the first (*ri son*) and I am the last (*ah ron*); besides me there is no god" (44:6bb; 41:4; 48:12). As scholars have observed, this formulation attests to the faith in Yahweh as the Creator who can declare ahead what he proposes to do and bring to fulfillment his stated purpose (44:7; 26f; 46:9b-10).[22]

The relationship which exists in Second Isaiah's thought between Creation faith and redemption may be seen in the way he uses the exodus motif.[23] The exodus motif like the Creation motif occurs many times in Second Isaiah, for he is, above all, a poet who uses metaphors drawn from almost all of Israel's traditions and then merges and blends them with kaleidoscopic effect in his message. It is therefore difficult to come to a correct assessment of the function of any one motif in his thought by simply collating these images and then evaluating them. Rather, we should concentrate on extended statements where any one motif predominates. Three passages—43:14-21, 48:3-8, and 46:8-11—are particularly important for our understanding of the way in which the exodus motif functions in Second Isaiah. In 43:14-21, he introduces Yahweh as the One:

> ...who makes a way in the sea,
> a path in the mighty waters,
> who brings forth chariot and horse,
>   army and warrior,
> they lie down, they cannot rise,
> they are extinguished, quenched like a wick.

Having made this explicit reference to the exodus, Yahweh then requests Israel to forget that past event:

> Remember not the former things,
>   nor consider the things of old.
> Behold, I am doing a new thing;
>   now it springs forth, do you not perceive it?
> I will make a way in the wilderness
>   and rivers in the desert.

Second Isaiah quite clearly perceives a discontinuity between the past salvation history of Israel, which began with the exodus, and the new event which Yahweh is about to perform. We may understand better the nature of this discontinuity by examining briefly the message of the pre-exilic prophets. Although Amos and Hosea hold open the possibility that Israel may repent and thus preserve the covenant relationship with Yahweh, they see the present trend as heading toward total disaster for Israel. Thus, for Amos, the imminent fall of Samaria would mark the end of Israel's salvation history which began with the exodus.

> Hear this word that Yahweh has spoken against you, O people of Israel, against the whole family which I brought up out of the land of Egypt:
> You only have I known of all the families of the earth; therefore I will punish you for all your iniquities (Amos 3:1f.)

And for Hosea it would be the end of the covenant relationship when Israel is called "not my people" (*lo-ammi*) and "those with whom Yahweh will not maintain covenant mercy" (*lo-ruhammi*) (Hos. 2:6, 8). For Jeremiah and Ezekiel, too, the exile marks the decisive end of Yahweh's covenant presence with Israel, so that the former could understand a future restoration as possible only through the gracious act of Yahweh who will institute a *new* covenant with Israel (Jer. 34:31f.), and the latter perceives it as no less than a resurrection-event when the creative spirit of Yahweh will bring Israel back to new life (Ez. 37). Against the background of this prophetic preaching, we can perceive why Second Isaiah also sees a discontinuity between the past salvation history of Israel and the new event which Yahweh is about to perform. How then do we account for the pervasive use of the exodus motif in Second Isaiah's message in general, and in particular (46:8), where he seems to contradict himself by saying "Remember the former things?"

> Remember this and consider,
>> recall it to mind, you transgressors,
>> remember the former things of old;
> for I am God, and there is no other;
>> I am God, and there is none like me,
> declaring the end (*ah rit*) from the beginning (*mere sit*)
>> and from ancient times things not yet done,
> saying, "My counsel shall stand,
>> and I will accompl'sh all my purpose,"
> calling a bird of prey from the east,
>> the man of my counsel from a far country.
> I have spoken and I will bring it to pass;
>> I have spoken and I will do it.

The three participial clauses introduced by "declaring," "saying," and "calling" give content to the assertion, "I am God and there is none like me"; and the unit 9b-11a, introduced by *for* (*ki*) forms the basis for requesting Israel not to forget the former things. He who "from the beginning" (*meros*) and "from the foundations of the earth" (*mos dot ha ares*) created the world and its inhabitants (Is. 40:21f) is the One who declares the outcome of an event from its inception and accomplishes what he has intended. For Second Isaiah, this ability of Yahweh to act with absolute freedom was demonstrated pre-eminently in creation (46:10). And this ability is to be demonstrated in his power to summon Cyrus and accomplish the future deliverance of Israel through him (46:11).[24] In this context, the old exodus serves as a powerful reminder of the fact that Yahweh is the Creator-God who will accomplish what he has purposed. Is. 48:3-5 also confirms the correctness of our conclusion that for Second Isaiah the exodus motif functions to remind Israel that it is Yahweh alone who, in his sovereign freedom as Creator, can accomplish what he intends.

> The former things I declared of old,
> they went forth from my mouth and I made them known;
> then suddenly I did them and they came to pass.
> Because I know that you are obstinate,
> and your neck is an iron sinew and your forehead brass,
> I declared them to you from of old,
> before they came to pass I announced them to you,
> lest you should say, "My idol did them,
> my graven image and my molten image commanded them."

Thus, in Second Isaiah's thought, the motif of the exodus and the deliverance from Egypt serve to demonstrate Yahweh's ability as Creator to bring to fulfillment what he has promised. (See also the viewpoint of the contemporary Priestly Writer who considers the deliverance from Egypt as the fulfilment of the promise to the patriarch, Ex. 6:2-8; cf. Gen. 17:1-8). This truth remains although the particular history of Israel with Yahweh, which the exodus from Egypt initiated, has ended.

The motif of Creation, therefore, as Second Isaiah interprets it, is more than a backdrop against which the redemption of other peoples is to be understood. It has a more positive function. Creation faith affirms the absolute freedom of the Creator-God to do "the new thing" in history. In the Asian situation, the motif of Creation will provide us with the theological framework for confessing that in Asia God is realizing in a new way the promise of salvation given in Jesus Christ for all mankind. This task becomes all the more imperative in view of C. S. Song's observation that a particular era of Christian salvation history has ended; and we have to discover in a new way the significance of the redemption performed by God in Jesus Christ in 30 A.D. for Asia today. Furthermore, only the affirmation of God as Creator, who is doing "the new thing" in Asia, will give us the theological motivation for discerning the signs of hope in the emerging new historical realities in Asia, and to point to those signs in spite of their ambiguity.

Second Isaiah, in addressing his message of hope to Israel, uses a method which attempts to do justice to the radically new thing which Yahweh is about to do. In so doing, he introduces a theological break between the new event and Israel's past salvation history. However, in articulating the new thing that Yahweh is about to do, he does not ignore the past traditions of Israel, but *reinterprets* them so that they speak to the new situation. As scholars have observed, Second Isaiah uses the past traditions of Israel freely and creatively, emphasizing some (exodus, patriarchal traditions) and ignoring others (e.g. Sinai); combining originally distinct traditions (exodus and Creation), and reinterpreting traditions which are in danger of becoming extinct (the promise to David).[25] In so doing the old informs the new and the new illumines the old. May we not have here a model for "doing" theology which may be meaningfully appropriated in the Asian context? It would help us to see the relationship with the past not just negatively but also positively so that we may speak theologically of the creative activity of God within Asian historical realities. It would also help us to go back to our past traditions, both Christian and those of other faiths, and reinterpret them so that they speak meaningfully to the present. Here we must recognize the role that our Asian spiritual and historical traditions can play because these express the experiences of our people, both their hopes and their fears. Therefore, this is not a task which we as Christians should undertake alone, but it has to be a shared responsibility. Only then will we understand the manifold ways in which God is realizing in the Asian situation his promise of salvation for all mankind declared in Jesus Christ.

We have seen that Creation faith will enable us to ground our hope in him who is able to do the suprisingly new thing in history. From this perspective we can also undertake the task which lies before us, namely, to understand theologically the break with the salvation history of the past, implicitly in the old missionary enterprise, and yet reappropriate in a more meaningful way for our situation the significance of what God has done in Jesus Christ. If it is important to ground our hope in the Creator-God, it is equally important to ground our suffering in the pathos of the Creator-God. Let us first look at the issue which makes this necessary and then go on to a discussion of what we mean by the pathos of the Creator-God.

In his essay, *The Crucified God,* Jurgen Moltmann warns us of the dangers inherent in any kind of "God who acts in history" theology. We should heed his warning, because our approach to theology also falls within this category. He observes that both the individualist who strives for personal achievement and the revolutionary who attempts to bring in a new social order are success-oriented. Both negate suffering. For the former, suffering is an admission of failure, and those who suffer are marginalized. He even refuses to recognize the suffering which his own actions bring on others.

For the latter, suffering is directly attributable to an unfair system which has to be overthrown. Both consider God to be on their side, either blessing the enterprising man with success or expressing his wrath with the revolutionary. For both, God's way of negating suffering on the Cross is either to be domesticated within their respective viewpoints or discarded altogether.[26] Coming as we do from the context of Asian suffering with the conviction that the present system is intolerable and has to be negated, it is ever so easy to create our own god of success out of our drive for "a new order of things." Admittedly, suffering has to be negated and the present order changed if indeed hope and justice are to be realized. But unless we take seriously God's way of negating suffering, we will only be bringing in through the back door another form of the triumphalism which contributed in no small measure to the failure of the earlier Christian salvation history viewpoint. God's way of negating suffering is declared on the Cross; and it stands as an invitation to us. In the words of Paul,

Have this mind among yourselves, which you have in Christ Jesus, who, though he was in the form of God, did not count equality with God a thing to be grasped, but emptied himself, taking the form of a slave, being born in the likeness of men. And being found in human form he humbled himself and became obedient unto death, even death on the cross. (Phil. 2:5-8)

God negates suffering by himself becoming God-abandoned, oppressed man. Therefore, if we are to understand the Asian situation of suffering theologically, we must see it within the context of God's suffering love.

In terms of the biblical witness this emphasis is not found primarily in the exodus tradition, which we liberation theologians tend to seize on and appropriate into our context. Rather, it is found in the witness of the prophets to Yahweh who, as the Jewish theologian Abraham Heschel points out, did not have so much a new idea about God as a new grasp of the dimension of God's suffering or pathos.[27] God gets caught, so to speak, between the cross-fire of his demand for justice and his love for disobedient Israel. Thus, Amos pleads with Yahweh to hold back his wrath for Israel, for Israel is so small and cannot endure his judgment. Surprisingly, Yahweh hears him and changes his mind till such time as the demand for justice had to be inevitably expressed (Amos. 7:1-9). Hosea sees this debate within God himself, so that it becomes an expression of the pain of God.

How can I give you up, O Ephraim!
How can I hand you over, O Israel!
How can I treat you like Zeboim!
My heart recoils within me,
    my compassion grows warm and tender.
I will not execute my fierce anger
I will not again destroy Ephraim;
for I am God and not man,
    the Holy one in your midst,
    and I will not come to destroy.   (Hos. 11:8-9)

Jeremiah experiences in his own ministry the suffering love of God, though he himself does not quite understand it, and pours out his agony in his confessions.   But an understanding of God's suffering begins to emerge in a crucial passage which ends Baruch's story of Jeremiah's ministry.   In this oracle Baruch asks for the confirmation of his own success and is met with a response which speaks of the divine agony.

Thus says Yahweh,
    Behold, what I have built I am breaking down,
        what I have planted I am plucking up.
    And do you seek great things for yourself?
    Seek them not...but I will give you your life
        as a prize of war.... (Jer. 45:4f.)

Thus, within the prophetic consciousness there begins to emerge the realization of God's own suffering caused by the divine demand for justice, on the one hand, and, on the other, the love of God for his people.   Furthermore, they perceived, however dimly, that they had come to share in this divine suffering in their own ministry.

Second Isaiah more than any other prophet begins to deal theologically with the pathos of God.   On the one hand, God's pathos or his empathy with man is expressed in Creation faith.   He who created the world and ordered it with his justice actively cares for man in his smallness (40:12-31).   It is the Creator-God who is the basis of hope for the fainting and the weary (40:28-31).   This concern is to be manifested concretely in the future event of deliverance through Cyrus.   On the other hand, God's pathos finds immediate expression in Israel's ministry, when she is called to perform the task to which she has been elected, namely, to witness to Yahweh (43:10; 44:8).[28]   This ministry of Israel finds supreme expression in the figure of the "suffering servant"[29] who incarnates in his own suffering the pathos of God.   Since Jesus himself understood his own ministry in the light of the ministry of the suffering servant (e.g. Mk. 10:45) and passed on that ministry to his followers, let us examine the emphases which emerge in Israel's call to witness to Yahweh's creating and redeeming activity in history and see how these are interpreted in the ministry of the suffering servant.

For Second Isaiah the affirmation of Yahweh as Creator means not only that he can do the radically new thing in history, but that he is also judge. Although Israel's deliverance is not yet a present reality but a future hope, the gods who hold the people in bondage are brought to judgment. Yahweh challenges these gods in a lawsuit and strips away their claims. They are declared powerless because they have neither the insight nor the power to discern the past or to speak meaningfully of the future.

> Set forth your case, says Yahweh;
> bring your proofs, says the King of Jacob;
> Let them bring them, and tell us what is to happen.
> Tell us the former things, what they are,
> that we may consider them,
> that we may know their outcome;
> or declare to us the things to come.
> Tell us what is to come hereafter,
> that we may know that you are gods;
> Do good, or do harm, that we may be dismayed and
> terrified.
> Behold, you are nothing, and your work is naught;
> an abomination is he who chooses you. (41:21-24)

This pronouncement is made at a time when those in bondage are actually experiencing the terrible might and power of these gods. Yet, this pronouncement is not, so to speak, left on the sidelines till the future event of deliverance is accomplished. No, it has to be proclaimed now. The peoples who have either chosen to serve these gods or have simply succumbed to their power cannot speak. Israel, in spite of her own weakness, is called to declare that Yahweh alone is able to bring to fruition what he has promised and thus, by implication, these gods are transitory.

> Let all the nations gather together,
> and let the people assemble.
> Who among them can declare this,
> and show us the former things?
> Let them bring their witnesses to justify them,
> and let them hear and say, It is true.
> "You are my witnesses," says Yahweh,
> and my servant whom I have chosen,
> that you may know and believe me and understand
> that I am he." (43:9-10; cf. 44:8)

This is also our mission. We in Asia know how dangerous such witnessing is, for many of our brothers have been incarcerated in prisons and tortured for doing just that.

286

There is a second aspect to Israel's task of witnessing, which is more in the nature of a ministry.

> I am Yahweh, I have called you in righteousness,
> I have taken you by the hand and kept you;
> I have given you as a covenant to the people,
>> a light to the nations,
>> to open the eyes that are blind,
> to bring out the prisoners from the dungeon,
>> from the prison those who sit in darkness. (42:6-7)

This is a more subdued but necessary ministry: to share in the suffering of the marginalized and dispossessed, and to work toward the creation of situations within which justice can be actualized and hope can indeed become a reality.

To interpret election in this way as a task to witness to God's justice in Asia will invariably involve us in situations of suffering. To quote in modified form a saying of Mao Tse-tung, "Our oppressors are paper tigers. When the rains come they will be washed away. But make no mistake about the fact that they can bite!" But such suffering as it is interpreted in the Servant poems is no longer a personal protest against suffering, but is willingly endured, for the Servant shares in the suffering love of God himself. Yahweh has put his spirit upon him (42:1). Thus, while Israel is prone to despair (40:27; 48:14), the Servant remains undiscouraged (42:4; 50:7-9). Israel is inattentive and rebellious (42:18-25), but the Servant is attentive and suffers patiently (50:4-6; 53:7-9). Hence the Servant who is given as a covenant to the nations (49:6) performs his task in a self-effacing way.

> Behold my servant, whom I uphold,
>> my chosen, in whom my soul delights;
> I have put my spirit upon him,
>> he will bring forth justice to the nations.
> He will not cry or lift up his voice,
>> or make it heard in the street;
> a bruised reed he will not break,
>> and a dimly burning wick he will not quench;
> he will faithfully bring forth justice.
> He will not fail or be discouraged
>> till he has established justice in the earth;
>> and the coastlands wait for his law. (42:1-4)

The Servant who is called to witness to Yahweh is marred and broken, so that his mission seems hopeless and he himself is an object of ridicule (53:2f). But he persists in the confidence that Yahweh will vindicate him (50:8f.; 52:13015). Because the Servant is not anxious on his own account (53:7-9) and manifests this fact in his ministry, others recognize that it is for their sakes that he suffers: "Surely he has borne our griefs and carried our sorrows; yet we esteemed him stricken, smitten by God, and afflicted" (53:4; cf. v. 10). In the situation of Asian suffering and hope, we are called upon to see our participation as no less an undertaking than to share in God's suffering love for his creation. Only in this way can we, on the one hand, avoid a triumphalistic stance which draws attention to ourselves and, on the other, persist in our task as witnesses to what God in Jesus Christ is doing in Asia today.

In summary, we have attempted to see the task for theology in Asia from an Asian standpoint. In doing this we have kept as our focus the task of witnessing to Jesus Christ in Asian suffering and hope; for it is our conviction that it is only in addressing ourselves to this problem that a valid and relevant Asian theology will emerge. Having taken into account the issues emerging from a local situation, where groups of people are witnessing in a new way to the presence of Jesus Christ in Asian situations of suffering and hope, we have sketched in the last part of our discussion a framework for doing theology in Asia. Here we have given priority to the motif of Creation which permits us to perceive and articulate the activity of the Creator-God in our midst who is realizing in a new way the promise of salvation given in Jesus Christ. As yet, the signs of hope which point to this activity are hazy and perhaps ambiguous. But it is only on the basis of our confidence in the Creator-God that we can perform our task. On the one hand, this task means to proclaim the transitoriness and worthlessness of the gods of our oppression, at a time when Asians do experience their power over them, and to work toward the creation of situations where hope can indeed become a reality. Furthermore, this task can be seen in proper perspective only when we understand that it is a call to share in God's suffering love for his creation. On the other hand, there is the task for theology, however difficult the task might be, to perceive and articulate the nature and shape of the radically new thing which God in Jesus Christ is doing in our midst. Only in doing so can we see the signs of new hope. He who has called us is faithful to his promise; and above all he has given us himself as the surety of that promise. In that confidence we can go on.

[1] Choan-seng Song, "The New China and Salvation History—A Methodological Enquiry," *South East Asia Journal of Theology*, XV, 2 (1974), pp. 55f.

[2] "The Question of Excellence in Theological Education," an address to the Foundation for Theological Education in South East Asia, New York, Dec. 6, 1974. Subsequently published in *SEAJT*, XVI (1975), 55-58.

[3] S. Wesley Ariarajah, "Towards a Theology of Dialogue," *Dialogue* (New Series), (Colombo), III, 3 (Dec., 1976), 88-97. Also published in *Ecumenical Review*, XXIX, 1 (Jan., 1977), 8-11. See this article for a longer discussion of the problem of the authority of the Bible in the context of dialogue with other faiths.

[4] "The Old Testament Basis for the Christian Mission," *The Theology of the Christian Mission*, ed. Gerald H. Anderson (New York: McGraw Hill, 1961), p. 29.

[5] *The Missionary Nature of the Church: A Survey of the Biblical Theology of Mission* (London: Lutterworth, 1962), pp. 66, 94-103.

[6] See in particular "The New China and Salvation History—A Methodological Enquiry, *SEAJT*, XV, 2 (1974), pp. 52-67; *Christian Mission in Reconstruction—An Asian Attempt* (Madras: The Christian Literature Society, 1975); and "From Israel to Asia—A Theological Leap," *Theology* (March, 1976), pp. 90-96. See also the Niles-Song-West debate in *Occasional Bulletin*, I, 3 (July, 1977), 9-15.

[7] "From Israel to Asia," p. 92.

[8] Ibid., p. 91.

[9] *Mission in Reconstruction*, pp. 19-35.

[10] "The New China," p. 55.

[11] Ibid., p. 57.   [12] "From Israel to Asia," p. 94. Italics mine.

[13] See Robin Boyd, *An Introduction to Indian Christian Theology* (Madras: The Christian Literature Society, 1969), pp. 89ff.

[14] See in particular the evidence discussed in M. M. Thomas, *The Acknowledged Christ of the Indian Renaissance* (London: SCM Press, 1969).

[15] "From Israel to Asia," p. 94.   [16] Loc cit.

[17] "The Theological Problem of the Old Testament Doctrine of Creation," *The Problem of the Hexateuch and Other Essays* (Edinburgh: Oliver and Boyd, 1966), p. 142.

[18] Ibid, p. 134.   [19] Ibid, p. 131.

[20] P. B. Harner, "Creation Faith in Second Isaiah," *Vetus Testament* XVII (1967), pp. 298-306, argues against von Rad that in Second Isaiah creation has an independent status. Edgar W. Conrad, *Patriarchal Traditions in Second Isaiah* (unpublished Ph.D. dissertation, Princeton Theological Seminary, 1974), also shows that in Second Isaiah's thought creation is independent of redemption.

[21] "A Stylistic Study of the Priestly Creation Story" (article to be published in a forthcoming Festschrift for Walther Zimmerli).

[22] See in particular Walther Eichrodt, "In The Beginning," *Israel's Prophetic Heritage*, ed. B. W. Anderson and W. Harrelson (New York: Harper & Bros., 1962), pp. 1-10

[23] See Bernhard W. Anderson, "Exodus Typology in Second Isaiah," *Israel's Prophetic Heritage*, pp. 177-195 for a full discussion of the Exodus motif in Second Isaiah, and pp. 187ff. where he shows that the "former things in Second

Isaiah are the events of Israel's *Heilsgeschichte*, pre-eminently the old exodus."

[24] Walther Eichrodt, "In The Beginning," pp. 4ff.: "The power to summon Cyrus is deduced here, as in 44:24ff.; 48:12-15, from the primordial majesty of Yahweh the Creator, who can make known from the beginning that which has not yet been created (v.10a) and who therefore causes the end to be proclaimed from the very beginning."

[25] Edgar Conrad, *Patriarchal Traditions*, pp. 1ff.

[26] Jurgen Moltmann, "The Crucified God" *Theology Today*, XXXI (1974), pp. 6-18. See also his book by the same title (SCM, 1974).

[27] *The Prophets* (New York: Harper & Row, 1963), chaps. 12 and 18.

[28] Edgar Conrad, *Patriarchal Traditions*, demonstrates that Second Isaiah grounds Israel's election not in the deliverance at the Sea but in the patriarchal traditions which contain the theme of divine promise. He goes on to show that just as Abraham was called to be the recipient of a promise and to be a means of blessing to the nations, so too Israel is called to reappropriate that task to be the witnesses to Yahweh to the nations.

[29] See Bernhard W. Anderson, *Understanding the Old Testament*, Third Edition (New Jersey: Prentice-Hall, 1975), pp. 457-462, who shows that the Servant as both an individual and as a corporate personality ideally portrays Israel's role.

14

MODERNIZATION AND THE SEARCH FOR A NEW IMAGE OF MAN*

Emerito P. Nacpil

The invitation to present this essay carried with it the suggestion that it deal with questions roughly in the area of "the new humanity" and consider them in the light of the revolutionary character of our times—as experienced particularly in my part of the world—and the missionary task in the new world. In writing the essay I decided that perhaps the best way to carry out my assignment would be to deal with some aspects of the search for a new image of man resulting from the requirements of the modernization process in Asia and then consider some of the implications of a doctrine of the new humanity for this search. Such a project would illustrate one way of doing the missionary task in the developing world of Asian societies, namely, to involve the significance of Christian faith in the creative thrusts of social change.

Robert Sinai in his book *The Challenge of Modernization* (1964) makes two pertinent observations about Asian societies. First, "none of these societies has ever known what spring is: they have never experienced a sense of refreshment and renewal. . . . Asian history is the history of inert being without sufficient resilience to defy destiny." Second, "in Asia, man has always been part of a group, at all times subordinated to ends larger than himself, willing to lose himself in something immense, in a horde or in a dynasty, in a pyramid or a Nirvana. Asia never found what Europe discovered—man —individual, self-conscious, expansive, seeking, acquiring, and tormented."[1] These two observations are now in the process of being falsified. Asian societies are now launched in the process of revolutionary change which can mean their rejuvenation and renewal. Moreover, the process of rapid social change itself is breaking up

---

*Reprinted from *The Living God*, edited by Dow Kirkpatrick (Nashville: Abingdon Press, 1971), pp. 132-156.

the hard and immense collectivities in which man has been lost, driving him to assert openly and defiantly his freedom, dignity, and creativity.

MODERNIZATION IN SOUTHERN ASIA

I will use the term "modernization" to interpret the social change now in process in Southern Asia. The term "development," which is very much in vogue today, is also useful, but its stress falls on economic and technological factors, and I wish to emphasize equally the social and cultural. In using the term "modernization" I mean to indicate at least three characteristics of the revolutionary ferment in South Asian societies. The first is its *total* thrust. Beyond any doubt, economic and technological progress is decisive in any conception of modernization, and it is possible to emphasize only this factor. But the modernization process goes beyond this. It involves nothing less than the struggle for a new social order, a new "cultural ethos," and a new conception of man.[3] The second feature of the revolutionary ferment in Asia which I wish to indicate by the term "modernization" is its *direction*: it is from tradition to modernity.[4] C. E. Black writes:

When one considers modernization as a process...one thinks of it as a continuous series of changes accompanying the growth of knowledge and its effects on man's ways of getting things done. As a means of bringing a degree of order to the great complexity of human affairs, one may think of traditional societies as a pattern of inherited institutions or structures that is relatively static at the time that modern knowledge makes its initial impact on it. The effect of modern knowledge is to change the functions that traditional institutions must perform, and this in turn affects the institutions themselves. It is in this sense that the impact of modern functions on traditional institutions lies at the heart of the process of modernization.[5]

M. M. Thomas explains the movement from tradition to modernity as a movement from (1) "an ethos with a vision of an undifferentiated unity to the contemporary awakening which recognizes differentiation leading to a heightened sense of individuality," (2) from the concept of world-as-nature to that of world-as-history, and (3) from a sacred to a secular ethos.[6] Finally, the term "modernization" also indicates the radical and rapid nature of the change that is called for. The contemporary South Asian who is awake to the possibilities of development demands change and improvement not merely within his life-time but actually within the next few years.[7]

Perhaps it is useful at this stage to speak briefly of the motivations that are stimulating social change in the societies of Southern

Asia. To do this I have chosen to consider the goals or ideals of the modernization process as understood by these societies. Before mentioning them, a few comments by way of preface are in order. It is to be noted that most—if not all—of these goals or ideals of modernization are largely Western in origin and conception. They are in fact cherished traditions of the modernized societies in the West where they were first conceived and achieved. It is precisely on the irresistible authority of achievement that they are at present making a revolutionary impact upon the traditional societies of Southern Asia, although their initial influence occurred under the coercive framework of colonialism. (See K. M. Pannikkar, *Asia and Western Dominance*, 1959). But although these goals have come as external and powerful influences, they are, nevertheless, being appropriated by, and adapted to, the societies of Southern Asia. It is within the tensions brought about by this process of appropriation that there has arisen the search for a new image of man in Southern Asia. The process by which this adaptation is happening has been described by Gunnar Myrdal.[8] First they formed a decisive part in the ideologies of the liberation movements which won political independence for many of these countries. Then they were incorporated into the organic laws or constitutions of the new states, thus according them the privileged status of national goals and endowing them with the majesty of constitutional law. The governments based on these constitutions are thus under mandate to implement them. Then they became the official goals and primary models of the development plans of the various countries.[9] They have also been adopted as the platforms or programs of government or political parties. They are often rehearsed in policy speeches, in leading articles, in academic debates, and in public discussions. They have also become a decisive part of the ideology of nationalism. In view of all this, one can go as far as to say that they have become the "official creed" of these countries.[10]

Viewed against the background of the prevailing conditions in the countries of Southern Asia, the modernization ideals appear as new and radical and—to some—almost impossible of realization. The very effort to adopt them, understand them, and make them a decisive element in the social vision of Asian peoples—let alone succeed in implementing them—is itself unmistakable evidence for the radical nature of the change that is demanded in modernization. But the process of renewal has begun, and the Asians seem to want development badly enough to be ready to pay the price of it.[11]

What then are the modernization goals? Gunnar Myrdal has put them together in summary fashion in his monumental book *Asian Drama,* where he uses them as value premises by which to evaluate the problems and prospects of modernization in Southern Asia.[12]

(1) Heading the list as a general ideal is rationality.[13] This ideal demands that all courses of action or policy should be based on rational considerations. Inefficient traditional ways, superstitions, and fallacious reasoning must be abandoned. The scientific method must be applied and modern technology utilized to maximize production. The late Prime Minister Jawaharlal Nehru expresses adequately what is involved in this ideal of rationality:

> But we have to deal with age-old practices, ways of thought, ways of action. We have got to get out of many of these traditional ways of thinking, traditional ways of acting, traditional ways of production, traditional ways of distribution and traditional ways of consumption. We have got to get out of all that into what might be called more modern ways of doing so. What is society in the so-called advanced countries like today? It is a scientific and technological society. It employs new techniques, whether it is on the farm or in the factory or in transport. The test of a country's advance is how far it is utilizing modern techniques. Modern technique is not a matter of just getting a tool and using it. Modern technique follows modern thinking. You can't get hold of a modern tool and have an ancient mind. It won't work.[14]

From this it can be seen that the ideal of rationality implies nothing less than a "mental revolution."

(2) Next are ideals that have to do with economic development. These include at least three things. First is the goal of development and planning for development, both of which flow directly from the ideal of rationality.[15] Second is the need for increasing productivity, which is to be achieved primarily through improved techniques and intensive capital. Third is the ideal of raising the levels of living, which can be achieved partly by raising output per head. The improvement of levels of living is a necessary condition for higher labor input and efficiency and for those changes in abilities and attitudes requisite for maximizing productivity.

(3) Next are two ideals that deal with sociocultural change. One has to do with social and economic equalization.[16] There is no doubt that great social and economic inequalities exist in Asia, and the situation is getting worse in some countries as in the Philippines. One of the aims of modernization is to reduce these inequalities. The appeal of socialism and communism derives largely from their alleged capacity to remove these inequalities and bring about a "socialistic pattern of society" or a "classless society." The other goal

has to do with the need to modernize institutions and attitudes.[17]   The changes required here cover a broad area and are far-reaching in their implications.   Perhaps we can best grasp what is involved in the modernization of social institutions if we envisage the sort of social order that is the goal of the modernization process.   Myrdal indicates this:

What is envisaged is a united and integrated national community within which there is solidarity and "free competition" in a much wider sense than the term implies in economic analysis.   In such a national community the barriers of caste, color, religion, ethnic origin, culture, language and provincial loyalties would be broken down and property and education would not be so unequally distributed as to represent social monopolies.   A nation with marked social and economic equality, high social as well as spatial mobility, and firm allegiance of the whole population to the national community is visualized.[18]

What is required in the modernization of attitudes is indicated by the qualities that should characterize "the new man," who would be the citizen of the new social order in Southern Asia.   The list of characteristics as given by Myrdal includes the following:

(1) efficiency;
(2) diligence;
(3) orderliness;
(4) punctuality;
(5) frugality;
(6) scrupulous honesty (which pays in the long run and is a condition for raising efficiency in all social and economic relations) ;
(7) rationality in decisions on action (liberation from reliance on static customs, from group allegiances and favoritism, from superstitious beliefs and prejudices, approaching the rationally calculating "economic man" of Western liberal ideology) ;
(8) preparedness for change (for experimentation along new lines, and for moving around spatially, economically, socially) ;
(9) alertness to opportunities as they arise in a changing world;
(10) energetic enterprise;
(11) integrity and self-reliance;
(12) cooperativeness (not limiting but redirecting egoistic striving in a socially beneficial channel; acceptance of responsibility for the welfare of the community and the nation) ;
(13) willingness to take the long view (and to forgo short-term profiteering; subordination of speculation to investment and of commerce and finance to production, etc).[19]

295

As will be indicated in the next section, the realization of these qualities would involve a thorough overhaul of the traditional image by which the average Asian understands himself.

(4) Finally, there are a number of ideals connected with political modernization. The first of these is the ideal of national consolidation, which has to do with the development of a sense of national community and the establishment of "a system of government, courts, and administration that is effective, cohesive, and internally united in purpose and action, with unchallenged authority over all regions and groups within the boundaries of the state."[20] The need for this is easily demonstrated when one realizes that within most of the countries in Asia there exists a variety of races, languages, cultures, and religions, and that the peoples are separated by physical barriers such as long distances, mountains, and bodies of water which have not been bridged by effective infrastructures of communication. The second goal of political modernization is national independence and sovereignty. This ideal is most firmly asserted and constitutes the cornerstone of militant nationalism in Asia.

There is a debate going on whether political democracy should be held up as an ideal of modernization. Certainly most of the countries in Southern Asia started out with the ambition of being democratic nation-states, governed by the rule of law through representative assemblies constituted by free elections and universal suffrage. They guaranteed civil liberties and human rights. But early in their careers these countries were thwarted in their democratic ambitions by internal strife and economic dislocation. Today we have substitutes for democracy in Burma, Indonesia, Pakistan, Malaysia, Cambodia, and until recently, Thailand.* However, most of the countries who have found it necessary to resort to more authoritarian forms of government as an alternative to anarchy make the promise of eventual return to political democracy. Moreover, there is the experience of some countries tending to show that political democracy does not necessarily form an integral part of the system comprising the ideals of modernization. As Myrdal found out, "national independence, national consolidation, changes in institutions and attitudes, equalization, rise of productivity, rise and redirection of consumption, and, more generally, planning for development can be attained by an authoritarian regime bent on their realization."[21] But if there are doubts whether political democracy should be regarded as a part of the system of ideals of modernization—and Myrdal is

---

*This essay was written in 1970, prior to Martial Law in the Philippines..

convinced that it should not[22]—the idea that as broad a segment of the population as possible should become involved in the acceptance of the modernization ideals and thus secure popular cooperation and responsibility in their implementation is universally aimed at. Such popular acceptance and cooperation are necessary for generating the kind of social discipline and even austerity in living that are necessary for the effort of development to be rewarded with success.

THE IMAGE OF MAN REQUIRED IN MODERNIZATION

It would now be useful for our purposes to indicate the lines and hues of the image of man that is required by the modernization goals or ideals and to point out some of the difficulties in their realization arising from the traditional ways in which man has been understood in Southern Asia. Our reasons for doing this are twofold. To begin with, modernization in Asia will depend much on the emergence of a modernizing *elite* who are committed to these goals and reflect the image of a modern man in Asia. In addition, the resistance of the traditional culture converges precisely at the point of the understanding of man, provoking a ferment that has given rise to the search for an image of man for contemporary Asia. The illustrations I use are drawn mainly from the Philippines, which I know best.

(1) To begin with, modernization requires a type of man who knows how to live with the fact that change is the normal state of reality, including man himself, and that he must use change to his advantage and not be a mere victim of it. Man in the West has by and large learned to cope with change. He knows that nature evolves, that the form of human life is historical, that society can be changed not by divine visitation but by human effort, that reality responds to human purposes and activity, and that man has the knowledge, power, and tools to become a participant in the creative process of change.

One cannot say the same things without qualification about man in Asia. Observers of the Asian scene are almost unanimous in the opinion that the traditional Asian values encourage stability more than change. His model for nature is the land, and the land is always there—stable, unchanging, and indestructible. His model for the movement of time and, therefore, of life and history, is the cycle of seasons—of planting and harvesting. What happened in the past is what is happening in the present, and it is what will happen in the future. The *new* is not expected at all. His model for society is the village—and the Asian village has always been the same through all millennia—knit together by kinship bonds that run through many generations and by customs and traditions hallowed by the spirits of ancestors and the sanctions and rewards of religion. He views reality and himself with it as ruled by inexorable fate, and it is a fate that is not friendly to his interest and is not finally amenable to his feeble attempts to alter it. The image of the traditional Asian is that of a poor, emaciated, sluggish, but contented cow—a patient and pathetic victim of circumstance. If the Asian wants modernization and development—and there are unmistakable signs that he wants them—he must pay the price of letting this image of man go and develop the capacity to live with change and be innovative. Maurice Zinkin believes rightly that creative innovation is a requisite for development:

Nothing is more vital to development than a high propensity to innovate, a high level of willingness to accept and initiate change. The underdevelopment of Asia has to a considerable extent been due to its low propensity to innovate; the Asian peasant learnt how to grow his crops under the conditions of his village two thousand years ago. From then until this generation any experiment he might make was far more likely to end in crop failure and starvation than in riches. Naturally, therefore, Asia puts a heavy emphasis on custom and the ways of one's ancestors; naturally too the road to success has normally been through growing old in conformity. It is important, therefore, for the development of Asia that the capacity to innovate, especially the capacity to absorb and apply technological knowledge, must be given a higher place than it has been hitherto.[23]

(2) Modernization requires a type of man who is rational and pragmatic. C. E. Black rates the accumulation of knowledge and the methods of rational explanation by which it has been achieved as central to the growth of the modernization process.[24] And Richard Dickinson points out that development is possible only on the basis of a rationalist ethos:

The development concept is fundamentally rationalist, based on an implicit faith in the capacity of reason ultimately to unravel the knots which snarl progress. On a small scale the symbol of the development ethos is the Five Year Plan. It implies faith in the physical sciences to help man master nature, faith in the social sciences to help man understand human relationships and to arrange them to promote human welfare, and faith in men to act morally and rationally to build a more just and rational society.[25]

Again, it is not far from the truth to say that man in the West by and large typifies this image. It is he who has brilliantly succeeded in developing scientific methods of acquiring knowledge of nature, man, and the universe and has learned to apply effectively the vast knowledge he has accummulated to control his environment, conquer space, and improve the material conditions and cultural expressions of his life. As a result science and technology have revolutionized the ways in which man runs his affairs and the values he lives by. The social upheavals that are exploding in our cities and universities occur as a consequence of the confidence that man can produce a better world with the knowledge and power and tools at his disposal.

The dimensions of rationality in the image of modern man challenge some of the traditional ways of thinking in Asia. The challenge can perhaps be illustrated by the average Filipino's mental makeup and its relation to science. One of my compatriots has looked into this matter, and she has come out with some very interesting conclusions.[26] Of these I will mention three. The first is that the average Filipino is not much interested in and lacks the ability to handle ideas profitably.[27] In this sense the Filipino mental makeup typifies an aspect of the Oriental mind which "is a deifying and worshipping mind."[28] Nature for the Oriental mind is still enchanted with ancestors, spirits, and gods, and this prevents it from being analyzed and known and controlled in a scientific way. Secondly, the Filipino shares the Oriental disposition toward harmony and integration. Josefina D. Constantino says: "Nature and person... are made integrally one, harmoniously one with his natural surroundings."[29] As a consequence, the Filipino is not disposed to analyze, to distinguish, to identify and objectify—all of which are important in ordinary scientific work. Finally, the Filipino mind—like a typical Oriental—"has a strong myth-making power."[30] This is closely related to the Filipino's sense for the immediate and the concrete, for the here and now, but without the training for abstract and conceptual generalization which again is important in scientific thinking.[31]

If what is said here is by and large typical of the Asian mind, it is not easy to develop the sort of rationality conducive to development and modernization. The typical Asian today is more interested in the finished products of science and technology than in the conceptuality and method of thinking which constitute the essence of science and technology. It is easier, of course, to import scientific services and technological goods than the whole system of thought and values which lies at the core of a scientific and technological culture.

(3) Modernization requires a type of man who includes in his idea of goodness the values of material riches and tangible achievement. Matter is good, and its humanization is a means for the re-

finement of the human spirit. Money and resources are to be conserved and used for productive rather than consumptive purposes. The businessman is to be regarded as equally useful in society as the scholar and the saint. Manual activity and material achievement are values equally as good and useful as intellectual pursuits and spiritual or religious exercises.

These values have been partly responsible for the technological advance and economic affluence of the Western societies. Because they are regarded as a necessary condition for the modernization of Southern Asia, their adoption by the average Asian is urged vehemently by the modernizing elites such as the economists, the politicians, and the intellectuals. The shrill insistence with which they are urged upon the people is an indication of the strong resistance of the traditional indigenous culture.[32] For the Southern Asian traditionally regards matter as illusory, if not outright evil, and its subjection to human ordering is not regarded as particularly ennobling to the human spirit. Traditionally the average Southern Asian does not save much—for there is little or nothing to save in a subsistence economy—and the little he saves he spends on religious ceremonies, social festivals, and jewelry for his wife.[33] He does not think well of profit—to pursue it systematically even at the expense of good personal relations is to have a distorted sense of values. The businessman is usually associated neither with hard work nor with honesty. As Maurice Zinkin rightly observed, "the admiration of Asia still goes to goodness rather than to success."[34] The effect is that less effort is put on being successful without perhaps increasing the effort at being good. Manual work is not regarded as dignifying, and the farmer, the factory worker, the mechanic, the laborer are without social prestige. In short, the culture of Asia has made a virtue out of poverty!

It is clear that for economic development to be sustained in Southern Asia, some of its noneconomic values must be changed in favor of those that make for increased productivity such as those in the West. At the same time, however, there is in Asia a nervous fear of Westernization arising out of the logic of nationalism and the desire for cultural identity. This dilemma underscores the urgency of the search for a new image of man in Asia.

(4) Modernization requires an image of man which underscores the view that man is an individual, personal self who is free to make decisions for himself in his manifold relations based on reason and conscience, and has certain rights which have to be recognized and

guaranteed. As a person he is to be valued and distinguished from the world of things and functions (i.e., from the world of nature). The integrity of his otherness as an individual in community with others must be respected. His potentialities for selfhood and creative achievement and making a useful contribution to the improvement of the quality of corporate life must be given full play in their development and realization. This ethic of human dignity and personal self-realization is characteristic of Western civilization. Whatever may have been the excesses of Western individualism, the image of man as a free, individual, personal self existing in competition with others has been a powerful catalyst in releasing the tremendous human energy, venturesome spirit, and creative intelligence with which the West has been developed.

I suppose not many Asians would dispute the fact that such an understanding of man is also necessary in Asia if the potentialities for creativity, which no one would doubt the Asian shares with men of other cultures, are to be developed and harnessed for the purposes of modernization and development. However, in the process of appropriating such an image of man many in Asia have run up against considerable difficulties in some elements of the traditional culture. Man in Asia is not primarily an individual person radically distinct from, but rather an organic part of, nature, family, and tribe. He is moored inextricably to kin and village. These natural ties are further hallowed by the unquestioned authority of tradition and custom. And this authority is further reinforced by the sanctions and rewards of religion, which in Asia is a dominant force of conservatism, continuity, and stability in society. The interests of his kin and village are his primary loyalty, and he must conform to the values and standards of his primary group to the point of submerging his individuality and sacrificing his personal interests or ambitions. To illustrate this: There is a woman member of our faculty whom we had groomed to go to the United States for further studies in her field, which is music. She is thirty-one years old, single, and living with her parents. For two years we scrounged for funds for her travel, scholarship, board, books, and allowances. She had been given leave for two years and was set to go in August. Within a month of her departure her father came to inform us that he and his wife decided not to let their daughter go. We asked him why, and he could not give us a satisfactory reason beyond telling us that they were afraid she might get sick and lonely and no one would take care of her. I talked to the woman and she told me she wanted very

301

much to go. We of course encouraged her in this and asked her in so many words to assert her right as a mature person, that it is her life which she must live after all, etc. She wanted to do all this, but—as she put it—it is not easy to go against the decision of her parents. In a situation like this—and this is not an isolated or exceptional case—it is difficult for the individual to emerge into the full light of mature, creative, and independent selfhood.

(5) Modernization requires an image of man who participates in society as a responsible member. Modern man regards society not as something divinely given, nor fixed by nature, nor chained unalterably to tradition, nor bound completely to the status quo. He looks upon it as a human product, capable of being reordered not only on the basis of order and harmony but, as M. M. Thomas suggests, "of the relation between responsible persons, within the framework of a creative tension between order, freedom and justice and the conviction that social, political and religious institutions are made for man and for the fulness of his personal life in a community of persons."[35] For this reason modern man has developed a civic consciousness beyond his family, village, and tribe and inclusive of the whole nation. He works at his job, serves in the civil service, or participates in political activity not merely to further his personal ambitions and promote his family interests, but to contribute to public welfare and nation-building. He knows that he is to be employed on the basis of qualification and not of good connections; he accepts the validity of evaluating performance in terms of competence and achievement and not in terms of smooth interpersonal relationships; he acknowledges the wisdom of applying impersonal criteria on a universalistic scale to eliminate nepotism and graft and to rationalize activity to cope with the demands of more complex and larger operations made necessary by an industrializing society.

These are attitudes and values which to some extent are new and not readily understandable to the average man in Southern Asia. Let me illustrate this in terms of the Filipino in his social world. The Filipino is born usually into a rather large family which consists of three segments: the nuclear family, the kinship family composed of relatives on both sides of the parents to the nth degree, and the ritual family made up through the *compadrino* system. Within this large family are roles, statuses, duties, and privileges and rights which are defined and prescribed by custom. The Filipino's social world is thus primarily structured by kinship relations, and for the most part he never really gets out of this kinship structure. Thus, he approaches the wider social world on the model of the family. He feels obligated to employ a relative who is not qualified for a job. A great deal of nepotism and graft in public and business life has been traced to this factor.[36] An apparent lack of civic consciousness and concern for the national interest is partly due to narrow family and kinship loyalties. Moreover, the Filipino seeks social acceptance —a value he prizes highly—through a system of personalized methods. He seeks to transform nonfamily social relations into the pattern of family relations. To do this he is prepared to sacrifice values such as clarity in communication, honesty in expressing feeling or opinion, and the pursuit of definite results or achievement. He has difficulty distinguishing ideas from personal feelings, and he often confuses criticism of the former with the latter. He attempts to personalize what had better remain impersonal, such as legal procedures, objective norms, bureaucratic operations, administrative standards, and institutional structures. The results are often disastrous. To live effectively in a modernizing society, the Filipino obviously must learn to operate not only through personal relations but also through impersonal structures and incorporate into his norms objective standards of efficiency and competence. He must learn to rationalize his activity to achieve maximum results with a minimum of effort and cost.

I hope that what I have said so far illustrates the profound tension generated by the confrontation between the image of man required in modernization and the image of man in the traditional cultures of Southern Asia. It is this situation of conflict which has provoked the search for a new image of man in Asia. In the Philippines there is a great deal of public discussion on the "profile of the new Filipino." In Singapore there is much talk about the image of the twenty-first century Singaporean.

The tension generated by this confrontation is reflected at various levels. Psychologically it is reflected in the split-leveling of the psyche of most educated Asians. Consciously they affirm the values of modernization and the image of man it requires. Unconsciously, however, they still operate by and large on the basis of the values of the traditional culture and the image it entails. Culturally it is reflected in the juxtaposition of two cultural forms—the modern and the traditional. Often on the same narrow street are to be found a huge American car of the latest model and a horse-drawn vehicle, both fighting for the right of way in crowded traffic. Socially it is

ed in the existence of only two socioeconomic classes, the rich
e poor; and the alienation between them is getting worse.
ɪnere is no middle-class nor a middle-class mentality in most Asian
societies.

In the search for a new image of man, it is quite clear that the
traditional image has to be altered, without—it is hoped—giving
away some of the values it has found essential for human life and
dignity. It is also clear that the modernizing image of man will not
be swallowed hook, line, and sinker, not only because the response
of the indigenous culture has been for the most part selective but
also because this image of man is itself changing under the pressure
of a quest for a meaning of life deeper and more ennobling than mere
material affluence. But it is not clear what the new image of man
will finally be. Perhaps it is not too much to say that it will include
at least such things as personal freedom, social justice, higher standards of living, and a sense of personal purpose and national identity
in a responsible society.

RELEVANCE OF A CHRISTIAN DOCTRINE OF THE
NEW HUMANITY

It seems to me the church has a contribution to make in the
revolutionary ferment in Asia. Among others, it can do two things.
First, it can help push the modernization process further along. Second, it can help provide a sense of direction for it. This means that
it should repudiate the traditional role accorded to religion in Asia,
namely, as a force for sociocultural conservatism, stability and order,
and a sanctifier of traditional values. It must rather become an
agent of social innovation and renewal on the basis of its message
and mission—a role it has not consciously sought so far. It can
serve this function partly by interpreting the Christian message in
all its scope in such a way as to help step up the process of social
change and provide creative thrusts for it. I take this to be the
function of Christian theology today in Asia.

I should like to illustrate how this might be done in terms of
one aspect of the Christian faith, namely, the doctrine of the new
humanity. I realize that this aspect of Christian doctrine has remained rather underdeveloped to this day. Leslie Dewart remarks
in his book, *The Future of Belief,* that Christian theism has suffered
underdevelopment in the history of theology. This judgment applies
also—though for different reasons presumably—to the doctrine of

the new humanity. But it has become crucial for our time, not only for us in Asia. As evidence for this, many of the themes recommended for study from the various sections of the fourth Assembly of the World Council of Churches seemed to converge precisely on the theme of the *humanum*. I do not promise to do here what has remained undone all these years. All I can do is to show how a doctrine of the new humanity can encourage the search for a new image of man in Asia and perhaps indicate some of the elements that can help shape it. I will attempt this at two levels.

The first is at the level of common humanity. When we speak of the new humanity it should be clear that there is only *one* human nature shared by both the old and the new man. In Romans 5:6-21, Paul draws a sharp material contrast between the First Adam and the Second Adam.

A point to note in this contrast is that one man represents the many in sin and alternatively one man represents the many in grace. There is a common human nature shared formally by Adam and Christ, although there is a sharp contrast in the material content of each. This one human nature formally identical in Adam and Christ is not destroyed or changed by sin. This means, as Barth suggests,[37] that "man is at once an individual and...at the same time... without in any way losing his individuality, he is the responsible representative of all men." The essential structure of human nature is that each man is for all men and all men are in each man.[38] For this reason Paul can speak of Adam as the type of the eschatological man, the one who is to come (Rom. 5:14). C. K. Barrett has suggested that Paul views history as gathering at "nodal points"—the points being outstanding figures who are not only great individuals in themselves but also represent the human race or sections of it.[39] Following this lead I want to suggest some representative types of man in the Bible who can become significant for the search of a new image of man in Asia.

First of all, there is the image of the man of faith who lives toward the future between promise and fulfillment. This type is represented by Abraham. There are two points here which I want to stress. For one thing, Abraham represents the man who desires to found a *new* nation in a *new* land and for a *new* purpose in world history. He can only do this by abandoning his primal ties with family, kindred, and country and, therefore, also of the culture and worldview of his own people. What Abraham did is exactly what every Asian has to do: to abandon family, tribe, religion, culture, and the past in search of a new social order, a new form of human life, a new purpose for history. Furthermore, Abraham sought the *new* as a promise in the future. For him the future is framed between promise and fulfillment, and life toward the future between promise and fulfillment is precisely the pilgrimage of faith. It is this orientation toward the future, as emerging from between promise and fulfillment and making room for creative effort, which can break the traditional temporal consciousness of the average Asian and transform it from a cyclic to a historical one. As already indicated earlier, the average Asian views time as moving in cycles. The past as the deposit of experience is the dominant category for interpreting the future which does not bring anything essentially different from the past. This view of time has veiled the future as a horizon of infinite possibilities. It has bred in the Asian a combination of the attitudes of fatalism, escapism, and improvidence which has crippled his ability to alter the existing state of things by personal initiative, rational planning, and purposive activity. Changing reality by creative effort is not yet an article of his credo. The future as promise breaks the cycle of time in a threefold way. It does this—as Moltmann suggests—by first contradicting the past by revealing to it something new which has not yet happened. The word of promise is always a judgment on the poverty of the past in the light of the possibilities of the future. Second, promise opens up the future and shapes it with a definite content in terms of which it can be grasped in anticipation. Promise reveals the future as a definite possibility awaiting realization, something new which the past does not have because it has not yet happened. The future then becomes more important and challenging than the past. It calls forth the boldness and creativity of freedom. Finally, promise creates a time-space between present promise and its future fulfillment. This time-space between promise and fulfillment is the time of opportunity, the time of creative work, the time of changing the status quo and remolding it into the possibilities of the future, the time of translating a dream into reality. Into this time-space are released, the possibilities from the future, and they must be grasped by faith and turned into reality by hard work. Promise, therefore, besides breaking the cycle of time, creates two important attitudes which enable one to live in the time-space it opens up. It creates faith, which repents of the past and hopes in the future; it creates a sense of responsibility in the present, which drives one into hard work by which reality is altered. Time now moves not only from past and present into the future, but aiso in reverse—the future comes to constitute the present and fill the past with new meaning. Time ceases being cyclic—it becomes historical time.

Another type of man which can very well become a part of the new image of man that Asia is seeking for is Adam as the steward or trustee of creation. Paul of course uses the figure of Adam as the representative of sin and disobedience. But in the priestly tradition of the Old Testament man is given the vocation of ruling over the created order, the animals, and the earth. His function is to rule, to subdue, and to procreate. Nature is man's dominion. The gods and spirits and cosmic powers which have reigned in it are usurpers. They have to be driven away and nature cleared of their alien presence and freed from divine qualities so that it may be restored to its true proportions as a creation of God and as the rightful domain of man as a steward of God. In contrast to the Greek view as expressed in the myth of Prometheus who had to steal fire from the gods in order to have the authority to conquer nature, the biblical view pictures God as giving to man this authority. Man is given the privilege to develop the means whereby he may "subdue" nature and care for it. He does not have to be punished for exercising this privilege as though it were an evil deed, as in the case of Prometheus who was chained to a rock in the Caucasus by Zeus to become a victim of the elements. On the contrary, man's commission to be the subduer and tiller and keeper of nature is part of the meaning of creation as good.

Man's calling to dominate nature has to be seen in the context of the ambiguous relation between man and nature. On the one hand, man is clearly subject to the powers of nature. He is a part of it. He is nurtured by it not only in his body but in his spirit. Nature not only provides man with a habitat and food; it offers him aesthetic delight and meditation, companionship, consolation, and inspiration. Man is also threatened by nature. The average Asian is literally aware of this truth. A great deal of his profound feeling that the universe is hostile comes from his experience of the terrors of nature, from typhoons, floods, droughts, earthquakes, volcanic eruptions, famine, and disease. But the fact that he is subject to the powers of nature constitutes precisely the challenge to subdue it, and the history of civilization indicates that the threat of nature has played no small part in compelling man to control nature and to humanize it.

On the other hand, man transcends nature and has the capacity to exercise dominion over it. The biblical view of man is quite clear about man's distinction from the rest of creation. He appears as the crown of creation in Genesis 1. Of all the creatures, he alone is made in the image of God. He alone is given the vocation to reflect God's sovereignty through his dominion over nature. For in man self-consciousness, rationality, moral sense, creative freedom, and all the ingredients of personalness have made their appearance in reality. In man nature has ceased to act merely naturally and spontaneously and unconsciously. In man nature has begun to act freely and intelligently and responsibly. Man therefore is no longer bound to act merely naturally. He must recreate nature in order that it might become the work not only of God's hand but also of *his* hand. He must know it, for only when he knows how nature behaves and under what conditions will he learn to work not only *with* it, but also *upon* it and thus to control and reshape it. Thus, he can fertilize the soil, increase the varieties and quality of plants (such as a new breed of rice which is causing what somebody has called "the green revolution" in Asia), improve the stock of animals and preserve their species, produce food and medicine, and make a trip to the moon.

The amazing fact of it all is that nature of which man is a part responds to human scientific investigation and technical control. The unconscious ends of nature are now subject to man's conscious planning and guidance and transformation. This is the great turn in the history of evolution: man who is the product of nature's evolution has now the knowledge and the power and the technique to guide not only nature's but his own evolution.

There is no doubt that man's destiny to dominate the earth is increasingly being fulfilled by means of science and technology. The contemporary Asian will certainly avail himself of this means. Speaking theologically, there ought to be no contradiction between Christian faith and science and technology, although the historical connection has been indirect. Christian faith clears nature of its sacred qualities and commissions man to know and master it through his creative freedom. Man is a fellow worker with God in the ongoing creative process. From this viewpoint, Christian faith provides a theological perspective for the Asian's desire to master his environment through science and technology.

But the perspective must be more than merely supportive; it must also be critical. For technology is not an end in itself. It asks for goals which can endow it with meaning and direct its processes.

Moreover, man's destiny is not simply to control nature. He has a responsibility for developing himself and his community. What he does with nature affects him considerably, for ill or good. For through man's interaction with nature, human culture develops. Because human culture is of man and for man, its meaning lies in man and his growth toward more humanity. In this connection, it is necessary to ask whether the kind, aims, and consequences of the technical domination which man exercises over nature do honor not only to his vocation as a trustee of creation but also to his being as a person in community with other persons.

This leads us to consider briefly another type of man—the liberator and the legislator represented by Moses. The Exodus from Egypt, the house of bondage, under the leadership of Moses is a paradigm of all liberation movements. It stands for the fact that human dignity consists in freedom. In this sense each man must be his own Moses, restlessly seeking his freedom to be himself by overthrowing any shackle of oppression and indignity. For freedom is not simply the absence of any objective situation of oppression. It is not only freedom of choice. It *is* freedom to be human. Being man and being free are identical.

But Moses and his horde of wandering Hebrews discovered that freedom can be lost in anarchy and chaos as well as in tyranny. The peoples and nations of Asia are learning this lesson, too. Freedom can thrive only in some form of community and order maintained by the discipline of justice and law and the reconciling power of love in the dynamic framework of an open and responsible society. Discovering the shape of such a society and establishing it remain the tasks of contemporary Asia, as indeed of all the world.

The point of all that I have said so far about man is that our common human nature impels us all to seek its future possibility, to fulfill its part in the creative process, and to secure its freedom to be itself. Man in Asia cannot do less if he is to remain human. To the extent that this happens our common humanity prefigures the man who is to come, the *true* man. For nothing in true human nature is alien to the new humanity. As Barth says, "What is Christian is secretly but fundamentally identical with what is universally human."[40] But we know that we do not fully succeed in this enterprise. Man falls short of his possibility; he abuses his stewardship of creation; he misuses his freedom and loses it in anarchy or tyranny, or slavery of various sorts. The type of "man the sinner"—helpless, godless, sinful, and an enemy of God, subject to judgment, condemnation, and death—must too become part of the new image of man that Asia is seeking for, qualifying every other element that goes into its making. To the extent that this happens, the new image of man in Asia will have need of the man who is to come, the *new* man.

The next thing I want to say is that there is something in the new humanity which is much more than the mere formal sharing of the same human nature between the First and the Last Adam. Paul's phrase "how much more" in Romans 5 points to a sharp material contrast between Adam and Christ, between human existence in Adam and human existence in Christ, and between man in sin against God and God being for man in Christ. The contrast is summed up in the statement that "where sin increased, grace abounded all the more, so that, as sin reigned in death, grace also might reign through righteousness to eternal life through [the one man] Jesus Christ our Lord" (Rom. 5:20b-21 RSV). The difference is between death and life. Put in another way, what is involved in the "how much more" is spoken of by Paul in terms of "new creation" (II Cor. 5:17; Gal. 6:15; cf. I Cor. 7:31).

The language of "creation" is certainly inclusive, and we cannot pretend we can deal with all that it means or implies. In Paul it is certainly connected with man: If any man is in Christ, he is a new creation. For a man to be "in Christ" amounts to a new beginning, not just for the individual but for the whole human race precisely because Jesus Christ is truly and fully man in the sense that he is the one man who is for all men and is all men in the one man. He is fully and truly an individual man and at the same time fully and truly a corporate man. Moreover, he is both of these in the true relations of being human—in relation to God, to himself, to nature and culture, and to fellowman in society. Furthermore, he lives truly and fully what is required in all these relations. But the beginning in Christ is as primordial as the old one, and it sets one in the horizon of the hope of sharing the glory of God. The event that begins the new creation and the new humanity in it is the resurrection of Jesus Christ from the dead.[41] The resurrection of Jesus constitutes a fundamental alteration in the character and movement of history; it is the beginning of the end; it is the dawn of a new age.

To begin anew in Christ means to begin to be what God intends man to be, namely, to be in his image, i.e., to be truly and fully man. It is not proper to look for God's image in man, for it is not God's image which is in man. Rather, man is in the image of God. And the image of God is not some human quality or capacity such as reason, or conscience, or answerability. The image of God is Jesus Christ (II Cor. 4:4; Col. 1:15). He is the one man who lives human nature truly and fully as God has intended it to be from the beginning. Precisely as true man he reflects God truly. For man to be in Christ is to be "conformed" to Christ, i.e., to become what he already is and will yet become in Christ by all the means and in all the relations and with all the life at his disposal. The Christian and the church represent the new humanity in Christ.

Now, if it is true that Jesus Christ is the true man and that his resurrection is the new beginning for all men to become true men in him, what is there in the man Jesus Christ which man can now begin being and doing? In what sense is the man Jesus true man which the resurrection vindicates? I cannot give a full answer here. But I can give you the answer of Jesus to John the Baptist. When John the Baptist sent two of his disciples to inquire of Jesus whether he was in fact "he who is to come," the reply of Jesus was: "Go and tell John what you have seen and heard: the blind receive their sight, the lame walk, lepers are cleansed, the deaf hear, the dead are raised up, the poor have good news preached to them" (Luke 7:19-22 RSV). If Asia is looking for the image of the true man, then it is in some such activity which the true man did that it may yet find the answer.

REFERENCE NOTES

[1] Robert Sinai, *The Challenge of Modernization* (New York: W. W. Norton, 1964), p. 46.

[2] Wilbert E. Moore, *Social Change* (New Delhi: Prentice-Hall of India (Private) Ltd., 1965), p. 89: "What is involved in modernization is a 'total' transformation of a traditional or pre-modern society into the types of technology and associated social organization that characterize 'the advanced, economically prosperous, and relatively stable nations of the Western world" Cf. C. E. Black. *The Dynamics of Modernization* (New York: Harper Torchbook, 1966), p. 6.

[3] Cf. M. M. Thomas, *The Christian Response to the Asian Revolution* (London: SCM Press, 1966). Gunnar Myrdal, *Asian Drama*, 3 vols. (New York: Pantheon, 1968).

[4] Cf. A. B. Shah and C. R. M. Rao, ed., *Tradition and Modernity in India* (Bombay: Manaktalas, 1965); Robert N. Bellah, ed.. *Religion and Progress in Modern Asia* (New York: The Free Press, 1965); Thomas. *The Christian Response to the Asian Revolution*. Black defines modernization as the "process by which historically evolved institutions are adapted to the rapidly changing functions that reflect the unprecedented increase in man's knowledge, permitting control over his environment, that accompanied the scientific revolution." *The Dynamics of Modernization*, p. 7. Cf. the definition given by Moore, *Social Change*, p. 89.

[5] Black. *The Dynamics of Modernization*, p. 55.

[6] M. M. Thomas. "Modernization of Traditional Societies and the Struggle for a New Cultural Ethos." *The Ecumenical Review*. October, 1966. pp. 426-39.

[7] Cf. Maurice Zinkin, *Development of Free Asia* (London: Chatto and Windus, 1963), p. 3.

[8] Myrdal, *Asian Drama*, I, pp. 54-55.

[9] A good example is the case of the Philippines. The Filipino official who was mainly responsible for the success of the self-sufficiency in the rice production program of the Philippines said this in a speech: "It is not surprising that in our efforts to solve our economic problems, we have patterned our program of action after the development programs that have proven successful in the modern industrial societies of today. We have emulated their techniques of production, their pattern of allocating national resources, their development projects, and their public investment programs. Our knowledge of the economic achievements of the industrialized world have had the salutary effect of saving us from the costly process of experimentation, which we would have experienced, had we been left to fend for ourselves. In addition, the apparatus of modern technology which has been developed by the industrial countries, is now at our disposal. It is an accepted economic fact that technology, properly harnessed, is the potent instrument of economic growth." "The Consequences of Development," in *The Manila Times*, May 12, 1969.

[10] Cf. Myrdal, *Asian Drama*, I, p. 54; cf. The Magna Charta of Socio-Economic Development of the Philippines adopted by the Philippine Congress, 1969.

[11] Cf. Zinkin, *Development for Free Asia*, p. 3.

[12] Myrdal, *Asian Drama*, I, pp. 49-69; Vol. II, Part 4.

[13] Ibid., I, p. 57.

[14] Cited by Myrdal, *Asian Drama*, I, pp. 57-58, n. 3.

[15] Ibid., p. 58.   [16] Ibid., pp. 58-59.   [17] Ibid., pp. 60-62.

[18] Ibid., p. 60; cf. M. M. Thomas, *The Christian Response to the Asian Revolution*, pp. 35-65.

[19] Ibid., pp. 61-62.   [20] Ibid., p. 63.

[21] Ibid., p. 65.   [22] Ibid., p. 65, n. 2.

[23] Zinkin, *Development for Free Asia*, p. 8.

[24] Black, *The Dynamics of Modernization*, p. 11.

[25] Richard Dickinson, *Line and Plummet: The Churches and Development* (Geneva: World Council of Churches, 1968), p. 33.

[26] Josefina D. Constantino, "The Filipino Mental Make-up and Science," *Philippine Sociological Review*, January 1966, pp. 18-28.

[27] Ibid., p. 20.   [28] Ibid., p. 21.

[29] Ibid.   [30] Ibid.   [31] Ibid., p. 36.

[32] Cf. Robert N. Bellah, *Religion and Progress in Modern Asia;* Myrdal, *Asian Drama*, I, pp. 71-125.

[33] Cf. Zinkin, *Development for Free Asia*, pp. 5-33; Bellah, *Religion and Progress in Modern Asia*, pp. 34-38.

[34] Zinkin, *Development for Free Asia*, p. 11.

[35] Thomas, *The Christian Response to the Asian Revolution*, p. 68.

[36] Cf. Ruben Santos-Cuyugan, "The Changing Philippines: A Problem of Cultural Identity," *The Chronicle Yearbook*, 1961, p. 101.

[37] Karl Barth, "Christ and Adam," *Scottish Journal of Theology* (Occasional Papers), 1963, pp. 43-44.

[38] Ibid., p. 5.

[39] C. K. Barrett, *From First Adam to Last* (New York: Scribner's, 1962), p. 92.

[40] Barth, "Christ and Adam," p. 43.

[41] Cf. Robin Scroggs, *The Last Adam* (Philadelphia: Fortress Press, 1966), p. 92.

312

15

MODERN MAN AND THE NEW HUMANITY IN JESUS CHRIST*

M. M. Thomas†

The primitive church, in the light of the Easter and Pentecostal experiences which gave it birth, identified the Crucified Jesus with the expected Messiah (the Christ). It interpreted the redemptive purpose in history in terms of the New Cruciform Humanity of Jesus Christ.[1] Jesus Christ is the New Man through whom a New Humanity is created after the image of God (Col. 3:10). He is the true Adam, through whom all mankind is continually reconciled to God (II Cor. 5:19), and all creation is being perfected (Rom. 8:18-21). He bears a Movement of the Spirit leading to the Ultimate Future[2] of God's relation to man and nature, the consummation of the Kingdom where "God shall be all and in all" (I Cor. 15:20-28; Eph. 1:1-10).

What are some of the significant points at which the traditional theological formulations of the Christian faith have been challenged to revision by its having to relate the New Man in Jesus Christ to the problems of community and self-understanding of modern man? There are several which may be mentioned.

1. THE CREATIVE PROCESS AND THE REDEMPTIVE HISTORY

Christianity has been compelled to reinterpret the traditional myths of Creation, Fall, and Redemption in new terms. Myths and symbols are the mother-tongue of religion to speak of God and the basic condition of man in relation to God,[3] but they have to be trans-

---

* Chapter VI from the author's *Man and the Universe of Faiths* (Madras: Christian Literature Society, 1975), which was one of three preparatory volumes for the All-Asia Consultation.

† Dr. Thomas is a Research Fellow and Director Emeritus of the Christian Institute for the Study of Religion and Society in Bangalore, India, and is former Chairman of the Central Committee of the World Council of Churches. He is the author of *The Acknowledged Christ of the Indian Renaissance; The Secular Meaning of Christ,* and other important books.

lated into doctrines and insights differently at different times. The traditional Christian doctrines of the relation between nature, man, and God which underlie the myths of Creation, Fall, and Redemption were formulated at a time, as Teilhard de Chardin has pointed out, when men generally thought of nature and society in rather static terms; and today when we know them as a dynamic process they need reformulation to make them tools of discerning Christ's presence and for participating with him in the process.

The first chapters of Genesis conceive of Creation and Fall as having taken place at the primal beginnings of the human race. The story emerged in the prophetic period to provide the background for the movement of redemption in history and its final consummation. As the Dutch Catechism[5] puts it: "God's concern for his sovereign power—this was Israel's earliest experience. It first knew God as deliverer. It was only when the world took on greater dimensions in their eyes that the people began to realize that it was from their Savior God that all things came. God was then seen as the Creator, as is splendidly expounded in the lyric of Creation in Genesis."[6] And if all things came from God and were "very good," evil had to be interpreted only as the result of a Fall. In Genesis 3-11, "primeval history recounts a Fall four times over; the eating of the forbidden fruit, the murder of a brother, the corruption of Noah's contemporaries, and the building of the Tower of Babel"[7] and man's whole environment, social and natural, is involved with him in the Fall. Evidently, the Old and the New Testaments and the Fathers of the church accepted an original Divine Creation and an original Human Fall as primeval events in the beginnings of human history, and saw redemption as a Restoration of humanity and through humanity the whole creation to the original state of Adam and Eve in the Garden of Eden before sin entered human existence. This way of expressing the basic condition of man in relation to God was inevitable in a determinist understanding of the universe. But ours is an age which has acknowledged the truth of a continuous dynamic evolution of nature, man and society; therefore, the Christian church in its enlightened teaching ministry recognizes the necessity to translate the biblical stories of Creation and Fall into insights regarding "the basic elements of all human encounter with God," without making them "a description of the beginning of mankind."[8] It means that "the authentic enlightenment" is to be brought "in the course of things and their culmination; it is better to say, God creates, than to say, God created." This is also true of sin. The truth is that man "sins

314

and becomes corrupt. The sin of Adam and Eve is closer than we imagine. It is our own selves." As the biblical story indicates, "sin has to do with human freedom; freedom grew in man and hence sin."[9] Indeed, in the creative process, matter-energy evolves through life and mind to the spirit,[10] which in man involves a sense of self and freedom. And man encounters a transcendent spiritual reality impinging upon his spirit; this is the reality of God. After the emergence of man, he is co-creator with God; and man's spiritual response is the focus around which the creative process continues to move forward in history.[11] In this context, sin means that man in the freedom of the spirit turns from God to his own self as his center and chooses false purposes of life and worships idols (Rom. 1:21-23), thereby betraying the true destiny of the world of man and nature. Thus sin is primarily related to the spirit in man and not to the brute in him. Therefore, it may be assumed that as history progresses bringing man to higher stages of heightened vitality and apprehension about self and the world, every stage experiences a new "fall" expressing itself in new forms of misdirection and perversity. Thus the experience of heights of creativity and depths of destructivity in our age can be interpreted best within the framework of Creation and Fall. It brings not only moral ambiguity but also tragedy into the spiritual dimension of the creative process.

Let us not however forget that it was the vision of Redemption that gave the prophets their insight into Creation and Fall. So also, the Christian doctrines of Creation and Fall are not accounts of the genesis of the world, either scientific or metaphysical, but are a working backwards from the Christian vision and experience of the Redemption of creation in Jesus Christ. Braaten, following Pannenberg, speaks of creation occurring from its end; it is an interpretation of the world looked at from "its neogenesis in the arrival of God's creative future in the resurrection of Jesus—the prolepsis of new creation." "Creation is the world in motion towards its fulfilment in the coming *eschaton*. The eschaton is the creative power, the inner dynamic, of the world in process, of the history of mankind towards its integration in the Lordship of Christ."[12] Therefore the picture of the modern human situation in terms of tragic destiny is not prior to but follows the recognition of the redemptive forces of what we have called the New Cruciform Humanity in Jesus Christ, which is at work through the Holy Spirit grappling with the destructive forces and overcoming them.

This brings to the forefront the question of the relation of the creative historical process to its final fulfillment, that is, the nature of Christian eschatology. Martin Buber, the Jewish philosopher, distinguishes between the "prophetic" eschatology of Israelite origin and the "apocalyptic" eschatology of Iranian origin, and discusses them in relation to Christianity[13] in the summary of his position in his address to a gathering of Christian Mission representatives in Stuttgart, in 1930, and other writings given in Cohen, *Martin Buber*.[14] According to Buber, the apocalyptic eschatology despairs of redeeming the world of evil and envisages its abandonment by God, who supplants it by a new world entirely different from it in nature; but the prophetic eschatology promises the end of time as a consummation of the created order where its hidden perfection will be realized, not by God alone, but by God and man together, turning through history to the future, that is, by the saving power of God working in history to resist man's contrariness and strengthening man's contribution to salvation. Buber thinks that Pauline eschatology and, following him, all Christian eschatology is apocalyptic and not prophetic, and that apocalypse often releases the demons of gnostic temptation.

Buber's definitions of the prophetic and the apocalyptic eschatologies, or the historical relation of Iran, Israel, and Christianity to them need not detain us. It is perhaps truer to facts to say that there has always been an element of the apocalyptic in the prophetic and vice-versa; and that in Judaism as well as throughout the history of Christianity there has been a swing between the prophetic and the apocalyptic eschatologies as Buber defines them. But the point to note is that we are here in the realm of the crucial debate about the relation between Creation and Redemption, between Nature and Grace, which has been a central theme of Christian theology throughout. Where Redemption is seen as continuous with Creation, it leads to a shallow view of evil; and when they are totally separated the gnostic idea of a historical spirituality appears. The Cross and the Resurrection of Jesus Christ interpreted as the "end" of history within history and as the inauguration of a movement of renewal of creation with its promise of a consummation in which all things will be summed up in him, certainly is more prophetic than apocalyptic; it turns "through history to the future" or rather, it brings the Ultimate Future into the midst of history to take hold of the present, every present, enabling man to be redeemed to make his contribution to the salvation of the world. St. Paul even speaks of men "filling up that which is lacking in the sufferings of Christ"

(Col. 1:24). The history of the Cruciform Humanity created in Jesus Christ is eschatology in human history, transforming it from within. It is both continuous and discontinuous with the creative process; continuous with it in so far as the creative process is the raw material of the New Man in Christ, discontinuous because at every stage of the process it needs to be judged and recreated by the Spirit to be made part of it. Even the modern man has to be renewed in this way, but when so renewed, he contributes something new to the Future of Man.

In his essay on "God in Nature and History"[15] Hendrik Berkhof deals with this question of eschatology and says: "In the old controversy between history and consummation, the greater truth is on the side of continuity." He points out that in fact "discontinuity serves continuity," for God's own liberating work of historicising of life can end "only in its glorification; its presentation in a wider context." This finds expression in the idea of mankind reigning with Christ in consummation: "Consummation will mean a new and far more thoroughgoing display of man's freedom and dominion." And so the picture the New Testament gives of the historical process of Creation, Fall, and Redemption is "the image of a great movement from lower to higher, going through estrangement and crisis, but also through atonement and salvation, and so directed toward its ultimate goal, a glorified humanity, in full communion with God, of which goal the risen Christ is the guarantee and the first fruits." This is not unlike Canon Raven's exegesis of Rom. 8 on the process of Creation, incomplete and frustrated, groaning for renewal, with God's Spirit involved and sharing that agony and inspiring and actualizing "our efforts" and bringing to birth the children of God,[16] or Teilhard de Chardin's picture of the creative process moving to the Omega Point, but Berkhof's thought has a greater recognition of the crises and tragedies, and therefore of transcendent divine "atonement and salvation" realized at every stage of the process, as well as at the end of it.

2. THE PEOPLE OF THE MESSIAH

The Christian theology of Messianism is compelled to grapple anew with the definition of the People of the Christ (Messiah) and their divine election, in the context of a new vision of the universality of Jesus Christ and the unity of mankind. This is perhaps the crucial theological task facing Christian ecumenism.

The affirmation "Jesus is Messiah" means that the life, death,

317

and resurrection of Jesus is the center of the historical movement of fulfillment of the divine purpose of the whole world; and that the history of the people acknowledging it and awaiting the promise inherent in it, signifies the power and the presence in the world of the divine goal, namely the transformation of the kingdom of this world into the Kingdom of God and his Christ. The relation between the particularism of the Church, the People of the Messiah, and the universalism of the End is radically raised at this point. No doubt the question of this relation has always been raised and has always been answered in terms of mission. It still remains the answer. But it is the nature of mission that needs restatement today in the light of the self-understanding of modern man and his struggle for a pluralistic world community.

In a discussion of the theology of Messianism, Paul Lehmann accepts the premise that the church and the world have the same center: Jesus Christ. He quotes Visser't Hooft: "The Church is the inner circle, the world the outer circle, both together are the realm over which Christ is King,"[17] and Karl Barth: "Existence outside Christ is, rightly understood, already a still hidden but real existence in him" because "the relationship between Adam and all of us was already ordered so as to correspond to our present and future—namely the relationship between Christ and all of us."[18] Therefore the mission of the church is a revealing of what is hidden, a revealing which is not merely gnosis, but redemption involving victory over evil and transformation of the world. Lehmann sees the story of the eucharistic community which acknowledges the Person of Jesus as Lord and identifies itself with his self-offering to the world, as "the penultimate chapter" of the divine-human movement of redemption in history. "Here is a laboratory of maturity in which, by the operative (real) presence and power of the Messiah-Redeemer in the midst of his people and through them of all people, the will to power is broken and displaced by the power to will what God wills," that is, "the power to be and stay human." He continues: "The Christian *Koinonia* is the foretaste and sign in the world that God has always been and is contemporaneously doing what it takes to make and to keep human life human."[19] Lehmann goes on to point out that, while the distinction between the church and the world is fundamental, the boundary between them is not easily defined: "The difference between believers and unbelievers is not defined by church membership or even in the last analysis by baptism. The difference is defined by imaginative and behavior-

318

al sensitivity to what God is doing in the world to make and to keep human life human, to achieve the maturity of men, that is, the new humanity."[20]

In this connection, we may note the approach of Vatican II to the nature of the link and the distinction between the Catholic Church and the world outside. "The Dogmatic Constitution of the Church," while reaffirming that the Catholic Church is the central stream in the movement of salvation in world history, recognizes the closest link with the whole community of the baptized Christians, and in the next outer concentric circles come the Jews who share the same covenant and promises "from whom Christ was born," and then those "who acknowledge the Creator" especially "the Moslems who, professing to hold the faith of Abraham along with us, adore the one and merciful God" and "those who in shadows and images seek the unknown God"; and in the further outer circle linked to the center are those who "sincerely seek God" and strive to live according to "the dictates of conscience."[21] In the "Pastoral Constitution of the Church in the Modern World," this last group is divided into two— first come those who "acknowledge God and preserve in their traditions precious elements of religion and humanity" and then those who "cultivate beautiful qualities of the human spirit but do not yet acknowledge the source of these qualities."[22] Of course all these spiritual links are set within the framework of a double movement of the church's mission of preaching and service to all mankind and humanity, and conversion of men to Christ in his church.

It is significant that here there is no attempt to define rigidly the boundary of the people who are in communion with Christ. Nevertheless, in the whole approach, the distance to the center seems to be measured more by the credal and religious expressions of faith, rather than by that of "imaginative and behavioral sensitivity to what God is doing" for man in Jesus Christ. Nor does the approach give full recognition to the traffic across the boundaries of religious and secular faiths which has been going on in the world, and which has introduced dynamic changes in all the faiths. However, in some other places, Vatican II cuts across this neat picture of saving center with near and distant relatives. For example, the Pastoral Constitution says, "Since Christ died for all men, and since the ultimate vocation of man is in fact one and divine, we ought to believe that the Holy Spirit in a manner known only to God offers to every man the possibility of being associated with this paschal mystery."[23] Such recognition of "the possibility" of those outside the church to be "associated with the paschal mystery" through the operation of the Holy Spirit "in a manner known only to God," inevitably conceives the Community of Faith as wider than the church. While we shall speak of the Crucified and Risen Jesus Christ acknowledged by faith in the Christian *Koinonia* as its structured nucleus, we have to acknowledge a larger unstructured stream of a *koinonia*-in-Christ or a "Communion in the Messiah" (to use the suggestive title of a study on the relation between Judaism and Christianity by Lev Gillet[24]), spiritually continuous with it.

The "lamb slain" who is "on the throne" at the End is present "from the foundation of the world" (Rev. 13:8). The Cross, or the self-emptying redemptive love of God revealed in Jesus has been the central dynamic of all history. John V. Taylor even goes further when he sees the principle of the Cross, of life through self-sacrifice, present and at work side by side with the principle of self-aggression in the whole creative process including that of nature and society. He says, "The free obedience of Jesus, his dying for us all and his rising again, are both history and universal reality."[25] It is the Crucified and Risen Jesus who is our evidence that "we are citizens of a forgiven universe," and that Being-in-Christ is the "primary and essential condition of man's existence." This is clearly declared in the New Testament hymns of Creation in John 1, Colossians 1, and Hebrews 1, and in the Creeds, where "all things" are seen as having been created through Christ and by him, and as subsisting in him, and oriented toward him. Such a universal presence of Christ also posits the possibility and even the reality of men being saved "not by relating only to that historical life, death, and resurrection in which the pattern was made plain once and for all, but by relating also to that pattern wherever it emerges" in the tissue of historical existence—not merely religious existence, but just human existence, religious or secular; not only in contemporary experience, but also in the whole history of mankind. This is what gives validity to the talk of the Unknown Christ[26] and the Anonymous or Implicit Christianity[27] and the Latent Church (Tillich) with reference to certain streams and trends in the religious and secular history and experience of mankind. But the historical Cross remains the clue, the criterion of discernment of the stirrings and positive responses of faith to the Universal Cross; and, therefore, as Schillebeeckx said, they are "the initial stage—something which of its nature requires to grow to completion"[28] in the acknowledgment of the dialectic between the historical and the universal in Jesus Christ.

We may speak of three kinds of implicit faith-response to Christ without explicit acknowledgment of Jesus as the Christ, being included in the wider Communion in the Messiah. First, the pattern of secular self-giving love and forgiveness, with an openness to the realm of transcendent forgiveness; second, a faith in the Holy with the expectation of a Divine Mediator or the atonement of suffering Messiah; and third, a recognition of the Person of Jesus as the ultimate pattern of the Messiah to come. In this connection, we may refer to what C.F. Andrews wrote in a paper presented to the Tambaram meeting of the International Missionary Council in 1938, about the mission of the church. He said, it involved "not merely [quickening] those who are dead in trespasses but also [welcoming] with joy his radiant presence in those who have seen from afar his glory."[29] The church's recognition of and dialogue within this wider *koinonia*-in-Christ is spiritually necessary for both. On the one hand it prevents the church from a spiritual egoism which arrogates to itself the right to decide who belongs to the messianic people, and it also brings to the church an awareness of hitherto unexplored insights and facets of life in the Holy Spirit. On the other, the encounter with the Person of Jesus Christ will prevent commitments to the universal Christ-principle and the way of the Cross from being perverted into a legalism and used as an instrument of self-justification.

3. TOWARD A SECULAR FELLOWSHIP IN CHRIST

C. F. Andrews says that Jesus' parable of the Last Judgment in Matthew 25 translates the Christ-centeredness of the Communion in the Messiah basically as commitment to "active love due to the least of those whom he calls his brethren." There is not only "no mention of any outward profession of a Creed," but also "those whom Christ counts as his own in the parable hardly know that they belong to him at all."[30] In other words, the final test of faith-acknowledgment of the death and resurrection of Jesus Christ is seen in men's participation in the work of the Holy Spirit in building tissues of genuine "human" community within and between the communal groupings of men in history, as signs of the ultimate Kingdom to come. The eucharistic community and the wider Communion in the Messiah are sacramental signs of it; but they are really credible only in so far as they express their eschatological hope in action, in *praxis*, by mediating the spiritual dynamic of the New Humanity in Christ through their concern for human community. Jurgen Moltmann says, "It is the Christ-event that first gives birth to what can be theologically described as 'man,' 'true man,' 'humanity'—neither Jew nor Greek, neither bond nor free, neither male nor female (Gal. 3:28). Only when the real, historic, and religious differences between peoples, groups, and classes are broken down in the Christ-event in which the sinner is justified does there come a prospect of what true humanity can be and will be. The path leads here from the historic and unique to the universal, because it leads from the concrete event to the general in the sense of eschatological direction."[31] The Message of the Uppsala Assembly of the World Council of Churches speaks of this Christ-centered concern for a "human" community thus, "Christ wants his Church to foreshadow a renewed human community. Therefore, we Christians will manifest our unity in Christ by entering into full fellowship with those of other races, classes, ages, religions, and political convictions in the place where we live."[32] In our pluralistic world, it envisages a "full fellowship" across all boundaries including the religious, as the goal of the church's witness to the renewal of humanity in Christ. The point was stated clearly by Dag Hammarskjold at the Evanston Assembly of the World Council of Churches in 1954. He quoted the following words from the Report on the Main Theme of the Assembly, "The Cross is that place at the Center of the world's history... where all men and all nations without exception stand revealed as enemies of God...and yet where all men stand revealed as beloved of God, precious in God's sight"; and he added, "So understood, the Cross, although it is the unique fact on which the Christian Churches base their hope, should not separate those of the Christian faith from others, but should instead be that element in their lives which enables them to stretch out their hands to peoples of other creeds in the feeling of universal brotherhood which we hope one day to see reflected in a world of nations truly united."[33] The idea of a "Christ-centered secular ecumenism" or of "a secular fellowship in Christ" has come to the forefront of Christian thinking today.

This idea is indeed very new. The theological and other presuppositions underlying it need much further exploration. No doubt, some insights in that direction have emerged in the discussions on "secular Christianity," "political theology," and "theology of religions"; and a theology of the human and of the human community which grapples with the realities of modern pluralism and ecumenism and the social and spiritual self-awareness underlying them is gradually taking shape. Charles Raven has reminded us that *koinonia,* the word for fellowship, has three meanings: community, communion, and communitarianism. All the three are relevant goals not only for the church but also for secular society. Of these Raven says, "We've tried to escape the third: it's time we realized that it is inherent in the other two and in the word itself."[34] The secular human fellowship informed by Christ should struggle to achieve, not merely inter-personal relations of love, but also structures of communitarian social living. It means voluntary pioneering experiments of "communes," but also politics aimed at liberating the poor and the oppressed and bringing the resources of technology and organization and the power of the state to serve justice among men in society.

A most potent source of strife in the world is religion itself. As Wilfred Cantwell Smith puts it, "Religious diversity poses a moral problem because it disrupts community." He points out that "unless men can learn to understand and to be loyal to each other across religious frontiers, unless we can build a world in which people profoundly of different faiths can live together and work together, then the prospects for our planet's future are not bright."[35] Religious traditions and secular ideologies pursuing their ends of saving and unifying the world armed with political, social, and cultural power, have the worst record of holy crusades and aggressiveness; and conversely all political, social, ideological, and cultural conflicts have been made more ruthless by the spiritual fanaticism introduced by the religions involved. Therefore it is significant that religions (and more especially Christianity) are developing a positive Christian attitude to the process of secularization of state and society in the modern world. There is a growing consensus among Christian theologians about accepting the secular state and society as the norm for Christians to work for.

Lesslie Newbigin justifies this norm on the basis of "the integrity of the human person," affirmed in God as Creator meeting man in Jesus "with a truth which is finally authoritative but not coercive." This implies for societies the guarantee of religious liberty as a fundamental right of every man and also the ensuring of "the proper integrity of the secular order."[36] He also points out that the dangers to humanity arising from a self-absolutization of the Christian religion are best countered by taking seriously the secular order. "There you have the true God-given reminder to the Church that it is still *in via* and cannot treat itself as the absolute vice-regent of God on earth. I do not believe that we shall go back on that insight."[37] Kenneth Cragg, while affirming the necessity of "political secularity" and the concept of the secular state, seems less conscious of the threat of ecclesiastical religious absolutism and state with established religion to the integrity of persons and the secular order, and is therefore more ambiguous about the validity of this "insight"; he finds it hard to shed the norms of Corpus Christianum and Corpus Islamicum, perhaps because he feels that the only alternative is that of a "closed" state-enforced secularism.   Charles Davis is committed to the idea of the secular state, but doubts the viability of "secular society"; nevertheless he believes "a pluralistic open or secular society" offers the best chance of carrying out the Christian mission in the present situation.   He argues it thus:

"When men differ as they do about ultimate truth, the only acceptable social order is one in which men do not try to impose their beliefs upon others by compulsion, whether physical or political or social, but decide to live in harmony on the basis of intelligent reasonableness, a willingness to listen to others and discuss problems, a desire to reach agreement by persuasion and a constant respect for all individuals and groups."[38]

Christians can contribute to the viability of such an open political and social secularity, provided they do not accept it to mean withdrawal from political and social witness into a purely private personal religion. No doubt, the theocratic mode of witness is not available, nor is it desirable because history is proof that the theocratic mode of the Constantinian and medieval era of furthering the Christian social mission through sacralized political power had turned out to be spiritually perverted and inhuman. In secular society the witness to the New Humanity in Christ and its redemptive power for politics, society, and persons take a different mode, namely the instrumentality of believers gathered in voluntary congregations and scattered in secular groups in civil society. Even so, it remains a witness to the Lordship of Christ over all creation and all human life. Johannes Metz speaks of the necessity of a "political theology" which is engaged in "the deprivatizing" of Christian spirituality and theology.[39] As Gibson Winter has said, a secular pluralistic society "desperately needs a Church which can participate in its public life without acting as a faction in search of private advantage."[40] In this connection the distinction between the sacred and the holy, between consecration and sanctification which Catholic theologians make[41] seems important. The church should not sacralize or consecrate the secular world by bringing it under the ecclesiastical order of the institutionalized religion, but it has the mission to sanctify

324

it by bringing it under Christ's redemptive spiritual power so that it may fulfill its secular human purpose.

Here some words of J. M. Lochman seem to sum up beautifully the direction in which Christian theology and mission in a secular society should be moving. Speaking of the theology that emerged in Czechoslovakia between 1948 and 1968, Lochman characterizes it as "a theology of the exodus, of dialogue and of change." He explains it thus:

In its *form*, it is a biblical theology, the thought of the exodus, concerned about God's commitment to man in history, trying in thought and action to interpret this commitment into the perplexities of history and society today. In its *approach*, it is a theology of dialog—the dialectical thought of pilgrims who do not claim ready-made dogmas and blueprints but who think and live as socratic evangelists, in honest give-and-take with their fellow pilgrims. In its *social perspective*, it is a theology of the Kingdom and of its righteousness, challenging all the justice and injustice of human laws and orders and opening the possibilities of creative change.[42]

It is very much a theology of participation with others in society and dialog in depth with them on the truth of man and society in Christ. Incidentally, what happened in Czechoslovakia in 1968 is a reminder about the insecurity which struggle for open secular society faces everywhere; only in some situations the threat comes from state-establishment or re-establishment of religious theocracy rather than from that of a closed dogmatic secular ideology. Nevertheless, the fact that all religious and secular ideologies are struggling with the humanization of the same modern forces, and the same modern spirit, dialog among them, leading to a consensus about an open secular pluralistic state and society as a historical ideal or norm, is not impossible.

One could go further and speak of Christian participation with others in the construction of one or more open and dynamic ideologies of secular humanism, which will provide guidance and framework for building a common secular human future. For Christians, such ideologies and the future envisaged will be fragmentary signs of the New Humanity given to all mankind in Christ; and their awareness of the *eschaton* will help keep the ideologies open, self-critical, and capable of constant revision and development. Karl Rahner discusses this question at several points in his *Theological Investigations* in relation to modern man's ability and duty to build human community by using his powers of "actively planning, shaping and directing the future—not merely individually but collectively—by self-manipulation and actively modelling his environment." Men and women can open themselves to "God's absolute future," says

Rahner, only "by concretely anticipating the concrete future which is to be produced." Since the emancipation of the secular world is something which has arisen out of the Christian understanding of God and Incarnation of the Logos itself, "the creation of a human future is not something optional for the Christian, but is the means by which he prepares himself, in actuality and not merely in theory, for God's absolute future." "The Kingdom of God only comes to those who build the coming earthly kingdom. In doing this, they use the continually new materials put at their disposal in succeeding ages," and "the Christian knows no better than other men just what this concrete provision (created by man so that he may be ready for what cannot be created) looks like, what form it ought to take, and how it is to be produced. In this matter he is on the same level as everyone else. He is obliged both to enter into a dialog with his fellow-builders of a common future, and also to involve himself in a struggle for the concrete future, since it is not theoretically deducible, can only be decided and implemented as a result of a 'struggle' and even violence." This being the case, in the building of a "secular humanism of the Christian qua Christian" there is no reason why Christians and non-Christians among whom "in the future Christians live everywhere as diaspora," should not "both plan together for the future which is unknown to both of them." He asks: "Why not try together to come to a clearer awareness of those hoped-for aspects of the future, which have as yet been anticipated only dimly—justice, freedom, dignity, unity and diversity in society?" "No doubt," he adds, "the Christian's secular humanism in keeping itself open to God's absolute future, implies certain formal structures in this concrete, intramundane future too."[43] We may make the comment, that so long as keeping the structures and ideas of secular humanism open to the ultimate future is not merely a Christian concern but also a demand of genuine humanity and should be approached as such, there is no reason why it should be called "Christians' Secular Humanism." Indeed, if it is the result of the Christian dialog with other men on man and society, the insights derived from Christianity, other religions, and the secular disciplines and ideologies are built into it. Of course the Christian will keep it under constant criticism and reinterpretation in the light of the New Humanity in Christ, but still it remains an idea of secular humanism which provides a common framework for active participation of men in building human community in a pluralistic situation.

Even when institutionalized religions have no control over the machinery of the state and the structures of society, and have withdrawn a good deal from public into private realms of personal and family life and relations or from public into voluntary modes of social and political witness, organized religious communities maintain religious and social distance from each other and are preoccupied, each with its own narrow communal interests and religious pursuits. Speaking of Christianity, the Kandy Consultation of 1967 on Interreligious Dialog, recognized that "there is far too much Christian communalism and ghettoism in both West and East," which militate against "human solidarity with all fellowmen, no matter what their color, culture, faith, or unbelief."[44] Van der Bent's comment is relevant here: "Continuing to affirm first of all its identity as a community *set apart* from other communities, instead of continually finding its identity as a peculiar community *in the midst* of other communities, the Church lags behind in the ecumenical movement."[45] This is similar to Cantwell Smith's observation that the conflict over "Christian exclusivism" which traditional doctrines have engendered, has militated against its traditional moral imperative toward "reconciliation, unity, harmony, and brotherhood among all men."[46] Therefore, within the context of the common struggle for an open secular human community and of the dialog on the ideas and structures of a secular humanism to reinforce it, Christianity cannot escape grappling with the theology of religion and religious pluralism. Here, of course, we come to a dimension of secularization and ecumenism which is more controversial.

Strange as it may seem, the dialectical theology of Karl Barth, Emil Brunner, and Hendrik Kraemer[47] which emphasizes the transcendence of the Word and Deed of God in Jesus Christ over all religions and quasi-religions of mankind has provided the basis for a radical relativization of all religions, including Christianity and also of atheism; and its understanding of Jesus Christ as the humanism of God[48] rejecting and electing all mankind in Jesus Christ points to a transcendent power which can renew them all.

Hegel's relativism conceived other religions as early stages of the religious development of mankind, which are totally abandoned by history now that the absolute religion of Christianity has emerged.[49] The later Troeltsch's relativism saw all religions as valid expressions of religion in varied cultures with Christianity itself as valid only in integral relation with the historical individuality of

327

Western culture.[50]   There are ideas of religious relativism based on conceiving all religions as imperfect forms of the Formless Spirit realizable only in mystic vision.   John Hick speaks of different religions as the inhistoricization of God's *agape* in the history of different peoples.[51]   The more recent thinking among the Roman Catholic theologians sees the other religions as valid means of divine salvation in a theologically "pre-Christian" situation.[52]   The newness of the Barthian approach is that it is a Christocentric relativism which relativizes all expressions of religiosity radically.   Therefore consistent with our general approach to God and man in this study, it is perhaps the most fruitful theological starting point to interpret religions including atheistic quasi-religions.

Man's selfhood is poised between nature and spirit.   Therefore it is impossible to isolate it from its involvement either in the processes of nature or the realm of religions and ideologies, which are structures of meaning and sacredness.   Man is both *homo religiosus* and *homo ideologicus*.   Created by God and alienated from him, man has idolatries and ideals which, like law in the N.T. Thought, have a dialectical character; on the one hand they point to God whom he has defied but cannot escape, and on the other they point to the condition of man as running away from God to find his own self-justification and involved in endless self-frustration.   And like law, religions are fulfilled and abrogated by Jesus Christ.   The "abolition of religion" in Christ, as Barth calls it, will be realized fully in the "end."   Meanwhile, there are two paths open.   One, suggested by Bonhoeffer,[53] is of a secular or religionless interpretation of Christian faith and the Person of Jesus Christ as "the Man for Others." We do not know exactly what he means by "religionless Christianity"; religionlessness, in its complete sense belongs to the "eschaton," the Ultimate Future; there is no temple in the City of God (Rev. 21:22).   There is a partial realization of this eschaton even now; and there is no doubt that Christian faith has created a spiritual ferment which has contributed a great deal to the process of secularization in our time, which involves the abolition of religious control of state, society, and culture in the name of liberation of human creativity.   But such realization remains always limited and partial; to assume otherwise is to deny that we are still saved by hope.   Religions will continue to have sway over men's lives till the "end"; and if religions are rejected, secularist quasi-religions will take their place.   Therefore the only path open for us is the second one, namely to be involved in religion with the hope of its abolition in Christ always present. It means a theological relativization of all religions in the name of the Grace of God in Jesus Christ. That is, people are "already" released from the absolute claims of religious and quasi-religions, in so far as they are caught up in the New Humanity of Christ through implicit or explicit faith; in being open to the judgment of God at the Cross, they become increasingly receptive to the power of the Risen Christ and his humanity, and to entering into dialog with other religions within the context of a concern for "human" fellowship. In fact, here the two processes of secularization and relativization converge.

It is along this line that Paul Devanandan seeks to interpret the relation among Christ, Christianity, other religions, and secular humanism. On the one hand, he sees the Western impact with its mixture of Christian and secular humanism producing a ferment of reformation and humanization in all non-Christian religions and discerns in it the presence and pressure of Jesus Christ. He says, "We may not forget that among men of faith who are adherents of renascent religions as well as those who profess no faith at all, there exists a common universe of discourse based on spontaneous reactions to the totality of life. We are all involved in a common social crisis, tied together by a community of interests; our common humanity serves as a common denominator; and on the frontiers of renascent faiths, doctrinal barriers no longer foreclose commerce. The outburst of newness of life in the resurgent non-Christian religions is due to increasing traffic across the border."[54] He adds that the dynamic of Christ and his New Humanity in the renascent religions lies not in the reaffirmation of their "classical theology" but in their response to the "new anthropology." Devanandan points out that "the primary question that is of dominant concern to the modern Hindu thinker is the nature and destiny of man; what is man and whither is he bound?" It is at the level of these new anthropological questions raised by modernity that the non-Christian world is opening (or consciously closing) itself to the reality of the new man in Christ. Therefore, citing Van Leeuwen, Devanandan says,

Perhaps the time has come now for us to focus our attention on the human aspect in God's redemptive act—on man as he really is, the creature for whose sake Jesus Christ died and rose from the dead. The burden of our message to the non-Christian world would then relate, in this generation certainly, to the Christian view of man and his destiny.[55]

As for the relation between Christianity and other religions, he speaks of the New Humanity in Christ as the source of their reconciliation. Preaching on the Cross abolishing the wall of partition between Jew and Gentile, he says,

The word of the Cross needs to be preached today in the conviction that because Christ rose again, what man calls religion—the reign of the law—is of the earth earthy, of the old things to pass away. This is a daring thought and it may well be fraught with dangerous heresy, but Christians of this generation may give heed to it. As we enter a new era in world history, we need to question ourselves whether we witness to a Gospel that perpetuates the very enmity which God in Christ had destroyed or do we proclaim the word of reconciliation.[56]

If the Word of the Cross is to be the basis of inter-religious reconciliation, the religion of Christianity must be distinguished from Christ and relativized, enabling Christ to reform, and take form within, all religions. Edward Schillebeeckx points out that "the religious claim (of the Church), her 'claim to exclusiveness,' on the basis of Christ's promise, is made relative by the fact that she is still eschatologically-oriented—still on the way in history toward the Kingdom of God and not yet identical with the Kingdom of God."[57] Does it not imply the possibility of the formation of Christ in other religions? This, no doubt, is a "daring thought," but something which we see happening. But is it theologically valid?

Today we recognize universally the possibility and even the necessity of Jesus Christ taking form in different cultures and re-forming them from within. That is, we have come to see Christ as transcending the culture of Western Christendom, able to relate himself creatively to other cultures. Since cultures are traditionally molded inwardly by the spirit of their respective religions, the idea of Christ's transcendence has to be extended to include religions. If Jesus Christ transcends the Christian religion, as its judge and redeemer, it opens up the possibility of Christ reforming all religions and informing himself in them. Herein we are acknowledging the theological validity of attempts at expressing the meaning of the Cross in terms of the indigenous religious traditions other than Christian, and in that process renewing the indigenous traditions themselves to become the vehicle of Christ and his divine humanity. As already stated, all the religious traditions of the world are in various stages of renaissance and reformation, through which they are seeking to redefine themselves under the impact of the spiritual self-understanding of the modern man, and under the urge to provide the spiritual foundation for the struggle for human community. It is within this framework that Christ, and the church as the fellowship in Christ, must take shape, calling for the transformation of all religions and the conversion of men in integral relation with their religions, to Jesus as the Christ of God.

Indeed, the theological possibility of this conversion is inherent (though not worked out) in Karl Barth's idea of Christianity turning from being "unbelief" to become the "true religion," through opening itself to the judgment and grace of God in Jesus Christ, on the same pattern of the sinner getting justified. He says, "The abolishing of religion by revelation need not mean only its negation, the judgment that religion is unbelief. Religion can just as well as be exalted in revelation, even though the judgment still stands. It can be upheld by it and concealed in it. It can be justified by it, and—we must at once add—sanctified."[58] Of course Barth refers to such a possibility of conversion to "true religion" only for Christianity, because of its openness in faith to the judgment and promise of the revelation of God in Christ. But we cannot see why the same justification and sanctification through openness to Jesus Christ in faith cannot be open to other religions on Barth's own theological premise. In fact, does not the renascence of non-Christian religions today signify a certain openness of this kind, as Devanandan has said? In this context, Panikkar's idea of Hinduism (and other religions) passing with Jesus Christ "through death to resurrection," and rising again as a new creation in Christ has validity.[59]

Of course, Panikkar does not start with religion as the creation of godless man, and Christ as the abolisher of religion as Barth does. He takes the other side of the dialectic and starts with what he calls the "Catholic Christic perspective" which sees "the ontic mediatorship of Christ" as present in all religions, and with the understanding that Jesus Christ came "not to found a religion and much less a new religion, but to fulfill all justice (Matt. 3:15) and to bring to its fulness every religion of the world" (Matt. 5:17; Heb. 1:1ff.). Therefore, just as Western Christianity is "the ancient paganism, or to be more precise, the complex Hebrew-Hellenic-Graeco-Latin-Celtic-Gothic-Modern religion *converted* to Christ more or less successfully," Indian Christianity should be "Hinduism itself converted—or Islam or Buddhism, whatever it may be."[60] To our mind, Barth's starting point is theologically more realistic since it takes the rebellion against God involved in religions more seriously than Panikkar; and Devanandan sees the significance of the ferment of secular humanism for the conversion of other religions to Christ more than Panikkar, who is too preoccupied with religiosity to recognize the Christian significance of the "new anthropology" in the meeting of

331

religions.[61]   Nevertheless, along the line of Barth and Devanandan, we can still arrive at Panikkar's conclusion.

The creativeness of the Barthian approach is that it relativizes not only religion, but also atheism and revolts against religion.   As Devanandan in his idea of reconciliation between Christianity and other religions, Lochman following Hromadka bases the idea of reconciliation between Christians and atheists on what the Cross of Jesus has done to abolish the middle wall of partition between the Jew and the Gentile; it is a "work of God" which cannot be destroyed by unfaith.   Man's denial of God "appears in the Bible only against this background, as something secondary, perverted, but also as something already overcome by God's faithfulness.   So atheism is not a hopeless ultimate step, but is something penultimate and in that sense relative."   In this view, atheism is "not simply disregarded, it is demythologized"; and it leads to the way of "Pro-existence" in which the Christian in a spirit of solidarity with the atheists under God's forgiving grace, gives up every self-justification and seeks to understand them in their basic humanity, its aims and intentions and existential frustrations, and enters into a partnership of common human concern.   Within this framework, Christians learn to listen to what God says to them through the atheists, and to articulate in a socratic manner the questions which Christ is asking the atheists from within their world of thought and aspirations.[62]

The theological relativization of atheism is taking place in other ways too.   The breakdown of the classical metaphysics and the allied concept of God in terms of which the Christian creeds have been formulated, makes it necessary for Christian theology to relativize and develop anew its own theism.[63]   Further, many protests against God could be interpreted as having arisen in the name of God—the God of Abraham, Isaac, and Jacob protesting against the God of the Philosophers; the God of Jesus against the God of the Pharisee; the God of the Crucified Messiah against the God of the Conquering Messiah.   The books of Job and Jonah and several Psalms in the Bible reject God at one level to affirm him at another.   Karl Rahner speaks of going behind the "categorical atheism" to the dimension of the existential commitment of the self, where in some cases he discerns a "transcendental theism elevated by grace."[64]   Evidently God versus godlessness does not correspond exactly to the theism versus atheism at the conceptual dimension; it has to be discerned in the light of the revelation of God in Jesus Christ.

In fact, it is such Christocentric relativization of Christianity and atheism which opens the door to their partnership in planning for the concrete future of modern society; and in this process, they not only help each other to unmask the false ideologies of self-interest and self-righteousness present in each and every distorting reality, but as already indicated elsewhere, also to build together relatively valid ideologies of secular humanism which affirm human dignity in society. Dialectical theology has rightly taken a negative view of ideologizing the Christian faith, but it must lead on to a positive attitude to creating utopias and ideologies open to the insights of the Christian and other religious and atheistic faiths as well as the social and human sciences. In his comment on a Church and Society statement on Images of the Future, Charles West says:

We need utopias projected by adventurous ideologists on the basis of convincing analysis of present trends, and leading to actions that engage us fully in their realization. We need pictures of how human community might be structured so as to be peaceful, hopeful, and loving, pictures which convince us by realistic analysis that we could get from here to there...we need visions of new forms of society which take account of the fact that we are by creation limited and defined in our relation to one another and to God, and will show how we can live in those relations responsibly and with hope that the powers pushing us around may be corrected into creative rather than destructive patterns.[65]

Van der Bent affirms his belief that "a creative and dialectic relationship between Ideology and Christianity" can be worked out in actual concrete situations to help Christians to "co-operate with others in efforts to work towards a greater intelligibility, and in this way to contribute to the well-being and unity of all men."[66]

The theological approach here presented hopes for the formation of Christ in communities committed to religious and atheistic ideologies and simultaneously in their re-formation in the light of Christ. It raises the problem of syncretism.

As Visser't Hooft notes in his book *No Other Name*[67] syncretism is a word which has been used in various senses.[68] Theologians as different as Von Harnack and Bultmann[69] and Russell Chandran[70] have used the word to denote the process whereby one religion utilizes and assimilates elements of other religions and cultures to communicate or embody its message. Visser't Hooft regrets this, because he would like to restrict the word to indicate a religion adopting elements from different religious traditions, without discrimination, and therefore without being able to adapt them to its original dominant spirit and structure, that is, what Hendrik Kraemer calls "the *illegitimate* mingling of different religious elements."[71] Pannenberg thinks that the original meaning of the word in Plutarch denotes a phenomenon, namely "the processes of reciprocity and integration in the relationship between cults, myths, individual gods, and whole religions," which the history of religions demonstrates. He adds that in spite of its bad reputation and the pejorative sense in which the word has been used in modern religious studies and classical philology based on a biased judgment about the phenomenon it designates, "it would make sense to hold on to the word and re-value it."[72] Since, after the Tambaram meeting of the International Missionary Council in 1939, the fear of syncretism has come to mean absolutization of Western Christianity (for which Kraemer himself is not responsible) leading to further self-isolation of Christian churches of the non-Western world from adherents of other religions in whose midst they live, there is great sense in Pannerberg's suggestion. But the warning against syncretism as defined by Kraemer and Visser't Hooft is indeed well-taken: it emphasizes radical Christo-centricity in the process of embodying the universal gospel and the church in societies and cultures as well as in secularized and religious communities.

Pannenberg points out how the emergence of the Israelitic idea of God, itself is an illustration of a discriminating syncretic process. The traditions of the Kenite Yahweh of Sinai, the god of the Exodus, the gods of the Patriarchs, as well as the god of heaven El, "have grown together into the form we know from the Old Testament as the God of Israel"; and "the driving force behind the fusion of all these figures may well lie in the manifest exclusivity that characterized Yahweh from the very beginning." This characteristic could mean, in confrontation with other deities, either identification or struggle, since the way to a pluralism of gods mutually supplementing each other closed." Baal, of course, was "bitterly opposed" but Yahweh gained victory "only by usurping specific functions Baal had possessed."[73] The dominant discriminating universal principle which had the characteristic exclusivity for Primitive Christianity was indeed "the Person of Jesus and the redemptive ascent of his death and resurrection." The religion and law of Israel was christologically interpreted and assimilated into the church of Christ. The formula "logos incarnate in Jesus" expressed for the church of the Fathers "the universal relevance of what happened in Jesus," and provided "the inexhaustible assimilative and regenerative power of Christianity." Thus, says Pannenberg, Christianity "not only linked itself to Greek philosophy but also inherited the entire religious tradition of the mediterranean world."[74] And today when Christians

are confronted with a world-wide pluralism of religious and secular
faiths and cultures and ideologies, Christo-centricity means, as Kraemer has rightly said, the recognition of "the relativity of our own
accustomed religious, cultural, and ecclesiastical apprehension and
patterns" and the eagerness to seek in "the beliefs and expressions"
of the peoples of the world "the elements that can serve as a human
starting point" for the unveiling of Christ and his significance.[75]
This is indeed a Christ-centered syncretic process which is to be wel-
comed.

REFERENCE NOTES

[1] Rosenstock-Huessy, *The Christian Future*, Scribner's Sons, 1946, p. 168.
[2] "Future of God" is a phrase often used by the theologians of hope. This is
legitimate only if our discourse is confined to God's being-in-relation-to-the-
world.
[3] Gustaf Aulen, *The Drama and the Symbols*. London: Society for the
Promotion of Christian Knowledge (SPCK), 1970.
[4] Vide Garaudy, *From Anathema to Dialogue*. Collins, 1967, p. 46.
[5] *A New Catechism*. New York: Burns & Oats, 1967.
[6] Ibid., pp. 488-9.   [7] Ibid., p. 262.
[8] Ibid., pp. 261, 3.   [9] Ibid., pp. 263-4.
[10] Harold K. Schilling: *The New Consciousness in Science and Religion*.
London: Student Christian Movement (SCM), 1973, p. 28.
[11] Charles Raven, *Creator Spirit*. London, 1927. Teilhard de Chardin,
Phenomenon of Man. Collins, 1960.
[12] Carl Braaten, *The Future of God*. Harper & Row, 1969, p. 104.
[13] See Martin Buber. *Between Man and Man*. London, 1947, pp. 141-144.
[14] Cohen, *Martin Buber*. London, 1957, pp. 70-71, 78.
[15] Vide Henrik Berhof in *Study Encounter*, Vol. I, No. 3, 1965.
[16] Charles Riven, *Christ and Modern Opportunity*. London: SCM Press,
1956, pp. 35-6.
[17] Paul Lehmann, *Ethics in a Christian Context*. London: SCM Press,
1963, p. 116.
[18] Ibid., p. 119.   [19] Ibid., p. 101.   [20] Ibid., p. 117.
[21] Sections 15 and 16, *Documents*, pp. 33-35.
[22] Section 92, *Documents*, p. 306.
[23] Section 22, *Documents*, pp. 221-222.
[24] Lev Gillet: Lutterworth Press, 1942.
[25] John V. Taylor, *The Go-between God*. London: SCM Press, 1973, p. 180.
[26] R. Panikkar, *The Unknown Christ of Hinduism*. London: Darton, Longman & Todd, 1974.
[27] Karl Rahner, *Theological Investigations*. VI. 32. "Anonymous Christians," pp. 390ff.; Charles David, *God's Grace in History*, pp. 75-76.
[28] Schillbeeckx, *Christ the Sacrament*, pp. 178-179.
[29] Chaturvedi and Sykes, *C.F. Andrews*. Allen & Unwin, 1949, pp. 310ff.
[30] "The Hindu View of Christ," (1939), *International Review of Mission*
pp. 259-264.
[31] Jurgen Moltmann, *Theology of Hope*. London: SCM Press,, 1967, p. 142.
[32] The Uppsala Report 68, p. 5.
[33] *Ecumenical Review*, July 1956, p. 402.
[34] Charles Raven, *Christ and Modern Opportunity*. London: SCM Press,
1956. p. 73.
[35] W. C. Smith, *The Faith of Other Men*. N.Y. & London: Mentor Book,
1965, pp. 115, 116.

[36] Lesslie Newbigin, *A Faith for This One World*. London: SCM, 1961, pp. 64-65.

[37] Ibid., p. 83.

[38] Charles Davis, *God's Grace in History*, pp. 61-62.

[39] Op cit., Johannes Metz, p. 110.

[40] *The New Creation as Metropolis*, p. 145, quoted in Schillebeeckx, *God the Future of Man*. Sheed & Ward, 1969, p. 127.

[41] M.D. Chenn, Ref. in Davis, op. cit., pp. 53-55.

[42] J. M. Lochman, *Church in a Marxist Society*, p. 115.

[43] IX. "Christian Humanism," pp. 200-202; Also V. "Christianity and the New Man," pp. 135ff.

[44] See A. J. Van der Vent, *The Utopia of World Community*. London: SCM, 1973.

[45] Ibid., p. 102.   [46] W.C. Smith, op. cit., p. 118.

[47] Owen C. Thomas (Ed.), *Attitudes Toward Other Religions*. London: SCM, 1969, pp. 93-114.

[48] Karl Barth, *The Humanity of God*, Collins, 1961.

[49] Owen C. Thomas, op. cit., see Paul Tillich, p. 117 and Ernst Troeltsch, p. 77.

[50] Ibid., see Troeltsch, pp. 83-84.

[51] John Hick, *God and the Universe of Faiths*. London: MacMillan, 1973. pp. 148-164.

[52] Joseph Neuner (Ed), *Christian Revelation and World Religions*. London: Burns & Oats, 1947. Eugene Hillman: *The Wider Ecumenism*. London: Burns & Oats, 1968. H. R. Schlette: *Towards a Theology of Religions*. London: Burns & Oats, 1966.

[53] *Letters and Papers from Prison*, Ed. Bethge, London: SCM, 1947.

[54] *Preparation for Dialogue*. Bangalore: CISRS, 1964, pp. 190-199.

[55] *Christian Concern in Hinduism*. Bangalore: CISRS, 1961, p. 106.

[56] *I Will Lift Up Mine Eyes*. Bangalore: CISRS, 1961, p. 106.

[57] *God the Future of Man*, London: Sheed & Ward, 1969.

[58] Op cit., Owen C. Thomas, see, Karl Barth: *Church Dogmatics*, Vol. I, 2, (Ed.) Bromley and Torrance, T. & T. Clark, Edinburgh, 1956.

[59] Panikkar, *The Unknown Christ of Hinduism*. London: Darton, Longman and Todd, 1964, pp. 57-60.

[60] Joseph Neuner (Ed.), op. cit., pp. 168-169.

[61] Panikkar, op. cit., p. 9

[62] Lochman, op. cit., pp. 159-169.

[63] Leslie Dewart, *The Foundations of Belief*, London: Burns & Oats, 1969.

[64] *Theological Investigations*, IX, p. 163.

[65] "Church and Society—Three Reports," in *Study Encounter*, Vol. VII, No. 3, 1971.

[66] Van der Bent, op. cit., pp. 115:116.

[67] Visser't Hooft, *No Other Name*. London: SCM, 1973.

[68] Ibid., pp. 10-11.   [69] Ibid., p. 12.   [70] Ibid., p. 123.

[71] Hendrik Kraemer, *The Christian Message in a Non-Christian World*, Edinburgh House Press, 1938, p. 203.

[72] Wolfhart Pannenberg, *Basic Questions in Theology*, Vol. II, London: SCM, pp. 85-86.

[73] Ibid., pp. 86-87.   [74] Ibid., pp. 88-89.

[75] Hendrik Kraemer, op. cit., pp. 343-344.

16

THEOLOGICAL EDUCATION TODAY*

A. A. Sitompul †

The purpose of this paper is to summarize and reflect upon the Lutheran World Federation (LWF) International Consultation on Theological Education, held in September 1975, at the Ecumenical Institute Bossey, Switzerland, whose task it was to wind up regional and national consultations previously held on the same subject.

Between 1971 and 1976 no less than ten national and regional consultations on theological education were held in various areas of the world with the active support of the LWF Department of Studies through its Office of Theological Education. Four of the consultations were held in Africa (Addis Ababa, May 1971; Accra, October 1971; South Africa, July 1972; and again Addis Ababa, July/August 1975). Three consultations were held in Asia (Parapat, Sumatra, September 1973; Madras, November 1973; and Hyderabad, November 1973); one was held in Latin America (Brazil, August 1972); one in Europe (Warsaw, April 1972), and one in the U.S.A. (St. Louis 1972), after which international consultations were held: one in Asia (Tokyo, Japan, 1975); and one in Latin America (Bogota, Columbia, 1976).

During the last international consultation new experiences were discussed and valuable proposals at regional and national levels made. Two major questions were focused upon through examination of certain case-studies and group discussions, namely: (1) What are some of the essential demands on theological education in a world where

---

* The major part of this chapter originally appeared in *Theological Education in Today's Asia,* edited by K. Rajaratnam and Adelbert A. Sitompul (Geneva: Lutheran World Federation. 1977), pp. 93-115.

† Dr. Sitompul is Director of the Office of Theological Education and Scholarship, Department of Studies, The Lutheran World Federation in Geneva.

human survival is increasingly being endangered daily and where, as a result of ever-growing violence and counter-violence, clear spiritual values, capable of being put into daily practice, are intensely needed? (2) What are to be the new features of a learning-teaching community in the context of a particular situation or of society as a whole?

One of the points greatly emphasized in the course of the Consultation was the need and urgency for supporting and developing full participation of Latin Americans, Africans, and Asians in the implementation and consolidation of more relevant and meaningful theological education for themselves. In this connection, it was stressed that the indigenous cultural background of people of a given church must, as far as possible, be respected when designing theological training for the whole people of God. However, it was rightly noted that the universality of the Christian faith might be jeopardized if cultural Christianity were overemphasized. It was, moreover, pointed out that an overstress on a people's cultural background could lead to an eventual weakening of ability for self-criticism.

The Bossey Consultation focused primarily on a selection of themes based on the findings of LWF-related national or regional consultations during the period 1971-75, and of the experiences of churches and theological institutions in three continents, namely, Africa, Asia, and Latin America. The themes dealt with were the following:

1. Theological Education for the Whole People of God
2. The Implications of Ecumenical Cooperation in Theological Education
3. Financially Viable and Independent Theological Education
4. Renewal of the Traditional Types of Theological Education
5. Introduction of Non-Traditional Types of Theological Education
6. New Methods of Theological Education

WHAT IS THEOLOGICAL EDUCATION FOR THE WHOLE PEOPLE OF GOD?

It was pointed out that until recently theological training was considered to be a privilege of pastors and theological professors. This attitude prevails in many churches even today in spite of the fact that many voluntary lay workers—men and women, adults and youth—are deeply involved in many tasks of the church which require some theological training. At the time of the Reformation, in the sixteenth century, the church had emphasized the need for educating the whole people of God, and the Reformation church spoke of the "priesthood of all believers." Later, this understanding of the nature of the church was either misunderstood or wrongly interpreted. The challenge of the church today, then, is to recapture the authentic meaning of that phrase, reflect on its implications for the life of the church, and live up to it. The misunderstood form is often justified by arguments based on a misinterpretation of our confessions. The office of preaching in the text of the Augsburg Confession (Article V) is not identical with the office of the ordained ministry. The way in which the ministry is conducted is a matter of church order. In all cases, however, the basic ministry of God's word in the world is entrusted to the whole congregation and this the Augsburg Confession refers to. Similarly, Article VII of the Augsburg Confession, in speaking about the congregation in which the gospel is being preached purely and in which the sacraments are being administered rightly, also refers to the basic ministry of the whole congregation.

The function of theological education has to be oriented toward equipping all church members for the ministry in various forms, and the professional ordained ministry is one of these forms. With a view to safeguarding that theological education shall pursue its true purpose, it is a matter of urgent necessity to examine critically the background and the motivation of traditional concepts which have cemented divisions in the church as, for example, the stereotyped division between ordained ministers and lay people, between men and women, rich and poor, educated and uneducated, old and young. A new theological interpretation of the church and its mission and of the ministry of the whole people of God to the world should be elaborated in order to pave the way for a reorientation in theological education.

The Accra Consultation (1971) stressed that the ministry should be more committed to teaching and preaching to the whole people of God in conformity with the New Testament view. The Head of the Church, the Lord and Savior Jesus Christ, ministers to his Body through the proclamation of the gospel in word and sacrament and builds up the Body for its ministry to the world, individually and corporately. This implies:

1. Serving our fellowmen in deeds of love and mercy.
2. Working for more just and humane structures in society.
3. Shaping the mind of the church and of the world around programs of justice and peace.

Women should be encouraged to participate more and more in

339

church life and in theological education. The Bossey Consultation unanimously acknowledged that the presence and involvement of women in theological education has so far been seriously neglected in many parts of the world. Many theological schools have either no women students at all or very few of them. The problem becomes even more serious and complex when it is realized that in numerous churches the question of ordination of women who have completed theological training is not entertained. Often these women end up teaching religion in schools instead of serving parishes as ordained pastors. They are not being trained for ordination, but to become Bible preachers, parish workers, social workers, or school teachers. In many churches women are discriminated against on the basis of their sex. It is essential, therefore, that future theological interpretation of the relationship between men and women should focus more on the "new creation in Christ" rather than on the Genesis account of Creation and the Fall.

A great deal more needs to be done by churches in order to bring about full participation of women in every sphere of church ministry. Women and men should serve the whole community in equal partnership, fully sharing their gifts and resources with one another. Notwithstanding the fact that at certain times and places women may be far more able than men to minister to women, the tendency to call women to minister only to women and children must be avoided as much as possible.

In considering how theological education for the whole people of God can best be implemented in practice, the International Consultation made the following suggestions:

(1) That on the boards of theological education, laity, including men, women, and youth, should be admitted as full members.

(2) That women should be elected constitutionally on all levels of church administration and not simply selected or co-opted as a privileged concession.

(3) That women should be included on all commissions and committees of the Lutheran World Federation.

(4) That our task as Christians regarding women is to initiate a change within the structures of the church in favor of their full participation in church life as well as in society.

THE IMPLICATIONS OF ECUMENICAL COOPERATION IN THEOLOGICAL EDUCATION

Ecumenical cooperative structures in theological education are

340

possible in the universities and union colleges. Federative models of theological education, such as the "cluster" seminaries (St. Louis 1972) are realizable at denominational and interdenominational levels. These cooperative patterns for theological training must be initiated, decided, and carried out by the local churches and the concerned seminaries if they are to be relevant and meaningful.[1] It was pointed out that:

...cooperation in theological education must be based on real needs if it is to be appealing and convincing. A statement of such needs, in line with biblical teachings, doctrinal convictions, educational trends and local situations must be carefully worked out. Cooperation in theological education must emphasize equality, mutuality and oneness if it is to be durable and strong. Differences between participating groups must be respected and their similarities should be emphasized, and the special interests of each, particularly of the smaller schools, should be taken care of in every way possible.[2]

Effective ecumenical cooperation, the Consultation argued, must be:

...based on the need to realize concretely our God-given oneness in Christ. Diversity and multiplicity in the Church may be a manifestation of the variety of the gifts of the Holy Spirit (I Cor. 1,12), but human divisiveness and sectarian factionalism are a scandal—a denial of our baptismal unity. Christian divisions also hamper the witness of the Church because they misrepresent to the world the nature of the Gospel as proclaiming one Lord for all people.[3]

Cooperation is needed both at the international level and in the local church. The local church should take the lead, if possible. However, in case cooperation is brought about by the seminary, the congregation (local church) should be encouraged to participate fully in the initiation, discussion, and implementation of cooperative programs.

The Hyderabad Consultation advocated making "use of local resources and organizing lay participation and training." Cooperation should also involve the exchange of personnel, equipment, and information. Fruitful discussion, dialogue, and possible reinterpretation and reapplication of the traditions of the Lutheran Church to the complex problems of our time can be achieved by bringing together people from North America, Europe, Asia, Africa, and Latin America.

The Warsaw Consultation stressed the importance of the "exchange of ideas and experiences of the various theological training systems in the European churches." Increased cooperation along these lines is necessary and will contribute meaningfully to a better service of the churches.

A variety of factors which stand in the way of ecumenical cooperation were noted and dealt with during the International Consultation:

(1) The historical traditions to which the churches belong.

(2) Political, social, racial, and economic conditions prevailing in a country.

(3) Financial questions.

(4) The question of identity.

(5) Adherence to familiar organizational structures.

(6) Theological and doctrinal differences.

FINANCIALLY VIABLE AND INDEPENDENT THEOLOGICAL EDUCATION

It was pointed out that theological education is dangerously dependent on foreign funds (over 70% of its income comes from the West) or on historically developed patterns of state support (Tokyo, 1975). The question was therefore raised whether theological education will always be dependent on such outside sources as congregational members, churches, mission boards, or states.

It was acknowledged that finance and power are often closely related. The church that supports a seminary tends also to control or dominate it in one way or another. Thus, in spite of all that has been said to the contrary, financial support from outside—be it a mission board or foreign church—tends to subject the receiving church or seminary to some foreign influence and domination. Dependency of the seminary on financial support from outside tends to discourage interest, involvement, and responsibility of the local congregation. Thus, the whole matter of dependency has to be seen in the light of the complex interaction of different but related power structures.

What steps, then, should the seminary take in order to achieve a measure of financial independence or interdependence? In Latin America, Africa, and Asia, the theological institutions and seminaries are usually considered instrumental to the church; therefore, self-reliance is extremely difficult to realize. Even if financial independence could be realized in practical terms, it would still be inadvisable as long as the seminary remains a servant of the church. It is imperative that the local church be educated and convinced that theological education is an integral and indispensable part of its life and work and that it is duty-bound to give support to the seminary in whatever way possible.

The Lutheran Theological Seminary in Hong Kong, for instance, is in the process of making new experiments in establishing healthier financial conditions and convincing the church that theological education is no longer only an enterprise of overseas mission bodies, but an integrated function of the church. The Seminary has taken various measures such as:

(1) Cutting down the number of staff personnel.

(2) Reducing non-essential expenditures.

(3) Revising the bookkeeping system.

(4) Introducing student fees and student voluntary services.

(5) Offering secretarial services to churches on a payment basis.

(6) Renting unused buildings, etc.

The most important step the Seminary in Hong Kong took in 1971 was the attempt to bring the sponsoring church into closer involvement. The Seminary Board of Directors was broadened to include both clergy and lay people; the curriculum was extended to try to meet the various needs of the church; bulletins were issued from time to time to inform the congregations about developments and financial problems; and Seminary "open-day" was held regularly for church members. In 1971 funds were raised amounting to about $2,000, and in 1972 this figure doubled. In 1973 the local revenue was 150% more than the previous years. In 1974 local contributions and other income increased by 30%.

Researches in Africa, Asia, Latin America, the South Pacific, and Caribbean area[6] show that viability of theological education can be secured by:

(1) Local church contributions.

(2) Fee revenue and pooling of student earnings.

(3) Endowment involving labor and participation of faculty and students.

(4) Combined sources of revenue.

(5) Subsidies of church-related universities and colleges.

(6) Use of foreign subsidies.

(7) Capital projects.

(8) Alternative patterns.

(9) Training of Faculty (up to doctoral level) at regional/national schools.

Meaningful incentives and ideas were contributed at the Bossey Consultation as to how the seminaries should achieve cooperation with and financial independence from the church. The church/congregation must identify with the seminary by recognizing theological education as an integral and indispensable part of its life and work and by accepting the dual role of the seminary as servant and prophet. Some of the practical ways in which the church/congregation,

343

especially in Latin America, Asia and Africa, can help, were set up as follows:

    (1) Have a regular budget for theological education in the church/congregation.

    (2) Sunday collections and money collected through special fund-raising appeals could be given to the seminary.

    (3) Professors and students, as members of the teaching-learning community, could serve churches/congregations by collecting gifts which might be used to benefit the seminary.

    (4) Certain available church resources could be used to serve the seminary (*e.g.*, renting buildings).

In order to overcome financial problems and to renew the seminaries' structures, the International Consultation proposed that:

    (a) Congregations support students they send to the seminary.

    (b) Whenever possible, students could work and bring the money to a central fund which should then be used as part of the seminary budget.

    (c) The students and the professors can take part in agricultural projects or in other productive projects.

    (d) Student fees should be introduced and encouraged.

    (e) Congregations can also make an extra effort to offer scholarships.

    (f) Some courses can be dropped, depending upon the immediate need of the church/congregation and society.

    (g) Students can work during the day and attend classes at night, thus enabling them to pay school fees.

    (h) Alumni can be encouraged to contribute monies, to teach some subjects, and become involved in the total life and growth of the institution.

    (i) Staff from a nearby university or theological college can offer full or part-time service to the seminary.

    (j) The seminary can offer multi-level or mutually complementary courses to the society at large. As a result of the seminary's service to the society, the state can undertake to finance the activity.

RENEWAL OF THE TRADITIONAL TYPES OF THEOLOGICAL EDUCATION

Why is a renewal of the traditional types of theological education important although they may no longer satisfy the needs of the churches today, neither in Latin America, Africa, and Asia, nor in Europe and North America? Theological education must be able to meet the concrete contemporary needs of the church and of society. The Third Mandate Program of the TEF, "Ministry in Context," applies authentic contextualization to theological education in three vital aspects:

1. to encourage relevant and indigenous theological reflection and expression;
2. to examine and experiment with theological curricula and teaching methods; and
3. to analyze and experiment with seminary forms and structures.

The criteria of contextualization mean wrestling with the message of the gospel within given contexts, namely the environments of socio-politics, religion, culture, and economics.

It was highlighted[7] that theological education, which is worth the name, must relate to the social, political, and economic environment of a concrete life situation in critical and self-critical awareness. Constructive criticism and self-evaluation would inevitably enhance the ability of the institution to play its prophetic role in the church and society more responsibly. It should be clearly understood that the importance of criticism and self-criticism is to keep the theological school on the alert and to help it to become a better servant and more effective prophet in the community. These being the premises, the seminary has to try to come to grips with concrete problems at the grass-root level.

SOCIETY AND WORLD IN CONTEXT. The dual role of contextual theological education is very important: on the one hand, as an instrument of prophetic function and, on the other hand, as a servant of the church. A theological school is expected to live, teach, and act as a servant of the church, but at the same time—as an organ of the church—it shares with it a prophetic responsibility in the society and in the world. The seminary is not the only fountain of prophecy, even though it is expected to play a prophetic role within the church and within the community in which it is situated. The seminary must also listen and be open to what the church, the community, and the society have to say in terms of faith, justice, freedom, poverty, and oppression.

It has been observed that poverty is an oppressive structure which cannot be adequately dealt with by acts of charity to individuals. Root causes of poverty must be exposed and solutions found. Many Christians in Latin America, Africa, and Asia have the conviction that part of the Christian action and mission in the world is precisely to fight these oppressive structures in favor of more humane social justice. What about the heavy contrast between the church of the poor and the church of the privileged? How should we adequately tackle our responsibilities in theological education in the face of this challenge?

CULTURAL CONTEXT. Theological education should encourage indigenous theological reflection and expression in context. Both the Addis Ababa and Bossey Consultations stressed the importance of curricula related to a given culture, because the effective communication of the gospel is always incarnated in a particular cultural setting (context) in which our churches have been placed by God. Those things that have been "imported" from other and our own cultures (i.e., hymns, liturgies, institutional structures, educational methods, etc.) should be closely examined to determine whether they hinder or further the impact of the gospel.

It was noted that the indigenization of theology on the basis of a given culture must, inevitably, raise the question of what is the Christian understanding of creation, of the world, of the individual, and of the natural order of society. What do we understand by the universality of Christ? How does one indigenize without necessarily neglecting the universal dimension of the Christian faith? Some theologians are already worried by the extent to which Christianity has been indigenized in Western Europe and North America. The real danger for the church that gets so deeply immersed in cultural Christianity is that it gradually loses its ability to be self-critical and fails to play a worthwhile prophetic role in society. Therefore, the challenge to the church—particularly in the developing countries —is how to ensure that our Christian theology is both indigenous and universal, and to keep an appropriate balance between the two.

The task of theological education is, therefore, to deal with the question of how Christ can be incarnated in man in each locality, in the nation, in the continent, in the world and, indeed, in each generation. Universal Christian theology cannot be properly and concretely expressed outside the various contextual interpretations of the meaning of the gospel. Wherever we are on the globe—east, west, north or south—what we need to do is to help one another to come to a full understanding as a learning community in world-wide ecumenical dialog, of what God's act in history—to deliver, liberate, and save his people—means in real human situations.

The Bossey Consultation recommended that, as theological education relates its issues to social and political life, informs about

346

Christianity at large, and points to the great commission for the extension of the Christian gospel, more emphasis and intensification be placed on the missiological dimension in all parts of the curriculum. In the future, theological institutions must aid the churches in setting up a forum to engage in critical cross-cultural study of confessing Christ in the cultural context.

INTERDISCIPLINARY EDUCATION. Several of the previously held consultations (Brazil, Parapat, Madras, Hyderabad), up to the Bossey Consultation, recommended that theological education programs work out a curriculum that not only includes traditional theological studies, but also other sciences such as basic sociology, psychology, anthropology, politics, and pedagogics; and that, at the same time, theological institutions open their doors and offer their services in providing theological training to social workers, teachers, doctors, psychologists, and professional workers of other disciplines.

The interdisciplinary Seminar on Urban Industrial Concerns in Africa,[8] held in Nairobi in 1974, brought together participants from many parts of Africa and from different churches, including Roman Catholics. They combined academic theological reflection with the use of other sciences and field work and provided a model as to how various churches could cooperate on a broad regional/continental basis. Training should take place both in the classroom of the seminaries and in the prospective field of activity of the student. Experience and reflection should guide.

SPECIALIZATION—TEAMWORK. The Consultations in Brazil and Parapat underlined the necessity of specializing in scientific-theological work. The Brazil Consultation stated that seminaries are also responsible for continuing and deepening theological research in their churches and should offer talented students the opportunity of specializing in scientific-theological work. It was suggested that the pastor should be in a position in a variety of fields—but without taking over the role of a specialist—to share in the practical day-to-day work of parishioners, thereby facilitating dialog and creating fellowship in real life situations. It advocates teamwork among pastors, but they should not hesitate to solicit the presence and advice of specialists, such as social workers, psychologists, etc. Everybody in the parish should be given the opportunity to contribute to the community according to his/her gifts. Ministry must no longer be the monopoly of the pastor. Teamwork among ministers of different confessions should also be encouraged, and/or in cooperation with lay people.

347

In the pluralistic community/society teamwork in theological education, thus understood, should comprise not only academically trained ministers, but also—otherwise in the church service—integrated specialists such as catechists, evangelists, women preachers, teachers, lay preachers, etc., to propagate the Word in the world.

The Accra Consultation and the Parapat Consultation stressed the need for specialization in scientific-theological work as well as in other disciplines for a meaningful theological education, and the study of administrative concerns such as management, stewardship, communication, agricultural programs and community development, medical aid, social work, and scientifics for higher schools. A thorough renewal of traditional forms of theological education along these lines was recommended and accepted by the Bossey Consultation, namely, training for administrative functions, urban industrial courses, mass media, and clinical pastoral education.

NON-TRADITIONAL TYPES OF THEOLOGICAL EDUCATION

Non-residential forms of theological education come under these categories; they are not institutionally bound to theological schools. The Addis Ababa (1971 and 1975), Parapat, and Bogota Consultations recommended that the residential theological education curriculum be extended, shaped, and adapted to serve as an adequate T.E.E. (Theological Education by Extension) program. The Mekane Yesus Seminary and its Board have resolved to improve the T.E.E. program according to the criticism that has been formulated against it.

T.E.E. programs, or programs similar in pattern, have been—or are in the process of being set up—not only in Latin America, but also by the Lutheran churches in Africa (Addis Ababa; possibly in Tanzania), and in Asia (Madras, Hong Kong, Manila, and Indonesia). They come into existence in response to an urgent need: in view of a lack of trained churchmen/women, it is imperative to prepare candidates for ministry and leadership in church and society and to provide continuing education for pastors and evangelists also, by means of in-service training. The program aims at minimizing the problem of shortage of ministers, leading its trainees to a non-professional or non-paid ministry, or a "tent-making ministry"; and at promoting members of the church as elders/presbyters, counselors, teachers, and lay preachers for the work in the congregations.

T.E.E. programs aim at giving students certain advantages, such as the following:[10]

(1) The student can study without leaving his family.

(2) The student lives in his/her local community and actively participates in the work of his/her congregation.

(3) The student puts his/her study into practice.

(4) The student simultaneously grows educationally and economically.

(5) The student becomes accustomed to supporting him/herself while serving his/her church at the same time.

T.E.E. is a viable teaching system for churches with limited financial resources and knowledge.

However, the disadvantages of T.E.E. should also be mentioned, namely:

(a) Receiving less on-going spiritual care and intellectual stimulation or scientific theology, which are important to challenge a dialog with other ideologies, religions, and technologies of our modern world.

(b) Less facility in utilizing libraries for research and in other resources considered as helpful and basic in the learning process.

(c) Limitation on programmed texts and qualified persons to prepare texts.

(d) Limitation in communicating world-wide experience within a given congregation and the difficulty for the trainee to move outside his/her congregation.

Nevertheless, T.E.E. meets the needs of the church today, especially in Latin America, Africa, and Asia; and it is to be hoped that T.E.E. curricula set up in Latin America, Africa, and Asia are not copying Western models.[11] It is somewhat surprising that some of the T.E.E. handbooks are still entirely in the wake of disciplines and curricula as practiced and set up by the church in Europe. This is by no means a value judgment of Western theological academics. The criteria valid for the Western theological institutions are simply not always applicable and adequate to stimulate and challenge the living theology in particular societal situations in Latin America, Africa, and Asia.

Topics and subjects of theological education must be contextual with a given cultural, societal, and human situation. It is understandable and intelligible that the curricula of theological education in the developing countries should emphasize a theology of dialog (denominations, religions, ideologies), a theology of cultural context, a cultural theology, a political theology, and a missiological theology besides a biblical theology. The churches of Africa and Asia examined and discussed at their WCC Consultation in Bossey (June 1976), "The African and Asian Contribution to Contemporary Theology": Biblical Theology, Pastoral Theology, Political Theology, Cultural Theology, the Theology of Dialogue, and Missiological Theology.

Theological education must deal with "Church Theology" as well as with "Scientific Theology."[12] I mean that church theology is not an individual theology which we find in well-formulated published statements. It should rather be a living theology, an interpretation, a dialog of church members (including lay people) based on their daily struggle in life and on their faith. In the West, theology is mainly considered a monopoly of theological educators. They are thinkers or researchers, but lack pragmatic experience and are frequently not sufficiently involved in the activities of the church and of society. They know the church and its problems only theoretically. They often have a one-sided knowledge lacking the substance of life. Church theology is important because all church members are fully involved, as they struggle and make decisions together. It is an enlivened theology involving the whole human being. Taking into account that church growth is in direct relation to our faithfulness to the gospel and to our daily spiritual renewal, the permanent updating of the programs of the church's theological education—and the inclusion of political and socio-economic-related subjects in them —should only be done within the spiritual and theological dimensions of our task (Bogota's Consultation).

This is the reason why the curriculum of theological education —and specifically of the T.E.E.—must contain topics adequately related to the main challenging problems a given church and society are facing. Theological Education must be able to equip the whole people of God—both ministers and lay people. The "Theology of Liberation," for example, is relevant to Latin American existence and history. The curriculum must prepare the students to enter into a critical and creative dialog with the "Theology of Liberation"; some of its aspects are "conscientization," "christological concentration," "revolutionary Jesus," "the anonymous poor," "marginal Jesus," "self-reliance," etc.

Synthetical models of theological education, such as T.E.E. combined with traditional residential training, are considered efficacious and commendable for continuing education of normally trained pastors (Warsaw Consultation); for elders and evangelists, for "auxiliary pastors"[14] in Brazil. These synthetical models serve also the purpose of training lay people and help the pastor to develop in the trainee a sense of church vocation and secular service. The Bossey Consultation, therefore, recommended to the Lutheran churches "that they use T.E.E. as a useful complementary method, together and combined with the traditional residential form of theological education and that they provide the qualified persons to make such programs possible."

Another form of non-traditional theological education is the "tent making" (self-supporting) ministry. Full-time ministry in the parish parallel to a lucrative secular occupation was practiced for centuries. Paul and most of the rabbis, like Hillel, Shammai, Akiba, Johanan, did not receive any fixed salary; they had to do some other kind of work to earn a living. Spyridon, bishop of Tremithus in Cyprus was a shepherd; Basil, a manual worker; sub-deacon Quadrangesimus in Buxentum, Italy, was also a shepherd; presbyter Severus was a winegrower. They all had to combine the ministry with a secular occupation, and this was not considered exceptional.[15]

The Addis Ababa Consultation in 1971 as well as in 1975 suggested the immediate review of present forms of ministry in Ethiopia, in favor of the "tent-making" ministry: "The tent-making ministry training is for teachers, doctors, nurses, dressers, farmers, merchants, soldiers, administrators, pastors, evangelists, deacons and for everyone who wants to serve God and his fellow-men throughout his life independently from salary."

For the voluntary and tent-making ministry the Addis Ababa Consultation (1975) recommended to the Executive Committee of the churches in Ethiopia, since these types of ministry are urgently needed to enliven the church, that gifted preachers be encouraged to commit themselves and that the church study how to equip devoted Christians in secular professions for such a ministry.

In dealing with the problems of paid ministry, the Addis Ababa Consultation (1975) recommended that:

(1) A committee to study the viability of theological education be set up to the end that a paid ministry be financed from the social and economic base emerging in a self-reliant church in a socialist society;

(2) That the same committee study the necessity and possibility of secular training for students of theology and for pastors and evangelists already employed by the Church;

(3) That proper and careful handling of church property and

351

finances be emphasized to the extent that it enhances greater contributions by members leading toward self-reliance. The tent-making ministry is available not only for Latin America and Ethiopia, but also for the churches world-wide. The Bossey Consultation recommended that tent-making ministry be used in areas where there is a shortage of pastors or where socio-politico-economic conditions do not allow for full-time pastors or other church workers.

The Consultation further recommended that non-traditional types of theological education be implemented, namely, clinical pastoral education, theological education in small groups of action and reflection, and new interdisciplinary ecumenical models of theological education such as the pilot project "Interdisciplinary Seminar on Urban Industrial Concerns in Africa," in 1974, and "cluster" seminaries (USA Consultation, 1972). These forms of theological education endeavor to make the best possible use of both scientific theology and the practical involvement of total human abilities to the benefit of the community and society.

New Methods of Theological Education

All the consultations, whether on the regional, national or international level, aimed at renewing the patterns, types, functions, and methods of theological education. They acknowledged that theological education, as now practiced, cannot meet effectively and responsibly the needs and interests of the church/congregation—the whole people of God.

The reasons for the inadequacies in theological education are manifold. One main reason is that, while in many countries all over the world essential socio-political changes have been achieved, corresponding reforms in the theological education system are frequently either still missing or insufficient. Under the impact of innovative trends toward more effective justice and real life opportunities, certain values inherent in our respective cultures are questioned; our churches and institutions are affected and recognize the necessity to abandon right hierarchial structures. These insights involve a slow process of experimentation and reorientation.

In some continents, nations and churches gained independence a long time ago. However, the systems and methods of education, including theological education, have not changed much. In South Africa the system is examination-oriented and forces the student just to collect and accumulate knowledge. Memo-technical methods of learning make this form of education non-creative, uncritical, and

352

non-involved. No personal effort is made to understand a problem fully, solve it, and gain new insights. Students are not led to develop their critical faculties; they think that the studies they do in class are complete in themselves and that there is no need to develop these subjects further on their own. They merely take notes and return the indoctrinated material at examination time. In Brazil the seminary was compared to a flower-bed:[16] plants must be nourished and encouraged to grow. The task of theological education is not to indoctrinate the student, but to help him grow in character and spiritual maturity, to develop his responsiveness and inner freedom, and to deepen his faith and sense of mercy.

Self-education and discussion are relatively seldom used, preference being given to attending lectures rather than reading books or doing research in a particular field. This situation is not specific to South Africa. The conditions are similar in other parts of Africa, Asia, and perhaps in parts of Latin America. The traditional lectures can be meaningfully complemented and enlivened by tutored groups working on a specific subject. The interaction of theory and practice, experience and reflection, involves forms of training such as field practice, internships, research, and tutoring with audiovisual material.

In Sweden "Parish-related study projects" started in October 1975. This new approach allows for a variety of combinations in the theological field of study. The professors, traveling from parish to parish, offer "parcels" of theological studies to be worked on invidually through reading certain books, local study group discussions, and attending lectures at the university. A final test completes this parish-related training.

Private leisure time study can be carried out through group study, group projects or in traditionally structured seminaries, workshops, and small community groups. Group dynamics (Brazil Consultation) is another meaningful teaching-learning instrument or "Juku" type Seminary: personality education (Tokyo 1975).

The case-study method is a new educational model implemented at the Berkeley Case-Study Method Institute. It represents the adaptation to theological education of non-theological modes and models of professional training (e.g. law, business, administration, psychology, social work, etc.). It is basically an inductive and integrative method. This form of educational training starts with a "case"—a cross-section or "incident" of society and, through group discussion in class-rooms at laboratories, is used by itself or in connection with other cases as the basis for constructing general principles or formulating various possible general strategies or courses of action.

The "group study" method, applicable also to theological training, is developed and practiced at the Aarhus Ecumenical Centre, at the Berkeley Theological Center, and at the Gurukul College, Madras. They organize leisure time gatherings for students, youth, and lay people to dialog on essential topics. They also provide consultative services and training courses. In the Hyderabad Theological College survey it was found that study methods are taught to students gathering data on Christian and other religious communities related to social, political, educational, economic, and religious needs and resources.

The different methods or disciplines related to interdisciplinary exchange programs/foreign exchange programs of personnel are all preparing for different forms of ministry for the whole people of God according to the gifts and talents of the candidates.

As pointed out at the Madras Consultation, the student must be prepared for a prophetic ministry. I would add that he should equally be trained for the ministry of the "priesthood of all believers" to fully meet the challenges of his prophetic call in theological education. Teaching methods should focus on achieving in the student a sound balance between well-integrated knowledge and spiritual maturity and they should stimulate critical and creative thinking, thereby enabling him/her to analyze his/her own experiences in the light of God's revelation in the Scriptures.

ASIAN PROGRAM FOR ADVANCED STUDIES (APAS) AS A NEW MODEL

APAS represents a new approach to meeting the needs of the churches with an emphasis on "grass roots" participation and development. The scope remains broad, although the emphasis is on theological research, studies, and training programs to fill the gap existing between the rigid seminary education and the ever-growing needs of congregations in a changing society.

The purposes of the APAS project are to foster the renewal of the churches' theological understanding and to further their witness to the gospel in particular contexts. The program aims to help strengthen the witness of the churches in their local situations, to encourage regional interaction, and to contribute by its concepts and its working style to Christian unity and ecumenical cooperation.

The program does not aim at an expansive new institution and structure with permanent establishment, but rather is geared to program-oriented cooperative efforts on a decentralized basis with a wide margin of autonomy, a minimum of structure, and a maximum of flexibility. In pursuance of its task and within the limits of the available resources, APAS considers undertaking work in the following areas of service:

1. Research relevant and meaningful to the needs of a given locale and church, long term or short term, in the Biblical, missiological, historical, cultural, social, inter-cultural, inter-religious, and communication fields.
2. Intensive program of continuing education for lay and clerical participants of the churches, as a part of the leadership training.
3. Any form of improvement of theological and Christian education of the churches.
4. Scholarship and exchange program at both professional and student levels, between/among Asian countries as well as with the partners in other continents.
5. Various types of special study seminars, institutes, workshops, and consultations with systematically organized programs, which may also be cross-cultural and inter-religious in nature.
6. Development of libraries.
7. Upgrading theological institutions.
8. Encouragement of advanced theological or related study programs in an Asian context. When the specific situation warrants, cooperative programs with other existing programs of the same nature may be encouraged.

There are now 10 areas/units of APAS: Korea, Japan, Hong Kong-Taiwan, India, Indonesia, Malaysia-Singapore, The Philippines, Papua, New Guinea, Australia, and Jordan. The ongoing programs are, namely:

Korea: A brief training for lay leadership was held; specialized training was conducted for Christian writers. Research in music for liturgy in the Korean context was started. The first translation of Luther's large catechism into Korean language was begun.

Japan: Survey and research for mission and evangelistic work was begun.

Hong Kong-Taiwan: A number of programs were conducted here: in 1975 a church workers' study seminar, lay leadership training classes, a Theological Education Series, a Theological Lecture Series and a Christian Writer's Seminar; in

355

1976, a Youth Leadership Training Camp, a Lay Leaders' Seminar series, a Program of Research on Church History and Christian Education, and an exchange scholarship program.

India: Gurukul Theological College's Programs were totally geared to the aims and program of APAS: research, pastors' refresher courses, lay training, Theological Education by Extension, and Communication. A Consultation for Lutheran-Non-Lutheran professors and a "Liberal-Conservative Dialog" on church and mission were conducted.

Indonesia: A seminar on "Confessing Christ in the Cultural Context" (1976) was conducted and a Workshop on "Indigenous Worship and Music" (1977) is planned.

The Philippines: A National Pastors' Wives Retreat and a workshop on "Contextualizing Faith and Life" were carried out.

Malaysia-Singapore: A study of church growth and lay activity in relation to local congregations was instituted.

Australia: The Lutheran Church of Australia has been initiating steps to conduct a Theological Conference among the member churches in Australia, Papua New Guinea, and Indonesia (North Sumatra) in 1978. The aim of this Conference is to search for a platform for training of church leaders and church workers among the above-mentioned churches, and to set a new program of joint action on church ministry and trans-national mission as well as among theological educators.

Jordan: In the year 1977 the individual units are meeting to prepare local input to the Asian Seminar on Mission for 1978.

Many of the research methods, reports, and findings of the consultants proved to be useful for the needs of various churches beyond the areas/units within the Asian program and some were picked up and used even outside of Asia. The program provided a positive contribution to existing ecumenical program and cooperation among denominations—Lutheran and others.

PROJECT STUDY "CONFESSING CHRIST IN THE CULTURAL CONTEXT"

Since our last International Consultation on Theological Education, held in Bossey in 1975, one of the main emphases of our office's work lies on the LWF/DS study project "Confessing Christ in the Cultural Context." The general purpose of the study is to help the churches and their institutions in their search for fundamental self-understanding, based on and centered in the Bible, yet related to a given cultural and social setting (contextualization), to enable them to deal more maturely with programs of indigenization and cross-cultural concerns, and to promote a contextualized theology and self-reliance in a critical, constructive, and redemptive way.

More specifically, the project aims at linking cross-culturally team research undertaken at theological institutions in South Africa, the Federal Republic of Germany, Indonesia, Japan, the U.S.A., and possibly France and Madagascar, and to encourage and promote sharing of information, dialog, and critical evaluation.

Reports and findings of these workshops, seminars, and consultations will eventually be assembled, together with research papers presented by individually working scholars, with a view to publication for distribution to all member churches and associated institutions.

Further, a WCC/LWF-sponsored colloquium was held at the Ecumenical Institute Bossey from July 2 to 8, 1977 on the subject "Confessing Christ in Different Cultures" with a large participation of theologians from African and Asian countries. A similar colloquim, focusing on the same theme, is planned for 1978.

Aim and purpose of the colloquim is:

a) to continue the contact and fellowship initiated when African and Asian theologians met for the first time in June 1976;

b) to clarify and share with one another our images and experiences of Christ as they come through our various cultural contexts;

c) to wrestle with the meaning and proclamation of Christ in the contemporary situations in which the church finds itself in Africa and Asia today;

d) to lift these culturally "conditioned" images of Christ to a global and ecumenical level of our understanding and experience of Christ. We shall try, for example, to search for the emergence of an ecumenical christology which arises out of the creative interplay of "regional" or "contextual" christologies in a universal context.

357

REFERENCE NOTES

[1] Cf. Albert Greiner, "Unser Reformatorisches Erbe in der Theologischen Ausbildung"; paper read at Warsaw's Consultation, 1974.

[2] Andrew Hsiao, "Ecumenical Co-operation and Financial Independence in Theological Education," a case study on Chinese Seminaries in Hong Kong; paper read at Bossey's International Consultation 1975.

[3] Ibid.

[4] Herbert M. Zorn, *Viability in Context, The Theological Seminary in the Third World—Seedbed or Sheltered Garden?* (London. 1975), p. v.

[5] Hsiao, loc. cit.   [6] Zorn, op. cit., pp. 14-25.

[7] J.B.M. Kiwovele, "Critical and Self-Critical Awareness of the Interrelationship between Theological Education and the Social, Political and Economic Environment," paper read at Bossey's International Consultation 1975; cf. G. Nagy, "Theologie de Diakonie—Ausbildung und zum Dienst der Kirche in einer saekular'si'erten Gesellschaft"; paper read at Brazil's Consultation, 1972.

[8] "The Church and the City, Training for Urban Ministry in Africa." a Report on the Interdisciplinary Seminar on Urban and Industrial Concerns in Africa, 1975; cf. G. Ebeling, *Studium der Theologie-Eine enzyklopaedische Orientierung*, J C.B. Mohr (Paul Siebeck), (Uni-Tascchenbuecher 446), (Tuebingen, 1975), pp. 166-167.

[9] S. Meincke, "Perspektiven pfarraemtlicher Taetigkeit im Latin Amerika von Heute und Morgen"; paper read at Brazil's Consultation 1972.

[10] The advantages of Theological Education by Extension were experienced by the Mekane Yesu Seminar in Ethiopia, paper read by Teklehaimanot Woldeyiorgis at Addis Ababa's Consultation 1975; and the Augsburg Seminar in Mexico, paper read by R. Hoeferkamp: "Ist es erforderlich, dass alle Pfarrer eine gruendl'iche theologisch—w'ssenschaftliche Ausbildung genossen haban?" Brazil's Consultation 1972; as well as the Lutheran Church in the Philippines, cf. *Handbook of Theological Education by Extension* (Manila. 1973), pp. 3-4.

[11] Cf. F. Ross Kinsler, "Extension: An Alternative Model for Theological Education " in: *Learning in Context* (London: TEF. 1973), pp. 27-49.

[12] Cf. Trutz'Rendtorff - Eduard Lohse. *Kirchenleitung und wissenschaftliche Theologie, Theologische Existenz Heute*. Nr. 179 (Chr. Kaiser Verlag, Muenchen 1974). pp. 60-62. Cf. Ivar Asheim, "Grundfrage der Pfarrausbildung Heute"; paper read at Warsaw's Consultation 1974.

[13] P. Hoffman, "The Problem of a Paid Ministry in a Self-Reliant Church in a Socialist Society"; paper read at Addis Ababa's Consultation. 1975.

[14] Arno Dreher. Brazil—"Theological Education by Extension," an interview, in *Lutheran World*, Vol. 22, 4, 1975, pp. 334-336.

[15] Cf. L. Vischer, "The Ministry and a Secular Occupation." in *New Forms of Ministry*. edited by David M. Paton (Edinburgh. 1965). pp. 36-54.

[16] Karl Hertz. "Neue Methodologie in der theologischen Ausbildung"; paper read at Brazil's Consultation 1972.

[17] Cf. K. Bridstone, "Teaching Theology by the Case Method"; paper read at Bossey's International Consultation 1975, in *Theological Education Within the Whole People of God—New Methods, Forms and Functions in Theological Education*, edited by A. A. Sitompul (Geneva, 1976), pp. 14-19.

APPENDICES

A. LEADERSHIP IN THE CONSULTATION

B. PARTICIPANTS

Appendix A

ALL-ASIA CONSULTATION ON
THEOLOGICAL EDUCATION FOR CHRISTIAN MINISTRY IN ASIA
March 13-21, 1977, Makati Hotel
Metro-Manila, Philippines

LEADERSHIP IN THE CONSULTATION

Keynote Speaker—Dr. Shoki Coe (Taiwan)
> Director, Theological Education Fund

Bible Study Leaders

> Dr. Preman Niles (Sri Lanka)—Old Testament
> Rev. Ben Dominguez (Philippines)—New Testament

Lecturers and Responders

1. Dr. C. C. Kim (Korea) on "Man and Nature"
   Rev. Hsien-chih Wang (Taiwan), Responder
2. Fr. Catalino Arevalo, S. J. (Philippines) on
   "Man in Society and History"
   Dr. Kosong Srisang (Thailand), Responder
3. Dr. Kosuke Koyama (Japan, New Zealand) on
   "Man and the Holy"
   Rev. K. C. Abraham (India), Responder

Panel Speakers

1. On Program of Theological Education
   Dr. Shoki Coe—Program for Theological Education (WCC)
   Dr. Adelbert Sitompul (Indonesia) on Asia Program for Advanced
   Studies and Theological Education in LWF
   Dr. Emerito P. Nacpil (Philippines)—The Critical Asian Principle
   and the SEAGST

2. On Relations in and Structures for Theological Education
   Dr. Andrew Hsiao (Hong Kong)—A nore suitable Regional
   Structure: Reflections on JRPC
   Dr. Arnold Come (U.S.A.)—The Pacific Basin Network

Workshops

1. Workshop I—Man and Nature
   Chairman : Dr. Akira Demura (Japan)
   Secretary : Dr. Wesley Ariarajah (Sri Lanka)
   Consultants: Dr. C. C. Kim (Korea)
   Rev. Hsien-chih Wang (Taiwan)

2. Workshop II (Group A)—Man in Society and History
    Chairman : Dr. Masao Takenaka (Japan)
    Secretary : Prof. Kyung Bae Min (Korea)
    Consultants: Fr. Catalino Arevalo (Philippines)
                Rev. Raymond Fung (Hong Kong)

3. Workshop II (Group B)—Man in Society and History
    Chairman : Dr. P. V. Premasagar (India)
    Secretary : Rev. Denis Dutton (Malaysia)
    Consultant : Dr. Shoki Coe

4. Workshop III—Man and the Holy
    Chairman : Dr. C. D. Jathana (India)
    Secretary : Dr. James Veitch (New Zealand)
    Consultants: Dr. Kosuke Koyama (Japan)
                Rev. K. C. Abraham (India)

Steering Committee

Members of the Planning Committee
Officers of Workshops (Chairman, Secretary, Consultant)
Presiding Officers During Sessions—appointed at the Consultation
                        by Steering Committee

Worship Leaders

Opening Service—Dr. Robert Fukada (U.S.A., Japan)
                Dr. Yong Ok Kim (Korea)
Closing Service—Dr. T. V. Philip (India)
                Dr. Ching-fen Hsiao, preacher
Daily Worship and Evening Prayers—appointed at the Consultation
                        by Steering Committee

Planning Committee

Dr. Yap Kim Hao (CCA)
Dr. Shoki Coe (TEF)
Dr. Robert Fukada (NEAATS)
Dr. T. V. Philip (BTE)
Dr. E. P. Nacpil (ATSSEA)

Organizing Secretary: Dr. Emerito P. Nacpil

Appendix B

ALL-ASIA CONSULTATION ON THEOLOGICAL EDUCATION FOR CHRISTIAN MINISTRY IN ASIA
March 13-21, 1977

PARTICIPANTS

AUSTRALIA

1. Dr. Graeme Ferguson
Principal
United Theological College
420 Liverpool Road
Enfield, N.S.W. 2136
Australia

BANGLADESH

2. Rt. Rev. B.D. Mondal
St. Thomas' Church
54 Johnson Road
Dacca-1, Bangladesh

HONG KONG

3. Dr. Andrew Chiu
Concordia Theological Seminary
68 Begonia Road
Yau Yat Chuen, Hong Kong

4. Rev. Joe Dunn
(alias Tang Shiu Ming)
Christian Study Centre
Tao Fong Shan
Shatin, N.T., Hong Kong

5. Rev. Raymond Fung
Hong Kong Christian Council
57 Peking Road, 4th Floor
Kowloon, Hong Kong

6. Dr. Andrew Hsiao
Lutheran Theological Seminary
Box 20, Shatin, N.T., Hong Kong

7. Dr. James Pan
Theology Division
Chung Chi College
Chinese University of Hong Kong
Shatin, N.T., Hong Kong

8. Rev. Lo Shek Wai
Lutheran Theological Seminary
Box 20, Shatin, N.T., Hong Kong

INDIA

9. Rev. K. C. Abraham
St. Mark's Cathedral
1 Mahatma Gandhi Road
Bangalore-1, India
United Theological College
17 Miller's Road,

10. Mrs. Leelamma Athyal
Bangalore 560046, India

11. Rev. J.W. Gladstone
Kerala United Theological Sem.
Kannammoola: Medical College
P.O. Trivandrum 695011,
Kerala, India

12. Dr. Emmanuel E. James
Principal
North India Theological College
106 Civil Lines
Bareilly 243001, U.P., India

13. Dr. C. D. Jathana
Principal
Karnataka Theological College
Balmatta P.O., Bangalore 575001,
India

14. Rev. Narendra John
Union Biblical Seminary
Yeotmal 445001, Maharashtra,
India

15. Mrs. Anaamma Joseph
Malloothara House, Tholashery
Tiruvalla, Kerala, India

16. Miss Saroj Sabita Mitra
South India Biblical Seminary
Box No. 20, Bangarapet 563114
Mysore, India

17. Miss Mathuri Mukhuti
William Carey Stury &
Research Centre
14/2, Sudder Street
Calcutta-700016, India

18. Rev. George Niñan
BUILD
11, Sujata Co-operative
Housing Society
1st Floor, S .V. Road: Bandra
Bombay-400050, India

19. Dr. T. V. Philip
Director
Senate of Serampore College
P. O. Serampore: Dist. Hooghly
W. Bengal, India

20. Dr. P. V. Premasagar
    Principal
    Andhra Christian Theological
    College
    Lower Tank Bund Road,
    Near DBR Mills
    Secunderabad-500003, A.P., India

21. Rt. Rev. C. Selvamony
    C.S.I. Bishop
    Nagercoil, Tamilnadu, India

22. Rev. G.R. Singh
    Leonard Theological College
    Jabalpur-482001, M.P., India

23. Rev. M. Thomas Thangaraj
    Tamilnadu Theological Seminary
    Arasaradi P.O.: Madurai-625010,
    India

24. Rev. Philipose Thomas
    Orthodox Theological Seminary
    Kottayam-686001, Kerala, India

25. Mr. Zaihmingthanga
    Aizawl Theological College
    Aizawl, Migoram, India 796001

INDONESIA

26. Miss Henriette Lebang
    Sekolah Tinggi Theologia
    Jalan Proklamasi 27, Jakarta
    III/20, Indonesia

27. Dr. O Messach
    Aip. KS Tubun 253
    Post Box 2683
    Jakarta-Pusat, Indonesia

28. Dr. Judowibowo Poerwowidagdo
    Sekolah Tinggi Theologia
    "Duta Wacana"
    Jalan Dr. Wahidin Sudirohusodo 21
    Yogyakarta, Indonesia

29. Rev. R. Radjagukguk
    Fakultas Theologia, University
    of Nommensen
    Jalan Asahan 4
    Pematang Siantar
    Sumatera, Utara, Indonesia

30. Dr. Nicolaas Hadjawane
    Sekolah Tinggi Theologia GPM
    Jalan Pancasila
    P.O. Box 15, Ambon, Indonesia

31. Rev. Luther Zwingli Raprap
    Executive Secretary
    PERSETIA
    Jalan Proklamasi 27
    Jakarta-Pusat, Indonesia

32. Rev. Hermogenes Ugang
    Akademi Theologia GKE
    Jalan Jenderal
    Sudirman 8, Bandjarmasin
    Kalimatan, Indonesia

33. Rev. Josef P. Widyatmadja
    Jalan Tagore 41, Solo
    Indonesia

JAPAN

34. Prof. Akira Demura
    Tohoku Gakuin University
    1-3-1 Dohi Sendai-shi 980
    Japan

35. Prof. Robert M. Fukada
    Doshisha University School of
    Theology
    Kyoto, Japan 602

36. Prof. Shigeo Hashimoto
    Doshisha University School of
    Theology
    Kyoto, Japan 602

37. Rev. Mitsuhiro Inukai
    Fukuyoshi Kaneda-cho
    Tagawa-gun
    Fukuoka-ken 822-12, Japan

38. Prof. Naohira Kiyoshige
    Japan Lutheran Theological
    Seminary
    3-10-20 Ohsawa Mitakashi
    Tokyo 181, Japan

39. Prof. Yoshinobu Kumazawa
    3-10-30 Ohsawa Mitakashi,
    Tokyo 181, Japan

40. Mr. Shiro Kusumoto
    3-10-30 Ohsawa Mitakashi
    Tokyo 181, Japan

41. Rev. Takafumi Mukai
    Kwansei Gakuin University
    School of Theology
    1-155 Ichiban-cho, Uegahara
    Nishinomiya-shi 662, Japan

42. Rev. Hiroshi Ohmiya
    Asagaya Church
    5-18-10 Asagaya Kita
    Suginami-ku, Tokyo 166, Japan

43. Miss Kasuko Oyama
    Hisayama Ryoikeun
    1869 Aza Kuhara
    Hisayama-cho Kasuya-gun
    Fukuoka-ken 811-25, Japan

363

44. Mr. Ikuzo Suzuki
The Central Theological College
1-12-31 Yohga Setagaya-ku
Tokyo 158, Japan

KOREA

45. Dr. Chong Nahm Cho
President
Seoul Theological Seminary
101 So Sa Dong, Bucheon City
Kyunggi Do, Korea

46. Rev. Hyang Rok Cho
President
Hankuk Theological Seminary
129 Soo Yoo Dong Sang
Do Bong Ku, Seoul, Korea

47. Dr. Chung Chun Kim
Professor
Hankuk Theological Seminary
129 Suyu-Dong, Sungbuk-ku
Seoul, Korea

48. Dr. Yong Ok Kim
Director
KAATS
Box 45 West Gate Post Office
Seoul, Korea

49. Dr. Kwang Shik Kim
Professor
Mokwon Methodist College
24 Mok Dong, Daejeon, Korea

50. Prof. Kyung Bae Min
Yonsei University School
of Theology
134 Shin Chong Dong
Seoul, Korea

51. Dr. Pong Bae Park
Methodist Theological Seminary
Box 45 West Gate Post Office
Seoul, Korea

52. Dr. Jong Sung Rhee
President
Presbyterian Theological
Seminary
353 Kwang Jang Dong
Sung Buk-ku, Seoul, Korea

MALAYSIA

53. Rev. Denis Dutton
2 Jalan Wesley, Kuala Lumpur
05-05, Malaysia

54. Rev. Ricky Ling Tung Leh
P.O. Box 8, Sibu
Sarawak, Malaysia

NEW ZEALAND

55. Dr. Kosuke Koyama (Lecturer)
University of Otago
P.O. Box 56, Dunedin
New Zealand

56. Dr. Frank Nichol
University of Otago
Knox College, Dunedin
New Zealand

PHILIPPINES

57. Rev. Henry Aguilan
National Council of Churches in
the Philippines
P.O. Box 1767, Manila
Philippines

58. Fr. Catalino Arevalo (Lecturer)
Loyola House of Studies
P.O. Box 4082, Manila
Philippines

59. Rev. Thomas Batong
Lutheran Theological Seminary
P.O. Box 16, Baguio City
Philippines

60. Dr. Domingo Diel, Jr.
The College of Theology
Central Philippine University
P.O. Box 231, Iloilo City
Philippines

61. Rev. Benjamin Dominguez
(Bible Study Leader)
Union Theological Seminary
P.O. Box 841, Manila
Philippines

62. Mrs. Elizabeth Dominguez
Union Theological Seminary
P.O. Box 841, Manila
Philippines

63. Bishop Soliman Ganno
St. Andrew's Theological
Seminary
P.O. Box 3167, Manila
Philippines

64. Fr. Henry Kiley
Saint Andrew's Theological
Seminary
P.O. Box 3167, Manila
Philippines

65. Dr. Emerito P. Nacpil
(Organizing Secretary)
Director
Association of Theological
Schools in South East Asia
P.O. Box 841, Manila
Philippines

66. Dr. Levi V. Oracion
Union Theological Seminary
P.O. Box 841, Manila
Philippines

67. Dr. Valentin S'toy
Silliman University
Divinity School
Dumaguete City 6501
Philippines

SINGAPORE

68. Dr. Yeow-Choo Lak
Trinity Theological College
7 Mount Sophia, Singapore 9

69. Rev. Michael Tan Chew Weng
Trinity Theological College
7 Mount Sophia, Singapore 9

70. Dr. James Veitch
Trinity Theological College
7 Mount Sophia, Singapore 9

SRI LANKA

71. Rev. Wesley Ariarajah
5 Boswell Place
Colombo 6, Sri Lanka

72. Rev. L. Nihal Ranj'th Fernando
Methodist Mission House
Thummodera, Nattandiya,
Sri Lanka

73. Rev. Kingsley Muthiah
Methodist Mission House
Puttur, Sri Lanka

74. Dr. Preman Niles
(Bible Study Leader)
Theological College of Lanka
Pilimatalawa, Sri Lanka

75. Rev. J. V. Ratnam
The Parsonage, Lindulla
Sri Lanka

THAILAND

76. Dr. Kamol Arayaprateep
Thailand Theological Seminary
P.O. Box 37, Chieng Mai
Thailand

77. Rev. David Luo
Bangkok Institute of Theology
301 Soi 31 Sukhumvit Road
Bangkok, Thailand

78. Dr. Vithavas Khongkhakul
72 Susarn Lane, North
Sathorn Road, Bangkok 5,
Thailand

TAIWAN

79. Rev. Chuang, Tsai-ming
Director
Kachsiung Counseling Center
No. 61 Chio-ju, 2nd Load
Kaosiung City, Taiwan
R.O.C.

80. Dr. Hsiao, Ching-fen
Tainan Theological College
115 Tung Men Road
Tainan, Taiwan

81. Mr. Hsu, Hsing-jen
Principal
Kuwang Hua Girls' High School
41 Sheng Li Road, Tainan
Taiwan, Republic of China

82. Dr. Paul Shang-hsin Liao
Taiwan Theological College
20, Lane 2, Sec. 2,
Yang Teh Ta Road
Shihlin, Taipei, Taiwan

83. Miss Tsai, Su-cheng
Student
Tainan Theological College
115 East Gate Road
Tainan, Taiwan, R.O.C.

84. Rev. Wang, Hsien-chih
Minister
274-19, Youth Road
Tainan, Taiwan, R.O.C. 700

85. Rev. Weng, Hsiu-kung
Acting General Secretary
Presbyterian Church in Taiwan
3 Chungshan, S. Rd., Taipei
Taiwan, R.O.C.

86. Dr. Ivy Chou
Executive Director
Foundation for Theological
Education in South East Asia
13 London Road, Bromley,
BRI IDE, Kent. England

87. Dr. Shoki Coe
Director
The Theological Education Fund
13 London Road, Bromley,
BRI IDE, Kent, England

88. Dr. Arnold Come
San Francisco Theological
Seminary
San Anselmo, California 94960
U.S.A.

89. Dr. Douglas Elwood
St. Andrew's Theological Sem.
P.O. Box 3167, Manila
Philippines

90. Dr. L. D. Fullerton
Principal
Methodist Theological Hall
Queen's College
University of Melbourne
Parkville, Victoria 3052
Australia

91. Dr. Yap Kim Hao
General Secretary
480 Lorong 2, Toa Payoh
Singapore 2

92. Rev. Roy Sano
Asian Center for Theology
and Strategy
Pacific School of Religion
1798 Scenic Avenue
Berkeley, California 94709
U.S.A.

93. Dr. Adelbert Sitompul
The Lutheran World Federation
Department of Studies
P.O. Box No. 66
Route de Ferney 150
1211 Geneva 20, Switzerland

94. Prof. Masao Takenaka
Doshisha University
School of Theology
Kyoto C02, Japan

95. Dr. Wilhelm Wille
Evangelisches Missionwork
Mittelweg 143, D2000 Hamburg
Germany

96. Dr. Toshitsugu Arai
Secretary of Education, CCA
CCA 480 Lorong 2, Toa Payoh
Singapore

97. Fr. Stephen Bevans, SVD
Archdiocesan Major Seminary
Vigan, Ilocos Sur
Philippines

98. Rev. Ronald Biel
Director of TEE
Lutheran Church, Philippines
P.O. Box 507, Manila

99. Rev. Ruben O. Caldito
P.O. Box 507, Manila
Philippines

100. Mr. Jerry Folk
Director
Shalom Centre for Continuing
Education
827 S. Spring Avenue
Sioux Falls, 57104
U.S.A.

101. Dr. Alex J. Grant
Yu-Shan Theological Institute
Li-yutan, Shou Feng
Hualien, Taiwan

102. Ms. Lee Hung-Chong
Hong Kong Christian Council
Metropole Building, 4th Floor
57 Peking Road, Kowloon
Hong Kong

103. Dr. Hanns P. Keiling
Silliman Divinity School
Dumaguete City 6501
Philippines

104. Rev. Esmeraldo A. de Leon
P.O. Box 1772, Manila
Philippines

105. Rev. Dr. Wilhelmus A. Roeroe
Fakultas Theologia Ukit
Tomohon, Sulut
Indonesia

106. Rev. Henry P. Silbor
Director of Alumni Affairs
Philippine Baptist Theological
Seminary
P.O. Box 7, Baguio City
Philippines

107. Mr. Amir H. Silitonga
Union Theological Seminary
P.O. Box 841, Manila
Philippines

108. Dr. Grover Tyner
President
Philippine Baptist Seminary
P.O. Box 7, Baguio City
Philippines

109. Rev. Rowland Van Es
Silliman University
Dumaguete City
Philippines

110. Dr. Lourdino A. Yuzon
The Divinity School
Silliman University
Dumaguete City 6501
Philippines

Other Orbis books . . .

THE MEANING OF MISSION

José Comblin

"This very readable book has made me think, and I feel it will be useful for anyone dealing with their Christian role of mission and evangelism." *New Review of Books and Religion*
ISBN 0-88344-304-X CIP   *Cloth $6.95*

THE GOSPEL OF PEACE AND JUSTICE

Catholic Social Teaching Since Pope John

Presented by Joseph Gremillion

"Especially valuable as a resource. The book brings together 22 documents containing the developing social teaching of the church from *Mater et Magistra* to Pope Paul's 1975 *Peace Day Message on Reconciliation*. I watched the intellectual excitement of students who used Gremillion's book in a justice and peace course I taught last summer, as they discovered a body of teaching on the issues they had defined as relevant. To read Gremillion's overview and prospectus, a meaty introductory essay of some 140 pages, is to be guided through the sea of social teaching by a remarkably adept navigator."
National Catholic Reporter
    "An authoritative guide and study aid for concerned Catholics and others." *Library Journal*
ISBN 0-88344-165-9   *Cloth $15.95*
ISBN 0-88344-166-7   *Paper $8.95*

THEOLOGY IN THE AMERICAS

Papers of the 1975 Detroit Conference

Edited by Sergio Torres and John Eagleson

"A pathbreaking book from and about a pathbreaking theological conference, *Theology in the Americas* makes a major contribution to ecumenical theology, Christian social ethics and liberation movements in dialogue." *Fellowship*
ISBN 0-88344-479-8 CIP   *Cloth $12.95*
ISBN 0-88344-476-3   *Paper $5.95*

LOVE AND STRUGGLE
IN MAO'S THOUGHT

Raymond L. Whitehead

"Mao's thoughts have forced Whitehead to reassess his own philosophy and to find himself more fully as a Christian. His well documented and meticulously expounded philosophy of Mao's love and struggle-thought might do as much for many a searching reader." *Prairie Messenger*

ISBN 0-88344-289-2 CIP · *Cloth $8.95*
ISBN 0-88344-290-6 · *Paper $3.95*

WATERBUFFALO THEOLOGY

Kosuke Koyama

"This book with its vivid metaphors, fresh imagination and creative symbolism is a 'must' for anyone desiring to gain a glimpse into the Asian mind." *Evangelical Missions Quarterly*

ISBN 0-88344-702-9 · *Paper $4.95*

ASIAN VOICES
IN CHRISTIAN THEOLOGY

Edited by Gerald H. Anderson

"A basic sourcebook for anyone interested in the state of Protestant theology in Asia today. I am aware of no other book in English that treats this matter more completely." *National Catholic Reporter*

ISBN 0-88344-017-2 · *Cloth $15.00*
ISBN 0-88344-016-4 · *Paper $7.95*

FAREWELL TO INNOCENCE

Allan Boesak

"This is an extremely helpful book. The treatment of the themes of power, liberation, and reconciliation is precise, original, and Biblically-rooted. Dr. Boesak has done much to advance the discussion, and no one who is interested in these matters can afford to ignore his important contribution." *Richard J. Mouw, Calvin College*

ISBN 0-88344-130-6 CIP · *Cloth $4.95*

THE CHURCH AND
THIRD WORLD REVOLUTION

Pierre Bigo

"Heavily documented, provocative yet reasonable, this is a testament, demanding but impressive." *Publishers Weekly*

ISBN 0-88344-071-7 CIP   *Cloth $8.95*
ISBN 0-88344-072-5   *Paper $4.95*

WHY IS THE THIRD WORLD POOR?

Piero Gheddo

"An excellent handbook on the Christian understanding of the development process. Gheddo looks at both the internal and external causes of underdevelopment and how Christians can involve themselves in helping the third world." *Provident Book Finder*

ISBN 0-88344-757-6   *Paper $4.95*

POLITICS AND SOCIETY
IN THE THIRD WORLD

Jean-Yves Calvez

"This frank treatment of economic and cultural problems in developing nations suggests the need for constant multiple attacks on the many fronts that produce problems in the human situation."

The Christian Century
ISBN 0-88344-389-9   *Cloth $6.95*

A THEOLOGY OF LIBERATION

Gustavo Gutiérrez

"The movement's most influential text." *Time*

"The most complete presentation thus far available to English readers of the provocative theology emerging from the Latin American Church." *Theological Studies*

"North Americans as well as Latin Americans will find so many challenges and daring insights that they will, I suggest, rate this book one of the best of its kind ever written." *America*

ISBN 0-88344-477-1   *Cloth $7.95*
ISBN 0-88344-478-X   *Paper $4.95*

MARX AND THE BIBLE

José Miranda

"An inescapable book which raises more questions than it answers, which will satisfy few of us, but will not let us rest easily again. It is an attempt to utilize the best tradition of Scripture scholarship to understand the text when it is set in a context of human need and misery."

Walter Brueggemann, in Interpretation

ISBN 0-88344-306-6 *Cloth $8.95*
ISBN 0-88344-307-4 *Paper $4.95*

BEING AND THE MESSIAH

The Message of Saint John

José Miranda

"This book could become the catalyst of a new debate on the Fourth Gospel. Johannine scholarship will hotly debate the 'terrifyingly revolutionary thesis that this world of contempt and oppression can be changed into a world of complete selflessness and unrestricted mutual assistance.' Cast in the framework of an analysis of contemporary philosophy, the volume will prove a classic of Latin American theology." *Frederick Herzog, Duke University Divinity School*

ISBN 0-88344-027-X CIP *Cloth $8.95*
ISBN 0-88344-028-8 *Paper $4.95*

THE GOSPEL IN SOLENTINAME

Ernesto Cardenal

"Upon reading this book, I want to do so many things—burn all my other books which at best seem like hay, soggy with mildew. I now know who (not what) is the church and how to celebrate church in the eucharist. The dialogues are intense, profound, radical. *The Gospel in Solentiname* calls us home."

Carroll Stuhlmueller, National Catholic Reporter

ISBN 0-88344-168-3 *Vol. 1 Cloth $6.95*
ISBN 0-88344-170-5 *Vol. 1 Paper $4.95*
ISBN 0-88344-167-5 *Vol. 2 Cloth $6.95*